MW01119778

Humber College Library
3199 Lakeshore Blvd. West
Toronto, ON   M8V 1K8

World stages, local audiences

Manchester University Press

theatre
theory · practice
· performance ·

series editors
MARIA M. DELGADO
PETER LICHTENFELS

advisory board
MICHAEL BILLINGTON
SANDRA HEBRON
MARK RAVENHILL
JANELLE REINELT
PETER SELLARS

This series will offer a space for those people who practise theatre to have a dialogue with those who think and write about it.

The series has a flexible format that refocuses the analysis and documentation of performance. It provides, presents and represents material which is written by those who make or create performance history, and offers access to theatre documents, different methodologies and approaches to the art of making theatre.

The books in the series are aimed at students, scholars, practitioners and theatre-visiting readers. They encourage reassessments of periods, companies and figures in twentieth-century and twenty-first-century theatre history, and provoke and take up discussions of cultural strategies and legacies that recognise the heterogeneity of performance studies.

The series editors, with the advisory board, aim to publish innovative challenging and exploratory texts from practitioners, theorists and critics.

also available

World stages, local audiences

Essays on performance, place, and politics

PETER DICKINSON

HUMBER LIBRARIES LAKESHORE CAMPUS
3199 Lakeshore Blvd West
TORONTO, ON.   M8V 1K8

Manchester University Press
Manchester and New York

distributed in the United States exclusively by Palgrave Macmillan

Copyright © Peter Dickinson 2010

The right of Peter Dickinson to be identified as the author of this work has been asserted by him in accordance with the Copyright, Designs and Patents Act 1988.

Published by Manchester University Press
Oxford Road, Manchester M13 9NR, UK
and Room 400, 175 Fifth Avenue, New York, NY 10010, USA
www.manchesteruniversitypress.co.uk

Distributed in the United States exclusively by
Palgrave Macmillan, 175 Fifth Avenue, New York,
NY 10010, USA

Distributed in Canada exclusively by
UBC Press, University of British Columbia, 2029 West Mall,
Vancouver, BC, Canada V6T 1Z2

British Library Cataloguing-in-Publication Data
A catalogue record for this book is available from the British Library

Library of Congress Cataloging-in-Publication Data applied for

ISBN 978 0 7190 8174 3   hardback

First published 2010

The publisher has no responsibility for the persistence or accuracy of URLs for any external or third-party internet websites referred to in this book, and does not guarantee that any content on such websites is, or will remain, accurate or appropriate.

Typeset by Servis Filmsetting Ltd, Stockport, Cheshire
Printed in Great Britain
by MPG Books Group, Bodmin

for Richard,
as always,
and for Alana, Amy, and Joanna,
my three muses

CONTENTS

FIGURES

ACKNOWLEDGEMENTS

This book is the product of conversations I have conducted, both in person and inside my head, with many people over the past few years. I outline some of my imagined interlocutors at greater length in the introduction. For agreeing to be a 'live' audience (however virtually and/or fleetingly) to my evolving ideas on performance and place, I am grateful to Susan Brook, Clint Burnham, Henry Daniel, Jeroen de Kloet, Jeff Derksen, Jill Dolan, Harry Elam, Gillian Evans, Karen Ferguson, Tom Grieve, Hong Hao, Jamie Hilder, Jean Graham-Jones, Rosalind Kerr, Ric Knowles, Carolyn Lesjak, Helen Leung, Jisha Menon, Sharon Rosenberg, D'Arcy Saum, Diana Solomon, Jackie Stacey, and Susan Stryker.

My partner, Richard Cavell, has listened more patiently and steadfastly than anyone. He has also accompanied me to most of the performances discussed in this book and, as both a native Vancouverite and a spatial theorist, generously shared with me his extensive knowledge and unique perspective on the city we call home. For daily making that home a better place to live, I owe Richard the world.

The editorial and production staff at Manchester University Press have been a joy to work with. I thank everyone there who has had a hand in seeing this book into print. Particular thanks must go to the two anonymous reviewers of my original manuscript, and to Maria Delgado and Peter Lichtenfels, joint editors of the 'Theatre: theory – practice – performance' series in which the published version appears; all four readers' enthusiasm for my work, and cogent suggestions for revision, were gratefully received and helped me to address more clearly my own hoped-for audiences.

I am especially indebted to all of the artists and photographers who have generously allowed me to reproduce images of their work, often free of charge, in the pages that follow.

Earlier, much abbreviated versions of chapters 2, 3, and 4 have appeared in the following journals: *Text and Performance Quarterly* 28:3 (2008); *Theatre Journal* 57:3 (2005); and *torquere* 6 (2004).

Many of the ideas explored in this book were first tested in front of, or inspired by, my students. Three of those students have made material contributions to its production, and for that reason alone the work is better than it ought to be. To Alana Gerecke, Joanna Mansbridge, and Amy Zhang I offer my sincere thanks, and most profound admiration.

Introduction: near and far

In the framework of enunciation, the [city] walker constitutes, in relation to his position, both a near and a far, a *here* and a *there*. (Michel de Certeau[1])

Genealogies of performance attend not only to 'the body', as Foucault suggests, but also to bodies – to the reciprocal reflections they make on one another's surfaces as they foreground their capacities for interaction. (Joseph Roach[2])

It is Sunday, 29 April 2007, International Dance Day, and I am leaning against a bus shelter on the corner of Burrard and Georgia Streets in downtown Vancouver. It is a gorgeous, sunny spring day, and like many in the city I have willingly given myself over to happy, aimless afternoon *flânerie*, zipping up my Fred Perry jacket, tightening the laces on my favourite maroon Adidas trainers, affixing my iPod headphones, and thus toting my global brand names like so many talismans content to wander the chicer boulevards and gaze in local storefronts, performing my idleness with what I imagine my fellow pedestrians recognise as professional aplomb. In truth, however, my perambulations do have a purpose, an end point, a destination. I have arrived at this

1 Michel de Certeau, *The Practice of Everyday Life*, trans. Steven Rendall (Berkeley: University of California Press, 1984), p. 99 (de Certeau's emphasis).
2 Joseph Roach, *Cities of the Dead: Circum-Atlantic Performance* (New York: Columbia University Press, 1996), p. 25.

particular corner, positioned myself next to this particular bus shelter, and turned myself from *flâneur* to loiterer because I have been tipped off by a former student that she and several others will be performing a site-specific dance theatre piece here as part of a series of public events, performances, displays, workshops, and impromptu happenings taking place throughout the city in celebration of International Dance Day. All I have been told is that the piece, called *What the Hell?*, is a structured improvisation for seven dancers (some of them, like Alana, alumni from my university), that it has been choreographed and workshopped by Lee Su-Feh, Artistic Director of the local company battery opera, and that it will last approximately 50 minutes. Still, the information is enough to make me feel like I am aligned with the performers in a special way, that our shared knowledge of the eventness of the events about to unfold separates us in some fundamental sense from the general masses milling about, who will come together as an audience only unwittingly, a coincidence of timing and physical proximity, and in whose anticipatory faces I read only eagerness for the arrival of the next bus, not the beginning of a potentially transformative performance experience.

At the appointed hour I spot Alana weaving her way through the crowds crossing Georgia Street. She sits down on the grass outside Christ Church Cathedral, next to a woman her age. The two start chatting. Then stretching. Then breathing rhythmically. Is this the start of the performance? I can't tell for sure. And when exactly were Alana and her friend joined by the other men and women? Was my view really obscured that long? Or was I distracted by other scenes of city life competing for my attention – the horn blasts issuing from an impatient driver waiting to turn left onto Georgia; a heated argument between an older couple (tourists, I surmise) about which bus to take; a posse of shirtless skateboarders issuing forth as if out of thin air, parting waves of pedestrians like the sea, careening down Burrard in their own magical ballet? Whatever the case, when I return my gaze to the spectacle I am *supposed* to be watching, there are suddenly four women and two men on the grass, each now breathing, arching their backs, lifting their torsos and legs, reaching their arms skyward – a sequence of repeated movements that starts to attract the attention of other passers-by. But first another distraction: a delivery man is struggling to pull a red dolly laden with packages up the steps of the cathedral, to the right of the dancers. This time, however, I'm confident he is part of the show. Sure enough, his entrance seems to be the signal for the corps of dancers, moving as one on the grass, to spill out onto the sidewalk and, eventually, to splinter off into a succession of duos and trios, their explorations

1 Left to right: Ali Robson, Billy Marchenski, Chris Wright, and Alana Gerecke perform Lee Su-Feh's improvised public dance *What the Hell?*, Vancouver, International Dance Day, 2007

of the intimate spaces between each other's bodies and between those bodies and the built environment making of the wide plaza between the Cathedral and Burrard Street a caravansary theatre, a mobile civic stage (see figure 1). And of the pedestrians, now weaving in and out of their orbits, now pausing to take in the action, a temporary audience. Who am I to say that their experience of the performance is any less authentic than my own? When, near the end of the piece, I am suddenly placed in the surprising (certainly to me) position of improvising a set of embraces with one of the dancers, I am being rewarded not for the singularity of my presence as audience member, but rather for the *duration* of that presence, my static performative pose next to the bus shelter having attracted its own sort of reciprocal attention.

The place of performance

These days it seems like there is a 'World Day' for almost everything, with UNESCO and other NGOs asking otherwise disparate and disconnected peoples around the globe to find common cause in locally celebrating, commemorating, or cogitating various artistic pursuits (dance or theatre), health and environmental crises (AIDS and global warming), or hoped-for political outcomes (peace). (The Internet and other new media technologies have abetted the possibilities for such worldliness at the same time as they have dispersed and diffused the local sites of its performance, with the 'LIVE SEARCH' buttons on our respective tool-bars launching audiences and our real-time bodies into virtual space.) I single out my *local* experience of this particular *world* event as a way into the main focus of this book: how the performance of place, and the place of performance, can lead to a political engagement with issues of larger global concern. In other words, I am interested in exploring, through the essays that follow, how local aesthetic experiences relate to, and even provide a model for, how one attends to the world socially.

Performance, or live art, is uniquely situated to engage with such questions because its present-tenseness forces audiences to consider carefully – and often to confront viscerally – the role of context, not just the 'what' or 'how' of performance, but the 'where', 'when', and ideally 'why' of performance, of what it means to come together as an audience in the first place, and what other non-proscribed, as-yet imagined social relationships might be posited within and beyond this otherwise random connection to the work being performed. To put this another way, unlike other forms of institutional or social organisa-tion (such as work, family, or nationhood), the very ephemerality of performance, its necessary contingency, asks us to ponder reflexively the ways we are obliged to each other as a constituency, one whose attachments and interests are temporary, discretionary, speculative, and plural, to be sure, but also embodied, emotionally adhesive (whether positively or negatively), and ideologically overdetermined. This 'double unfolding' of audience consciousness, in which Herbert Blau sees individual subjectivity forming an 'equivocal dialectic' with historical process, thus means that audience perceptions and connec-tions are also spatially (and politically) re-deployable, a performative response to the response solicited by the performance event itself.[3] As Blau writes,

> The audience . . . is not so much a mere congregation of people as a body of thought and desire. It does not exist before the play but is *initiated* or *precipitated* by it; it is not an entity to begin with but a consciousness

---

3 Herbert Blau, *The Audience* (Baltimore: Johns Hopkins University Press, 1990), pp. 25-6. See also Susan Bennett, *Theatre Audiences: A Theory of Production and Reception* (New York: Routledge [1990]; 2nd edn, 1998), in which she posits audience formation and response at the nexus of a similar double interaction between the outer frame of culture, including its various interpretive communities and horizons of expectation, and the inner frame of performance, including its 'overcoded' production strategies and ideologies.

constructed. The audience is what *happens* when, performing the signs and passwords of a play, something postulates itself and unfolds in response.[4]

As such, I see performance participating in a world-making project of the sort theorised by critics such as Jill Dolan and José Muñoz, among others.[5] That is, performance can and, I believe, should involve the transformation of the specific forms and contours of intimacy and identification that come from being part of a local theatrical public sphere into a potentially radical re-imagining of global citizenship as an activation of still more spectacular forms of counter-publicity. As my own experience of International Dance Day shows, performance – as a way of doing and an excuse for gathering – always includes more people than can be identified, always spatially exceeds the end-time of its elaboration, always produces modes of feeling and sentiment that will not be circumscribed by nor ever be commensurate with the performed object, let alone the object of performance. I should note, in this regard, that the objects which constitute my own performance archive and the methodology which mobilises their performative analysis in this book are very broadly defined, ranging from specific textual analyses and close readings of works of theatre, visual art, and social and religious ritual, to larger discursive comparisons of competing performances of promotion and protest that accompany global sporting events like the Olympics or World Cup, political and historical dramas like wars and narratives of national or cultural memory, local organising around urban development and sustainability, public displays of grief and the work of mourning, and even debates about climate change. To borrow a distinction from the influential performance studies theorist Richard Schechner, in this book I give equal attention to 'make-believe' performances, those pretend acts of dress-up and role-playing that we associate, for example, with the fictional world of the stage, and performances that are aimed more at 'making belief', 'real-world' dramas that, in their unfolding, enact a particular vision of that world.[6] To the extent that belief in that vision might be *more* or *less* acceptable to different audiences depending on their *place* in the world, accounts for the competing social formations

---

4 Blau, *The Audience*, p. 25.
5 See Jill Dolan, *Geographies of Learning: Theory and Practice, Activism and Performance* (Middletown: Wesleyan University Press, 2001); and *Utopia in Performance: Finding Hope at the Theater* (Ann Arbor: University of Michigan Press, 2005). See, as well, José Estaban Muñoz, *Disidentifications: Queers of Color and the Performance of Politics* (Minneapolis: University of Minnesota Press, 1999), especially pp. 195–96.
6 Richard Schechner, *Performance Studies: An Introduction* (New York: Routledge, 2002), p. 35.

and political identifications that will inevitably emerge in response to or alongside such performances. As my analysis of a quintessentially 'make-belief' performance like the Olympics in the next chapter attests, place-based narratives of national boosterism, global censure, and local activism inevitably overlap and collide when discussing the myriad elements and constituencies that help produce, and in turn are affected by, such a grand spectacle.

Questions of place have long informed both the structure and content of modern drama, mostly in terms of what Una Chaudhuri has perceptively diagnosed as a 'geopathology' of plot and character divided between home and exile, or what she calls 'a *victimage of location* and a *heroism of departure*'.[7] In the chapters that follow I survey many such thematic and representational engagements with place, both theatrical and non-theatrical, both near and far. However, I am much more concerned in this book with analysing performance (again, broadly defined) as an 'evental site' of the sort theorised by the French philosopher Alain Badiou. That is, I take the performance event to be emblematic of those radically contingent situations, as described by Badiou, that have the potential to interpellate being, rupturing the established order of things and ideally producing a new 'militant' (politically, aesthetically, erotically, etc.) consciousness,[8] one that is analogous to Blau's discussion of the audience as a body of thought and desire produced at once in the moment of happening *and* the moment of response. Crucially, for Badiou, this new consciousness is a 'place-based consciousness'; it is politically transformational, and thus distinguishable from the ideological interpellation of state apparatuses or the normalising and naturalising conditions of globalisation, only to the extent that the evental site retains its local specificity. As Badiou summarises, 'Every radical transformational action originates in a point, which, inside a situation, is an evental site'.[9] And here, too, I see the particular site of the performance event (an intersection in Vancouver, a bar in Beijing, a theatre in London, a football pitch in Japan) providing an important link between Badiou's typology of situational being and the work of spatial theorists like Doreen Massey, David Harvey, and Arif Dirlik, who have attempted (albeit using differently contested analytical paradigms) to

7 Una Chaudhuri, *Staging Place: The Geography of Modern Drama* (Ann Arbor: University of Michigan Press, 1997), p. xii.
8 Alain Badiou, *Being and Event*, trans. Oliver Feltham (London: Continuum, 2006), pp. xii–xiii.
9 *Ibid.*, p. 176. The term 'place-based consciousness' is Arif Dirlik's; see his 'Place-based imagination: globalism and the politics of place', in Roxann Prazniak and Arif Dirlik (eds) *Places and Politics in an Age of Globalization* (New York: Rowman & Littlefield, 2001), p. 15.

redirect attention to the local politics of place as a way of countering the economic and social asymmetries attending discourses of globalism that triumphally proclaim the obliteration of the distance – and difference – between places.[10] As a world-making project, this works reciprocally in two directions: on the one hand, I am contending that a locally produced piece of community theatre can inspire its neighbourhood audience, for example, to connect their place-based behaviour to an issue like global climate change; at the same time, I want to suggest that events played out on the world stage (wars, acts of terror, religious gatherings, natural disasters, sporting contests, human-rights protests) can never be inter- preted apart from the local constituencies to whom and through whom they are being mediated, even if only electronically. In other words, to the extent that I am making a case in this book for the way performance practice overlaps with political praxis as a project aimed at re-making the world, I am likewise arguing that we must never lose sight of the *place* of that overlap.

Badiou, a playwright in addition to being a philosopher, has himself 'rhapsodised' (in typically French high theoretical fashion) on the 'iso- morphism' between theatre and politics, noting that the two are linked in terms of their mutual 'fidelity to an event', one that is situation- ally contingent and temporally impermanent; as Badiou puts it, what matters is not whether politics or theatrical representation can be said to exist, but rather that each '*takes place*'.[11] For this to occur, both require an audience, a public, a spectator, who is called upon (or, in Badiou's words, 'summoned') to transpose the 'analytic' elements of eventness (actors, set, text, design, etc.) into a 'dialectics' of play, whereby a partic- ular state of affairs and/or affair of the state provokes an ethical response on the part of even the laziest of spectators, who must either accede to or resist the version of truth being staged.[12] These demands alone account for the world-making project that I, along with Badiou, see as being a priori a part of theatre and performance. 'Because', as Badiou states, 'under these conditions, theatre makes it known to you that you will not be able innocently to remain *in your place*'.[13]

Hence the particular relevance of beginning to map the local con- tours and global concerns of this book via a site-specific performance in

10 See Doreen Massey, *Space, Place, and Gender* (Minneapolis: University of Minnesota Press, 1994); David Harvey, *Spaces of Capital: Towards a Critical Geography* (Edinburgh: Edinburgh University Press, 2001); and Dirlik, 'Place-based imagination'.

11 Alain Badiou, 'Rhapsody for the theatre', trans. Bruno Bosteels, *Theatre Survey* 49:2 (2008), pp. 191, 192.

12 *Ibid.*, pp. 194–5.

13 *Ibid.*, p. 199.

my hometown that was meant to double as a celebration of international artistic solidarity. For the essays that follow – some begun before, some finished after, that date, and each analysing performances I experienced both at different venues throughout the city and in places (real and virtual) decidedly further afield – all take as their focus recent political events played across various world stages that nevertheless have local referents decidedly more proximate to the actual street corner on which I found myself that April day. Starting with Christ Church Cathedral itself, from whose pulpit the West's ongoing war on terror has been vociferously condemned at the same time as the Anglican rite of blessing same-sex unions has been vigorously defended (see chapter 2). A block east along Georgia Street, between Hornby and Howe, is the north concourse of the Vancouver Art Galley, where just a month earlier organisers of the 2010 Winter Olympics had installed a giant clock counting down the days, hours, and minutes to the start of the Games, and which has since become a focal point for anti-Games protests targeting poverty, housing and sustainability issues specific to Vancouver's urban core, as well as human rights and environmental abuses in China, host of the 2008 Summer Olympics (see chapter 1). The steps on the south side of the gallery, along Robson Street, have also historically served as a local gathering place, where tourists watch myriad street performers, skateboarders, and graffiti artists; protesters of all stripes assemble in advance of a march; and sports fans, again of all stripes, launch their victory celebrations. The area is especially frenzied during any World Cup summer and increasingly year-round as Canada's combat role in Afghanistan persists, producing a confluence of diasporic/migrant communities whose sentimental interests and attachments often overlap in startling ways (see chapter 3). Finally, at the westernmost tip of Georgia Street lies the entrance to Stanley Park, an oasis of green within Vancouver's conurbation about which locals are fiercely protective, but which nonetheless bears the memorial scars of a violence (both human and meteorological) that is global in its causes and reach, and painfully local in its effects and consequences (see chapter 4 and the coda). My methodology, then, is best summed up by the epigraphs which preface this introduction, with me consciously building on the genealogical approach of Joseph Roach, who is in turn adapting the spatial theories of Michel de Certeau. Thus, in the ensuing chapters I walk readers through my city and various affiliated sites of performance that announce their congruency – if not always their adjacency – with sometimes more (the Vancouver East Cultural Centre or the Brooklyn Academy of Music), sometimes less (Studio 58 or Bar Obiwan) geographical specificity, in order to construct a performance genealogy of the past and the present, the near and the far, the placeless and the place hoped-for, that will provide an embodied repertoire of acts, memories, and performative substitutions with which we might circumnavigate, and even intervene in, world politics. The fact that de Certeau's and Roach's respective remarks are made in the context of discussions of a pre-9/11 New York City and a pre-Katrina New Orleans is not lost on me and, indeed, I incorporate both of these world stages, both of these global spaces of (dis)location and (dis)embodiment, within my ruminations on local response and responsibility in this book.

Another way of approaching what I'm getting at here is through that famous dictum from the 1960s: 'think globally, act locally'. In an age of ever-accelerating globalisation and increasingly situated responses to its effects, it may seem somewhat quaint, nostalgic even, to trot out such a tired axiom. Nevertheless, this book is premised on the never-more urgent need to take seriously its familiar two-part injunction. More specifically, as I hope to demonstrate in the chapters that follow, the spatial-temporal relation here posited between perception/ intellection and action, between imagining a future where and when and doing the work of the present here and now, requires an understanding of how performance and the 'performative' (a term I also deploy quite expansively in this book) dialectically inform the double imperative in this instance. Here, I am guided in my thinking as much by *Hamlet* as by ACT UP, as much by Brecht and Boal as by J. L. Austin and de Certeau. That is, just as we have seen via Badiou that any individual *act* (of which we may take the pledging of an oath, the walking of a city, or the staging of a play to be equally exemplary) depends for its success and power, for its 'doing', on the place or context of its enunciation, so might we understand the collective *activity* or even *activism* that potentially results as a tactical 'making do' – in de Certeau's formulation of that phrase – of the placelessness and powerlessness that comes from mutually acknowledging 'the space of the other' (of which I take membership in any audience also to be exemplary).[14] Again, I am following the lead of critics like Muñoz and Dolan, who in riffing on Austin's discussion of the linguistic performative in *How to Do Things with Words* (a text I take up, in more depth, in chapter 2), have called for an examination of the 'performativity of *or* in performance'[15] – that is, an understanding of performance as not simply being *about*, or a representation *of*, something, but as *doing* or *enacting* something,

---

14 De Certeau, *The Practice of Everyday Life*, p. 37.
15 See Muñoz, *Disidentifications*, p. 200; Dolan, *Utopia in Performance*, pp. 5ff.; and J. L. Austin, *How to Do Things with Words* (New York: Oxford University Press, 1962).

including potential political change. In other words, I am interested, with this book, in exploring how the local (or localised) experience of, or participation in, performance (be it a theatrical production, a sporting event, a religious ceremony, or a political demonstration) translates into the thinking through and doing of a progressive global politics that produces, in turn, material change – how, in effect, performance *re-stages* the world.

Exploding frames, engaging politics

Of course, as Shakespeare reminds us, performance has always been in the business of taking the world as its stage (and, yes, I do consider a production of *As You Like It* in chapter 2): from early-modern and eighteenth-century representations of colonial contact to contemporary performance studies theorists' various (inter)disciplinary investments in 'intercultural' or 'transcultural' performance.[16] Indeed, one might say that it is through performance, rather than Area Studies or Comparative Literature, that we come closest to an approximation of 'planetarity' as Gayatri Spivak has recently proposed that term as a 'species' of radical alterity and differentiation capable of doing battle with the politically abstracting and culturally homogenising forces of globalisation.[17] And yet as Roach and Diana Taylor have separately pointed out, performing the planet has historically involved a rather unequal exchange of otherness, with both the European theatrical avant-garde (cf. Brecht, Artaud, and Grotowski) and the nascent North American academic discipline of performance studies as it came to be influenced by cultural anthropology (represented especially by the collaborations between Victor Turner and Richard Schechner in the 1980s) incorporating non-Western performance traditions and rituals within their aesthetic practices and/ or universalising theories of social drama without a reciprocal risking of methodological expertise or, indeed, the narrative positionality and economic purchase that comes from maintaining a structural stake in First Worldism.[18] (This is an issue, especially as it relates to what

16 See Victor Turner, *The Anthropology of Performance* (New York: PAJ Publications, 1986); Lisa Wolford and Richard Schechner (eds), *The Grotowski Sourcebook* (New York: Routledge, 1997); Patrice Pavis (ed.), *The Intercultural Performance Reader* (New York: Routledge, 1996); and Richard Schechner, *Between Theater and Anthropology* (Philadelphia: University of Pennsylvania Press, 1985).

17 Gayatri Chakravorty Spivak, *Death of a Discipline* (New York: Columbia University Press, 2003), pp. 72–3.

18 See Diana Taylor, *The Archive and the Repertoire: Performing Cultural Memory in the Americas* (Durham, NC: Duke University Press, 2003), pp. 8–11; and Joseph Roach, 'World Bank Drama', in Wai Chee Dimock and Lawrence Buell (eds), *Shades of the*

Spivak has called the 'planet-talk' subtending the discourse of 'unexamined environmentalism',[19] that I will return to in the coda to this book.) To the extent that '[w]e are all in the picture, all social actors in our overlapping, coterminous, contentious dramas', Taylor advocates taking seriously the scope of that picture's frame (which, in her case as a Latin Americanist, is at least hemispheric, if not completely planetary), constantly revising our critical methodologies 'through engagement with other interlocutors as well as other regional, racial, political, and linguistic realities both within and beyond our national boundaries'.[20] I am the first to admit that, in promulgating a theory of performance in/of/as the world in this book, I do all too little of what Taylor counsels, with the cosmopolitan, diasporic theatrical subjectivity I am attempting to project in these pages frequently betraying an all too narrow provincialism – something the interdisciplinary, multi-campus International Performance and Culture Group of the University of California has politely critiqued me for in connection with an earlier published version of chapter 3 (although would that they had, in doing so, spelled my name correctly).[21]

In my defence, I am suggesting here that a focus on the local can, paradoxically, produce its own exploded frames, its own 'exponential future', to borrow the title of an important recent art show here in Vancouver that I reference in chapter 1. The local spaces of performance, and the persons within whom it is embodied, constitute sites where broader political engagements and movements of the sort envisioned by Taylor might be initiated. Localness, in this way, gets transposed back into a concept of worldness, of being in and of the world, by virtue of performance's double structure of address: that is, the particular *place* of its production, and the multiple *spaces* of its reception, recognition, and redistribution, an experience or 'practising' of place that de Certeau calls 'a relation to the world'.[22] Let me be clear: I don't wish to overstate the role that local spectacle might play in helping to remedy complex world conflicts and crises, or, heaven help us, even securing and sustaining global justice. But to the extent that, as Taylor reminds us, spectacle – in the Debordian sense – represents a series of social relations mediated by images, it can theatricalise and make newly compelling for local

Planet: American Literature as World Literature (Princeton: Princeton University Press, 2007), pp. 174–5.

19 Spivak, *Death of a Discipline*, p. 72.
20 Taylor, *The Archive*, p. 12.
21 The International Performance and Culture Research Group of the University of California, Letter to the Editor, *Theatre Survey* 47:2 (2006).
22 De Certeau, *The Practice of Everyday Life*, p. 117.

audiences various scenarios of present-day political turmoil, as well as historicise how that turmoil very often reenacts the past.[23] Here it is worth pausing to consider Taylor's useful parsing of the 'metonymic relationship' between *scene* and *scenario*. Writing with reference to the scenarios of 'discovery' and 'conquest' that continue to haunt the plot of the Americas, and to overdetermine various social dramas enacted within that plot, Taylor notes that whereas we can think of 'scene' as referring to a physical location or environment (be it a street corner or a proscenium stage), 'scenario' encompasses the setup and the action that frame and activate our interpretation of that scene. In other words, the scenario, as an embodied 'act of transfer', *relocates* us as spectators, placing us 'within its frame, implicating us in its ethics and politics'.[24]

Let me attempt to get at the relevance of Taylor's comments to my own study by describing another recent performance in Vancouver that I participated in. The scene, this time, was a hair salon in the city's east end rather than a street corner downtown; the scenario, at least in its external concept, or setup, involved fifty-odd local adults – myself included – agreeing to have their locks shorn, shaped, styled, and quite possibly dyed by a group of eager ten- and eleven-year-old schoolchildren in front of a live public audience, and preserved for posterity by an array of constantly flashing digital cameras. Programmed as part of Vancouver's 2008 PuSh International Performing Arts Festival, a two-week showcase of live art held every January (and overseen with remarkable energy and curatorial vision by local arts impresario Norman Armour), *Haircuts by Children*, as the event was so prosaically titled, was Darren O'Donnell and his Toronto-based company Mammalian Diving Reflex's (MDR) latest example of anarchic civic performance, or what O'Donnell prefers to call 'social acupuncture'. Deriving equally from O'Donnell's training in traditional Chinese medicine and his work as an activist and artist interested in re-energising both democracy and the theatre as truly participatory forms, the social acupuncture experiments of MDR work through tactical applications of pressure to different parts of the social body, working to redirect the circuitry and redistribute the energies of that body toward long-term, system-wide repair. As O'Donnell sees the most debilitating symptom of the breakdown of democracy in our society to be the steady erosion of opportunities and spaces for 'unstructured discourse', the basic modus operandi of MDR is to bring strangers together in public situations and to force them to talk

---

23 See Taylor, *The Archive*, p. 13; and Guy Debord, *Society of the Spectacle* (Detroit: Black and Red, 1983), p. 4.

24 Taylor, *The Archive*, pp. 29 and 33.

to each other, 'needling' us toward unfamiliar – and frequently uncomfortable – social *interactions* that then might lead to related political
interventions.[25] O'Donnell summarises MDR's mandate as follows: 'We
are interested in using social acupuncture to short-circuit familiar social
networks and formations to create something unexpected and fully
influenced by chance – an artistic civic engagement that uses the city as
raw material'.[26]

With each successive civic engagement, O'Donnell and MDR have
sought to expand the contexts of and for social intimacy at the same
time as they have steadily ramped up their participatory stakes: from
enlisting random strangers in conversation on the street (*The Talking
Creature*); to knocking on various front doors in a neighbourhood and
requesting a look around inside (*Home Tours*); to somehow convincing
all the patrons of a busy downtown bar to play a potentially salacious
party game from their adolescence (*Spin the Bottle*). For the initial performance of *Haircuts*, O'Donnell and MDR worked with grade 5 and 6
students from Parkdale Public School in Toronto, training them, with
the aid of a professional stylist, to cut and style hair, and then turning
them loose on a brave roster of adult volunteers who had signed up for
half-hour appointments scheduled over two successive days at the Milk
International Children's Festival for the Arts in May 2006. Testing the
limits of the trust we place in children by reversing the standard generational power dynamics, the performance, which O'Donnell notes is
explicitly 'framed as a call to allow children into the political process',[27]
asks us to consider, in turn, the ways in which our society routinely *dis-
enfranchises* children within a multiplicity of domestic and institutional
settings, including families and schools. This question, of global relevance, takes on added local resonance when one considers that Parkdale
is a particularly poor inner-city neighbourhood in Toronto, made up of
mostly working-class, immigrant families, and plagued by longstanding
drug- and gang-related violence.

To find the equivalent neighbourhood in Vancouver one has to
travel, ironically, to the suburbs, specifically to the notorious Whalley
region of Surrey, which is among the most ethnically and linguistically
diverse regions in the Lower Mainland of British Columbia (featuring an
especially large population of South Asian immigrants), and which also
boasts the highest crime rate. Additionally, the Surrey School District

25 For a fuller description of O'Donnell's performance politics and aesthetic, see his
    book *Social Acupuncture: A Guide to Suicide, Performance, and Utopia* (Toronto:
    Coach House Books, 2006), especially pp. 48–51.
26 *Ibid.*, pp. 94–5.
27 *Ibid.*, p. 85.

has a reputation within the province for being extremely conservative and censorious, its recent history of deciding what is in the best interests of its students including the banning of a series of children's books featuring same-sex parents and the cancelling of a planned 2005 production of *The Laramie Project* at a local high school.[28] However, in choosing as his co-creators the grade 5 and 6 students from Broadview Elementary, O'Donnell was actually tapping into a tested pool of youth creativity, with several students from the same school having earlier worked with local documentary filmmaker Nettie Wild in creating a series of short digital videos for the National Film Board of Canada.[29] Not that this inspired me with heaps of confidence as I made my way, along with my camera-toting partner, Richard, to my scheduled appointment. I am known, among my friends and colleagues, as someone particularly invested in the way his hair looks (it changes colour and styles frequently, and requires a lot of product, all of which I pay for accordingly); as such, I made sure, in inviting said friends and colleagues to witness my shearing, that they understood what a sacrifice I was making in the name of performance.

In the end, I needn't have worried. My stylists, Sam and Jamal, were wizards with the scissors. Initially their eyes lit up when they saw the ersatz faux-hawk I was then sporting, and I could tell they very much wanted it to come off. But then we talked about what I was looking for, and we very quickly came to mutual agreement: a light trim and thinning on top and a much closer cropping with the razor on the sides and at the back. I then took my glasses off (without which I am virtually blind), sat back, and placed myself (literally) in their hands. In retrospect, the scenario unfolded as a kind of double mimesis, with me – as actor *and* spectator – framed at once by the stylist's mirror into which I occasionally squinted to catch a measure of Sam and Jamal's progress, and by the multiple camera frames pointed towards me – as anthropological specimen – by avid audience members both amazed and appalled at my willing submission to such a power reversal. This, in turn, produced two further scenarios that competed for my attention, and that bring things back to the main concerns of this book. On the one hand, I congratulated myself on my own small contribution to the empowerment of this cohort of kids, with the seriousness and pride they were so obviously taking in their work leading me to encourage Sam and Jamal,

28 See David Reevely, 'Surrey school board rejects same-sex books', *Vancouver Sun* (13 June 2003), p. B6; and Gary Mason, 'Hate is a learned behaviour', *Globe and Mail* (24 September 2005), p. A9.

29 See 'Tales from Bridgeview: web stories made by kids', National Film Board of Canada, www.onf.ca/webextension/bridgeview (accessed January 2008).

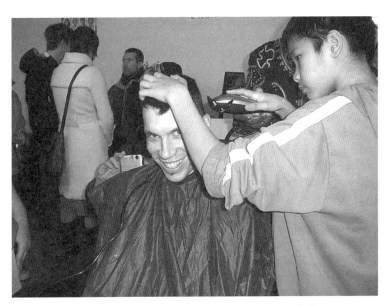

2 The author getting shorn as part of Mammalian Diving Reflex's *Haircuts by Children*, PuSh Festival, Vancouver, January 2008

in particular, to be even bolder in their designs (a little more came off the top, a few more racing stripes of temporary colour went down the middle); in this way, I saw this performance-cum-social experiment as potentially filling an important gap in the imaginative lives of a group of kids whom local institutional structures had long ago left behind in very material ways. At the same time, I had to keep reminding myself that I was, in the end, getting a free haircut, and not a bad one at that (see figure 2). Indeed, the flip side of social apprenticeship and dialogue in this scenario is economic exploitation. After all, these were not Equity actors earning a basic union wage. Moreover, the predominantly racialised make-up of most of the child-stylists and the equally predominant whiteness of most of the adult-clients and audience members necessarily raises questions and images of child labour, an issue which compels, as per Taylor's terms, a performative act of transfer back out into the world, and a confrontation with the various ethical and political claims that world makes daily upon us.

Liveness/livability

This dialectics of performance's geography, its historical exploitation of the tension between the performance of local embodiment and the politics of global abstraction, contribute to what Michel Foucault has identified as the modern world's heterotopic conjuring 'of other spaces' in order to represent, contest, or invert what remains illusory and/or compensatory about the 'real places' of power and knowledge in our society, and to imagine those placeless spaces (utopias) where we might *unrealise* some of our more oppressive social structures.[30] This is also what makes performance so conducive, in my mind, to modelling what, again after Foucault, we might call an ethical aesthetics, or 'an aesthetics of existence'. In his philosophical and personal explorations of the 'use of pleasure' for the 'care of the self' in the last years of his life, Foucault returned again and again to the idea that developing radical new styles of and for living required first of all attending to one's own self-fashioning in the same way that an artist devotes himself or herself to the creation of a new work of art.[31] But such performances of the self require, as part of their 'ethical response', not to mention their 'theory of responsibility', an audience, the doing or redoing of one's self presupposing, in Judith Butler's recent reexamination of Foucault's ethical account of himself, an 'undoing' by another: 'we must recognize that ethics requires us to risk ourselves precisely at moments of unknowingness, when what forms us diverges from what lies before us, when our willingness to become undone in relation to others constitutes our chance of becoming human'.[32]

Such moments of unknowingness, of undoing, of becoming human, occur again and again in the theatre, and here my guide remains – steadfastly, insistently – Peggy Phelan. In arguing for why the 'liveness' of live art matters, Phelan does not naively valorise some unmediated notion of 'presence', as some have critiqued her for suggesting, but rather

30 For Michel Foucault's influential formulation of his concept of 'heterotopia', see his 'Of other spaces', in Nicholas Mirzoeff (ed.), *The Visual Culture Reader* (New York: Routledge [1998]; 2nd edn, 2002), pp. 229–36. Importantly, in contrasting heterotopias from utopias, Foucault does note state, as some have supposed, that the two concepts are opposed or antithetical; rather, as 'counter-sites', heterotopias serve as 'a kind of effectively enacted utopia in which the real sites, all the other real sites that can be found within the culture, are simultaneously represented, contested, and inverted' (p. 231). Thus, I see my application of heterotopia to performance (something Foucault himself peripherally explores in the essay) as coextensive with Dolan's discussion of 'utopian performatives'. For a somewhat different application of Foucault to the places of theatre, see Chaudhuri, *Staging Place*, p. 5.

31 See Michel Foucault, *The History of Sexuality, Volume 2: The Use of Pleasure*, trans. Robert Hurley (New York: Vintage, 1990); *The History of Sexuality, Volume 3: The Care of the Self*, trans. Robert Hurley (New York: Vintage, 1990); and *Ethics: Subjectivity and Truth*, ed. Paul Rabinow, trans. Robert Hurley *et al.* (New York: New Press, 1997).

32 Judith Butler, *Giving an Account of Oneself* (New York: Fordham University Press, 2005), pp. 135 and 136.

points to the fact that the live event allows for 'the response of the other', opening up 'the possibility of both the actor and the spectator becoming transformed during the event's unfolding'.[33] It is at this point, for Phelan, that 'the aesthetic joins the ethical', and, I would argue, where her discussions of 'liveness' in performance link up with Butler's theorisations of 'livability' as that which (similar to Giorgio Agamben's notion of 'bare life') 'establishes minimum conditions for a livable life with regard to human life'.[34] Both Butler and Phelan are formulating their theories very much in the shadow of 9/11, seeking to account for how that event's performative and political exposure of the fragility or 'precariousness' of life might, paradoxically, serve as the starting point for a new ethics of human response and social responsibility (something I return to, via Butler and Phelan, in chapter 4). In doing so, it is perhaps no accident that both turn to Emmanuel Levinas's concept of face-to-faceness as that which most fundamentally reduces any concept of being *in* the world to the proximate, to a local encounter with another that necessarily changes one's view *of* the world.[35] Here again, I would argue, along with Phelan, that performance has much to teach us. As she writes,

> If Levinas is right, and the face-to-face encounter is the most crucial arena in which the ethical bond we share becomes manifest, then live theatre and performance might speak to philosophy with renewed vigor. So far the language of this conversation has been largely nonverbal. Becoming fluent will require practice, patience, humility, and the recognition that the social body, like our own all-too-human body, is both stronger than we guessed and unbearably tender. The connection between the social body and the mortal body is defiantly metaphorical. The metaphorical link, however, is fused by the literal physical body – whether the body of a suicide bomber or of an earnest artist – as its actions and inactions make vivid the drama we face every moment of this, our dismaying young century.[36]

33 Peggy Phelan, 'Performance, live culture and things of the heart: Peggy Phelan in conversation with Marquard Smith', *Journal of Visual Culture* 2:3 (2003), p. 295. Phelan is responding here, in part, to Philip Auslander's critique of the theory of the 'ontology of performance' she put forth in the last chapter of *Unmarked: The Politics of Performance* (New York: Routledge, 1993); see Auslander, *Liveness: Performance in a Mediatized Culture* (New York: Routledge, 1999). For similar comments by Phelan on live performance's facilitation of the possibilities of mutual transformation, see her 'Marina Abramović: witnessing shadows', *Theatre Journal* 56:4 (2004), p. 575.

34 See Phelan, 'Marina Abramović', p. 575; Judith Butler, *Undoing Gender* (New York: Routledge, 2004), p. 226; and Giorgio Agamben, *Homo Sacer: Sovereign Power and Bare Life*, trans. Daniel Heller-Roazen (Stanford: Stanford University Press, 1998).

35 See Phelan, 'Marina Abramović', pp. 574 and 577; Judith Butler, *Precarious Life: The Powers of Mourning and Violence* (New York: Verso, 2004), pp. 128–51; and Levinas, *Ethics and Infinity*, trans. Richard A. Cohen (Pittsburgh: Duquesne University Press, 1985).

36 Phelan, 'Marina Abramović', p. 577.

When I first began writing the essays that make up this book in the spring of 2003, with a near simultaneous stab at what would eventually become chapters 3 and 4, I had no idea that they would eventually cohere (if, indeed, they do cohere at all) into an argument about the co-extensiveness and co-implicatedness of performance, place, and politics. I only knew that I needed to attempt to make sense of the 'dismaying young century' in which I suddenly found myself, and of the local and global confluences of unexamined violence (an unprovoked gay bashing in my city's most famous park; an unauthorised invasion of a country half way around the world) and equally unexamined celebration (a bonanza of same-sex weddings in North America and Europe; Olympic fever in Vancouver and Beijing) that I was increasingly witness to. Performance seemed to be the best way to do this, not least because its 'critical temporality', that is, its suspended or provisional constitution of a temporary public within a particular moment and a localised space, serves as an especially useful way to intervene into the pressing issues and debates that subtend what David Román has identified as the 'contemporary', one that 'engages with the past without being held captive to it and that instantiates the present without defining a future'.[37] It is, I think, no coincidence that post-9/11 there has emerged a wave of books published by respected scholars (including Román, Dolan, Taylor, and others) who have attempted to make sense of the urgent times in which we all now live through performance. The essays in this book are governed by a similar sense of urgency, and with the exception of the concluding chapter, they are arranged in the reverse chronological order of their composition in order to give readers a sense of the past, present and, dare I say, future performances that have contributed to the evolution of my own global politics, and to my experience of the local embodied genealogy of my city.

Local/global genealogies

That genealogy begins, in chapter 1, with a detailed account of the preparations Vancouver has been making in gearing up to play host to the world at the 2010 Winter Olympics. As sports journalists and cultural pundits love to remind us, there is perhaps no bigger world stage than the Olympic Games, when tribal nationalisms join forces with late

37 David Román, *Performance in America: Contemporary U.S. Culture and the Performing Arts* (Durham, NC: Duke University Press, 2005), p. 1. Jill Dolan likewise argues that the unique temporality governing performance, its being in some fundamental sense 'out of time', goes hand in hand with its utopic qualities; see Dolan, *Utopia in Performance*, pp. 13–14.

capitalism, neo-liberal individualism, cultural tourism, gender bina-
rism, the modern security state, and local weather patterns to produce a
two-week media showcase of drug and judging scandals, political grand-
standing, corporate sponsorships, regional boosterism, heart-tugging
human interest stories, spectacular opening and closing production
numbers and, very occasionally, sublime moments of athletic excellence.
Befitting a festival that owes its origins to ancient Greece, the Olympics
are resolutely Aristotelian in their privileging of plot and their emphasis
on narrative arcs, be it an athlete's back story, a nation's past and present
history, a given sport's evolution, or the ritual aspects of various ceremonies. One of those narratives, I contend in this chapter, has to do with
place, from the competition fostered between cities during the initial
bidding process through to the development, re-design, and re-branding
of the eventual host city's built environment. In the process, local economic, social, and cultural issues relating to the overall sustainability
of an Olympic city might come in conflict with larger symbolic representations of place that a host nation wishes to project to the world. A
comparison of Vancouver's Olympic preparations with those of Beijing
yields interesting results, in this regard. In undertaking this comparison,
I am less interested in each Olympics as a performance 'event' (hence the
publication of this book prior to the opening of the Vancouver Games)
than in the performative dynamics of various local, national, and international responses and responsibilities related to the *organisation* of the
event. These range from, in the case of Beijing, abstract evaluations of
progress that are applied differentially (i.e. economically vs. socially and
politically) depending on one's national or global relationship to China,
to, in the case of Vancouver, more measurable, but no less fraught,
indices as corollary investments in arts and culture and a purported
commitment to expand affordable social housing in a real-estate market
made even more grossly inflated by an Olympics building frenzy.

   That market, of course, has a history, one that is bound inextricably
with China, starting with the Gold Mountain men who came across the
Pacific to build Canada's railway in the nineteenth century, and then
were taxed for deciding to stay. More proximately, there is a connection
to be made to China via Vancouver's last major hosting of the world
during Expo 86; that event marked an important moment in the city's
emergence as a Pacific Rim destination ripe for capital investment and
real-estate speculation, much of it fuelled by wealthy Hong Kong business tycoons nervous about the colony's scheduled reversion to rule by
mainland Communist China in 1997. China's rapid ascent to global
superpower – undoubtedly a major factor in the country being awarded
the 2008 Summer Olympics – is, in other words, visibly evident in local

transformations to Vancouver's skyline. Thus, in this first and longest chapter, I attempt to provide a template for the critical methodology employed in the rest of the book by using the performance genre of the showcase to analyse various media spectacles, works of community theatre, museum and gallery exhibitions, signature architecture and urban design, displays of cultural branding, and the competing optics of pride and protest accompanying the preparations for both Olympic events, in turn asking how this relates to larger questions of urban sustainability, national mythologising, and global human rights in the narrative of place promotion which is always the real performance goal of any Olympic Games. I structure much of this analysis around a more focused discussion of one high-profile Chinese artist, Ai Weiwei, who very publicly opted out of Beijing's official Olympic narrative, reading the local/global interfaces of audience and event operating in several of his photographic, video, and installation pieces alongside similar performance-based conceptual work produced by Canadian and local Vancouver artists such as Rebecca Belmore, Edward Burtynsky, Alex Morrison, David Rokeby, and Althea Thauberger. To the extent that those interfaces, in the case of Beijing and Vancouver, map an embodied history of what, after Roach, we might call the 'circum-Pacific world', and in particular the Asian Pacific diaspora, the chapter begins with a short detour through Sydney, Hong Kong, and Shanghai.

In chapter 2 my focus remains transnational, but I move, at least initially, from an east–west to a north–south axis. There, I examine the politics of same-sex marriage in Canada and the United States along-side its performative representation on stage and in the media in both countries, and the world at large. I argue, via Elizabeth Freeman, that marriage as an institution bestowing rights upon private individuals needs to be decoupled from the wedding ceremony, a ritual event that asks a participatory public to avow, or disavow, the form and force of its connections with each other, and with various state apparatuses in or against whose name those connections are made. In so doing, I ask whether or not a queer performance of 'I do' can function simultane-ously as a performatively queer 'I do not', especially as such a statement may signify an active/activist disidentification with the transnational (in)security state that has grown up in North America post-9/11 and the invasion of Iraq? I attempt to answer this question by first re-examining the deconstructive and dramaturgical uses to which J. L. Austin's most famous example of performative utterance has been put by queer theory; next by surveying the (same-sex) marriage plots of a number of theatri-cal productions (of plays by Shakespeare, Charles Mee, Paul Rudnick, and Terrence McNally, among others) performed both Off-Broadway and by local Vancouver companies; and finally by analysing in depth the ongoing *Love Art Laboratory* 'performance art wedding' project initiated by Annie Sprinkle and partner Beth Stephens in 2004, one that uses the queer wedding ceremony, and the potential counter-publics produced by it, to put in place a different sort of repeating with respect to the violence of war. I conclude this chapter by expanding my geopolitical focus, outlining some of the local/global dynamics of the debate surrounding the blessing of same-sex unions in the worldwide Anglican Communion, and returning to Austin to discuss how, in the Church of England at any rate, acts of blessing share some performative and political overlaps with acts of repentance.

Local audiences can be migrant, even migratory, audiences, and in chapter 3 I demonstrate how this is so by going travelling with Tony Kushner and David Beckham. Specifically, I examine Kushner's celebrated and controversial play *Homebody/Kabul* alongside the recent career of the world's most famous footballer, in order to argue that live theatre, like global sporting culture, can function as a site of transnational connection and local transformation. Using Gilles Deleuze and Félix Guattari's concept of nomadology as a way of negotiating between the globally relative and locally absolute claims of history, I situate Kushner's evolving gloss on the 'war machine' that is Afghanistan within the context of my own deterritorialised and itinerant responses to two separate productions and one staged reading of the play (in London, New York, and Vancouver, respectively) between 2002 and 2008. These responses are further juxtaposed with the contests between discourses of globalism, nationalism, and migrancy that have routinely emerged in the media in connection with David Beckham, especially in the lead-up to the 2002 World Cup, and following his trades to Real Madrid in 2003 and the LA Galaxy in 2007. Beckham is not paradigmatically a nomad, but the sport he plays, and the fans who follow its theatrics, resist easy conscription by the State, even as powerful a governing body as FIFA. Thus, an analysis of Beckham's travels, both on and off the field, serves to contextualise the confluence of the local and the global, the personal and the political, that simultaneously mobilises my reading of Kushner's play. Taking my cue from the Homebody herself, I suggest that this reading needs to be more migratory than armchair, especially within the context of Canada's ongoing combat role in Kandahar and the ever-expanding global war on terror more generally.

In chapter 4 I return to questions of remembrance and forgetting, mourning and melancholy, that critics like Phelan, Roach, and Butler posit are at the heart of live performance, the life of cities, and human life itself. I do so by first offering an account of a range of different built and embodied memorials in Vancouver as they enact, comment on, and at times revise a recent history of anti-female, anti-immigrant, and anti-gay violence in the city. I then go on to examine a series of local – and specifically theatrical – performances of mourning whose respective Vancouver stagings between 1993 and 2005 speak to my own evolving memorialisation of the city in which I live, and to a larger genealogy of global queer witnessing that, in the face of what I call heteronorma-tive historiography, perforce remains ephemeral and diffuse, but no less generative, agential, or agitational as a result. Among the artists I discuss in this context are the Canadian dancer/choreographer Margie Gillis and the American playwright Paula Vogel, women who have both sought to memorialise their respective brothers' AIDS deaths in endur-ing performance works. The chapter concludes with an analysis of the 2002 Vancouver productions of two plays – Terrence McNally's *Corpus Christi* and Moisés Kaufman and Tectonic Theater's *The Laramie Project* – forever associated with the 1998 murder of Matthew Shepard, but equally resonantly for local audiences with the savage gay-bashing of Aaron Webster in Stanley Park in the fall of 2001. Drawing from Butler's ruminations on Sophocles' *Antigone*, and her related query in *Precarious Life* about what counts as a grievable life, I ask how, in mourning Shepard and Webster, we are to remember their killers, our other broth-ers? How, too, to move beyond the melancholic whiteness that might be said to encompass many locally constituted queer theories of mourning (my own included)? In posing these difficult questions, I seek once again to expand the dialectics of place at play in this book, this time calling upon recent dance-theatre works created by UK-based DV8 Physical Theatre and Stan Won't Dance, whose debut performance piece, *Sinner*, is a complex re-membering of the 1999 nail-bombing of the Admiral Duncan, a gay pub in Soho.

The dynamic and dialectical relationship between the local and the global that animates the central concerns of this book is nowhere more evident than in the performative effects of, and political responses to, climate change. The results of centuries' worth of unfettered (though unequal) fossil fuel and carbon emissions are, for example, observable by audiences in places as geographically distant and geologically dis-tinct as the Canadian Arctic and sub-Saharan Africa. Extreme weather affords us all a front-row seat on the world, and thus in the coda to this book I use a severe wind storm that blew through Vancouver in the fall of 2006 to roam near and far in my assessment of the equally extreme action that seems needed in order to save our planet. In so doing, I refer-ence an outdoor play production, a dance performance, and a series of community theatre forums in Vancouver; Al Gore's LIVE Earth concert series; Google Earth, satellite imaging, and website animation associated with the tracking of climate change; the recent UNFCC Conference in Bali; and Paul Chan and the Classical Theatre of Harlem's celebrated 2007 production of *Waiting for Godot* in post-Katrina New Orleans. Approaching climate change through performance, I argue, demonstrates in compelling and starkly theatrical ways how, as both local actors in and global spectators to what many are suggesting might be Earth's final act, we cannot, *pace* Didi and Gogo, remain unmoved.

As I mentioned earlier, the chapters, in their sequencing, map a reverse chronology of their composition that opens out, inevitably, onto a very uncertain future. They also enact, spatially, the necessary tensions between a vigilant global spectatorship and the equally robust local activism I see constituting performance's balancing of and mediation between place and politics, audience and event. Thus, while the book begins, in the next chapter, with its most expansive discussion of performance's engagement with the world, it gradually progresses toward a more focused treatment of the local, if only as a way of adequately assessing our place in and responsibilities to the world. The spatial/temporal dialectic animating the organisation of this book also mirrors, coincidentally, the life of a performance; that is, we can say that chapter 1 sets the stage for the performance, chapter 2 analyses the specific doing of the performance, chapter 3 travels with the performance as it tours, chapter 4 looks at how we remember the performance when it ends, and the coda discusses what new actions, meanings, and performances need to come from those ends. This performative trajectory was only pointed out to me at the end of the writing of this book – by my research assistant, Alana, who has been with me every step of the way on this project. And that speaks, finally, to another fundamental thread of connection I am trying to delineate in these pages.

Reconstituting kinship (queerly)

When I come together with others – in Vancouver or elsewhere – to take in a performance, I am increasingly conscious that the bonds we tentatively (and temporarily) form, in our collective gathering as an audience, enact a fundamental reconstitution of kinship relations. For me, that reconstitution is effectively a queer one. By this, I do not mean to trade on the theatre's reputation as a queer-friendly profession (although neither do I wish to dismiss this out of hand); rather, I am positing that the theatre, like queerness, is a space of connection and contestation, where performers and audiences are able to rehearse and experiment with different sentimental attachments, stranger forms of intimacy, new narratives of embodiment and political participation. And here I must acknowledge the centrality of queer theory to what I see as place-based performance's fundamental relation to a politically progressive under-standing of global citizenship in the succeeding chapters. Indeed, one way of thinking about the local logics (and logistics) of the worldmaking project sketched in the pages of this book is as a partial attempt to queer normative patterns and premises of kinship as they have historically been used to shore up arbitrary and counter-productive cross-cultural divisions based on blood, language, gender, national belonging, race and ethnicity, or religious affiliation. Instead, if we admit – like the Greeks (who knew a thing or two about theatre as well) – that citizenship has a sexual and bodily dimension, and if, following from this, we further imagine global citizenship to be a network of relations and obligations based on, among other things, an ethical accounting of subjective auton-omy *and* shared corporeal responsibility, then we can begin dismantling arbitrary public/private, us/them divisions closer to home, starting with citizenship's key economic and institutional prop, the family. As I attempt to demonstrate in the succeeding chapters, performance – the doing of it, the reacting to it, and the writing about it – provides us with another family model altogether, one for which we may take what is so fraught, contestatory, fragile, and ultimately unknowable about being part of an audience as exemplary.

This is not to deny that audience relations in the theatre are often initially sustained by shared aesthetic taste, geography, identitarian affiliation, or socio-economic status. But it is also to contend that those relations can be transformed, during the course of a performance, through what Victor Turner has identified as 'communitas', a tempo-rary levelling of social hierarchies into the unstructured, stateless equal-ity of mutual participation in a ritual event.[38] Again, there are obvious overlaps here with many explicitly queer performance rituals, and Jill Dolan has analysed with careful insight in her recent book *Utopia in Performance* how Turner's theories can help to illuminate LGBT per-formance practices and community formations, and what, in turn, those practices and formations have to teach us about transforming the hope for a better world into the political alliances and 'queer' (in the sense of productively despoiling the status quo) friendships best placed to achieve real change.[39]

In what follows, I have made an effort to foreground my own

---

38 See Victor Turner, *Dramas, Fields, and Metaphors: Symbolic Action in Human Society* (Ithaca: Cornell University Press, 1974), p. 274.
39 See Dolan, *Utopia in Performance*, pp. 10–12.

moments of 'queer' audience-affiliation by describing in detail not only particularly transformative ones, but also by naming, where appropriate, those persons who, whether by accident or by design, have become part of my performance posse. Such acknowledgements are, I know, conventionally located in the prefatory apparatus of most scholarly books and I have abided, for the most part, with that convention. But, in keeping with the dynamic and dialectical performance geography I am trying to map in this particular book, I also want to expand here, at the end of this introduction, on some of the people – both near and far – I am especially obliged to in thinking through the connections between performance, place, and politics. Starting with my partner, Richard Cavell, who is a key presence throughout these pages. Sometimes dragged, sometimes doing the dragging, Richard reminds me, through his *continued presence* in my life – and, perhaps more to the point, in line beside me for the theatre – how both the intentional and arbitrary dramas in our own relationship are connected to the human condition of wanting and waiting for a better world. Other friends, colleagues, performers, and innumerable strangers I've sat down next to have likewise reminded me how a group of 'unruly bodies' can come together to imagine new ethical arrangements and political commitments in the space of performance, and I have tried to single out as many of them as possible in these pages.

Equally, when I read and write about performance I have become more and more aware of being part of a community, an audience, one whose peculiar mix of intellectual, professional, and personal entanglements also offers alternate ways to think about kinship, especially regarding questions of knowledge inheritance and/or transmission. My work has been profoundly influenced and, I like to think, productively enhanced, by the scholarly example of a range of performance studies theorists – many of them queer – who, in setting out to forge a new academic discipline, have likewise sought to make structural changes to the world at large. And so to them, as well, I have made a conscious effort in what follows to acknowledge my debt in ways both big (sustained applications of and conversations with their work) and small (various stylistic allusions, including epigraphs and chapter titles). But let me be even more explicit here in naming (or re-naming, as most have already been identified in this introduction), up front, some of the critics who, most without their knowledge, have become my ideal interlocutors. Diana Taylor and Joseph Roach have taught me how performance's repertoire of embodied enactments is key to understanding the relationship between local memory and world history, especially as this is connected to the life (and death) of cities; moreover, the centres that they respectively oversee

– the Hemispheric Institute of Performance and Politics at New York University and the World Performance Project at Yale – demonstrate that it is possible to bring the local and the global, the performative and the political, together within institutional settings like the university. Jill Dolan, through her scholarship, her institutional service (especially as former chair of the Performance as Public Practice Graduate Program at the University of Texas at Austin) and, above all, her wonderfully provocative and wide-ranging Feminist Spectator blog, models the very activist spectatorship she theorises as the foundation of a vibrant and truly pluralist theatrical public sphere. Richard Schechner has been an invaluable guide in his mapping of the field, and in helping me to distinguish between the 'is' and 'as' of performance. José Muñoz and David Román have shown me that one can write from a community, and for a community, without presupposing the cultural, ideological, or political fixity of that community. Jen Harvie, Helen Gilbert, and Joanne Tompkins have provided exemplary models for how one might write about national performances – and performances of nation – while simultaneously attending to the transnational, and the local. Closer to home, Canadian scholars like Susan Bennett and Ric Knowles have served as key guides and mentors in my study of audience relations and the performative dynamics of memorialisation, respectively. Even closer to home, colleagues Diana Solomon and Jisha Menon, in their respective examinations of female comedy in the eighteenth century and the performative violence of India's partition, and in their ongoing discussions with me about the local performance scene in Vancouver, have helped refine my thinking about performance, place, and politics immeasurably. Likewise, Jerry Wasserman has taught me much about how one remains actively involved in and communicates with different performance publics. Last, but certainly not least, Peggy Phelan, in her passion for live performance, and in the risks she takes in analysing its ethical dimensions, provides a model for performative critical writing (which, I would argue, is simultaneously an engaged political writing) to which I can only aspire in these pages.

Finally, as a teacher I know first-hand how a local audience can come together – in surprising, haphazard, and often difficult to measure ways – to rethink the world. Many of the ideas in this book have been tested in front of my students, been inspired by their intellectual and social examples, or revised as a result of their performative and political critiques. Knowledge as embodied practice, the live/d experience of social interaction and dialogue, the ways we are obliged to each other (if only for an hour) as ethical subjects, are nowhere more palpable for me than in the classroom (and perhaps most especially in those moments when I think I've failed). Would that I could single out here all of the students who have challenged and changed me. Instead, let me close this introduction by mentioning three who have had a special impact on this study. Joanna Mansbridge, currently completing a Ph.D. on Paula Vogel at the City University of New York's Graduate Center, is the first person I go to when I want to know what's hot performance-wise in New York City. She sees everything – from Marina Abramović uptown at the Guggenheim to Nicky Paraiso downtown at La Mama – and she redacts what she sees with precision and critical acuity. Joanna has been indispensable in comparing notes on productions we have both seen in New York, and in filling me in on equally relevant ones I couldn't get to. She has also been a generous long-distance reader of my work and a delightful dinner and theatre companion when Richard and I make our annual pilgrimage to the Big Apple.

Before she went on to do an interdisciplinary MA in Globalisation Studies, Amy Zhang wrote a superb undergraduate Honours thesis on Kushner's *Homebody/Kabul* under my direction. Many of the ideas we discussed about the play inform my argument in chapter 3. Following a research internship at the Montreal-based Rights and Democracy organisation in the summer of 2006, Amy moved to Beijing, where she worked first for the UN and then for Greenpeace on various sustainability projects, including ones directly related to the Olympics. Like Joanna in New York, Amy was my eyes and ears in China in the lead-up to the 2008 Beijing Games, then, along with her partner D'Arcy, my host when I finally made my way to the city in June of that year. My conversations with Amy about the human and environmental toll wrought by the Olympics – not to mention the artists, activists, and local citizens I met through her – have aided me immeasurably in my comparative analysis, in the next chapter, of the multiple spectacles on offer in Vancouver and Beijing's respective Olympic bids.

Finally, and most importantly, this book would have been greatly impoverished without the active collaboration and ongoing dialogue provided by Alana Gerecke. I have known Alana for more than four years now: as a student of generous and wide-ranging intelligence; as a research assistant of unparalleled industry and insight; and, above all, as a performer of exceptional ability and creativity. During this time, we have carried on an extended conversation about performance theory, live art, community practice, and participatory politics that has, it is fair to say, changed the way I think, and that has influenced the direction of this book in very material ways. For example, my earlier discussion of the connections between Phelan's theorisation of the ethics of live art and Butler's formulation of a concept of 'livability' owes much to Alana's own expert examination of the performative overlaps in each writer's theories. Alana's diligence in unearthing important research discoveries from my always shifting performance archive, not to mention her admirable editorial and intellectual acumen in reading through various drafts of these pages, has saved me from many an embarrassing oversight or error. Moreover, as a practising dancer and choreographer, Alana has also challenged me to connect my often abstract claims about the political possibilities afforded by the theatrical public sphere to the material conditions of artistic production and reception. Alana's own work performing and researching site-specific art in Vancouver has provided me with an inspiring model for connecting local civic engagements of and with performance to a larger global politics of creative counter-memory.

It is only fitting, then, that just as I was completing final revisions to the typescript of this book Alana and I should find ourselves together again on a street corner participating in another roving theatrical performance by battery opera. This time, however, the work, called *Lives Were Around Me*, was by Lee Su-Feh's producing partner, David McIntosh. And this time we were both members of the audience, one purposely restricted to an intimate group of three, and committed, regardless of weather, to following McIntosh and later performer Adrienne Wong (alternating with Paul Ternes) as they led us on an hour-long guided walking tour of the historical centre of Vancouver. Except that the text for this tour was freely adapted from James Kelman's *Translated Accounts*, an abstruse, Kafkaesque novel made up of monologues detailing instances of surveillance, arrest, detention, and torture carried out in an unnamed police state. The effect was deliberately disorienting, forcing us to reexamine a part of the city that I suggest at greater length in subsequent chapters is already overdetermined with meaning, not to mention over-policed by various state apparatuses invested in the interpretation of that meaning. Then, too, the juxtaposition of textual site and cited text necessarily prompted me to import other spaces, other world stages (near and far) as dramatic referents, some of which made me feel more, some less, vulnerable; none of which gave me any clearer sense of my bearings. But, as Alana reminded me, the performance was less about retrieving a singular archive of place than it was precipitating an encounter with the full repertoire of its experiences.[40] In this respect, the neighbourhood did not disappoint. Lives *were* around us. We, *too*, had an audience. All we had to do was look.

40 For a distinction between archival (representational, institutional) and repertory (ephemeral, embodied) knowledge as it relates to performance, see Taylor, *The Archive*.

1

One world, two cities: Olympic showcases in Beijing and Vancouver

The Beijing Olympic Games will fully express the common aspiration of the Chinese people to jointly seek peace, development and common progress together with the peoples of the world, and it will highlight the fact that the 1.3 billion Chinese people of 56 ethnic groups, along with 50 million overseas Chinese, are all most enthusiastic participants in the Beijing Olympic Games. (From the official website of the Beijing 2008 Olympic Games[1])

Vancouver is Canada's Pacific gateway. Like the Olympic Movement itself, Vancouver looks outward to the world beyond. Its location halfway between Asia and Europe and its embrace of multiculturalism uniquely position Vancouver to host the world. (From the introduction to the *Vancouver 2010 Bid Book*[2])

Just as winning the Olympic gold medal represents the pinnacle of achievement for an athlete so, by extension, gaining the nomination to stage the Olympics is the highest accolade that a city can now attain in the game of place promotion . . . [N]o other festival approaches the Olympics in the extent to which sporting stadia become the setting for pure theatre. (John R. Gold and Margaret M. Gold[3])

1 'Goals & concepts', *The Official Website of the Beijing 2008 Olympic Games*, http://en.beijing2008.cn/bocog/concepts/index.shtml (accessed May 2008).
2 'Introduction', *Vancouver 2010: The Sea to Sky Games*, www.vancouver2010.com/resources/PDFs/BidBook_Intro1.pdf (accessed February 2008).
3 John R. Gold and Margaret M. Gold, *Cities of Culture: Staging International Festivals and the Urban Agenda, 1851–2000* (Aldershot: Ashgate, 2005), p. 140.

For his contribution to the 2006 Sydney Biennale, curated by Charles Merewether around the theme 'Zones of Contact', China's most celebrated contemporary artist, Ai Weiwei, created *World Map*, an 8-metre long, 6-metre wide, and 1-metre high installation that used 2,000 layers of precisely cut cloth to construct and fit together in the manner of a jigsaw puzzle a replica international atlas. Given the media interest in Ai's high-profile collaboration with Swiss architects Jacques Herzog and Pierre de Meuron on the design of what was to be the architectural centerpiece of the 2008 Beijing Olympics, the Bird's Nest Stadium, viewers might be forgiven for initially reading *World Map* as a cynical marketing stunt, high-end advertising for the benign globalism of sport as trumpeted by the official slogan of the Beijing Games: 'One World, One Dream'. However, Ai, famous for giving the finger to Tiananmen Square, among other public spaces and world monuments, in a 1997 series of photographs called *Study of Perspective*, has never been one to toe the official party line, even when enforced as rigidly as the Communist Party of China's (CCP). Indeed, little more than a year later, in August 2007, Ai would publicly condemn the Olympics as a glorified propaganda exercise sponsored by a one-party state,[4] an incident whose performative consequences I return to in a later section of this chapter.

In fact, *World Map* is more in keeping with past works by the artist that likewise engage with the nation as at once an imaginary cultural construct authenticated by a global consumer market *and* as a real physical entity monitored by local government. So, for example, Ai is famous for deliberately destroying pottery from the Han and Ming Dynasties (more on this below), or defacing it with bright paint and logos from Coca-Cola; and in his *Map of China* series he carves monumental sculptures of the 'official' geographical mass of the People's Republic (including Taiwan) out of beams salvaged from Qing Dynasty temples. As with *World Map*, these objects' abstract metaphysical representations of place are interrupted, challenged, and rendered mutable by an audience's local – and very tactile – encounter with the medium of their performance: latex, wood, felt. As such, the fabric used in Ai's Biennale piece, and the time and effort required to cut, pile, and fit it, speak to the conflicting and situationally contingent layers of history, politics, and economics that continue to circumscribe the contact zones available between nations in this age of globalisation, with China's ability to

---

4 See Jonathan Watts, 'Olympic artist attacks China's pomp and propaganda', *The Guardian* (9 August 2007), www.guardian.co.uk/world/2007/aug/09/china.artnews (accessed July 2008).

stage a media event as extravagant as the Beijing Olympics, no less than its ability to serve as primary manufacturer to the worldwide garment industry, dependent on abundant local supplies of cheap labour.

At the same Sydney Biennale, Vancouver-based Anishinabe–Canadian artist Rebecca Belmore, about whom I talk at greater length in chapter 4, exhibited *America 2006*. Combining textile work with sculpture, the installation saw her stitch together by hand fragments from the flags of all the countries of the Americas in a manner that at once served as a witty comment on the United States' diminishing geopolitical influence within the hemisphere (its flag ended up next to Venezuela's) and as a serious indictment of the dispossession and cultural genocide of the continents' Indigenous peoples. In Belmore's work, 'contact' thus has a very specific historical referent, and to the extent that all territory in the Americas might still be considered occupied or colonised space, borders per force remain arbitrary and transferable. And allegiance to a flag can only be defined in terms of instrumental outcomes, a point I will also return to in connection with local First Nations' protests to the 2010 Winter Olympics in Vancouver.

A performance event like the Olympics trades equally in images of global cosmopolitanism and tribal nationalism, and most often via recourse to the very emblems used by Ai and Belmore in their respective installations: a map of the world, and various countries' individually brandished flags. As crucially, what these works also demonstrate is that it is local audiences' embodied and place-based engagements with the different symbolic registers of the national and the global that provide both international art fairs *and* international sports showcases with their real drama. In other words, the 'dream' of worldliness is revealed to be nothing less, and nothing more, than the sum of one's material location in the world. And it is here, as this chapter seeks to argue – in part by examining additional conceptual, photographic, and performance art pieces by Ai and others – that we see the city emerge to challenge the nation as the key site of local performative inquiry and global political connection.

Coincidentally, Richard and I were having drinks on a patio in Sydney in June 2003, enjoying spectacular views of the Harbour Bridge and the Opera House, when our server, upon learning where we were from, informed us that Vancouver had been picked by the International Olympic Committee (IOC) to host the 2010 Winter Games. It seemed strangely appropriate to be receiving this news Down Under, during the antipodean winter season, with Sydneysiders huddled under heat lamps in what for us were relatively balmy conditions, on par with what we might expect back home during our increasingly temperate summers. I deal at greater length with the performative consequences of Vancouver weather patterns (especially recent distressing departures from the norm) at the end of this book. Here, at the outset, let me dwell a bit further on Sydney's relevance to the specific concerns of this chapter, and to the local/global approach to performance, place, and politics that this book seeks to model. That relevance has as much to do with the fact that Sydney had only narrowly beat out Beijing for the right to host the first Summer Olympics of the new millennium on a controversial fourth ballot held by IOC members in 1993,[5] as it does with comments made by the cab driver who drove Richard and I from the airport into town upon our arrival. Passing Sydney Olympic Park en route, I asked the cabbie what the venues were now used for. 'Blasted if I know, mate', came the reply. 'Friggin' white elephant, if you ask me'.

The fate of purpose-built venues has historically proven to be a telling indicator of the local impacts of Olympic Games on host cities. Do they revitalise and renew urban neighbourhoods? Or do they become derelict eyesores for nearby residents and money-pits for municipal governments? Are they long-term legacy projects designed to bolster the economic infrastructure and quality of life of poorly serviced inner-city communities or outlying suburbs? Or are they really short-term social engineering experiments, targeting for 'retraining' and/or displacement the largely poor, working-class, immigrant, and ethnic minority residents who live in these areas? And can even the best possible outcome ever justify the expense? Choosing to centralise a majority of Olympic venues, as well as the Athletes' Village, in one self-contained area, organisers of the Sydney Games helped to minimise transportation, organisational, and other logistical problems that are wont to plague events of this size. In so doing, they also transformed the former polluted industrial wasteland of Homebush Bay into a new, environmentally friendly sports complex that became the showpiece of Sydney's so-called Green Games, and that was meant to revitalise the area, post-Olympics, into a vibrant new residential neighbourhood and leisure destination. However, in the years immediately following the Olympics, 'it resembled a ghost town . . . and its vast expanses were frequently empty. With relatively few major events in the largest stadia, transport to the Park was sporadic, making it less accessible and attractive to the public'.[6] Since our visit in 2003, this picture has changed somewhat, with the area attracting elite teams to its sports complexes and increasing public

5 Alan Riding, 'Olympics to Sydney; Beijing's bid fails for 2000 Games', *Montreal Gazette* (24 September 1993), p. D1.
6 Richard Cashman, *The Bitter Sweet Awakening: The Legacy of the Sydney 2000 Olympic Games* (Sydney: Walla Walla Press, 2006), p. 153.

patronage of its recreational and cultural facilities.[7] And in terms of its performative remediation of place post-Olympics, Sydney continues to offer instructive lessons for other host cities, including Beijing (which has also followed a centralised construction model for its showcase venues), Vancouver (whose Athletes' Village, in a former industrial area known as False Creek South, has been targeted for a high-profile 'greening' of the sort undertaken in Homebush Bay), and London (which is hoping to do for the Lower Lea Valley in 2012 what Canary Wharf did for the Docklands in the 1980s).

There are any number of additional ways in which the 2000 Sydney Olympics serve to inform my comparative analysis of Beijing and Vancouver as Olympic host cities in this chapter: for how they showcased (via Ian Thorpe, Cathy Freeman, and others) Australia's emergence as a global sporting power and the collective pride taken in that prowess; for how the 'made-for-media' message-making[8] and symbolic pageantry of the opening and closing ceremonies linked strategic displays of ethnicity and Aboriginality to larger performances of nationhood and cultural branding that could be exported to a global audience; and for how the *business* of spectacle extended beyond the two-weeks of the Games themselves, influencing various pre-Games arts festivals and post-Games legacy projects. All these considerations are ripe for performance studies analysis, and have been so approached by a wealth of scholars studying different Olympics from the modern era. But, as per the brief discussion of Sydney Olympic Park that stemmed from our cabbie's apparent throwaway remark, all are also part of a larger narrative about the political economy of place.

That is the main narrative I wish to tell in this chapter and helps to explain why, in using the Olympics to contextualise, at the outset of this book, Vancouver's place in the world (including its strategic location along the Pacific Rim and its historical relationship with China), I am especially concerned with integrating an analysis of selected works of artistic production and performance within a larger discussion of the performance of eventness itself, that is, the marshalling of local histories, communities, material realities, and symbolics required for the successful staging of a media spectacle of the size and scale of the Olympics. For if the global television audience for the actual sporting showcase seems to come together as a performance public only fragmentarily united around shared time zones, athletic preferences, national fervour, or

7   Michael Geller, 'Sydney's sustainability suburb', *Vancouver Sun* (10 March 2007), p. L2.
8   I borrow this phrase from Alan Tomlinson; see his 'Olympic spectacle: opening ceremonies and some paradoxes of globalization', *Media, Culture & Society* 18 (1996), p. 586.

choreographed displays of fireworks, then the different sites of performative action and activism (from urban sustainability to human rights)
produced through the *organisation* of that showcase also tell us something about how counter-publics are formed not just in spot-lit scenes
played on the world stage but also as a result of the behind-the-scenes
mechanics and practicalities of local staging. Beginning in this way, I
am attempting at once to outline the scope of performance studies as
a method of critical analysis and a tool for political critique, and to
demonstrate how my discussion of the local dynamics of Vancouver
performance here and elsewhere in the book might be relevant to practitioners and scholars in other parts of the world – be it a London gearing
up for 2012, or an Edinburgh or Glastonbury or Venice or Sao Paulo
winding down annually or bi-annually from its local showcase festival.
Let me return briefly to Sydney – and to my own sense of geographical *dis*-placement while there – in order to articulate more clearly how
Beijing fits into this equation.

In Sydney I kept experiencing déjà vu. The Harbour Bridge reminded
me of the Lion's Gate back home, the vast expanse of green known as
The Domain of Vancouver's own urban oasis, Stanley Park. The ocean
we share also gives each city a rich supply of accessible sandy beaches.
Then, too, Canada and Australia's linked colonial past, and the forced
relocation of Aboriginal peoples that forms its shameful backdrop,
means that Vancouver and Sydney are home to large numbers of urban
Aboriginals, many of whom live in poverty and/or, by necessity, are
involved in prostitution or the drug trade. The centres for these activities
are the Downtown Eastside (DTES) in Vancouver and the Kings Cross
area of Sydney, both home to controversial safe injection sites, and
both subject to increasing pressures related to gentrification. As Pacific
Rim cities, Sydney and Vancouver also have large Asian populations,
with Chinese immigration to both cities dating back to the nineteenth
century and momentarily spiking in the years leading up to the 1997
transfer of Hong Kong back to the People's Republic of China. Finally,
it is worth remembering that Sydney and Vancouver are both lifestyle
cities with extremely inflated real-estate markets, large parts of which
are controlled by offshore interests or holding companies.

In fact, it is the connection between the migratory flows of the
recent Chinese diaspora and the equally migratory flows of global
financial capital that at last brings me to the main point of departure
for my comparative analysis of the Beijing and Vancouver Olympics in
this chapter, showcasing how both cities (and others besides, including
Sydney, but also Hong Kong and Shanghai) form part of an economic
and geopolitical nexus of Pacific Rim property speculation and urban

redevelopment. Indeed, in terms of the performance of place, and its local/global significations, one must not underestimate the relationship between 'mega-events' like the Olympics and what Kris Olds, with particular attention to Vancouver, has called urban mega-projects (UMPs). UMPs are 'large scale (re)development projects composed of a mix of commercial, residential, retail, industrial, leisure, and infrastructure uses', often built on abandoned inner-city tracts of land (derelict ports, old railway yards, reclaimed industrial sites), and usually oriented around signature buildings that help re-brand the global visual iconicity of cities.[9] Similarly, 'mega-events', according to Maurice Roche, are 'large-scale cultural (including commercial and sporting) events which have a dramatic character, mass popular appeal and international significance', and which are likewise designed to project a particular global image of the host city, repositioning that city 'in the world of global inter-city and economic competition'.[10] In other words, the mega-event and the mega-project both demonstrate how, in late modernity, the performance of local public cultures is always already mediated by global economic forces, producing what Olds refers to as a 'relational geography', in which the particularity of place is deterritorialised and dispersed – unevenly and contingently, to be sure – along an ever-fluctuating network of performative flows (capital, money, commodities, labour, migration, tourism, information, images, etc.), and manipulated by hidden actors, usually powerful elites.[11] The heads of the Beijing Organizing Committee for the Games of the XXIX Olympiad (BOCOG) and the Vancouver Organizing Committee for the 2010 Olympic and Paralympic Games (VANOC) – Liu Qi and John Furlong, respectively – are, after all, CEOs of registered corporations, with all of the insider business access, tax loopholes, and potential conflicts of interest, that incorporation normally entails.[12] Yet, an analysis of the practices of embodied spectatorship and participation at the local level reveals that different constituent audiences often have very different political investments in the sustained performance of place that comes with what Roche calls an Olympics' 'event horizon', that is, its 'long-term (pre-event) causes/motivations and (post-event) effects'.[13]

9   Kris Olds, *Globalization and Urban Change: Capital, Culture, and Pacific Rim Mega-Projects* (Oxford: Oxford University Press, 2001), p. 6.
10 Maurice Roche, *Mega-Events and Modernity: Olympics and Expos in the Growth of Global Culture* (London: Routledge, 2000), p. 10.
11 Olds, *Globalization and Urban Change*, pp. 8–9.
12 To this end, questions were raised in the media when it was discovered that VANOC was registered as a federal lobbyist but not as a provincial one; see Jeff Lee, 'Who is lobbying who [*sic*] is the name of the game', *Vancouver Sun* (30 May 2008), p. A3.
13 Roche, *Mega-Events and Modernity*, p. 11.

In developing his theory of the 'sociology' of mega-events, Roche focuses his attention not just on the Olympics, but also on the historical legacy of World Expositions,[14] and in terms of the specific 'event horizon' governing my comparison of the Beijing and Vancouver Games, it is worth contextualising my argument a bit further by first looking back to the 1986 Expo in Vancouver and forward to the 2010 Expo in Shanghai. Connecting both events are the ongoing UMPs that resulted from the successful host city selection process, not to mention legendary Hong Kong business tycoon and property developer Li Ka-shing's strategic involvement in some of the more significant of those projects. After all, it was Li, chief shareholder and managing director of the property development firms Cheung Kong (CK) and Hutchison Whampoa (HW), who together with his eldest son Victor (a Canadian citizen) formed the private development firm Concord Pacific in 1987 with the aim of buying and developing the former Expo 86 lands on the north side of Vancouver's False Creek. The deal was a controversial one, not least because the British Columbia Enterprise Corporation, created by the newly reelected Social Credit government in the months following the close of Expo with the express purpose of privatising various provincial assets, announced that the 82-hectare parcel of land would be sold in one piece, thereby excluding local small-scale property developers from the list of prospective buyers; because of BC Economic Development Minister Grace McCarthy's rumoured less-than-arms-length involvement in encouraging Li to acquire the property; and because the financial arrangements negotiated by Li and the BC government – including deferred payment schedules and the province's absorption of the costs of cleaning up contaminated sections of the site – effectively meant that Concord Pacific acquired the land for less than half of what they themselves agreed it was worth.[15]

In the twenty years since the sale of the land to Concord Pacific, and in particular since the Li family transferred their majority stakeholder status in the firm to Terry Hui in 1993, the area has been transformed into one of the most densely populated downtown neighbourhoods in North America, and has become a model, in terms of urban planning, for similar developments targeted at the globe-trotting super-rich around the world.[16] And yet this global performance of place has come

14 The comparison makes historical as well as analytical sense, as in the early days of the modern Olympic movement, World Fairs served as the main events around which Baron de Coubertin and the IOC organised their fledgling sports competitions. This was, for example, the case in Paris in 1900, in St Louis in 1904, and London in 1908.

15 See Olds, *Globalization and Urban Change*, pp. 107–8 and 122.

16 To this end, former Vancouver senior planner Larry Beasley has been recruited by the government of Abu Dhabi to recreate the 'Vancouver Model' (high-density

at a local price – quite literally – with an increasing lack of affordable housing in Vancouver's urban core resulting in a form of enclosure that sees companies like Concord Pacific at once encroaching on and seeking to contain the social blight of the DTES, for example, through a phalanx of luxury condominium towers, most of whose units are owned internationally. As the city now looks across the water, to South False Creek, site of the 2010 Athletes' Village, and earmarked for major redevelopment thereafter, it would do well – especially in the current bear market – to seek alternative models of place promotion, ones that better reconcile local integration with global destination.

While Li's primary investment interests in Shanghai relate to the operation of container ports in the Mingdong and Pudong districts, HW's property development wing has sought to capitalise on the real estate potential associated with the extraordinary urban transformation of Shanghai into a global financial, high-tech, transportation, and trade zone centred around the Pudong New Area Project and the Lujiazui Central Finance District. Specifically, HW has a number of grand luxury property and hotel developments currently in various stages of development throughout these two areas. However, unlike Vancouver, the major development initiatives in Shanghai since the 1980s have been fuelled by the economic (and political) engines of Beijing, rather than Hong Kong. Arguably it is the Chinese government's desire to see Shanghai overtake Hong Kong as the major financial capital of Asia and, consequently, regain some of the glory of its cosmopolitan past that explains an architectural re-branding of a city now in eclipse of Tokyo as the stand-in for urban futurity in Hollywood films.[17] Something similar has happened in Beijing, in connection with the building of various signature Olympic venues, about which I will have more to say below. As yet, however, there have been no local protests in Beijing of the sort organised in Shanghai at the beginning of 2008 around the proposed extension of the city's high-speed magnetic levitation, or maglev, train through residential neighbourhoods. Taking the form of peaceful 'strolls' through city streets, and modelled on similar actions undertaken protesting the construction of a large chemical factory in the port city of Xiamen, these demonstrations have targeted what was to have been a centerpiece of Shanghai's ultra-modern, high-tech projection of itself to the world in

buildings combined with lots of green space and pedestrian-friendly walkways) in the oil-rich emirate. See David George-Cosh, 'The man who built Vancouver has grand plan for Abu Dhabi', *National Post* (12 April 2008), p. FP1.

17 For the full historical and social background to this phenomenon, see Olds, *Globalization and Urban Change*, pp. 141–239. See, as well, Jeffrey N. Wasserstrom, *Global Shanghai, 1850–2010: A History in Fragments* (New York: Routledge, 2008).

2010, and have left authorities flummoxed as to how to respond.[18] The actions of these protestors, together with those of grieving parents who have launched class-action lawsuits over children killed in the collapse of an elementary school during the Sichuan earthquake, or from drinking milk tainted with melamine,[19] indicate something of a sea change in Chinese politics since 1989, with a newly emancipated and financially leveraged middle class overtaking students and workers in demanding more accountability of their national government at the local level.

A telling sign that Shanghai's 2010 World Expo is seen within China as a showcase event as – if not more – significant as the Beijing Olympics is the fact that a clock counting down the Expo's opening in August 2010 was installed in Shanghai's People's Square in February 2003, more than a year before a similar clock counting down the Beijing Olympics was installed in Tiananmen Square in September 2004.[20] Of course it was an earlier countdown clock in Tiananmen, this one ticking off the days to the transfer of Hong Kong sovereignty in 1997, that established the precedent of symbolically showcasing the future-oriented temporality of China's emergence as a major player on the world stage. And if, in this regard, the coming out party that is the Beijing Olympics is being measured in the West – as an indicator of China's *social progress* – against the brutal suppression of the pro-democracy movement in Tiananmen in 1989, in China the timing of the Olympics arguably has much more to do with celebrating the country's amazing *economic progress* in the thirty years since Deng Xiaoping opened the door to global markets as part of the reform policies implemented in 1978.

While no countdown clock was put in place in anticipation of Expo 86, one was installed in February 2007 in front of the Vancouver Art Gallery to inaugurate the three-year countdown to the 2010 Olympics. The clock was an Omega, the official timekeeper of both the Beijing and Vancouver Games, and this is as good a metaphor as any for the compression and consolidation of the local specificities of space and time into the unreal, non-material scapes and flows of globalisation. But the well-orchestrated ceremonial unveilings of these various clocks

18 See Maureen Fan, 'Shanghai's middle class launches quiet, meticulous revolt', *The Seattle Times* (26 January 2008), p. A1.
19 See Edward Wong, 'Parents of schoolchildren killed in China earthquake confirm lawsuit', *The New York Times* (23 December 2008), www.nytimes.com/2008/12/23/world/asia/23quake.html (accessed December 2008); and 'Families file suit in Chinese tainted milk scandal', *The New York Times* (21 January 2009), www.nytimes.com/2009/01/21/world/asia/21milk.html (accessed January 2009).
20 Jeffrey N. Wasserstrom, 'Protests and propaganda during China's Olympic year', Centre for Chinese Research Workshop, *Staging the Beijing Olympics: Visions, Tensions, and Dreams*, University of British Columbia, 12 May 2008.

3 Clockwise from top left: countdown clocks in Beijing, Vancouver, and
Shanghai

also speak, metonymically, to the relevance of a performance studies
approach to the Olympics as a mass public spectacle that, to adapt Guy
Debord, obliges one to participate in an abstract construction of the
world at the same time as it separates one from the concrete material
conditions of the local as it is produced by that world (see figure 3).[21] To
this end, in his influential analysis of the Olympic Games as 'a special
kind of cultural performance', John MacAloon builds upon Debord (and
Victor Turner) by adopting a multi-genre approach to the 'distinctive
forms of symbolic action' contained within and produced by the event

21 Guy Debord, *The Society of the Spectacle* (Detroit: Black and Red, 1983), p. 46.

as a 'performance system'.[22] These genres include 'spectacle' (the eye-popping visual extravaganzas of the opening and closing ceremonies); 'festival' (the joyous celebrations and public displays of festivity that accompany the Olympics as a mass gathering, some of which may be more programmatic – e.g. official Cultural Olympiads – and some more spontaneous – e.g. the winning athlete who does a victory lap around the track with his or her national flag); 'ritual' (the parade of nations, the lighting of the Olympic flame, the declaring of the event opened and closed, the athletes' and officials' pledges, the awarding of medals and playing of national anthems); and 'game' (the various sporting contests that supposedly form the foundation of the Olympics). MacAloon's genres are by no means discrete categories, and can often bleed into one another. Nor do they, as he himself states, 'exhaust the roster of performance types found in an Olympic Games'.[23] With this in mind, I want, in my own comparative analysis of the Beijing and Vancouver Olympics, to deploy as both a performance analytic and a potential tool for political critique a word that I have already invoked several times in this chapter: *showcase*.

I do so primarily because showcase, as a genre, helps to connect occasion with place, the performative with the exhibitionary,[24] through the act of public display, in this case not just of elite athletic skill, but also of modern urban aesthetics and an accompanying ethics of livability. This returns me to the earlier link I made between mega-events like the Olympics and mega-development projects that have transformed the respective built environments of Vancouver and Beijing. That is, a chief symbolic action performed by the former is to showcase the latter in the 'game of place promotion', providing visual evidence of a city's attractive and competitive position in the new world order and encouraging, in the process, tourism and further global investment. At the same time, the taxonomic (not to mention taxidermic) impulse that accompanies the museum showcase, for example, or, as per my discussion above, the World Exposition, points to the dialectical nature of such a performance genre; the specific and/or universalist principles or criteria informing the display of objects, locales, events, acts, peoples, and so on, may not be received as intended by different audiences, and may even provoke

---

22 John J. MacAloon, 'Olympic Games and the theory of spectacle in modern socie-
    ties', in John J. MacAloon (ed.), *Rite, Drama, Festival, Spectacle: Rehearsals Toward
    a Theory of Cultural Performance* (Philadelphia: Institute for the Study of Human
    Issues, 1984), pp. 258–9.

23 *Ibid.*, p. 242.

24 On exhibition and performance, see Roche, *Mega-Events and Modernity*, p. 9, who
    identifies these as sub-genres of the 'complex' of cultural forms of expression that
    merge in mega-events such as the Olympics.

a degree of scrutiny potentially detrimental to the success of the performance. As television broadcast statistics consistently bear out, events like the Olympics really do focus the eyes of the world on a given city, and not just for the two weeks of the Games themselves. Whether or not those eyes all share in the dreams being sold in and by that city is another matter entirely, and in the sections that follow my goal has been to examine the different local, national, and international investments and contradictions in the Beijing and Vancouver Olympics' showcasing – sometimes willfully, sometimes not – of questions relating to urban sustainability, cultural heritage, and human rights. In so doing, I discuss, among other topics, official policies on green building practices and the material realities of displaced and homeless local populations; performances of culture that receive national brand approval, as well as artists seeking to challenge what that brand might be selling; and the transnational mediation of protests in Tibet and First Nations and anti-poverty activism in British Columbia. In all cases, an ancillary goal has been, wherever possible, to give some sense of the response of different local and global actors and audiences to these issues by quoting from media and personal interviews where relevant.

This last point speaks to a final crucial element that the showcase genre allows me to highlight, namely my own shifting role as researcher in relation to the two Olympic cities under discussion. As an almost twenty-year resident of Vancouver, with an active interest in local politics, access to public documents and officials connected to the Games, and the opportunity to attend various community forums (both pro and con) and cultural events related to the Olympic preparations, my ability to collect, measure, assess, and, in turn, showcase in this chapter relevant data has been largely unfettered. Not so with Beijing, where linguistic and cultural barriers, my inability to penetrate BOCOG's publicity firewall, and a tenuous grasp of the overlapping and at times competing interpretive discourses and communities at play in the Chinese media and blogosphere reporting on the Games, has somewhat compromised – and necessarily influenced – my take on local, national, and diasporic responses to the performance and politics of place on offer in the 2008 Summer Olympics. At the same time, I have been able to draw on the knowledge and expertise of a number of important friends, colleagues, and collaborators. First and foremost, in this regard, is Amy Zhang, a former student who worked for Greenpeace China as lead author of their environmental assessment of the Beijing Olympics and who, together with her partner, D'Arcy Saum, put me up when I visited Beijing in advance of the Games. Amy and D'Arcy also introduced me to friends, co-workers, artists, and activists who in turn shared with me their views on the Olympic fever gripping their city. If, in the end, I have interpreted or applied the views of these individuals in ways that might seem anomalous or askew, this has as much to do with my own performative location with respect to Vancouver as it does with what might appear to be the non-locatability of my politics in relation to Beijing. Another way of saying this is that, in my analysis of the 'relational geography' connecting these Olympic host cities, I am aiming as well for a reciprocal temporality, demonstrating that Beijing's long march toward and lingering moment in the global spotlight is simultaneously part of Vancouver's history of local emergence as a showcase city, one subject to its own critique.

Showcasing sustainability: local paradoxes

In 2003, soon after being brought on board by Herzog and de Meuron as design consultant on the Bird's Nest, Ai embarked on a series of digital video works documenting the rapid urban transformation of Beijing. *INTERVAL* (2003) comprises 150 hours of video footage shot through the windshield of a single vehicle as it traverses every street within the circumference of Beijing's Fourth Ring Road over a continuous 16-day period. *Chang'an Boulevard* (2004) is an extended video essay on the main east–west axis through the city recorded in a manner akin to stop–motion animation. Finally, in *Beijing – The Second Ring* and *Beijing – The Third Ring* (both 2005), Ai captures CCTV-like footage of the notoriously gridlocked traffic on the two main arterial loops that encircle the centre of the city from each of the bridges that traverses them. Collectively, these works add up to a sobering environmental 'map' of a city seemingly in thrall to developmental sprawl, whatever the price. Still, it is the C-prints that make up Ai's *Provisional Landscape* series of photographs, undertaken during the same period, that I find most haunting, not least for their eerie beauty. In them Ai represents a spatially and temporally 'void' Beijing as a perpetual construction site, recording 'empty' images of areas targeted for redevelopment and repurposing in the lead up to the Olympics at the moment just after the old built environment has been demolished and just before work on the new one has begun, the detritus of the past a passive rebuke to dreams of future progress. The images, though much smaller in scale, are reminiscent of Canadian artist Edward Burtynsky's massive and visually stunning photographs of 'manufactured' industrial landscapes.

As a result of Jennifer Baichwal's award-winning documentary film on the artist, Burtynsky has become most famous for his towering portraits of several hallmarks of China's recent industrial progress, including the Three Gorges Dam.[25] However, *An Uneasy Beauty*, a solo exhibition of the artist's work that opened at the Surrey Art Gallery in January 2009 as part of the second Vancouver Cultural Olympiad to be organised in the lead-up to the 2010 Winter Games, reminded me that he has documented the visible evidence of our planet's collective consumption and waste at sites much closer to home. The show featured twenty-four images Burtynsky shot in western Canada between 1985 and 2007, including compositionally precise photos of oil sand extraction sites at Fort McMurray, Alberta, open-pit mines in northern British Columbia, and the container port of Vancouver. Designed and exhibited as a series, the photos trace both the material roots and the spectral routes of our dependence on non-renewable energy resources, a global fuel economy that leads from Alberta's oil fields, through Vancouver's port, to the bulldozers, heavy diggers, and forklifts awaiting start-up in Ai's photos of Beijing. The human-altered landscapes in Ai's and Burtynsky's photos are likewise linked in that they are devoid of bodies and yet paradoxically demand of their viewing audiences bodily engagement, a sensorially immersive accounting of how we are locally implicated in these 'placeless' spaces by the cars we drive, the food we eat, even the entertainment and sporting spectacles we attend. At the same time, both Ai and Burtynsky have separately stated that their work is not meant to be read as an overt judgment but rather as a kind of 'monitor' or 'point of departure for discussion',[26] not as political indictments but as performance indicators. In this, Burtynksy's lens, like Ai's, would find a rich resource of subject matter in the venue building sites of any number of recent or future Olympic host cities (including Vancouver and London), where IOC-imposed conditions around sustainability as a global philosophy and the local conditions for living sustainably are frequently at odds.

Following the 1994 Winter Olympics in Lillehammer, Norway, the IOC formally amended its Charter to include environmental and social sustainability as the 'third pillar', along with sport and culture and education, of the philosophy of life and the body it calls Olympism.[27] Theoretically, the linking of Olympism and sustainability has meant that each prospective host city since Lillehammer has had to outperform its

---

25 *Manufactured Landscapes*, dir. Jennifer Baichwal (Mongrel Media, 2006).

26 See 'Ai Weiwei: fragments, voids, sections and rings', interview with Adrian Blackwell, *Archinect* (5 December 2006), http://archinect.com/features/article. php?id=47035_0_23_0_C (accessed December 2008); and Robin Laurence, 'Landscapes beyond nature', *The Georgia Straight* (22–9 January 2009), p. 43.

27 For an – admittedly very partial – overview of 'the development of the Olympic Movement's commitment to protecting the environment', see Steven Maass, 'Going green', *Olympic Review* 64 (2007), pp. 31–7.

predecessors in trumpeting its green credentials and social commitments as part of its bid proposal. In practice, however, those commitments can seem more imagined and well-intentioned than real,
and it is highly debatable what role environmental best practices play
in the IOC's frequently mercurial and inscrutable decision-making
process in awarding the Games. Which is why Beijing's decision to not
only allocate an unprecedented US$ 12.2 billion to meet its ambitious
twenty-point environmental improvement plan,[28] but also to showcase
the 'Green Games' as one of three main themes of its Olympics (the
other two were 'High-Tech Olympics' and 'People's Olympics') raised
more than a few eyebrows among environmental activists and NGOs
around the globe. This was a country, after all, that still relied on coal
(the dirtiest of fossil fuels) for 70 per cent of its total energy consumption; that was putting new cars, responsible for 40 per cent of Beijing's
toxic air pollution, on the roads of its capital at a rate of 1,500 per day;[29]
whose water and sewage treatment systems were rudimentary at best;
that had no comprehensive controls for monitoring, controlling, and
reducing industrial waste disposal and pollution; where building codes
and practices were subject to the whims of corrupt local officials; and
that was sacrificing valuable farm land at unprecedented rates, displac-
ing countless local residents, and exploiting scores of migrant workers,
all for the sake of dubious mega-development projects like the Three
Gorges Dam.

Granted BOCOG's rhetoric around its environmental goals supposedly met or exceeded has seemed, at times, like a lot of smoke and
mirrors (quite literally in the case of its trumpeting of Beijing's so-called
'Blue Sky' days). It certainly ran counter to my own observations of
demolished *hutongs* and the generally poor living conditions of thousands of migrant workers charged with completing construction on
Beijing's Olympic venues. However, in the course of my research, and
in my conversations with various Western observers working with environmental NGOs monitoring the sustainability of the Beijing Games, I
was surprised to learn just how much concrete action China appeared
to be taking in working towards a more comprehensive post-Olympics
commitment to global climate change, as well as how the specific

---

28 United Nations Environment Programme (UNEP), *Beijing 2008 Olympic Games: An
    Environmental Review* (Nairobi: UNEP, 2007), pp. 26–8.
29 See Keith Bradsher and David Barboza, 'Pollution from Chinese coal casts a global
    shadow', *The New York Times* (11 June 2006), www.nytimes.com/2006/06/11/
    business/worldbusiness/11chinacoal.html (accessed July 2008); and Ted Conover,
    'Capitalist roaders', *The New York Times Magazine* (2 July 2006), www.nytimes.
    com/2006/07/02/magazine/02china.html (accessed July 2008).

'greening' of Beijing was being taken up in very material and performative ways at the local level. This paradox is just one of the many that has helped 'sustain' China's careful management of the Beijing Games (along with 'unrestricted' press freedom that excluded travel to Tibet and live broadcast from the Great Wall, or designated protest zones empty of protestors), not to mention its promotion of a 'harmonious' society, more generally.

Witness, in this regard, a visual spectacle as playful and seemingly benign as China's five official mascots, or *fuwa*; while each is colour-coded to represent one of the five Olympic rings, and each carries with it a traditional Chinese blessing, BOCOG has also connected the mascots to its overall environmental message by having them symbolise the natural elements. Thus blue Beibei, a flying fish, represents the sea; the black and white panda, Jingjing, represents the forest hills; the red Olympic flame is incarnated in the fiery Huanhuan; Nini, a green flying swallow, alludes to those elusive clear blue skies; and finally Yingying, a yellow Tibetan antelope, is the lone *fuwa* who does double duty, symbolising the grass-covered earth, but also signaling Beijing's commitment to a Green Olympics more generally.[30] All the more ironic, then, that it is arguably China's ongoing depredation of the grasslands in Tibet's Qinghai Plateau (begun during the Great Leap Forward of the 1950s, when much of the area was converted to unsustainable and non-irrigable cropland), and the consequent migration of traditional herders to cities such as Lhasa in search of work, that helped fuel the outburst of protests against a recently arrived and upwardly mobile Han middle-class in March of 2008.[31] Even more ironic, in this regard, is that a photo by Liu Weiqiang that was chosen by China Central Television (CCTV), the country's main broadcast network, as one of the top ten of 2006, and which showed a herd of Tibetan antelope running, in an apparent harmonious fusing of nature and technology, underneath a railway overpass carrying a highspeed train on China's newly built Qinghai-Tibet line, turned out to have been Photoshopped.[32]

30 'The official mascots of the Beijing 2008 Olympic Games', *The Official Website of the Beijing 2008 Olympic Games*, http://en.beijing2008.cn/spirit/beijing2008/graphic/n214068254.shtml (accessed July 2008).
31 See Yoichi Shimatsu, 'Tibetan cowboys' last stand: globalism sets grasslands on fire', *New America Media* (20 March 2008), http://news.newamericamedia.org/news/view_article.html?article_id=ee49c44cd49f7bca788fe2f284552696 (accessed July 2008).
32 Jane Spencer and Juliet Ye, 'China eats crow over fake photo of rare antelope', *Wall Street Journal* (22 February 2008), p. A1. My thanks to Graham Johnson and Tsering Shakya, participants in the UBC Centre for Chinese Research Workshop on the Beijing Olympics in May 2008, for drawing my attention to the issue of the Tibetan grasslands and the Photoshopped image, respectively.

In March 2008, the BOCOG media offices released, as part of their ongoing monthly published updates, a *Supplement on Olympic Commitments*. Produced, like most of BOCOG's printed media propaganda, in the form of a glossy colour magazine, the *Supplement* details, among other things, the steps Beijing has taken to ensure as green a Games as possible. These include employing rigorous environmental protection guidelines in its construction and renovation of venues (especially regarding energy and water conservation); improving public transport by building two new subway lines and a rapid transit link to the airport; improving overall energy efficiency and air quality in Beijing by transitioning from coal to cleaner energy sources, such as natural gas, geothermal energy, and wind; improving water quality and conservation by upgrading municipal reservoirs and sewage networks; implementing a new management system and building new disposal facilities for the processing of domestic and industrial waste; and increasing the overall green space of Beijing to more than 50 per cent of the city's total area by, among other things, an aggressive forestation plan focused on the massive 680-hectare Olympic Forest Park and the 76 competition and training venues.[33] BOCOG's ambitious and self-congratulatory claims are largely endorsed by two independent environmental reviews of the Beijing Games conducted by the United Nations Environment Programme (UNEP) and Greenpeace, respectively. Notwithstanding a large caveat about air quality contained in its report, UNEP is 'able to conclude that considerable effort has gone into fulfilling the letter and spirit of the promise . . . to deliver a "Green Olympics"'.[34] Similarly, Greenpeace notes that 'Beijing's tremendous efforts and investment in environmental initiatives for the 2008 Games have allowed many of the city's bid commitments to be met', leaving 'an important environmental legacy for the city of Beijing in areas such as transportation infrastructure, energy efficiency, and in the development of renewable energy, water, and waste treatment capacities'.[35] Yet while commending Beijing Olympic organisers for greatly superseding Athens in its environmental commitments, Greenpeace also outlines a number of missed opportunities that fall short of the more comprehensive approach taken in Sydney, including limited transparency and engagement with third-party stakeholders and NGOs, and a lack of independently verifiable

---

33 See BOCOG, 'Green Beijing, green Olympics', *Supplement on Olympic Commitments* (Beijing: BOCOG, 2008), pp. 36–45.

34 UNEP, *Beijing 2008 Olympic Games*, p. 14.

35 Greenpeace China (Amy Zhang, lead author), *China after the Olympics: lessons from Beijing: A Greenpeace assessment of the performance of the Beijing 2008 Olympic Games* (Beijing: Greenpeace China, 2008), p. 42.

data by which to evaluate fully and completely Beijing's environmental performance.[36]

Both reports by UNEP and Greenpeace also note that Beijing's Olympic commitments regarding sustainability were developed in consort with a larger eighteen-year 'Environmental Master Plan' for the greening of the city adopted in 1997 by the Beijing Municipal Government, while BOCOG chief Liu Qi was Mayor, and that the city's aggressive efforts, among other things, to phase out ozone-depleting substances a full six years ahead of China's national deadline has established important precedents for the rest of the country to follow.[37] No doubt the CCP's commitment in its most recent (eleventh) Five-Year Plan to a mandatory 20 per cent reduction of energy consumption per unit of GDP by 2010[38] was likewise influenced by Olympics-related optics. However, such measures simultaneously speak to a more expansive and complex internal dialogue about the environment and sustainability in China that is largely not being heard outside the country, and certainly not by the leaders of industrialised Western nations who admonish China – in the highly racialised terms of First Worldism – for its environmental abuses while prevaricating on their own unmet commitments to Kyoto and other global environmental protocols (about which I will have more to say in the coda). Indeed, as respected China-watcher James Fallows has recently reported, in the pages of *The Atlantic*, while China's environmental situation is undeniably 'disastrous', it is also 'improving': 'Everyone knows about the first part. The second part is important too. Outside recognition of where and why China has made progress increases the prospects that it will make further advances. Recognition also clarifies the most important obstacles, political and economic, to such progress'.[39] In this regard, one ironic benefit to the entire planet might in fact be the CCP's unevenly autocratic control of its citizens, and the degree to which it can count on more or less uniform adherence to its slogans and edicts. That is, when the tag-team of President Hu Jintao and Premier Wen Jiabao speak, at every turn (including in relation to the Olympics), of promoting a 'harmonious society', they are increasingly emphasising that economic prosperity cannot be sustained without concomitant investment in the environment. And while the recent global economic downturn might yet necessitate further revisions to the ultimate version of this message, it would appear that the Chinese

36 *Ibid.*, p. 4.
37 UNEP, *Beijing 2008 Olympic Games*, pp. 14–15; Greenpeace China, *China after the Olympics*, p. 11.
38 Greenpeace China, *China after the Olympics*, p. 11.
39 James Fallows, 'China's silver lining', *The Atlantic* (June 2008), p. 39.

government's official position – unlike that of many Western adminis-
trations – allows no room for climate-change skepticism.

However, there is equally evidence that many Chinese are not
waiting to be told to change their green habits; the aforementioned
protests in Xiamen and Shanghai reveal a growing environmental activist movement in China. And to judge by the number of Chinese web
pages, blogs and networking sites devoted to the environment (see, for
example, the 'Green Leap Forward' and 'China Dialogue'), local grassroots organising around sustainability issues, especially in urban centres
like Beijing, is thriving. My favourite of these electronic sites is China's
Green Beat (CGB; www.chinasgreenbeat.com). It's maintained by Zhao
'Shane' Xiangyu, a transplanted Beijinger from the coal-producing
northern Heilongjiang province, and John Romankiewicz, an American
expat in China on a Fulbright Scholarship; they write a blog and frequently appear together (along with their friend Sun Zhe) in quirky
homemade video podcasts that mix documentary footage and voiceover
with improvised scenes of sketch comedy to talk about local solutions
to various environmental problems (an interesting feature on Beijing's
famous three-wheeled bicycles, for example, puts the lie to a lack of comprehensive recycling programs in the city, and in one hilarious episode
the hapless Sun Zhe gets some tips on 'green dating'). As it happened,
while I was in Beijing the boys at CGB were collaborating with Beijing
International Theatre and Entertainment, a largely expat company that
performs in English, to stage *Lean, Mean and Green*, an improvised
sketch comedy show, at a popular local bar called Obiwan. Structured
as a reality-TV style competition between a group of rapacious indus-
trialists and their radical environmentalist counterparts, the teams are
forced to work together, in a series of increasingly whacky challenges, to
find solutions to the mutual sustainability of the economy and the environment. Using physical comedy, song and dance, slides, a surprising
amount of cross-dressing, and of course the dreaded audience participation, the energetic and cosmopolitan cast (including the ever-affable Sun
Zhe) light-heartedly skewered the ideologically entrenched positions
of both sides of the environmental debate. It was by no means great
theatre, but as we settled into a booth at a popular restaurant near the
Chinese Workers' Stadium (site of the Olympic football matches) after
the performance, Amy, D'Arcy, and I agreed that the thematic focus on
profligacy and waste found an interesting inverse formal corollary in the
down and dirty staging, one that was potentially instructive for China's
unique environmental situation. That is, the way this show was put
together – quickly, cheaply, and improvisationally – describes not only
the current popular perception of China's much-derided manufacturing

industry, for example, but also the solution to improving the overall environmental efficiency and sustainability of that and other industries. As Fallows puts it, 'the business of improving China's environment can be a very attractive business indeed'.[40]

These local successes notwithstanding, in the global visual spectacle of place promotion, all of China's real progress around the environment in connection with the Olympics inevitably ran up against the negative television optics of Beijing's omnipresent smog. Then, too, China's attempts to balance its rapid economic rise against consequent environmental depredation need to be measured against that third principle of sustainability, social development. And here, it must be noted, China has failed miserably. Left out of the reports by UNEP and Greenpeace are issues around the relocation and forcible eviction of residents in Beijing to make way for Olympic-related construction projects, and the exploitation of migrant workers engaged in completing those projects. According to the Geneva-based Centre on Housing Rights and Evictions (COHRE), as many as 1.5 million people will have been relocated in Beijing as a result of various 'urban development activities that were either accelerated, expanded or facilitated by the political imperative of "holding the best Olympics ever"'.[41] Forcible evictions have been widespread, with residents subject to abuse, intimidation, and even violence by developers and local authorities. Compensation packages have been grossly inadequate and the relocation of most affected residents to the outer reaches of the city, far from their places of employment, has meant that upwards of 20 per cent of them have crossed the line from 'having a sustainable low income livelihood to a genuinely precarious one'.[42] At the same time, the Chinese government has introduced new legislation restricting lawyers' abilities to represent groups of evictees, and those that have attempted to take on property developers and local authorities on these matters have tended to land in jail.[43]

Human Rights Watch (HRW) has been equally damning in its assessment of the treatment of the nearly two million migrant workers who toil in Beijing, many of them on Olympics-related construction projects. Based on interviews conducted at nine different building sites in Beijing between January and March 2007, and on follow-up interviews a year later, HRW issued a fifty-eight-page report just months before the start of the Games detailing the various abuses routinely endured by

---

40 *Ibid.*, p. 48.
41 Centre on Housing Rights and Evictions, *Fair Play for Housing Rights: Mega-Events, Olympic Games and Housing Rights* (Geneva: COHRE, 2007), p. 168.
42 *Ibid.*
43 *Ibid.*, p. 166.

migrant workers in China's capital. These include the regular proroguing of monthly wages in favour of end-of-year or end-of-project payouts that are invariably smaller than what workers are owed, if in fact they get paid at all; a lack of legally required medical and accident insurance, despite the incredibly high rate of injury and death in their working environments; inadequate, overcrowded, and unsanitary on-site housing, with upwards of twenty men sharing quarters designed for ten, often without heat in the winter and with no washing facilities; and, finally, coordinated harassment and violence should they attempt to seek redress for any of this.[44] While HRW places much of the blame for this social catastrophe at the feet of the Chinese government, it also reserves harsh criticism for the IOC, noting in particular that Olympic officials have a moral imperative to '[s]eek independent certification that all workers employed to construct venues for the 2008 Olympic Games in Beijing have not been the victims of wage exploitation, inadequate safety standards and other abuses'.[45] With new construction being the single most expensive, time-consuming, and globally scrutinised of host cities' Olympic preparations, and with most mega-development projects around the world these days requiring, in some form or another, the labour of migrant workers, this is a lesson in ethical accountability that Vancouver would do well to consider in showcasing its sustainable responsibilities.

Of course, when it comes to the environment, Vancouver has perhaps the opposite image problem from Beijing. As the birthplace of Greenpeace, the home of a new generation of affluent, multi-cultural eco-hipsters who have turned urban densification and eating locally into exportable lifestyle choices, and a city whose spectacular natural setting is alone responsible for landing it at or near the top of various annual livability indices, the popular global perception of Vancouver's green cred is more or less secure. Which perhaps explains the hubris behind VANOC's licensing agreement with the provincial government and the Insurance Company of British Columbia (ICBC) to rebrand the slogan contained on the special signature car licence plates issued in advance of the 2010 Olympics. 'Beautiful British Columbia', the benignly serviceable descriptor used since 1964, was replaced with the following superlative: 'The Best Place on Earth'. But paradise, it seems, carries with it both added premiums and an expiry date: in exchange for its six-year, $15-million sponsorship deal with VANOC, ICBC raised motorists' individual insurance rates by 3.3 per cent; and the plates themselves, which also

44 Human Rights Watch, 'One Year of My Blood': Exploitation of Migrant Construction Workers in Beijing, vol. 20, no. 3 (New York: Human Rights Watch, 2008), pp. 16–40.
45 Ibid., p. 5.

contain the 2010 Olympics' official logo, initially could only be renewed and displayed through 2012, when ICBC's deal with VANOC expires.[46]

However, along with such perceptions come added expectations, and it is perhaps no accident that on the official *Vancouver 2010* website (www.vancouver2010.com) the drop-down menu for the 'Sustainability' hot button contains the most items to click on. Indeed, VANOC is the first Olympics Organizing Committee to implement a self-reporting system on what it calls its 'sustainability performance', pledging to release five annual reports between 2005 and 2010 detailing the 'benchmarks' achieved and the 'progress' made during its 'lifespan', from 'planning and design, to construction, operations, convening the Games, then decommissioning and wind-down'. Each of these reports, of which two have so far been produced, is broken down into six main sections that together comprise VANOC's overall sustainability action plan: 'accountability'; 'environmental stewardship and impact reduction'; 'social inclusion and responsibility'; 'Aboriginal participation and collaboration'; 'economic development'; and 'sport for sustainable living'.[47] I don't propose to scrutinise in depth all of VANOC's reported claims regarding its 'performance' of sustainability. The use of local materials – including the very laudable recycling of pine-beetle infested waste wood from BC's decimated northern forests – and the attention to energy efficiency on the various Vancouver venues, together with minimising disturbances to natural ecosystems in Whistler, has been justifiably trumpeted, including by the IOC.[48] Building on the example set by Sydney, Vancouver Games organisers have also been working very hard to include members of the Four Host First Nations, on whose traditional lands the events are after all taking place, in all aspects of Olympics planning. I will have more to say about some of the cultural contradictions and internal disputes this particullar collaboration has yielded in the next section. For the time being, let me concentrate in the remainder of this section on what remains the most pressing social concern for Vancouver Olympic organisers and civic leaders, an area of sustainable *under*-performance that has prompted a lot of hand-wringing and finger-pointing by various local constituencies, and a definite image problem for the city in the lead-up to the 2010 Games.

46 As a result of the unexpected popularity of the plates, with a projected 100,000 to be sold by 2010, ICBC changed the terms of its original renewal agreement, and will now allow motorists to display the commemorative plates past 2012. See Jeff Lee, 'Licence plates prove hot', *Vancouver Sun* (13 June 2007), p. B4.

47 'Sustainability report', *Vancouver 2010*, www.vancouver2010.com/en/Sustainability/SustainabilityReport (accessed July 2008).

48 Rod Mickleburgh, 'VANOC wins praise for social conscience', *Globe and Mail* (28 February 2008), p. S1.

I am referring to the dearth of affordable social housing in Vancouver and the ongoing crisis of neglect with respect to the city's poorest inner-city neighbourhoods, particularly the notorious Downtown Eastside (DTES). The two issues are related and can be traced back, as I began this chapter by suggesting, at least in part to the city's hosting of its last big global mega-event in 1986. Indeed, before Vancouverites think about condemning Beijing for its relocation of residents in advance of its Olympics, we would do well to remember, as Kris Olds himself reminds us, that we sanctioned a similar policy of forcible evictions in preparation for Expo 86, with sources estimating that between 500 and 1,000 low-income residents were displaced, primarily from the DTES and adjacent neighbourhoods, to make way for tourist lodgings or various building projects.[49] At the same time, this area, already in economic decline for several decades owing to the loss of retail infrastructure that accompanied residential flight to the suburbs (especially by recent waves of Chinese immigrants, who were increasingly opting to settle in Richmond instead of historic Chinatown, immediately adjacent the DTES), was the unlucky beneficiary of clean-up drives trageting the sex and drug trades, then much more dispersed throughout the city, in advance of Expo. As a result, in particular, of the vice sweeps of the Davie Street corridor in the West End and the Mount Pleasant area on the east side, and with the open acknowledgment if not tacit approval of the police force, this underground economy became concentrated around a few square blocks of the DTES, with Main and Hastings, once anchored by its beautiful beaux-arts buildings, suddenly becoming a different sort of showcase, this one for urban blight and social decay. Other problems necessarily followed: a spike in homelessness (exacerbated throughout the 1990s with the rapid gentrification of nearby Gastown and Yaletown, and the conversion of many former single-room occupancy [SRO] units that rented by the day to luxury condos); a similar spike in HIV- and hepatitis-C infection rates; and serial violent crime that targeted mostly Aboriginal women and sex trade workers and that, as I detail at greater length in chapter 4, again seemed to have the tacit approval of the police.[50]

Successive municipal governments and mayors, including Philip

49 Olds, 'Canada: hallmark events, evictions, and housing rights', in Antonio Azuela *et al.* (eds), *Evictions and the Right to Housing: Experience from Canada, Chile, the Dominican Republic, South Africa, and South Korea* (Ottawa: International Development Centre, 1998), p. 4.

50 For a history of the neighbourhood, as told by the people who live and work there, see Leslie A. Robertson and Dara Culhane (eds), *In Plain Sight: Reflections on Life in Downtown Eastside Vancouver* (Vancouver: Talonbooks, 2005); and Paul Taylor (ed.), *The Heart of the Community: The Best of the Carnegie Newsletter* (Vancouver: New Star, 2003).

Owen, Larry Campbell, and Sam Sullivan, have paid various degrees of lip-service to the revitalisation of the DTES, attempting to counter the tide of upscale residential development by adopting various low-income housing strategies, including a one-to-one SRO replacement policy and the trading of height restrictions for agreements from developers to include a mix of social housing units in their plans.[51] In 2001, Owen, in conjunction with the provincial and federal governements, also formally adopted the Four Pillars Drug Strategy, coordinating the city's official drug policy around the related issues of prevention, treatment, harm reduction, and enforcement. It is the third pillar, harm reduction, that has proved the most controversial, as most of the publicity has focused on the opening, in September 2003, of North America's first supervised safe injection facility, Insite, in the heart of the DTES. This pilot project required a special Health Canada drug law exemption, one that expired at the end of June 2008. The City of Vancouver and Vancouver Coastal Health, which operates Insite, applied to the Canadian government for an extension of their exemption, and won a temporary reprieve when the BC Supreme Court struck down parts of Canada's drug laws earlier the same year. But despite a wealth of statistical evidence supporting an increase in detox enrollments and reduced rates of needle sharing and public injections, and despite the support of both levels of government in BC, the majority of Vancouver residents, and the Canadian Medical Association, there is every likelihood that the ruling federal Conservative Party, pending the results of its appeal of the BC Supreme Court decision, will permanently close Insite.[52]

This particular battle is just one of several local scenarios connected to the fate of Vancouver's 'derelict residents' in advance of the Olympics that informs James Long's recent play *The View from Above*, where global climate change combines with local class warfare to produce, in the words of one character, 'a socio-meteorological incident'. In the play, it's 2012 and it has been raining non-stop for three years; the

51 Jessica Chen, 'Regeneration of Vancouver's inner-city neighbourhoods: planning for an inclusive Olympics', Centre for Chinese Research Workshop, *Staging the Beijing Olympics: Visions, Tensions, and Dreams*, University of British Columbia, 12 May 2008. My thanks to Ms Chen, Senior Planner with the City of Vancouver Planning Department, for sharing her perspective on Vancouver's homelessness problems with me.

52 André Picard, 'Supporting Insite unethical, Clement tells doctors', *Globe and Mail* (19 August 2008), pp. A1 and A5. The City of Vancouver's 'Four Pillars drug strategy' is outlined at www.city.vancouver.bc.ca/fourpillars (accessed July 2008). For a frontline account of the immediate history leading to the opening of Insite, see Nettie Wild's documentary, *FIX: The Story of an Addicted City* (Canada Wild Productions, 2002). At this writing, the federal government still had not made a decision on the renewal of Insite's special drug law exemption.

4 Tom McBeath (left) as Stuart and Kyle Rideout as Roland in the Ruby
Slippers/Théâtre la seizième production of *The View from Above* at
Performance Works, Vancouver, March 2008

Olympics have been cancelled and North Vancouver couple Stuart
and Marsha are barely getting by on stockpiled canned goods and the
occasional foraged vegetable, all the while clinging (quite literally) to
the hope that they can sell their house before it slides down the hill. But
they are also being terrorised by roving gangs of the drug addicted, the
homeless, and the mentally ill, who, having been rounded up and forcibly evacuated from the city in the lead-up to 2010, have now broken
out of their suburban asylums and have begun a mass migration back
into the city. Among their ranks is Stuart and Marsha's son, Roland, a
former junkie. The prodigal has returned home; he has brought friends,
and they're hungry.

In one especially vivid scene Stuart and Roland have a conversation in which father explains to son his own idiosyncratic take on
Vancouver's tipping point in terms of urban sustainability (see figure
4). Struggling to come up with an explanation for the soggy situation
in which they find themselves, Stuart makes no attempt to link the rain
to real-estate speculation, the attendant deforestation of Vancouver's
north shore, or an increase in fossil-fuel emissions from his daily
commutes to work alone in his car; instead, he latches onto a Dutch
study he has read which claims that when significant numbers of drug
addicts get together their combined dehydration somehow gives off an

electrical spark that causes a change in atmospheric pressure, resulting especially in persistent precipitation. Something else to blame the most vulnerable members of society for: the weather. A unique co-production between Théâtre la seizième and Ruby Slippers Theatre, the play actually premiered twice in the spring of 2008, once in French, and once in English. I attended performances of both productions, admiring, in particular, Patrick Pennefather's brilliant sound design, which managed to take something to which I thought I was acoustically inured as a Vancouverite – rainfall – and make it sound terrifyingly apocalyptic. But the true prescience of Long's play was confirmed to me only several months later when, in partial response to the astute and pointed questions about Vancouver's homelessness problem posed to BC Premier Gordon Campbell during his visit to the Beijing Olympics by a Chinese journalist educated at my university, city police forcibly removed several homeless people who had set up a temporary tent city in Oppenheimer Park; and when I subsequently read in the newspaper that the Mental Health Commission of Canada was set to pilot a project in Vancouver that would provide shelter and mental health and addiction treatment for as many as 300 homeless people from the DTES, and that would 'have the side effect of helping clear the poverty stricken area before the 2010 Winter Olympics'.[53] The future is now.

That future has much to do with the fact that significant new property development in the downtown core has nowhere else to go but east. All of a sudden it was in no one's economic interests to continue to ignore the DTES. This realisation, coinciding as it did with Vancouver's Olympic bid, prompted VANOC, the city, and the province to put together and sign a flurry of official agreements and statements committing them to a plan for the revitalisation of the DTES that included as much attention to community, commercial, social, and non-market housing infrastructure as it did to new development projects. The Vancouver Agreement, signed in March 2000, identified strategies for improving economic development, training and employment opportunities, affordable housing, and health and safety in the region regardless of the success of Vancouver's Olympic bid.[54] The Inner-City Inclusive Commitment Statement (ICI), signed two years later and accompanying the Olympic bid book that went forward to the IOC, contained five

53 See Mary Frances Hill, 'Homeless swept from tent city to hotels', *Vancouver Sun* (16 August 2008), p. B7; and Ian Bailey, 'Ahead of Games, Vancouver reaches out to Eastside homeless', *Globe and Mail* (15 September 2008), p. A1.

54 *Vancouver Agreement: Community Assessment of 2010 Olympic Winter Games and Paralympic Games on Vancouver's Inner-City Neighbourhoods* (February 2003), www.iocc.ca/documents/ICI_CommAssfinal.pdf (accessed April 2008).

housing commitments related to the Games: to start planning immediately for an affordable housing legacy; to protect existing rental housing
stock; to provide as many alternative forms of temporary accommoda-
tion for Winter Games visitors and workers as possible; to ensure that
no one is made homeless as a result of the Games; and to ensure that
residents are not involuntarily displaced, evicted, or charged unreason-
able rental increases as a result of the Games.[55] Once Vancouver was
awarded the Games, the City of Vancouver issued its Homeless Action
Plan in 2005, making 87 recommendations, including the creation of
8,000 additional subsidised housing units over the next 10 years.[56] This
particular commitment was echoed by two independent reports issued
by the Pivot Legal Society and the ICI Housing Table in 2006 and 2007,
respectively, both stipulating as a target goal the creation of 800 new
social housing units a year, and with the latter claiming that 'if hosting
the [Olympic] Games is to provide a significant, enduring, and visible
legacy, it should be to eliminate homelessness'.[57] In 2008 outgoing
Mayor Sullivan signed the EcoDensity Charter, a general statement of
principle regarding Vancouver's commitment to urban sustainability
that likewise purports to take seriously the affordable housing crisis
plaguing Vancouver's most vulnerable inner-city neighbourhoods.[58]
Finally, Sullivan's replacement as mayor, Gregor Robertson, who heads
a new left-of-centre coalition at city hall, and who campaigned on a
pledge to end street homelessness in Vancouver by 2015, created the
Homeless Emergency Action Team (HEAT) shortly after taking office,
opening three new low-barrier shelters that serviced 300 people a night
during an unseasonably cold stretch in December 2008.[59]

Yet despite the performative commitment in all of these reports
to use the opportunities created by the Olympics to solve Vancouver's
housing woes, among other social development issues, saying in this
case has so far added up to very little doing. This accounts, in no
small measure, for the D-grade awarded VANOC and the City by the

55 'Inner-City Inclusive Commitment Statement', *Vancouver 2010*, www.vancou-
    ver2010.com/resources/PDFs/CommitmentStatement_EN.pdf (accessed July 2008).
56 City of Vancouver, *Homeless Action Plan* (June 2005), pp. 28–9, http://intraspec.ca/
    hap05jun.pdf (accessed July 2008).
57 *Report of the Inner-City Inclusive Housing Table* (March 2007), p. 3, www.iocc.ca/
    documents/2007-02-27_ICIT_Final4_with_apps.pdf (accessed July 2008). See,
    as well, David Eby and Christopher Misura, *Cracks in the Foundation: Solving the
    Housing Crisis in Canada's Poorest Neighbourhood* (Vancouver: Pivot, 2006).
58 City of Vancouver, *Vancouver EcoDensity Planning Initiative*, www.vancouver-
    ecodensity.ca (accessed July 2008).
59 'New Vancouver homeless shelter program filled to capacity', *Vancouver Sun* (6
    January 2009), www.vancouversun.com/Life/Vancouver+homeless+shelter+
    program+filled+capacity/1148114/story.html (accessed January 2009).

Impact of the Olympics on Community Coalition (IOCC) in its May 2007 *Olympic Oversight Interim Report Card*.[60] As we shall soon see, the IOCC and affiliated community-based organisations working in the DTES have also opted to pursue Vancouver's perceived inaction on social housing through official human rights channels like the UN. Others are not awaiting the rulings that might result, with the direct action Anti-Poverty Committee, in particular, staging squats and sleep-ins at various DTES hotels scheduled for demolition or redevelopment, repeatedly and openly vandalising the Olympic Countdown Clock, and, in one inspired bit of lunacy that combined social activism and community theatre, leading a coalition of DTES interest groups in the 'Poverty Olympics'; events included the 'poverty-line high jump', with the bar set at well over three metres, and a long jump that required competitors to leap over bedbug-infested mattresses.[61] Vancouver social housing advocates were particularly outraged by the decision of Sullivan and his fellow right-of-centre Non-Partisan Association councillors to renege, shortly after taking power in 2006, on the previous municipal administration's commitment to use money from the city's $1.2-billion Property Endowment Fund to expand on one of the key social legacy commitments contained in Vancouver's Olympic Bid Book, namely that in the post-Games conversion of the False Creek South Athletes' Village (see figure 5) to a state-of-the-art green residential community (to be called Millennium Water), there would be a healthy mix of market and social housing units. Specifically, the previous left-of-centre COPE/Vision coalition presided over by Mayor Campbell recommended that the 250 units Vancouver bid organisers said would be set aside for social housing be upped to 660 (of a total 2,000 planned units), with an additional 660 to be priced slightly below market value in order to target lower- and middle-income groups. In other words, the plan was to make False Creek South – the last stretch of undeveloped waterfront property in the city – a model sustainable, mixed community, with the initial outlay of social, affordable, and market housing in the area to be divided up equally in thirds. However, at the recommendation of City Manager,

---

60   The IOCC is 'a broad-based independent community coalition whose mission is to mitigate the negative impacts of the 2010 Winter Olympic and Paralympic Games and to advocate for a rich post-Games, community-based legacy'. In addition to raising concerns over evictions and failed housing commitments, the interim report card also identifies serious concerns in the areas of environmental sustainability, civil liberties, and public expenditure and transparency. See IOCC, *Olympic Oversight Interim Report Card: 2010 Olympic Games*, pp. 4 and *passim*, www.iocc.ca/documents/2007-05-07_OlympicReportCard.pdf (accessed May 2007).

61   Elianna Lev, 'Poverty Olympics carries the torch for social issues', *Globe and Mail* (4 February 2008), p. S2.

5 Construction on the 2010 Athletes' Village, South False Creek, Vancouver,
September 2008

Judy Rogers, who said the move would save close to $20 million and who
claimed '[t]he city does not have a shortage of affordable housing sites',
Sullivan's council reduced the number of social housing back down to
the original 250, and eliminated the affordable, middle-income units
altogether, arguing that Millennium Development Corporation could
be persuaded to build these units voluntarily.[62]

That looked increasingly unlikely when it emerged, in October
2008, that the developer was in fact unable to pay its construction
bills, and that the New York-based investment company providing
the private financing for the project stopped advancing funds in the
wake of an increasingly gloomy global economic forecast and its belief
that Millennium would likely default on its loan. This prompted an
emergency secret loan of $100 million by the city to Millennium under
Sullivan's watch that became the focus of great controversy and public
outrage during the 2008 civic election and that led, eventually, to Rogers'
firing and the city assuming de facto control of the project's development soon after Robertson was sworn in as mayor. The latter decision
required a legislative amendment at the provincial level to Vancouver's

---

62 See Frances Bula, 'City opts for less social housing in False Creek', *Vancouver Sun* (21
    January 2006), p. B11.

charter so that the city might be allowed to borrow unlimited amounts of money and seek a new financing deal at lower interest rates in order to complete the project on time, and at the least amount of risk to taxpayers, who, barring a sudden upswing in the collapsed real-estate market, would potentially be on the hook for close to $1 billion, almost the exact same size of the debt that Montreal was left with after the 1976 Summer Olympics, a bill that was only paid off in full 30 years later.[63] Coincidentally, as all this was playing out, the British government announced that it was also releasing hundreds of millions of pounds of contingency funds to keep construction of London's 2012 Olympic venues on track, with the lion's share – £326 million – likewise going to their own embattled Athletes' Village.[64]

Compounding the calamity of what might have been done differently about the economic financing and social legacy of the Athletes' Village in Vancouver is a similarly shortsighted dismantling of some of the basic infrastructure that already exists in the city around low-income housing. According to David Eby, co-author of Pivot Legal Society's aforementioned housing report, longtime DTES activist, current executive director of the BC Civil Liberties Association and maintainer of one of the best community watchdog blogs devoted to the 2010 Olympics, between December 2007 and April 2008 alone a total of 448 low-income housing units – mostly SROs – were lost as a result of nine building closures in the DTES.[65] This compares with a projection of only 557 additional SROs to be built in the same area before 2010, a net gain – by these numbers – of only 109 units. By contrast, 1,597 units of market housing are projected to be built in the DTES during the same period.[66] Several of those market units will be contained within The Greenwich, the latest condominium project by Concord Pacific (celebrating its twentieth anniversary in 2008) to be greenlighted by the city's Development

63 For a full accounting of the financing costs associated with Vancouver's Athletes' Village, see David Baines, 'The devil was in the details', *Vancouver Sun* (17 January 2009), p. A5. On Montreal's paying off of its Olympic debt, see 'Quebec's Big Owe stadium debt is over', *cbcnews.ca*, www.cbc.ca/canada/montreal/story/2006/12/19/qc-olympicstadium.html (accessed August 2008).

64 Owen Gibson, 'Government forced to bail out major Olympic projects', *The Guardian* (21 January 2009), www.guardian.co.uk/uk/2009/jan/21/olympics-2012-funding-bailout (accessed January 2009).

65 Pivot Legal Society (David Eby, Compiler), 'Backgrounder – Vancouver low-income housing closures December 2007 to date' (9 April 2008), www.iocc.ca/documents/LowIncomeHousingClosures.pdf (accessed May 2008).

66 Wendy Pedersen and Jean Swanson, *Nothing About Us Without Us: Interim Report on Community Visioning* (Vancouver: Carnegie Community Action Project, 2008), p. 2, http://ccapvancouver.files.wordpress.com/2008/07/ccapvisionwebsm.pdf (accessed August 2008).

Permit Board. The Greenwich's address will be 58 West Hastings Street, and its units will range in price from $300,000 to well over $500,000. The project's location in the heart of the DTES and its lack of mixed market and non-market housing units outraged community activists, who lobbied both the City and Concord Pacific CEO Terry Hui repeatedly to rethink their plans.[67]

The Concord Pacific connection takes us back, once again, to 1986 and even earlier in terms of the link between Chinese migration, mega-events, the historical performance of place, and urban development (and decline) in this particular region of Vancouver. For if, as a recent local newspaper headline suggested, quoting former Director of Planning Larry Beasley, and referring specifically to an Olympics-related revitalisation of our inner-city neighbourhoods, 'Vancouver's future [is] rising in the east',[68] then Chinatown's historical proximity and inter-connected destiny to the DTES should remind us that that future stretches at least as far as Beijing, where the literal bulldozing of the past should also give Vancouverites pause. Consider, in this regard, the fate of what is today the oldest surviving building in Vancouver's Chinatown, at 51 East Pender. Built in 1889 by Yip Sang, owner of an import–export business and co-founder of the Chinese Benevolent Association, the building is currently being renovated as a private art gallery that will house the collection of the city's most successful realtor.[69]

Showcasing culture: national brandings

As an exercise in the visual branding of a place and its people, there is perhaps no bigger stage than the Olympics. A host nation and city get to impress upon the world their cultural iconicity in myriad ways: through official logos and mascots; signature architecture; souvenir programmes and merchandise; various affiliated festivals, performances, and commissioned artworks; and, most spectacularly, the opening and closing ceremonies, where the spirit of friendly international competition signalled by the lighting of the Olympic flame is preceded by a calculated promotion of singular national heritage, most often by combining folk art pageantry (song, dance, and costuming) with visual effects

---

67 See Jackie Wong, 'City green-lights condo against community objections', *Carnegie Community Action Project Web Log* (8 July 2008), http://ccapvancouver/word-press/2008/07/08 (accessed July 2008).

68 See John Bermingham, 'Vancouver's future rising in the east', *Vancouver Province* (5 February 2006), p. A31.

69 See John Mackie, 'Yip family legacy lives on in renovation by condo king', *Vancouver Sun* (1 August 2008), p. A3.

of monumental scale. It should come as no surprise, then, that while cultural festivals have been associated, in one form or another, with the modern Olympics since their inception, it was Nazi Germany that, along with innovations like the torch relay (more on that below), established the template for linking youth, athleticism, ceremony, and national ideology in the choreographed displays of culture we have especially come to expect from the Olympics' opening and closing spectacles.[70]

Although, as we shall soon see, the parallels are at times uncanny, the too-easy comparisons with Nazi Germany tap into a far more historically embedded – and compensatory – discourse of 'yellow peril', and obscure the specific dynamics of how the Beijing Olympics have initiated a strategic programme of national branding that announces to the world China's newfound economic clout while also reminding us that the country is no mere *arriviste* in terms of its cultural heritage. That is, Beijing has sought to proclaim its (belated) modernity by aggressively pursuing and promoting its new *place* among the international avant-garde of world-class cities at the same time as it has carefully showcased its historical *timelessness* through various performative gestures and strategic references to Chinese antiquity and 5,000 years of tradition. Nowhere is this more evident than in the signature buildings Beijing has commissioned in the lead-up to the Olympics, including the National Stadium, the Aquatic Centre, the National Performing Arts Centre, the new CCTV building, and the new Terminal Three of Beijing Capital Airport. Each of these buildings has been designed by a major international architect or architectural firm (in order: Switzerland's Herzog and de Meuron; Australia's PTW Architects; France's Paul Andreu; Holland's Rem Koolhaas; and the UK's Sir Norman Foster). However, each project has also formally sought the input of local Chinese artists, architects, and designers – most notably, and controversially, Ai Weiwei – as native informants on everything from the ancient principles of *feng shui* to the traditional symbolic power accorded famous monuments in Beijing. Finally, the buildings that have resulted are spectacular visual landmarks whose nicknames and distinctive forms (Herzog and de Meuron's Bird's Nest, Andreu's Egg, Foster's dragon-like Terminal Three, Koolhaas's asymmetrical trapezoid) speak as much, if not more, to Westerners' clichéd understandings of Asian symbology as they do to Chinese people's investments in recognisable icons of culture. In short,

70 See Allen Guttmann, 'Berlin 1936: the most controversial Olympics', in Alan Tomlinson and Christopher Young (eds), *National Identity and Global Sports Events: Culture, Politics, and Spectacle in the Olympics and the Football World Cup* (Albany: SUNY Press, 2006), pp. 65–82; and David Clay Large, *Nazi Games: The Olympics of 1936* (New York: Norton, 2007).

6 Construction on the Bird's Nest Stadium in Beijing, November 2007

the Olympics have allowed Beijing to import a futuristic new skyline to match what is arguably its most valuable cultural export: its historical past.[71]

The spatial/temporal dynamics underscoring this process of architectural branding are especially on display not just in the design, but in the placement of the Beijing Olympics' two most recognisable landmarks, the Bird's Nest Stadium (figure 6) and the National Aquatic Centre or Water Cube. The two venues were inaccessible during my visit, cordoned off behind a heavily guarded perimeter fence as scores of migrant workers attended to last-minute plantings and grounds keeping. But even through barbed wire and under a heavy layer of smog, there is no denying the visual impact of these buildings. That impact is even more stunning at night, when thousands of lights placed within the Bird's Nest's complex web of steel girders and support columns turn the building into a sparkling piece of public sculpture, and when the translucent plastic exterior of the Water Cube is illuminated to reveal its walls of blue-green bubbles, or sea-foam. However, it is the siting of these two buildings, along with the more prosaic looking National Indoor Stadium, on the specially created Olympic Green that aligns them, quite literally, with what Susan Brownell, in her very useful discussion of how sports stadiums map onto national identity in Beijing, has identified as

71 I borrow, and adapt slightly, the import/export metaphor from Paul Goldberger; see his 'Out of the blocks', *The New Yorker* (2 June 2008), p. 70.

'the history of state power' in the city since the end of the Qing dynasty.[72] That is, the Bird's Nest and the Water Cube lie just beyond the northern end of Beijing's Fourth Ring Road, on either side of the central north–south axis that bisects the city, an axis that, as one heads south from the Olympic Green, encompasses some of the city's most important and recognisable cultural landmarks from China's imperial and communist pasts, including the Bell and Drum Towers, Jingshan Park, the Forbidden City, Tiananmen Square and Mao's Mausoleum, and the Temple of Heaven. This, of course, was the route that was traced in the opposite direction via the twenty-nine fireworks rings or 'footprints' that apparently lit up the Beijing sky from Tiananmen to the Bird's Nest Stadium at the outset of the opening ceremonies, but that turned out to have been mostly prerecorded and digitally inserted into the television broadcast.

So auspicious was the Olympic Green's planned location thought to be that the site was preserved from increasingly encroaching urban development by Beijing's municipal government even after the failure of its original bid for the Games in 1993.[73] However, in terms of *national* symbols of state power, Beijing Olympic organisers attracted a different kind of cultural scrutiny when they likewise opened the redesign of the central axis leading to the Olympic Green to an *international* competition. For the winner was none other than Albert Speer Jr, son of Hitler's anointed architect, who used the 1936 Olympics in Berlin as the launching pad for rebuilding, and rebranding, the capital of a new Germany. Given this coincidence it is perhaps to be expected – although by no means defensible – that critics have drawn connections between the political regimes of Nazi Germany and Communist China, and the 'totalitarian' architecture and urban planning those regimes are said to have inspired.[74]

A similar national/international nexus can be seen at work in the five Cultural Olympiads and various affiliated artistic programmes that preceded the Beijing Olympics. On the one hand, the Cultural Olympiads were used as occasions to showcase various ethnic Chinese traditions, folk arts, and pop culture, with touring productions, exhibits, and local performers from the provinces, as well as Hong Kong, Macao, and even

72 Susan Brownell, *Beijing's Games: What the Olympics Mean to China* (Lanham: Rowan and Littlefield, 2008), p. 73.
73 *Ibid.*, p. 89.
74 Nicola Smith and Flora Bagenal, 'Hitler architect's son redraws Beijing', *The Sunday Times* (12 August 2007), www.timesonline.co.uk/tol/news/world/asia/article2241705 (accessed July 2008); and Robert Macfarlane, 'Blitzed Beijing: why the Olympic city is set on abolishing its past', *Granta* 101 (spring 2008), pp. 79–94.

Taiwan, finding a hospitable reception in the capital city. At the same time, various high-profile international companies and artists were invited to Beijing and other parts of China to display their work under the auspices of Olympics-sponsored cultural exchange programmes, with the result that on a given evening in the months immediately preceding the opening ceremonies, Chinese audiences might choose from the Irish extravaganza *Riverdance*, the Broadway musical *Hairspray*, Cairo Opera's production of *Aida*, the Greek National Theatre's version of *Prometheus Bound*, or the Kirov Ballet's *Swan Lake*. As with most intercultural performance, the interface between an artistically cosmopolitan globalism and a culturally relative, even recidivist, localism can often prove a jarring and uneasy one.

So it was with my experience of two Olympics-related cultural showcases in Beijing. The first was the *Intangible Cultural Heritage* show that opened at Beijing's Cultural Palace of Nationalities the day before I arrived. Sponsored by China's Ministry of Culture, the show featured various folk artists playing traditional musical instruments, performing snippets of opera, drama, and dance, or displaying crafts and textiles. Alongside these celebrations of China's cultural diversity there were also several parallel museum exhibits devoted to different ethnic peoples and geographical regions of China, including one called 'Tibet of China: Past and Present'. Occupying two rooms, the exhibit was carefully stage-managed to convey to the viewer how primitive and hopelessly backward were the Tibetan people prior to their 'liberation' by Communist China in the 1950s. To that end, in the first room were scores of black and white photos showing the hardships, humiliations, and punishments endured by Tibetan 'serfs' during the first half of the twentieth century; the second room, by contrast, was filled with colour photos of free Tibetans enjoying the fruits of Chinese prosperity and modern technological innovation.

Ontological questions of the human and of how, in our current advanced technological age, the blurring and collapsing of the body/ machine divide might help us renegotiate relations between self and other were explored in much more nuanced and complex ways in a groundbreaking show of international new media art curated by Zhang Ga at Beijing's National Art Museum of China. Called *Synthetic Times*, and playing off BOCOG's dedicated themes of 'Hi-Tech Olympics' and 'People's Olympics', the show placed multi-media works by Chinese artists like Du Zhenjun, Xu Zhongmin, Xu Bing, Wu Juehui, and Miao Xiaochun alongside challenging and frequently interactive sound, video, digital, robotic, and computer installations, projections, sculptures, and immersive environments created by such international art world luminaries as Stelarc, Christoph Hildebrand, Edwin van der Heide, Anthony McCall, Jean-Michel Bruyère, and Mariana Rondon. Works were grouped according to four organising themes: 'Beyond Body' explored technological extensions of the physical body, testing the limits of subjectivity through bio-mediation; 'Emotive Digital' examined the ways in which machines and related electronic devices are becoming responsive creatures; 'Recombinant Reality' sought to break down old Cartesian dualisms through mixed, virtual, and acoustic environments; and, finally, 'Here, There and Everywhere' focused on how the Internet, especially, functions as a kind of 'planetary membrane'.

In this last category, I was especially gripped by Canadian artist David Rokeby's 'surveillance installation', *Taken*. A split-screen dual projection, Rokeby's piece uses infrared video cameras to capture and record in real time the movements of gallery goers; these are then projected onto the orange, right-hand side of the screen in overlapping twenty-second loops, a computer-generated, panoptical emplotment of all human activity in the room that is at once synchronous and sequential, as in the manner of most closed-circuit television monitors. Every now and then white boxes frame the heads of individual visitors; when this happens, the blue, left-hand side of the screen displays the faces of those singled out in close-up, adding randomly generated text to suggest their possible states of mind while under observation ('nervous', 'carried away', 'hungry', 'complicit'). These close-ups are in turn arranged as black and white thumbnails of the last 200 visitors to the room, and displayed at regular intervals, a taxonomy of our own self-monitoring. And if, as curator Zhang claims in her introduction to the catalogue accompanying the show, a 'new taxonomy' of the human needs to be written, then surely what Rokeby's work suggests is that – again to quote Zhang – 'the role of art is to ensure that the deliberation takes place not behind closed doors but in the recombinant arena of open space'.[75] As Zhang's choice of sporting metaphor implies, the Olympics have provided an impetus to initiate such a dialogue in China at the same time as they have given the state an excuse to increase security and surveillance, including conscripting local citizens as part of reconstituted, Mao-era neighbourhood committees. At the very least, this groundbreaking show – the first of its kind at China's premiere art institution – has gone a distance toward banishing the ghosts of social realism that have long dominated this particular cultural arena.

75 Zhang Ga, 'Synthetic times', in Fan Di'an and Zhang Ga (eds), *Synthetic Times: Media Art China 2008* (Beijing and Cambridge, MA: National Art Museum of China and MIT Press, 2008), p. 28.

Indeed, the Olympics have arguably allowed the Chinese state to cotton on at last to what the rest of the world has long known: contemporary Chinese art, especially photo-, video-, performance- and conceptual-based work, is a very hot commodity. Beyond the evidence of recent biennales, what especially bore this out for me was a local survey of contemporary Chinese photography that opened at the University of British Columbia's Morris and Helen Belkin Art Gallery (more on this important local art venue below) in January 2009 as part of the international offerings of Vancouver 2010's second Cultural Olympiad. *Action Camera: Beijing Performance Photography* traced the relationship between performance art and photography in China as both emerged from the underground scene in Beijing's East Village in the 1990s. That relationship, as the large-scale, professionally illuminated, and formally composed C-prints in the show attest, has little to do with documenting for historical posterity the officially discouraged and temporally ephemeral live public performances and body art actions of East Village pioneers like Ma Liuming, Rong Rong, Zhang Huan, and Xing Danwen. Rather, these and other artists are using the medium of the camera itself to stage agitprop performances of individual self-expression and collective national consciousness as highly choreographed, repeatable, and overdetermined with paradoxical meaning as any Photoshopped and digitally manipulated images released by the Chinese state in the lead up to the Olympics (and, significantly, many of the images in the show, including ones by Hong Hao and Li Wei, do in fact use Photoshop to achieve their performative effects). As curator Keith Wallace suggests in his catalogue to the show, this places a special onus on audiences in terms of negotiating between a locally distinctive and culturally specific versus globally assimilative and formally partial comprehension of the work.[76] For example, do we read Ai's contribution to the show, his 1995 triptych *Dropping a Han Dynasty Urn*, as a logical extension of the Duchampian questioning of the cultural value of art via the ready-made, or as an iconoclastic comment on Ai's part about the relative national worth bestowed by China on an historical past that predates the Cultural Revolution?

Of course, Beijing's legendary East Village has long since been superseded by the far more commercialised 798 Art District, a series of galleries and studios occupying various abandoned munitions factories in the Dashanzi area of Chaoyang that were built by East Germany (following Bauhaus-inspired designs) in the 1950s and 1960s. As Chinese artists started gaining increasing international acclaim in the early part

---

76 Keith Wallace, *Action-Camera: Beijing Performance Photography* (Vancouver: Morris and Helen Belkin Art Gallery, 2009), p. 68.

of this century, 798 attracted its own attention from dealers and tourists alike, with commercial galleries and amenities like restaurants, cafés, and shops popping up at an accelerated rate, thereby increasing rents and gradually squeezing out artists' studios. Indeed, during my visit what was formally a mass of unsigned roads and muddy pathways had been turned into a newly paved, freshly landscaped, and accommodatingly mapped Olympic destination, its appropriation as 'corroborative evidence' of Beijing's vibrancy and creativity signalled via its referencing on an official Olympic poster.[77] Not surprisingly, I soon discovered from Amy and D'Arcy that one consequence of 798's anointment as a 'Central Art District' along the lines of the Central Business District just to the south, was that the real cutting-edge work was now being made and shown in Caochangdi, even further to the northeast, and presided over by Ai's own China Art Archives and Warehouse.

As artist Hong Hao put it to me quite bluntly when I interviewed him in Beijing, the relationship between the Olympics and the contemporary Chinese art scene is one of differing market incentives, with the spotlight thrown by the lead-up to the Summer Games helping to fuel the international appetite for challenging conceptual work, and the Chinese government responding by flooding the domestic market with a lot of mass-produced, Olympic-themed representational painting, much of it referencing the Bird's Nest, or other recognisable symbols of Beijing's economic renaissance.[78] And yet, as the example of Ai has demonstrated, not all Chinese cultural producers have been willing to have their work conscripted as part of Beijing's official national brand. Stressing that he was hired by Herzog and de Meuron, and not the Chinese government, Ai, in making his public denouncement of the Beijing Games as a whole, also criticised those artists who would 'shamelessly [abuse] their profession' and neglect their moral responsibilities by agreeing to collaborate with such a regime.[79]

Singled out for special derision by Ai in his comments were his former Beijing Film Academy classmate, Zhang Yimou, and Stephen Spielberg, who at the time were still set to collaborate on the staging of the Beijing Games' opening and closing ceremonies. Very soon after Ai's public outburst, Spielberg withdrew his consultancy services, citing

77 Jeroen de Kloet, Gladys Pak Lei Chong, and Wei Liu, 'The Beijing Olympics and the art of nation-state maintenance', *China Aktuell* 2 (2008): p. 15.

78 Personal interview with Hong Hao, Beijing (15 June 2008). Ironically, Hong then proceeded to tell me how he had agreed to have a painting based on a photo of the Bird's Nest, and completed by his assistants, appear in an Olympics-themed exhibit in Germany.

79 Watts, 'Olympic artist'.

concerns over Darfur and China's support of the Sudanese government. For his part, Zhang – whose family, like Ai's, suffered under Mao, and whose early films ran afoul of Chinese government censors – shrugged off both Ai's criticisms and Spielberg's withdrawal, reiterating that he had 'no interest in politics' and that he took the Olympics assignment because he 'wanted to do something for the Chinese people'.[80] While I do not have the space to comment extensively on the elaborate spectacles that Zhang eventually produced to bracket China's Olympic coming-out party, I do want to note that they, too, preserved the aesthetic mix of international modernism and national tradition that I have suggested has characterised Beijing's entire performance of Olympics-related national branding. That mix was first of all incarnated in Zhang himself as impresario, with the historical subject matter of his most famous films (including *Red Sorghum*, *Ju Du*, *Raise the Red Lantern*, *Hero*, and *House of Flying Daggers*) standing comfortably alongside his reputation among international critics for his sumptuous cinematography and bold use of colour. Zhang then sought to extend this local/global aesthetic by wooing expat Chinese artists who have achieved recognition in the West to collaborate on key aspects of direction and design (such as visual artist Jennifer Wen Ma and choreographer Shen Wei), or else, like concert pianist Lang Lang, to participate as featured performers. In so doing, Zhang ensured that his tasked exploration of the ancient foundations of Chinese philosophy, aesthetics, and ingenuity would be presented in a suitably modern, culturally accessible, and visually cohesive manner.

The most watched portion of any Games, and routinely among the highest rated television events in broadcast history, Olympic opening ceremonies have, dramaturgically speaking, always been about striking a balance between competing performance styles – and scales: monumentality and intimacy (2,008 Ko drummers and 3,000 Confucian dancers versus a little singing girl); tradition and innovation (a parade of nations according to the Chinese alphabet versus Li Ning's spectacular aerial lighting of the Olympic flame); high art and kitsch (usually encompassed within one multi-octave singer, in this case Sarah Brightman); the real and the simulacral (again, that little singing girl, or those digitised fireworks footprints). Balancing, as well, at times complementary, at times competing, messages and symbols of local/regional, national, and supranational specificity, Olympic opening ceremonies have also typically sought at once to performatively reproduce and particularise a narrative

---

80   Quoted in David Barboza, 'Gritty renegade now directs China's close-up', *New York Times* (7 August 2008), www.nytimes.com/2008/08/08/sports/olympics/08guru. html?pagewanted=1&_r=1# (accessed August 2008).

of historical progress by 'mixing visions of a simple, untainted and yet retrievable past with the impact of new and sometimes alien forces, in an optimistic blend for the future'.[81] In Zhang's case, this meant excising completely any reference to the past sixty years of Communist rule – and especially the isolationist leadership of Mao – in favour of showcasing four inventions from Chinese antiquity – gunpowder, paper, printing, and the compass – that served to remind Western audiences of the country's global historical contributions and current technological and economic aspirations. And if some audience members nevertheless detected in the military precision with which these choreographed displays of historical pageantry were executed (by members of the artistic ranks of the PLA, no less) traces of the old strong-arm tactics and message management of the CCP, consider the memo from the Canadian federal government that was made public, following an access-to-information request, two days before the Beijing closing ceremonies; in it, the ruling Conservative Party, through the Department of Heritage, commits to investing '$20-million toward the opening ceremony of the [2010] Olympic Winter Games in order to ensure that the event adequately reflects the priorities of the Government and helps to achieve its domestic and international branding goals'.[82]

What those goals are remain unclear. Nevertheless, in terms of Vancouver's performance of culture in the lead-up to the 2010 opening ceremonies, organisers have faced a branding challenge at least as performatively complex as Beijing's attempts to balance modernity and tradition. Specifically, as has bedevilled so many public displays of Canadian culture outside Quebec in the years since Confederation, the question becomes how to represent iconographically a 'national' culture when no such singular entity is said to exist – beyond, that is, a 'mosaic' of many, or 'multi-', cultures, or an amalgam of various regional/natural references. The solution has, historically, *not* been to invent, holus-bolus, cultural pageantry on the order of the United States' Hollywood razzmatazz, but rather to appropriate, where possible, the traditions and symbols of Canada's Indigenous peoples. So it continues with the 2010 Winter Olympics. Despite Premier Gordon Campbell's reported displeasure at what he saw as the kitschy and clichéd display of 'hackneyed' regional stereotypes during an eight-minute segment promoting the 2010 Games at the closing ceremony of the Turin Olympics[83] (including

81   Tomlinson, 'Olympic spectacle', p. 592.
82   Quoted in Robert Matas, 'Ottawa aims to put its stamp on 2010 Games', *Globe and Mail* (22 August 2008), p. A1.
83   Miro Cernetig and Kevin Griffin, 'Premier cringes at Games ceremony that presented icy image of Canada', *Victoria Times-Colonist* (1 April 2006), p. A4.

a tableau of ice-fishing that was almost as bad as London 2012 organisers trotting out the double-decker bus, the brollies, and Beckham at the
Beijing closing ceremonies), VANOC has, since that time, continued to
promulgate – and profit from – the connections between Vancouver's
location on the West Coast and the area's rich Aboriginal heritage.

To be sure, that area tends to be rather expansive and free-floating,
and, consequently, the associated cultural references somewhat of a
hodge-podge. Thus we have as the Vancouver Games' official logo an
inukshuk named 'Ilanaaq' (Inuktitut for 'friend'), based on the traditional stone sculptures of Canada's northern Inuit peoples. More
geographically appropriate, if not entirely materialisable, are the three
mythical creatures derived from local Coast Salish legend that VANOC
is using as its official Olympic mascots: Miga is a sea bear, part Orca
whale and part Kermode or Spirit bear; Quatchi is a sasquatch, especially
popular in Haida storytelling traditions; and Sumi is a guardian spirit
who has thunderbird wings, an Orca hat, and black bear legs. In partnership with the Ministry of Transport, signage along the Sea-to-Sky
Highway connecting West Vancouver to Whistler is also being rede-
signed to incorporate First Nations art and culture, and to emphasise the
links between landscape, history, and memory. Finally, in the summer of
2008 a public art program was launched to commission specially created
artworks by First Nations artists that will be permanently installed in all
fifteen Olympic and Paralympic venues.[84]

For the most part, the Four Host First Nations (FHFN) participating in the Vancouver/Whistler Games – Lil'wat, Musqueam,
Squamish, and Tsleil-Waututh – have been cooperating in this process
of cultural appropriation, seeing in it a chance, in the words of FHFN
Executive Director and CEO Tewanee Joseph, to create and launch a
new Aboriginal brand on the international stage.[85] So far their marketing campaign has demonstrated a solid mastery of web-promotion and
product placement, using Facebook and YouTube to get their message
out, and their own website (www.fourhostfirstnations.com) to offer free
mobile ringtones and computer wallpaper, as well as pricier merchandise like T-shirts, hats, and luggage. The advance marketing is mostly
designed to ensure that international visitors to the Vancouver Olympics
stop by the 20,000-square foot FHFN 2010 Aboriginal Trade Pavilion
that will occupy the southeast corner of the downtown Queen Elizabeth
Theatre Plaza, and that will also serve as a 'stage to showcase Aboriginal

---

84 'Aboriginal participation', *Vancouver 2010*, www.vancouver2010.com/en/
Sustainability/AboriginalParticipation (accessed July 2008).
85 See Derrick Penner, 'Creating a first nations buzz', *Vancouver Sun* (28 July 2008), p.
B3.

Peoples and . . . culture to the estimated three billion television and internet viewers that will tune in to the Games at one time or another'.[86] Originally designed as a temporary structure, talks are currently underway with the City of Vancouver, as part of their Creative City visioning process, to determine whether the Pavilion might become a permanent feature of the post-Games cultural precinct that is being planned for the area (including a new home for the Vancouver Art Gallery and a long-discussed Coal Harbour Performing Arts Complex).[87]

A brand-new showcase for First Nations culture has already opened in Whistler. A short walk from the heart of Whistler Village, and across the street from the Fairmont Chateau, the three-storey, 30,400-square-foot Squamish Lil'wat Cultural Centre is strategically located to attract the thousands of international tourists who visit the resort town each year, and especially the crowds that will descend in even greater numbers during the 2010 Olympics. For an adult admission fee of $18, visitors are led by a docent on a tour of various indoor and outdoor exhibits devoted to both communities' cultural, linguistic, artistic, and ecological histories, including displays of ceremonial regalia, carvings, weavings, and drums, and replicas of their traditional communal dwellings, the wooden Squamish longhouse and the earthen Lil'wat istken. At the end of the tour, visitors are led to the gift shop, where, as the Centre's official website notes, they can purchase and '[t]ake home a piece of BC aboriginal culture'.[88] That culture's brand – at once standing in for the entire province – is historically and economically tied to nature, and so the souvenirs for sale include wooden carvings, cedar baskets, wool blankets and other weavings, and gold and silver jewellery.

The literal trading being done under the cultural banner of the First Nations brand was also very much on display in British Columbia's Olympic Pavilion in Beijing. Opened is the spring of 2008, and scheduled to welcome visitors through the duration of the Beijing Games, the Pavilion copped a prime location, just southeast of Tiananmen, and connected to Beijing's vast Exhibition Hall. However, this didn't necessarily translate into crowds of Chinese visitors pouring in following their obeisances at Mao's mausoleum. The morning I toured the Pavilion, the docents (mostly Chinese students who were going to school in BC) outnumbered the

---

86 Quoted from the description of the pavilion contained on the FHFN website; see Four Host First Nations Society, 'The Pavilion', www.fourhostfirstnations.com/pavilion.html (accessed July 2008).

87 *Ibid.*; see, as well, City of Vancouver, 'The creative city initiative', http://vancouver.ca/creativecity/ (accessed July 2008).

88 'BC aboriginal culture – gifts of two nations', Squamish Lil'wat Cultural Centre, www.slcc.ca/gift-shop (accessed July 2008).

paying customers, and they were sorely disappointed upon discovering I was actually from Vancouver. Apparently I already knew everything they were about to tell me. In truth, there was much about the Olympic marketing of my city and province in Beijing that surprised me, starting with the live Chinese Mountie wandering from room to room. Those rooms were arranged according to the five Chinese elements – metal, wood, water, fire, and earth – and after one took in the abundant Aboriginal iconography and got one's head around some of the more bizarre transnational cultural correspondences (especially fire symbolising the 'passion of the Canadian people'), one discovered that the real story being told here was about strengthening economic ties with China. Thus, the accompanying text and images, as with much 2010 Olympic promotional materials (see my second epigraph, above), emphasised BC's strategic position as 'Canada's Pacific gateway', detailed the thriving transportation and trade routes between Asia and the province, played up Vancouver's bustling container ports, and highlighted the region's abundant natural resources, including precious minerals like jade. An interactive video about Vancouver featured buttons to press called 'live', 'work', 'play', and 'invest', promoting the city as a lifestyle city and tourist destination, but also focusing on various real-estate and economic development projects, and touting hi-tech and video gaming as particular growth industries.

While the official mission of the FHFN Secretariat is to ensure that First Nations' 'languages, traditions, protocols and cultures are meaningfully acknowledged, respected, and represented in the planning, staging and hosting of the Games',[89] Joseph has likewise acknowledged that 'Our participation in the Olympic Games is really an economic exercise'.[90] However, there is by no means unanimity among BC's Aboriginal communities about the benefits of such participation, and at times internal divisions have threatened to spill over into violence. Indeed, Joseph, was himself charged with mischief and uttering threats against Donald Joe Mathias, an outspoken critic of the Squamish Nation's participation in the Olympics, after a dustup in April 2007 on North Vancouver's Capilano Reserve.[91] The Native Warrior Society (NWS) also maintains a website called No Olympics on Stolen Native Land (www.no2010.com), in which it openly calls for an escalating series of violent actions in advance of Vancouver's opening ceremonies. Members of NWS also claimed responsibility for what has so far proved to be the most daring

---

89 Four Host First Nations Society, 'Sharing our culture and stories with the world', www.fourhostfirstnations.com/index.html (accessed July 2008).

90 Quoted in Penner, 'Creating', p. B3.

91 He was subsequently acquitted of all charges; see Bethany Lindsay, 'Olympic exec not guilty in threat case', *North Shore News* (17 August 2008), p. 1.

and theatrical protest to the Games, namely the stealing of the Olympic flag flying outside Vancouver's City Hall on the night of 6 March 2007. Three days later a photo ran in the local media showing three balaclava-clad members of NWS standing in front of the distinctive rings of the white Olympic flag, fists raised, and holding aloft the equally distinctive red and gold flag of central Canada's Mohawk Warrior Society, as well as a photo of Harriet Nahanee. A seventy-one-year-old Nuu-cha-nulth elder, Nahanee was sentenced to fourteen days in jail in January 2007 for taking part in a 2006 protest against the destruction of West Vancouver's Eagleridge Bluffs as part of the Olympics-mandated expansion of the Sea-to-Sky Highway to Whistler. Ill with pneumonia at the time of her sentencing, Nahanee spent nine days in Surrey's notorious Pre-Trial Centre, primarily used as a men's prison, before being released to St Paul's Hospital, where it was discovered she was also suffering from lung cancer. She died less than a month later, with many outraged Native and environmental activists claiming that her unnecessary imprisonment contributed to her rapid decline. In a statement accompanying the photo, the NWS expressed solidarity with the 'courageous stand' of the 'elder-warrior' Nahanee and vowed to continue fighting 'the destruction caused by the 2010 Olympic Games'.[92] In this regard, it is the clearly visible Mohawk flag in the foreground rather than the fragment of the Olympic flag displayed in the background that is meant to give VANOC and FHFN members, along with all BC residents generally, pause. For it necessarily evokes memories of the violent uprisings in Oka, Quebec, in the summer of 1990, when plans to expand a golf course onto a burial ground and sacred grove of pine trees claimed by the Native community of Kanesatake prompted an armed stand-off that lasted seventy-eight days.

Local photo-conceptualist Alex Morrison appropriated and restaged this already iconic NWS image for one of his contributions to a recent exhibition of young Vancouver artists, also held at UBC's Belkin Art Gallery, from January to April 2008 (see figure 7). Called *Exponential Future*, the show attempts, according to Belkin Director and co-curator Scott Watson, 'to take the measure' of the local visual arts scene – and its global interfaces. It does so partly by thematising the work of cultural memory, investigating 'the relationship between works of art and historical consciousness in a time of general amnesia', and examining how '[w]e live amongst the ruins of imagined futures from the recent past'.[93] Certainly this would seem to apply to the process

---

92 See Suzanne Fournier, 'Native warriors admit to flag theft', *Vancouver Province* (9 March 2007), p. A6.
93 Scott Watson, 'Exponential future', in Julie Bevan, Juan A. Gaitán, and Scott Watson (eds), *Exponential Future* (Vancouver: Morris and Helen Belkin Art Gallery, 2008), p. 6.

7 Alex Morrison, *Friday March 9th 2007* (C-print, 71" × 84", 2008)

of calculated cultural theft by which Morrison has fashioned his own image. Showcased alone on the back wall of the Belkin's main exhibition room, the enlarged and (literally) reframed photograph asks the viewer to consider, much like the metonymy of flags and the mise-en-abŷme of Nahanee's brandished portrait in the original NWS image, the relationship between figure and ground – in this case, the literal ground on which the gallery stands. I refer to the fact that UBC is located on what, historically, is unceded Musqueam land and, more proximately, to the fact that at the time of the *Exponential Future* show Musqueam band leaders were just in the process of finalising a deal with the provincial government that would grant them title to approximately seventy-nine hectares of land surrounding UBC. This land includes the exclusive University Golf Club, which in 2005 the BC Court of Appeal declared had been improperly sold to UBC, and which the mostly white residents of the adjacent University Endowment Lands, in a fitting reversal of the Oka situation, feared the Musqueam would immediately want to develop.[94]

94 In fact, the deal prevents the Musqueam from developing the golf course until 2083 at the earliest. For a full account of the treaty particulars, and related local fallout, see Jack Keating, 'Musqueam members ratify treaty', *Vancouver Province* (12 March 2008), p. A7.

And lest we think that Morrison, in this artistic regifting, is exempt from the cultural economy of biting the hand that feeds, consider one more fact that relates to figure and ground: the show in which his work appears was, like the *Beijing Performance Photography* show that opened in the same venue almost exactly a year later, the recipient of financial support from VANOC as part of its Cultural Olympiad programme. To be sure, Vancouver Olympic organisers might in this case be forgiven for failing to scrutinise their cultural brand more closely; pushed back from original plans to launch in 2006, the inaugural 2008 Cultural Olympiad was late getting its submission, adjudication, and funding processes off the ground, and, as a result, decided to hand out grants to various artistic and cultural events that were already scheduled to coincide with the Olympiad's planned February–March timeframe. The one dedicated event organisers did manage to coordinate was a special 'countdown concert' headlined by Canadian indie darling Feist, who got her start as a performer on the world stage when, at age twelve, she appeared as one of 1,000 young dancers in the opening ceremonies of the 1988 Calgary Winter Games. Apparently this experience provided the inspiration for her ubiquitous *1234* video, which we have another cultural brand – Apple – to thank for searing indelibly upon our brains.[95]

Showcasing human rights: global mediations

There can be no doubt that Vancouver's hosting of the Olympics in 2010 has played a large role in motivating the BC government to revive the modern treaty process and settle as many outstanding land claims as possible with First Nations before the start of the Games.[96] Ditto the impetus for Prime Minister Harper's recent apology to Canadian Aboriginal peoples for the legacy of residential school abuse, and the even more recent push by provincial and territorial leaders to revisit the Kelowna Accord and kickstart talks begun there about tackling Native poverty.[97] Like Sydney in 2000, the one place Canada is most

---

95 Kerry Gold, 'Feist shines on the Olympic stage', *Globe and Mail* (14 February 2008), p. R7.
96 Unlike most of the rest of Canada, colonial administrators in nineteenth-century BC did not bother negotiating land title treaties with resident First Nations communities. The Nisga'a Treaty, signed into law in 2000, became the first modern treaty negotiated in BC, and established the basic template for most that have followed, including a one-time cash settlement, a form of self-government, and limited sovereignty over traditional lands and resource industries (such as fishing and forestry).
97 Doug Ward, 'A national call for healing; Harper takes step to atone for a "sad chapter in our history"', *Vancouver Sun* (12 June 2008), p. A4; and Sean Gordon, 'Revive Kelowna accord, leaders urge', *Toronto Star* (17 July 2008), p. A15.

vulnerable to being shamed on the world stage is in its treatment of First Nations peoples. Thus when VANOC CEO John Furlong and Canadian IOC member Dick Pound vocally denounced the protests that greeted China's international torch relay, claiming politics had no place in the Olympics,[98] it was hard not to think that they were being somewhat disingenuous, worrying instead about the negative publicity should similar protests occur in Vancouver in 2010. For, indeed, this is precisely what happened during the last Olympic torch relay run through Canada in the lead-up to the 1988 Calgary Winter Games. At that time, the Lubicon First Nation in Alberta, upset at relay sponsor Petro-Canada's oil mining on their traditional lands, organised protests at key points along the route.[99]

Despite protestations to the contrary by the IOC, and whatever its Charter might say,[100] the Olympic Games have always been political, at times violently so: witness Munich in 1972, or Atlanta in 1996. Even Pierre de Coubertin's spearheading of their revival was directly related to France's military humiliation during the Franco-Prussian War, and his belief that greater attention to athleticism would reinvigorate his country. Since that time, the Olympics have been cancelled by war three times – in 1916, 1940, and 1944 – with the countries held responsible for those events (Germany, Japan, and Italy) subsequently banned from competition until deemed suitably rehabilitated by the IOC. The IOC also banned Apartheid South Africa from competition between 1960 and 1988, and when New Zealand's rugby team made the mistake of touring the country in 1976, more than thirty African nations stayed away from the Summer Games in Montreal. Indeed, the era of rolling Olympic boycotts that peaked with the last gasps of Cold War posturing that tarnished Moscow in 1980 and Los Angeles in 1984 actually began not in Berlin in 1936 (where a proposed boycott over Nazi Germany's racial policies was averted at the last minute, largely due to the subterfuge of American Olympic Committee head Avery Brundage), but in Melbourne in 1956, which was beset by three separate protests: Egypt, Iraq, and Lebanon withdrew after Israel invaded Egypt; Spain, Switzerland, and the Netherlands after the Soviets invaded Hungary; and China after the IOC formally recognised Taiwan.[101]

98 See, for example, the comments made by Furlong in Gary Mason, 'Another sickening sight for the man planning Vancouver's version', Globe and Mail (8 April 2008), pp. A1 and A11.

99 'Olympic boycott worked, Lubicon say', Montreal Gazette (29 February 1988), p. A8.

100 According to the Charter, one of the roles of the IOC is 'to oppose any political or commercial abuse of sport and athletes'. See Olympic Charter (Lausanne: International Olympic Committee, 2007), p. 15.

101 For a comprehensive survey of the 'primacy of politics in the Olympic movement',

The question of the 'two Chinas' was hardly resolved at the Beijing Games; the Chinese Taipei Olympic Team marched in under their specially designed flag as they have done at every Olympics since 1984. There was no repeat of Sydney in 2000, when North and South Korea marched together for the first time, despite what some in both the CCP and IOC might have hoped. Nevertheless, the Korean analogy was one IOC President Jacques Rogge clung to for a long time, repeatedly defending the decision to award China Olympic hosting duties for 2008 by citing the 1988 Summer Games in Seoul as an example of how the Olympic movement can help speed up democratic reforms in developing nations with dubious human rights records. A military dictatorship when awarded the Games in 1981, South Korea had by 1987 rewritten its constitution and held its first free elections, bowing to internal prodemocracy demonstrations rather than face the possibility of losing the Olympics.[102] However, as Russia's invasion of Georgia on the eve of the opening ceremonies reminded many, the more appropriate analogy for Beijing in terms of politics and human rights might be Moscow in 1980. There is also the precedent of Mexico City in 1968, when just ten days before the opening ceremonies the army opened fire on students protesting Olympic over-spending, killing hundreds, and where open political displays by athletes (i.e., the Black Power salutes of Tommie Smith and John Carlos) were swiftly punished or suppressed.[103]

In this final section, my aim is not to single out China for special condemnation in sacrificing individual human rights – including those of public expression and assembly – to the supra-political stage managing of Beijing's collective Olympic optics. As noted Olympics critic Helen Jefferson Lenskyj usefully reminds us, the IOC, 'an autonomous, non-elected body', abets host cities' curtailment of basic civic rights by insisting that organisers play by their tightly controlled rules, including a guarantee that there will be no public protests in or adjacent to Olympic

from de Coubertin's militarism to a discussion of the dilemma of the 'two Chinas', see Christopher R. Hill, *Olympic Politics* (Manchester: Manchester University Press, 1992), especially pp. 31–55.

102   For an analysis of the 'applicability of the lessons of Seoul to Beijing', see David R. Black and Shona Bezanson, 'The Olympic Games, human rights and democratisation: lessons from Seoul and implications for Beijing', *Third World Quarterly* 25:7 (2004), pp. 1245–61. As late as April 2008, in chiding torch relay protestors for hectoring China about its human rights record, Rogge was still clinging to South Korea as a shining example of the processes of democratisation wrought by the Olympics that might yet be emulated in Beijing; see Roger Blitz and Richard McGregor, 'Olympics chief warns west', *Financial Times* (26–7 April 2008), p. 1.

103   On the legacy of the Mexico City Games, see Claire and Keith Brewster, 'Mexico City 1968: sombreros and skyscrapers', in Tomlinson and Young (eds), *National Identity and Global Sports Events*, pp. 99–116.

venues, or any behaviour that might be considered an affront to Olympic values (and valuation). Thus, Vancouver's Safe Streets Act, brought into effect in 2004, mimics similar anti-panhandling legislation passed in advance of the 1996 Atlanta Olympics and the 2000 Sydney Olympics.[104] Notwithstanding these built-in Olympic inducements toward authoritarianism, neither do I want to dismiss or diminish the severity of the abuses sanctioned by Chinese authorities and BOCOG officials, nor the degree to which those abuses increased following the arrest and detention of dissident Hu Jia in December 2007, escalated still more with the eruption of violent protests in Tibet in March 2008 and the rise of Uyghur separatist violence in Xinjiang, and continued even after the Games were over, especially for Lu Xiaobo and other signatories of the China 08 Democratic Manifesto. All of this has been well-documented by various respected organisations, including Amnesty International, which published a series of 'Countdown' reports on the Internet in the lead-up to the Games detailing the erosion of multiple freedoms, including of the press. To this end, when Amnesty's last report was released just a week before the start of the Beijing Games, international reporters already stationed in Beijing were unable to access it, despite Rogge's assurances only two weeks before that there would be no media censorship during the Olympics, and that the foreign press would be able to cover stories freely and fully while in China.[105] Rather, I want to suggest all too briefly by way of conclusion that Beijing's attempts to control not just the message of its Olympics ('One World, One Dream'), but also their mediation (via, among other electronic channels, the World Wide Web), returns us to the special applicability of the showcase genre in highlighting a fundamental asymmetry at the heart of local and global practices of place. That is, as noted China and Pacific Rim scholar Arif Dirlik has commented, in terms of the fostering of 'place-based consciousness', the spatially abstracted routes of globalisation are often pitted against the concrete locations and historical roots of everyday social and political activity.[106]

104   Helen Jefferson Lenskyj, *Olympic Industry Resistance: Challenging Olympic Power and Propaganda* (Albany: SUNY Press, 2008), p. 23. As section 51.3 of the *Olympic Charter* proclaims, 'No kind of demonstration or political or religious propaganda is permitted in any Olympic sites, venues, or other areas' (p. 98).

105   Amnesty International, 'People's Republic of China: the Olympics countdown – broken promises', www.amnesty.org/en/library/asset/ASA17/089/2008/en/8249b304-5724-11dd-90eb-ff4596860802/asa170892008eng.pdf (accessed July 2008); and Andrew Jacobs, 'China to limit web access during Olympic Games', *New York Times* (31 July 2008), p. A1.

106   Arif Dirlik, 'Place-based imagination: globalism and the politics of place', in Roxann Prazniak and Arif Dirlik (eds), *Place and Politics in an Age of Globalisation* (New York: Rowman and Littlefield, 2001), p. 15.

Thus, China's swift and brutal suppression of the protests in Tibet, for example, was read by most Western media – and certainly CNN – as evidence of China's failure to integrate itself successfully and fully within a global development narrative of capitalist modernity, where universal human rights necessarily follow upon economic prosperity. However, the subsequent protests against the torch relay in London, Paris, and San Francisco, among other international locales, were seen within China – and not just by the state-run news agency Xinhua – as further evidence of the West's ongoing marginalisation and isolation of the country. One can only imagine what might have happened had the torch visited Vancouver, which is home to many of the key organisers behind the pro-Tibet demonstrations on the Great Wall and in Greece, as well as the second-largest Chinese community in North America, which held several local counter-demonstrations in support of the Beijing Games in the spring of 2008.[107] As my colleague Zhao Yuezhi has recently put it, were China ever in fact to lift the 'great firewall' it has erected around the Internet, foreign web browsers might be quite shocked by what they read, with many popular – and populist – blogs trading in a nationalist discourse far more jingoistic and muscularly anti-Western than that promoted by the CCP,[108] and playing to an impatient and expectant generation of only children coming of age with no memory of Tiananmen, let alone the Cultural Revolution. Some of these referential paradoxes were underscored for me as a result of an informal email survey I conducted in June of 2008, asking Chinese students studying at my university to compare Beijing's hosting of the Summer Olympics with what – if anything – they had taken note of regarding Vancouver's preparations for the 2010 Winter Games. One young woman's response was particularly illuminating, framing the politics – and performance – of place at work in the two Olympic cities not simply in terms of differences in national temperament, or 'philosophy', but also, implicitly, in terms of a critique of neo-liberalism's abstract prioritisation of individual human rights at the expense of context-specific, or 'place-based', considerations of new models of collectivisation, even post-Maoist ones that have resulted in the (apparently willing) resettlement of her own family. I quote at length from her remarks:

107 See Miro Cernetig, 'Vancouver has a pivotal role in the Tibet debate', *Vancouver Sun* (19 April 2008), p. D4; and 'Chinese Canadians in Vancouver rally to support Beijing Olympics', *China Economic Net* (27 April 2008), http://en.ce.cn/National/Politics/200804/27/t20080427_15292385.shtml (accessed May 2008).

108 Zhao Yuezhi, 'Fanning the flame: the media and the communication of official and popular national discourse', Centre for Chinese Research Workshop, *Staging the Beijing Olympics: Visions, Tensions, and Dreams*, University of British Columbia, 12 May 2008.

Like millions of Chinese people in my generation, I have been waiting for the Beijing Olympic Games since I was 13 years old. Finally, I can see my home city shine on the world stage this summer. It's a feeling much more complicated than happiness or excitement. It is a feeling most Canadians will never be able to understand. It is more about . . . national pride and glory than having fun. It is about sacrificing individual freedom for the greater good of the country . . . I am sure you know all about the new Olympic venues being built in Beijing. But you might not know that tens of thousand[s] of citizens had to move away to make the land available for the venues. My family happened to be one of them and we were honored to do so, although we had to lose some money due to the resettlement . . . The difference between the Chinese philosophy and the Canadian philosophy is what the general public considers to be more valuable: individual freedom or . . . national pride. If half of the Beijing residents think they would not sacrifice their own interests for the country's most important event, the government would have more than ten million people blocking its way to success. In China, people who fight for individual rights might gain more property and glamour, but people who sacrifice their rights for the country gain more respect. It is a fresh image for me to see how Canadian people see their Vancouver Olympics . . . I saw people protesting against the Olympics on Commercial Drive, [saying] that it's a businessmen's money-making event . . . Athletes have to advertise through sponsors to get their funding. When I ask Canadian people how they feel about winning the right to hold the [W]inter Olympics, many of them don't even care.[109]

What lessons might such a complexly articulated statement hold for Vancouver, where, as this student suggests, we take for granted our right to protest as well as our right to disinterestedness? And how might thinking critically about both the real differences *and* the complex lines of historical connection in local audiences' responses to globally mediated sports spectacles like the Olympics in turn foster a particular politics of place that resists the universalist narratives of development (athletic, economic, social) championed by supra-national institutions like the IOC? Three rights challenges related to the 2010 Olympics offer one possible way to begin answering these questions by exposing the performative exclusions embodied within the very category of the human that such narratives are meant to uphold.

The first is a United Nations complaint filed against the federal government of Canada, the BC provincial government, and the City of Vancouver by three community-based NGOs working in the DTES – the Impact of the Olympics on Community Coalition, Pivot Legal Society, and the Carnegie Community Action Project – who built on the original

109 Personal email (6 June 2008).

research conducted by two University of British Columbia graduate students in Political Science, Michael Powar and Gayle Stewart. The petition states that all three levels of government are in violation of section 11.1 of the International Covenant of Economic, Social, and Cultural Rights (of which Canada is a signatory), which states that 'Parties to the Covenant recognise the right of everyone to an adequate standard of living for himself and his family, including adequate food, clothing and housing, and to the continuous improvement of living conditions'. Citing a litany of broken promises 'made to the low-income community about social sustainability during the bid process surrounding the 2010 Games', the claimants allege that the governments have failed in their responsibilities to provide adequate affordable and habitable housing to the neediest residents of Vancouver; that the homelessness crisis in the city has been exacerbated by development projects related to the Olympics (resulting in an alarming conversion of SROs); and that as the homeless population in the city is disproportionately represented by some of the most marginalised members of Canadian society, including people of Aboriginal ancestry, those with substance abuse problems, and the mentally disabled, this constitutes a systemic practice of discrimination.[110]

The second challenge also concerns Vancouver's 'street homeless' population; submitted to the BC Human Rights Tribunal in July 2008 by Pivot Legal Society, United Native Nations, and the Vancouver Area Network of Drug Users, it alleges that the Downtown Vancouver Business Improvement Association, together with Geoff Plant, in his role as Vancouver's Project Civil City Commissioner, have engaged in a targeted campaign of harassment against this population via their coordination of the Downtown Ambassadors, a roving 'public safety' force meant to combat 'street disorder' that is directly modelled on a similar 'hospitality force' put in place in Atlanta in advance of the 1996 Olympics. Contracted through a private security firm, the Ambassadors are Vancouver's more menacing version of Beijing's etiquette police, patrolling a ninety-block area radiating out from the DTES, on the lookout for 'suspicious' individuals, including those sitting or sleeping on sidewalks, binning in alleyway dumpsters, engaging in public drug use or alcohol consumption, panhandling, or otherwise failing to conform 'to the behaviour desired by businesses in the area'.[111]

---

110 IOCC, Pivot Legal Society, and CCAP, *No Place Like Home: Human Rights Council 1503 Procedure* (12 April 2008), pp. 8 and 4, http://noplacelikehomevancouver.org/pdfs/noplacelikehome.pdf (accessed May 2008).

111 Pivot Legal Society, United Native Nations, and VANDU, 'Submissions of the complainants', BC Human Rights Tribunal (17 July 2008), p. 6.

The complaint states that the Ambassadors' attempts to 'modify' this
behaviour – mostly by forcing targeted individuals to move – is a clear
violation of the right to equal public access and that, again because of
the social constitution of the targeted population, '[t]he grounds of
discrimination include race, colour, ancestry, and physical and mental
disability'.[112]

These first two challenges highlight some of the social groups left
behind when host cities harness their particular urban aspirations to
abstracted messages of Olympic inspiration: if human bodies can be
engineered – via equipment vested or drugs ingested – to go 'faster,
higher, stronger', then why can't the places those bodies reside? This
question was in part what informed my experience of local artist Althea
Thauberger's September 2008 site-specific performance event *Carrall
Street*, in which she threw a one-night live art spotlight (quite literally)
on a contact zone in the city that runs a scant six blocks – from the red-
brick buildings of historic Gastown, through the strewn hypodermics
of Pigeon Park, to the gleaming real-estate offices of Concord Pacific
on the north side of False Creek – but that in that distance maps a
fraught and polarising social history relating to the ethics of livability
and the politics of development in Vancouver. Thauberger is known
for performance-based video and photographic works in which she col-
laborates closely with different social communities (Canadian soldiers
and tree planters, US military wives, linguistic minorities in Northern
Italy, conscientious objectors in Germany) to explore the dynamics of
group consciousness and state control. For *Carrall Street*, Thauberger
worked with community groups with varied interests in the area
(housed and unhoused DTES residents, local service organisations,
artists and theatre directors, politicians and city planners); together,
they created both scripted and improvised scenes of social interaction
in which the roles of performer and spectator, local denizen and curious
passer-by would deliberately blur on a stretch of streetscape cordoned
off and brightly illuminated like a film set. For me, the piece's plainly
visible fictional scaffolding, and the highly telegraphed orchestration of
its 'scenes' (I was 'interviewed' by two very manic 'real estate agents')
threw into relief the different performance publics (between business
owners and low-income residents, artists and activists, tourists and
addicts, security guards and the street homeless) that are daily negotiated at a very local street level. In the process, Thauberger brought out
in ways often obscured by abstract policy discussions relating to the
proposed revitalisation of the area, the historical connections between

112 *Ibid.*, p. 3.

this particular street's past (as a tavern-lined, working-class byway connecting Vancouver's old port to Chinatown), present (as a thoroughfare
traversed on one end by visiting tourists and local hipsters negotiating
both the tack and trend of Gastown, and, on the other, by the homeless,
addicted, and mentally ill citizens of the DTES), and future (as a showcase street targeted for a controversial clean-up and beautification in
advance of the Olympics). Whether Carrall Street's latest incarnation as
a high-profile 'Greenway Project' is designed to stimulate the economy
of the area, as officials contend, or simply to provide more pleasant
direct access from Gastown to the downtown portion of Vancouver's
famed pedestrian seawall for Olympic tourists and the affluent new
residents that will hopefully follow in their wake, is open to debate. But
along with the restoration of Pigeon Park's concrete surface, the painting over of graffiti on adjacent walls, and the installation of new benches
and tables, the erection of high-powered street lamps is probably a clue
as to who is winning the contest between social engineering and the
protection of civil liberties.

Of course, the winners and losers that accompany such contests are
a reminder that the history of the Olympics mirrors the history of capitalist modernity, from their humble branch plant origins as an amateur
sideshow at World Expositions (themselves glorified trading shows) to
their steady growth as a powerful global industry run by professional
elites, fuelled by broadcast revenues and corporate sponsorships, and
riven by bribery scandals and competitive fraud. Even the poor return
of medals that is routinely cited (as it was again in Beijing) as evidence
of Canada's *lack* of serious investment in its sports industries is part of
this same developmental narrative. Yet as the final rights challenge suggests, such fundamental institutional inequities are actually built into
the very fabric of an *athletic* movement based on the cohesion of body
and world that has for most of its history done its best to ignore over
half of the bodies in the world, not to mention the various *social* and
political movements they have spawned. I refer to the fact that VANOC
was forced to defend itself against a high-profile, but ultimately unsuc-
cessful, lawsuit filed in BC Supreme Court by a coalition of international
women ski jumpers arguing that the IOC's decision to exclude their
event from the 2010 Olympics despite intense lobbying efforts constitutes sex discrimination.[113]

Whither sport. Despite its Charter's principled avowal that 'the
practice of sport is a human right' (and notwithstanding the noble

---

113 See Rod Mickleburgh, 'Female ski jumpers to sue VANOC for inclusion', *Globe and
     Mail* (21 May 2008), pp. S1 and S3.

efforts of former and current Olympians involved in the Right to Play aid organisation),[114] the Olympic Movement remains deeply entrenched within binaries of human difference. Sex and gender are chief among them (as hormone testing and controversies surrounding trans athletes routinely attest), but exclusionary divisions and categories based on race, class, sexuality, age, religion, physical mobility, and geography are just as persistent. Indeed, one of the main arguments in awarding Beijing the 2008 Olympics – that the world's most populous nation should have the right to host the world's premiere sporting event – seems slightly specious when one considers that most of the sports showcased at that event were invented by white European men at the height of colonialism. In the corporatised, bureaucratised, politicised spectacle of place promotion that is the Olympics, final medal tallies belie not just the unspoken story of 'performance enhancement', but also a long history of the global south, or the communist east, having to beat the West at its own game.

Whether art. In May 2008 Ai was back in Sydney for the first international retrospective of his work, also curated by Charles Merewether as a joint exhibition between the Sherman Contemporary Art Foundation and the Campbelltown Arts Centre, and meant to overlap with the 2008 Sydney Biennale. The show featured the world premiere of the video *Fairytale*, a three-hour documentary following from concept to realisation Ai's invited contribution of the same name to Documenta 12, the major survey of international art held every five years in Kassel, the small German town that was home to the Brothers Grimm when they collected and published their own famous tales. In Ai's piece we see the process behind his invitation and facilitation of the journey of 1,001 Chinese citizens to Kassel in the summer of 2007, where in groups of 200 over successive one-week periods, participants, having first been extensively interviewed on everything from their definition of a fairytale to whether or not art can change the world, lived and ate communally, toured the city and the Documenta shows in matching uniforms, and came together at the end of each day for various group demonstrations orchestrated by Ai. As in Thauberger's piece, participants acted both

114 *Olympic Charter*, p. 11. Right to Play began as a fundraising and athlete ambassadorial program at the 1994 Lillehammer Winter Games; today it is an international humanitarian organisation headquartered in Toronto that uses sports programmes to improve the health and quality of life of children in disadvantaged and war-torn regions around the world. See 'History of right to play', http://rtpca.convio.net/site/PageServer?pagename=rtp_History (accessed August 2008). Ironically, at this writing the organisation has been banned from advertising, as at past Olympics, at Vancouver's Athletes' Village owing to a promotional deal it recently signed with Mitsubishi, a rival of key Olympic sponsor GM; see Gary Mason, 'IOC sinks to new low by severing ties with charity', *Globe and Mail* (22 January 2009), p. S1.

as spectators and performers, conventional 'tourists' and exhibitionary 'specimens', the resulting spectacle designed at once as an experiment in cross-cultural exchange through art and as a more pointed local intervention into the West's fantasies of the history of collectivisation and social interaction in China. *Fairytale*, like Ai's *World Map*, thus reads as an interesting comment on a showcase event like the Olympics. The dream of global cosmopolitanism is always a game where the competing national and transnational stakes and scales of what it means to be human – and to be part of an audience to humanity – play out in local acts of display and concealment, celebration and protest, formation and fragmentation, competition and cooperation.

2

Love is a battlefield: the performance and politics of same-sex marriage in North America and beyond

[T]here is a productive non-equivalence between the institution of marriage and the ritual that supposedly represents and guarantees it. (Elizabeth Freeman[1])

This [gay marriage] is an issue just like 9-11[;] we didn't decide we wanted to fight the war on terrorism because we wanted to. It was brought to us. (Rick Santorum[2])

I have come to a kind of conclusion about gay marriage: we have to stop the war. (Bonnie Mann[3])

In November 2005, American queer performance artist and political gadfly Tim Miller brought his most recent solo creation, *Us*, launched at P.S. 122 in New York the previous September, to the Vancouver East Cultural Centre. It is in part a frenetic romp through the original cast recordings of the classic era of Anglo-American musical comedy – from *Gypsy* and *My Fair Lady* to *Oliver!* and *Man of La Mancha* (see figure 8). These shows, we learn, helped shape and define Miller's queer adolescent identity during an especially fraught period of American history,

---

1 Elizabeth Freeman, *The Wedding Complex: Forms of Belonging in Modern American Culture* (Durham, NC: Duke University Press, 2002), p. xv.
2 As quoted in Mariella Savidge, 'No, you don't: controversy continues to build over the right of gay couples to wed', *The Morning Call* (9 March 2004), p. E1.
3 Bonnie Mann, 'Gay marriage and the war on terror', *Hypatia* 22:1 (2007), p. 250.

8 Tim Miller in *Us*

when the nation, then as now, was divided over both foreign and social policy issues. Thus, Miller's reminiscences of how, as a sixth-grader in Southern California, he planned to flee to Canada to avoid the Vietnam draft (he was anticipating a long war) are related against the backdrop of Mitch Leigh, Joe Darion, and Dale Wasserman's 1965 Tony Award-winning adaptation of Cervantes, about another kind of national inquisition and mass exodus. And relating why, during the same period, he spoke with an English accent, Miller reveals a pronounced nostalgia for the homosocial communities of boy pickpockets and bachelor professors on offer in the most famous works by Lionel Bart and Lerner and Loewe, respectively.

Plus ça change. Indeed, given the invasion of Iraq and the debates over same-sex marriage rights that necessarily frame Miller's performance, *Us* is also, more proximately, a searing indictment, on the eve of its reelection, of George W. Bush's administration. As Miller hastens to point out at the start of the show, Bush's immigration and civil rights polices discriminate against bi-national same-sex couples, forcing Miller and his Scots-Australian partner, Alistair McCartney, to live with the very real possibility of having to relocate outside the USA in order to remain together (an issue Miller first explored in 1999's *Glory Box*). That possibility seemed to have been temporarily mitigated by the May 2008 California Supreme Court ruling in favour of same-sex marriage equality (although, as Miller himself quickly pointed out, state marriage laws in California don't automatically carry with them de facto immigration rights[4]). However, the success of Proposition 8, a ballot initiative nullifying the California Supreme Court decision and reaffirming marriage as the union of one man and one woman, somewhat dampened queer exuberance (in the US and elsewhere) over the election of Barack Obama as the next American President on 4 November 2008; it also once again threw Tim and Alistair's relationship – along with the newly registered marriages of thousands of same-sex couples (California, unlike Massachusetts, does not have a residency requirement for couples wishing to marry in-state) – into legal limbo. At the same time, given the local legal challenges and transnational rallies and protests launched by gay activists in the wake of Proposition 8's passing, *Us*, in serious danger of wearing out its performance shelf life, has suddenly become newly relevant.

Watching Miller's 2005 Vancouver performance of *Us* alongside my show-tune-loving partner, Richard, it was hard (despite our own pronounced ambivalence on the issue) not to feel smug and self-congratulatory, especially given how recently Canada, under Liberal Prime Minister Paul Martin, had legalised same-sex marriage in Bill C-38.[5]

---

4 See Miller's blog post on the ruling, 'California marriage equality' (19 May 2008), http://timmillerperfomer.blogspot.com/2008_05_01_archive.html (accessed September 2008).
5 Bill C-38, Canada's Civil Marriage Act, passed a third and final vote in Canada's

Miller played to such sentiments shamelessly, especially when, near the end of the show, he describes a visit to the Rainbow Bridge that connects Canada and the United States at Niagara Falls, and how this becomes the perfect metaphor for his own domestic situation. To the strains of Barbra Streisand belting out 'Don't Rain on My Parade', from *Funny Girl* (1964), Miller notes that his visit just happens to coincide with an annual tug-of-war contest waged between Canadian and American federal law enforcement officers. Imagining himself as the rope, Miller sees himself being pulled between both countries, not wanting to leave the land of his birth and his greatest artistic success, but, as the robust Royal Canadian Mounted Police's inevitable victory portentously suggests, finding that the escape route to Canada he planned at age ten may in fact have to be travelled after all.

Flash forward to June 2006. A year has passed since Canada's new Civil Marriage Act became law. However, the country has a new minority government, and Conservative Prime Minister Stephen Harper, acting on a campaign promise, and in defiance of polls that indicate a majority of Canadians support the new law, has vowed to re-open the debate around same-sex marriage by holding a free vote on the issue in late fall. Caught in the middle of the political hectoring and mudslinging that attends this announcement are two male RCMP constables from Nova Scotia, whose planned wedding (in the broad-brimmed Stetsons, distinctive scarlet tunics, black and yellow-striped breeches, and Strathcona boots that comprise the Mounties' full dress uniform) just happens to fall on the eve of Canada's 139th birthday. This coincidence is seized upon by gay activists as evidence of Harper being woefully out of touch not only with public opinion, but also with his own state apparatus. The 'Brokeback Mounties', as the two officers have been dubbed by more than one media wag,[6] are – to extend Miller's rope metaphor – suddenly being pulled rather than

House of Commons on 28 June 2005 by a margin of 155 to 133; it was approved by Senate on 19 July 2005 and officially became law the following day. Earlier the same month Spain's parliament also ratified same-sex marriage into law. The Netherlands and Belgium had previously legalised same-sex marriage in 2001 and 2003, respectively. South Africa (2006), Norway, and Sweden (both 2009) have since also enacted legislation recognising same-sex marriages among their citizens. The following countries allow the registering of same-sex domestic partnerships and civil unions: Andorra, Czech Republic, Denmark, Ecuador, Finland, France, Germany, Hungary, Iceland, Luxembourg, New Zealand, Slovenia, Switzerland, the UK, and Uruguay. In the US, Connecticut Maine, Iowa, New Hampshire, and Vermont have joined Massachusetts in permitting same-sex marriage. California, Hawaii, Maryland, New Jersey, Oregon, Washington, and the District of Columbia all permit same-sex civil unions or domestic partnerships. New York recognizes same-sex marriages entered into elsewhere.

6 See, for example, Alison Auld, 'Constables to wed, as Canada blogs', *Globe and Mail* (30 June 2006), p. A3.

doing the pulling, conscripted into the theatre of war that has consistently framed the debates around the formal recognition of different ways of loving on both sides of the forty-ninth parallel. I invoke this latter metaphor deliberately. For, just as the same-sex marriage issue in North America has largely – and quite strategically – been pitched as a battle for the very soul of civil society and social democracy in Canada and the United States, so was Harper's apparent pledge to rescue and redeem the sanctity of 'traditional' heterosexual marriage largely a tactical maneuver, a diversionary ploy. In this, Harper was following the lead of Bush, whose desultory support for a proposed constitutional amendment banning same-sex marriage failed to pass muster in the US Senate earlier the same month. According to *New Yorker* staff writer Hendrik Hertzberg, Bush's lukewarm endorsement of the legislation was a 'performance piece, a political pageant aimed at energizing the Christianist wing of the Republican "base" for the midterm elections while distracting public attention from the Iraq war'.[7] Likewise, Harper's barely believable posturing over the vote (which was soundly defeated on 7 December 2006, prompting the Prime Minister to declare the matter 'closed for good'[8]) was at once a cynical sop to the religious right in his party and a way of avoiding close public scrutiny of his government's decision, soon after taking power, to extend Canada's combat role in Afghanistan through to February 2009 (it has since been extended again through 2011). Playing, like Miller, to partisan local audiences, Bush and Harper enjoyed a momentary *coup de théâtre* around marriage that overshadowed the larger funereal dramas being played out on the world stage.

In this chapter, I want to explore, among other things, the language of love and war that has attended the performative representation, public reception, and private regulation of the North American same-sex marriage debate in various local, transnational, and global contexts since the 1980s. What is at stake, I ask, in the very performance of publicity and privacy inherent in the marriage ceremony itself? That is, how does the public declaration or assent of private persons to enter into a conjugal/domestic/legal relationship bring with it not only additional privacy rights but also enact (in a Habermasian extension of J. L. Austin) said persons' full entry into the 'bourgeois public sphere' via the performative utterance of 'I do'?[9] More to the point, how and why are those stakes

---

7   Hendrik Hertzberg, 'Distraction', *The New Yorker* (19 June 2006), p. 29.

8   See Gloria Galloway, 'Same-sex marriage file closed for good, PM says', *Globe and Mail* (8 December 2006), p. A1.

9   For Habermas' conceptualisation of the late-seventeenth-early-eighteenth-century 'bourgeois public sphere' as 'above all . . . the sphere of private people come together as a public', and as a space 'to engage . . . in a debate over the general rules governing

raised when such performances are opened up to what Michael Warner has called 'counterpublics of sexuality and gender'?[10] Are these counter-publics then at risk of being coopted, 'normalised', and de-radicalised, as Warner himself contends, by the very institutional structures they seek to transform?[11] Or might those institutions, including the institution of marriage, be exposed as only tangentially – and comparatively recently in modern history – connected to the discourses of heterosexuality and the family with which they are de facto aligned in popular political parlance? And might this, in turn, allow for a twenty-first-century *ritual* reinvention of the public sphere as a truly radical experiment in participatory democracy? As my italicisation of the word 'ritual' is here meant to suggest, in my analysis of these and related questions in what follows, I want to focus as much on the theatre of, and the different audiences hailed by, the performative representation of same-sex nuptials, as on the promiscuous political ideologies and affective embodiments underscoring their ceremonial acts. The acts of same-sex marriage I examine in these pages are, for practical and theoretical reasons, largely those confined to the stage; I do not attempt, in what follows, any sort of ethnographic account of individual couples' actual ceremonies.[12] Rather, I want to use the heterotopic, mimetic space of the theatre to examine how traditional definitions of marriage might be otherwise imagined, and how, in the process, a theatre public might be both radicalised and radically transformed.

Remember, in this regard, that among the key conditions and consequences that Habermas cites in the transformation of the monarchical public sphere into the bourgeois public sphere are the loss of the court as an audience for the king's embodied performance of his public authority, and the related privatisation, dispersal, and abstraction of that authority – via, among other things, the rise of print culture, changes in domestic architecture, increasingly interdependent mechanisms of sociability and commerce, and some fairly fundamental shifts in understandings of

relations in the basically privatized but publicly relevant sphere of commodity exchange and social labor', see his *The Structural Transformation of the Public Sphere: An Inquiry into a Category of Bourgeois Society*, trans. Thomas Burger (Cambridge, MA: MIT Press, 1989), p. 27. For Austin's isolation of the performative utterance 'as not, or not merely, saying something but doing something', and his use of the 'I do' from the marriage ceremony as a particular example of this kind of utterance, see his *How to Do Things with Words* (New York: Oxford University Press, 1962); this quote, p. 25. I will be discussing queer theory's felicitous *and* infelicitous uses of Austin and his most famous example of performative utterance at greater length below.

10 Michael Warner, *Publics and Counterpublics* (New York: Zone Books, 2002), pp. 57ff.

11 See Warner, *The Trouble with Normal: Sex Politics, and the Ethics of Queer Life* (New York: Free Press, 1999).

12 For more on this, see Suzanne Sherman (ed.), *Lesbian and Gay Marriage: Private Commitments, Public Ceremonies* (Philadelphia: Temple University Press, 1992).

intimacy and civility – onto a disembodied 'reading public'. This reading public exercised its critical judgment first and foremost from the home and its private spatial extensions (coffeehouses, clubs, salons), and, in its 'liberalist' manifestation, saw itself as a necessary bulwark not only against unwanted domination by the state, but also from potential social subversion by the masses.[13] Remember, too, that this period, in England at any rate, also witnessed the re-opening of the theatres under Charles II, and female actors' first appearances on the stage. And yet while Habermas is not all that concerned with the theatrical public sphere's relationship to, and at times radical dissent from, the critical debates of the reading public, nor with women's participation in the public sphere as a space of emancipatory possibility, I reach back momentarily to the long eighteenth century to remind us that the institution of marriage and the institution of the theatre have long exploited each other's structural instabilities and tragicomic potential, and that our current political moment is no different in this regard. From John Dryden's *Marriage à la Mode* and William Wycherly's *The Country Wife* to Nell Gwynn's most famous starring role as mistress to the King; from the mock marriage ceremonies that proliferated on-stage to the thriving clandestine marriage trade that actors participated in off-stage:[14] Restoration theatre demonstrates just how pliable the connubial state has historically proven to be – both in terms of its performative prescriptions and its public personifications.

Let me be clear: in no way do I wish to be aligned with the largely assimilationist social politics of neo-conservative public intellectuals like Andrew Sullivan, in the United States, or neo-liberal poster boys Kevin Bourassa and Joe Varnell, in Canada, who argue that same-sex marriage is a fundamental human right, bestowing upon queers that ultimate marker of full citizenship, access to official, respectable coupledom and family recognition.[15] But neither do I endorse without question the discourse of exceptionalism that seems to me to characterise much of the recent work of anti-social and anti-reproductive queer theorists like Lee Edelman and Judith Halberstam, among others, who claim that queers should not be insisting upon equal access to the laws of the state (including, and especially, those pertaining to marriage and the family),

13 See Habermas, pp. 31–3ff.
14 On the connections between the latter, see especially Lisa O'Connell, 'Marriage acts: stages in the transformation of modern nuptial culture', *differences: a journal of feminist cultural studies* 11:1 (1999), pp. 68–111.
15 See Sullivan's *Virtually Normal: An Argument about Homosexuality* (New York: Knopf, 1995) and his edited reader *Same-Sex Marriage: Pro and Con*, (New York: Vintage, [1997], revised edn, 2004); see, as well, Bourassa and Varnell, *Just Married: Gay Marriage and the Expansion of Human Rights* (Toronto: Doubleday, 2002).

but actively avowing their subcultural dissent from, and opposition to, the whole symbolic order and hegemonic social temporality those laws are meant to prop up.[16] I find much of this work, in its persistent striving toward rhetorical provocation, to be unduly narrow in scope and blinkered in focus, viewing questions of sexual citizenship within a predominately American (and largely presentist) frame of reference, and especially ignoring how the authors' own academic purchase already guarantees them access to many of the social benefits (shared health care, transferable pension plans, spousal hiring policies) 'ordinary' homosexuals (many of them working-class and racial minority) can only ever hope to tap into through some sort of legal recognition of the 'civility' of their unions.[17] Thus, I agree, on the one hand, with both Michael Warner and the Law Commission of Canada that we must move 'beyond' questions of conjugality and the whole 'recognition drama' in debating the terms of marriage as legal institution.[18] At the same time, I want to redirect our

16 See Lee Edelman, *No Future: Queer Theory and the Death Drive* (Durham: Duke University Press, 2004); and Judith Halberstam, *In a Queer Time and Place: Transgender Bodies, Subcultural Lives* (New York: New York University Press, 2005).

17 Consider, in this regard, the following caution issued by Biddy Martin in 1994 with respect to the 'anti-normativity' stance adopted by much queer theoretical work: 'In some queer work, the very fact of attachment has been cast as only punitive and constraining because already socially constructed, so that indifference to objects, or the assumption of a position beyond objects – the position, for instance, of death – becomes the putative achievement or goal of queer theory . . . An enormous fear of ordinariness or normalcy results in superficial accounts of the complex imbrication of sexuality with other aspects of social and psychic life, and in far too little attention to the dilemmas of the average people that we also are'. See Martin, 'Extraordinary homosexuals and the fear of being ordinary', *differences: a journal of feminist cultural studies* 6:2-3 (1994), p. 123.

18 See Warner, 'Beyond gay marriage', in *The Trouble with Normal*, pp. 81–147; the phrase 'recognition drama' is his, coined in the context of the exceedingly 'normative dimensions' of the relationships marriage names and affirms (i.e., the opposite-sex or same-sex monogamous couple), and all those other modes of affective and social belonging it excludes. As Warner puts it, 'One can easily imagine ceremonies with a difference – in which people might solemnize a committed household, ironize their property sharing, pledge care and inheritance without kinship, celebrate a whole circle of intimacies, or dramatize independence from state-regulated sexuality. A movement built around such ceremonies could be more worthwhile and more fun than the unreflective demand for state-sanctioned marriage. Indeed, some people already experiment in these ways. Why do they get no press?' (pp. 133–4). In December 2001, the Law Commission of Canada, established in 1997 as a tacit advisory board to the Canadian Parliament and Justice Ministry, submitted a report called 'Beyond Conjugality', which argued, among other things, that the functional realities of contemporary family and household configurations necessitated a fundamental rethinking of traditional legal definitions of marriages, going so far as to recommend the creation of a formal legal mechanism by which adult citizens could register the full panoply of their personal relationships and partnerships, including gay and straight couples, adult children living with parents, siblings or friends sharing a house, and so on. The report, alas, was shelved.

attention to the ritual dramas embedded within the gay wedding ceremony as theatrical production, one that stages, however tenuously and
temporarily, a 'participatory public' based on activist spectatorship. This
kind of spectatorship, according to Jill Dolan, takes the shared sense of
belonging fostered by the performance itself as a potential model for
other forms of social interaction, encouraging audience members 'to be
active in other public spheres, to participate in civic conversations that
performance perhaps begins'.[19] In shifting the focus from rights to *rites*,
I am following the lead of Elizabeth Freeman. In her book *The Wedding
Complex*, she argues compellingly that the 'forms of belonging' enacted
in the wedding ceremony and the formal legitimation enfranchised in
marriage law are not reducible to one another. Further, she contends
that multiplying 'the sites, scenes, and rituals' produced, on a small scale,
by the former can lead to 'participation in larger group endeavors' aimed
at remaking the world via means of social interaction not institutionalised by local state apparatuses.[20] As Freeman puts it,

> The power of the wedding lies in its ability to make worlds through doing
> symbolic and aesthetic work on affiliation, attachment, and belonging, and
> in the way it preserves exactly what it claims to renounce: cultural possibili
> ties for organizing social life beyond either the marital or mass imaginary.
> This constitutive contradiction between what weddings can do and what
> marriage law really does might be one reason people cry at weddings.[21]

To put this another way, and the main question I want to take up in
the remainder of this chapter, to what extent can a queer performance
of 'I do' function simultaneously as a performatively queer 'I don't'?
That is, how might we read the alternate forms of kinship enacted via
the queer exploitation and theatricalisation of what Chrys Ingraham has
called the 'wedding-industrial complex'[22] as signalling, in turn, a con-

---

19 See Jill Dolan, *Utopia in Performance: Finding Hope at the Theater* (Ann Arbor:
    University of Michigan Press, 2005), p. 11.
20 Freeman, *The Wedding Complex*, pp. 216 and 217. Mary T. Conway, in a trenchant
    performance studies analysis of the 1993 Fluxwedding of lesbian author Jill Johnston
    and her Danish partner Ingrid Nyeboe (about which I will have more to say below),
    likewise bemoans the 'aesthetic effects' that are overlooked when the 'ritual of *becoming* married' is subsumed within the institutional state of 'being' married: 'By seeing
    the possibilities of performance [in the ritual practice of becoming married], we can
    detect the importance of aesthetic practice in general, and a queer, critical aesthetic
    practice in particular, and how that practice might alter the ways we understand marriage and the subjects who produce and are produced by it'. See Conway, 'A becoming
    queer aesthetic', *Discourse* 26:3 (2004), pp. 167 and 168.
21 Freeman, *The Wedding Complex*, p. 44.
22 See Chrys Ingraham, *White Weddings: Romancing Heterosexuality in Popular Culture*
    (New York: Routledge, 1999), pp. 25–76.

scious disaffiliation and disidentification from other forms of coupling or private partnerships sanctioned by the state, including, and perhaps most especially in this case, the associated political and commercial relationships that shore up the 'military-industrial complex'? This returns me to my opening detour through Tim Miller and the proximate relationship between (North American) same-sex marriage and the (global) war on terror, and provides, as well, one possible answer to the question of why gay marriage now? In the transnational (in)security state that has grown up on this side of the Atlantic post-9/11 and the invasion of Iraq, where, in 2004, former Pennsylvania Republican Senator Rick Santorum called the defence of traditional heterosexual marriage 'the ultimate homeland security',[23] and where other right-wing pundits have linked the racial and sexual humiliation of prisoners at Abu Ghraib to moral liberalism at home,[24] one of the reasons local performances of queer weddings might attract so much scrutiny and debate is because their 'legitimacy', like that of the global political alliances formed or sundered through acts of war, depend, to paraphrase Judith Butler, on a shared acknowledgement of the vulnerability of *all* our attachments to others.[25] As Butler has noted elsewhere, in connection with Sophocles' *Antigone*, marriages, like funerals, are 'forms of doing' that performatively repeat and reinstate kinship as a scandalously public ceremonial relationship that is inherently equivocal and contingent.[26] This might be why so many of the theatrical representations of (same-sex) marriage I examine below are interrupted and/or framed by funeral rites. Coincidentally, this might also explain why in Catholic Spain and ethnically and religiously diverse South Africa, two countries with relatively recent histories of state-sponsored terrorism, same-sex marriage laws were adopted coincident with Canada's, and, all things considered, with relative ease. Out of the dirty wars of the past perhaps emerges an openness to new kinds of social intimacy. On the other hand, none of this accounts for

23 Comments made by Santorum on the floor of the US Senate following the defeat of a proposed constitutional amendment banning gay marriage, as quoted in Carl Hulse, 'Gay-marriage ban faces loss in early vote', *The New York Times* (14 July 2004), p. A19.
24 On this see especially Mann, 'Gay marriage', pp. 249–50.
25 See Judith Butler, *Precarious Life: The Powers of Mourning and Violence* (New York: Verso, 2004), pp. 20ff.
26 Judith Butler, *Antigone's Claim: Kinship Between Life and Death* (New York: Columbia University Press, 2000), pp. 57-8. I will have occasion to return to this text in chapter 4. Elsewhere, in arguing that the 'topic of gay marriage is not the same as that of gay kinship', Butler claims that marriage, as an institution, not only forecloses on other constitutive 'sexual possibilities that will never be eligible for a translation into legitimacy', but also constitutes them temporally as 'the irrecoverable and irreversible past of legitimacy: *the never will be, the never was*'; see Butler, 'Is kinship always already heterosexual?', in *Undoing Gender* (New York: Routledge, 2004), pp. 102 and 106.

why the US, which once shared with South Africa a prohibition against inter-racial marriage, has not learned similar lessons from its own historical civil rights struggles.

I explore the performative and political backdrop to these and other questions in three inter-connected sections. First, after briefly outlining some of the significant differences in the social, historical, and juridical contexts underscoring the same-sex marriage issue in Canada and the US, I review both the deconstructive and the dramaturgical uses to which J. L. Austin's most famous example of performative utterance has been put by queer theory; my aim here is to show how performance theory's own longstanding interest in questions of ritual and repetition contributes productively to a similar reimagining of the social relationships envisioned by and enacted in the wedding ceremony. In the next and longest section, I turn to discussions, representations, and enactments of same-sex marriage in recent theatre and performance art. After focusing briefly on Cheek by Jowl's and Charles Mee's queer takes on two of Shakespeare's more iconic marriage plots, I compare the New York premieres of Paul Rudnick's *Regrets Only* and Terrence McNally's *Some Men*, both conventionally realist dramas that anchored the 2006–7 subscription seasons at the Manhattan Theatre Club and the Second Stage Theatre. I conclude by examining in some depth the ongoing *Love Art Laboratory* project of the now five times married performance and visual artists Annie Sprinkle and Beth Stephens.

In direct response to both the 'violence of war' and the 'anti-gay marriage movement', and in collaboration with various friends, family, and communities, Sprinkle and Stephens have combined theatre, film, the Internet, activism, and, once a year, a 'performance art wedding', as part of a seven-year 'love-experiment' based on the themes and colours of the chakras, and structurally inspired by Linda Montano's 1984-98 durational performance piece *14 Years of Living Art*.[27] In January 2007, Sprinkle and Stephens' third wedding ceremony took place in Calgary, as part of One Yellow Rabbit Theatre's twenty-first annual High Performance Rodeo; it was the first time the event was open to the public (previous weddings in New York and San Francisco were by invitation only, although both ceremonies were streamed live over the Internet) and it also resulted in Sprinkle and Stephens becoming legally married for the first time. I examine, then, the intersection of local and transnational politics enacted in this latest ceremony, as well as the larger

---

27 All quotations from Sprinkle and Stephens related to their *Love Art Laboratory* wedding project are taken from their website of the same name (www.loveartlab.org), and will hereafter be cited parenthetically as loveartlab.org.

genealogy of feminist and queer ritual protest and activist spectatorship Sprinkle and Stephens' wedding archive is in dialogue with.

In the final section of the chapter, I attempt to broaden the comparative national and geopolitical focus of my analysis, as well as complexify my discussion of same-sex marriage as a civil institution, by turning my attention to the trans-Atlantic routes of dissension within the Anglican Church over the blessing of same-sex unions. Here, I explore the local/global dynamics of both the religious rites and the Religious Right that are never far from the same-sex marriage debate, in this case pitting liberal Anglican/Episcopalian congregations and leaders in North America against more traditional members of their own dioceses, the Church hierarchy in Canterbury, as well as Anglican provinces from the global south (Africa, Asia, and Latin America), which today comprise the majority of the worldwide Anglican Communion's 77 million members. The threat of schism and the internal civil war engulfing the Church was only narrowly – and temporarily – forestalled by Archbishop Rowan Williams at the 2008 Lambeth Conference in Canterbury, and to the chagrin of many has overshadowed other strongly united moral stands the Church has taken in the public sphere, including a searing condemnation of the war in Iraq. In addition to unpacking the theatrical spectacle that was Lambeth (and some of the local performative dynamics and audience pressures from within the UK at once framing and constraining Williams's role as spiritual leader and political impresario), I also examine some specific Vancouver connections to this growing crisis. These include Bishop Michael Ingham's decision, in 2003, to begin allowing the blessing of same-sex unions in the diocese of New Westminster (which encompasses Vancouver), as well as a staged reading I attended of *Articles of Faith: The Battle of St Alban's*, a 2001 docudrama by local playwright Mark Leiren-Young about another parish community in British Columbia that seceded from the Anglican Church over the same issue. Finally, I return to some of the legal and linguistic parsing of marriage-related performatives undertaken in the first section of this chapter by analysing how we might relate the Anglican Church's mooting of a binding Covenant to deal with, among other things, differences over same-sexuality, to the new obliquity governing personal status laws in Iraq under a largely *shari'a*-codified constitution, and to the incitement toward explanation, perhaps even repentance, contained within the act of blessing itself.

Performative trouble, or, the politics of normal

At one point in *The Normal Heart*, Larry Kramer's 1985 theatrical screed/*drama-à-clef* about the early days of the AIDS epidemic and the founding of the Gay Men's Health Crisis in New York, protagonist Ned Weeks turns to one of his friends and asks: 'Mickey, why didn't you guys fight for the right to get married instead of the right to legitimize promiscuity?'[28] And, indeed, the play itself ends, in a brutal undermining of traditional comic closure, with a mock-wedding ceremony performed between Ned and his lover Felix in the latter's hospital room mere seconds before his death from AIDS-related complications. Ten years later, Andrew Sullivan, then editor of *The New Republic*, wrote *Virtually Normal*, in which he likewise made 'equal access to civil marriage' (and a related lifting of the ban on military service, to which I will return) the 'centerpiece' of his political argument about ending the 'formal public discrimination' of homosexuality. In so doing, he advanced a conservative defence of the emotionally secure and economically stable anchor provided by marriage in the 'maelstrom of sex' and 'short-term relationships' to which gays and lesbians are otherwise prone.[29] Writing in *Time* magazine in 2003 shortly after the Canadian government decided not to contest the rulings of three provincial courts of appeal which all endorsed same-sex marriage (see below), Sullivan was still promoting the 'conservative case' for gay marriage, although his claims that it will lead to the 'domestication of unruly men' are often at odds with his own lifestyle.[30] In any case, by 2006 Kramer's own feelings on the subject of gay marriage had grown decidedly more ambivalent; in a revealing *New York Times* profile of his complicated and frequently acrimonious relationship with his brother, Arthur (the Ben Weeks character from *The Normal Heart*), Kramer finds little redeeming in the institution of marriage, and avers that he is '"amazed by how little support for gay marriage comes from gay people"', before admitting that he might consider getting married to his partner, David, if it meant he could 'take advantage of federal estate tax laws'. And all this as Arthur's law firm prepared to argue the case for gay marriage before the New York State Court of Appeals.[31] In fact, the inconsistencies in Sullivan's and Kramer's respective positions provide a fairly comprehensive roadmap

---

28 Larry Kramer, *The Normal Heart* (New York: Plume, 1985), p. 85.
29 Sullivan, *Virtually Normal*, pp. 178 and 182–3.
30 Sullivan, 'The conservative case for gay marriage', *Time* (22 June 2003), www.time.come/time/magazine/article/0,9171,1101030630-460232,00.html (accessed September 2007). In an earlier book, *Love Undetectable: Notes on Friendship, Sex and Survival* (New York: Knopf, 1999), Sullivan defended his own non-monogamy this way: 'Although I never publicly defended promiscuity, I never publicly attacked it. I attempted to avoid the subject, in part because I felt, and often still feel, unable to live up to the ideals I really hold' (p. 53).
31 Anemona Hartocollis, 'Gay brother, straight brother: it could be a play', *The New York Times* (25 June 2006).

to the constituent dramas (social, moral, financial) embedded within the same-sex marriage issue as a piece of political theatre in North America. At the same time, they point, more generally, to a process of increasing privatisation coincident with the 'normalisation' of homosexuality in the west since the 1970s.

In Canada that process began in earnest in 1967, encapsulated most famously in the public utterance used by then Justice Minister Pierre Trudeau in introducing legislation aimed at decriminalising homo-sexuality: 'There's no place for the state in the bedrooms of the nation'.[32] Thereafter, the right to privacy became a key weapon in the Canadian queer community's ongoing fight against systemic and institutional-ised discrimination in the public sphere, particularly with respect to police raids on gay bathhouses and the entrapment of men engaging in toilet sex throughout the 1970s and early 1980s.[33] It was not until 1985, when the main provisions enshrining equality rights in section fifteen of Canada's newly adopted Charter of Rights and Freedoms came fully into effect, that gays and lesbians in this country began seeking recourse through the courts to many of the public benefits (including immigra-tion rights, adoption and child custody rights, financial dependency, pension, and survivor benefits, and so on) enjoyed by married and common-law opposite-sex couples. This culminated in a 1999 Supreme Court of Canada ruling that in effect declared gay and lesbian couples were entitled to all of the financial and legal benefits associated with mar-riage, but that stopped short of opening up that institution to same-sex partnerships. Indeed, that same year the Canadian parliament enacted its own polite, northern version of the United States' controversial 1996 Defense of Civil Marriage Act when it introduced a resolution affirm-ing the definition of marriage as 'the union of one man and one woman to the exclusion of all others'.[34] However, there was really no stopping the judicial steamroller to which the same-sex marriage movement in Canada had pinned its hopes, and when, in 2002-3, the top courts of Ontario, British Columbia, and Quebec all declared the laws currently

---

32 Made in a televised interview broadcast on the CBC on 21 December 1967. See 'Trudeau's omnibus bill: challenging taboos', *CBC Digital Archives*, http://archives.cbc.ca/IDC-1-73-538-2671/politics_economy/omnibus/clip1 (accessed September 2007).

33 See Gary Kinsman, *The Regulation of Desire: Homo and Hetero Sexualities* (Montreal: Black Rose Books, [1987] 2nd edn, 1996), pp. 341–2; David Rayside, *On the Fringe: Gays and Lesbians in Politics* (Ithaca: Cornell University Press), p. 167; and Wendy Pearson, 'Interrogating the epistemology of the bedroom: same-sex marriage and sexual citizenship in Canada', *Discourse* 26:3 (2004), p. 142.

34 See Canada's House of Commons Hansard Index for the 1st Session of the 36th Parliament, www2.parl.gc/housechamberbusiness/ChamberHome (accessed September 2007).

prohibiting same-sex marriage unconstitutional, the federal government decided not to appeal those decisions.

Instead, the ruling Liberals prepared a draft bill extending marriage rights to same-sex couples, which it then promptly referred to the Supreme Court for review and comment. Specifically, the government asked whether the proposed amendments to Canada's civil marriage statutes fell under the exclusive legislative authority of the federal parliament; whether the proposal to allow same-sex couples the right to marry was consistent with the Charter of Rights and Freedoms; whether said Charter's guarantee of religious freedom protected religious officials from marrying same-sex couples if it violated their beliefs; and, rather absurdly, whether the current opposite-sex requirement for civil marriage was consistent with equality provisions set out by the Charter. In early December 2004, the Supreme Court of Canada answered in the affirmative to the first three queries, but pointedly refused to respond to the fourth, noting that the government's failure to appeal the earlier provincial rulings of Ontario and BC in effect meant that they already knew the answer.[35] With the passage of the Civil Marriage Act the following July, same-sex marriage finally arrived in Canada in a manner wholly consistent with the governing Liberal party's particular brand of performative politics, where the process of deliberation that precedes an instrumentalist Act of Parliament involved, in this case, not only disidentification from the thing being done but also an attempt at deauthorising who was doing it.

If the legalising of gay marriage in Canada appears to signal a benign endpoint in homosexuality's progress narrative from private aberrance to public acceptance, the American context proves just how performatively unstable the private/public distinction continues to be. To this end, the United States, which has always maintained an equally puritanical and prurient interest in the sex lives of its citizens, did not get out of the business of policing the bedrooms of the nation until 2003, when the Supreme Court, in *Lawrence et al. vs. Texas*, overturned the 1986 *Bowers vs. Hardwick* decision and declared sodomy laws, then still on the books in fourteen states, to be unconstitutional.[36] This points, in turn, to a fundamental difference in the historical projects of litigating equality in Canada and the US. Not only are the provisions enshrined in the US Constitution and Bill of Rights far more absolute than those

35 For a full summary of the events leading to the legalising of same-sex marriage in Canada, see Sylvain Laroque, *Gay Marriage: The Story of a Canadian Social Revolution* (Toronto: Lorimer and Co., 2006).
36 See 'Lawrence *et al.* vs. Texas', www.supremecourtus.gov/opinions/02pdf/02-102.pdf (accessed September 2007).

contained in their Canadian counterparts, but the aims and scope of the American judicial review process tend to be interpreted much more conservatively. Together with the difficulties involved in amending the US constitution (two-thirds majority approval by both levels of Congress *and* ratification by three-quarters of state legislatures) and the relative ease with which individual states can amend theirs – using referenda and other ballot initiatives at election time to overturn unpopular decisions of the court (cf. the aforementioned Proposition 8 in California, or, earlier, the fate of Hawaii's proposed gay marriage law) – this has meant only uncertain recourse through the courts for the American same-sex marriage lobby. And so, taking a page from other civil rights movements past and present, that lobby has turned instead to the court of public opinion, at the same time as it has sought the financial backing of wealthy private donors to advance its message. Curiously, however, at the April 1993 March on Washington, it was repealing the ban on gays and lesbians in the military, rather than same-sex marriage, that emerged as the key rallying point from a proposed LGBT civil rights bill.

Only in the wake of the perceived 'betrayal' by President Clinton in his 'Don't ask, don't tell' compromise did powerful national organisations like the National Gay and Lesbian Task Force, the Lambda Legal Defense and Education Fund, and the Human Rights Campaign turn to 'betrothal' as a queer cause to begin promoting in earnest. Never mind that Clinton betrayed the community's trust once again in signing the Defense of Marriage Act in 1996. Never mind that state after state lined up to enact similar statutes, nor that the Religious Right had by now rolled out its own well-oiled counter-publicity machine, a remarkably savvy inter-faith coalition whose most spectacular victory to date has been the grassroots campaign launched to ensure passage of California's Proposition 8. By framing the right to marry as a matter of private choice (without at all attending to the public consequences for those who choose not to exercise that right),[37] and by emphasising that such a choice (via the potential extension of inheritance laws, insurance coverage, income splitting, and the like) benefits not just individual homosexuals but the entire wealth of the nation, the mainstream gay and lesbian movement in the United States clearly feels it has a human drama that will play not only in liberal coastal outposts like Massachusetts and California, but also, with time, in the heartland. So, it would appear, does the most visible representative of change in America. To this end, it is worth noting that in outlining his support for the LGBT community as part of the Civil Rights Agenda posted to his *Change.Gov* transition

37 See Warner, *The Trouble with Normal*, pp. 97–8.

website, then President-Elect Barack Obama not only expressed his
support for full civil unions for LGBT couples, but also for the repeal
of the Defense of Marriage Act *and* the 'Don't ask, don't tell' policy,
stating that the latter has not only cost the US government 'millions of
dollars', but also potentially compromised national security (by, among
other things, leading to the firing of several hundred language experts,
many of them trained in Arabic).[38] And if, indeed, patriotism is measured and sustained in part by structures of feeling – however normative
– pertaining to the sanctity and protection of family and marriage, let
us not, then, admit impediments to alternative constitutions of those
arrangements.

Except those posed by the performative structure of the marriage
ceremony itself. Notably, political debates around same-sex marriage in
the North American public sphere since the mid-1990s have coincided
with the emergence of J. L. Austin's 1962 text *How to Do Things with
Words* – and especially his discussion therein of the exemplary 'I do'
utterances normally exchanged at weddings – as foundational to the
ongoing development and refinement of queer theories of performativity. Here I am referring especially to the pioneering work of Judith Butler
and Eve Kosofsky Sedgwick. In a pair of dialogically linked essays published in the inaugural issue of *GLQ: A Journal of Lesbian & Gay Studies*
in 1993, the two theorists redirect attention to the queer possibilities, and
infelicities, implicit in Austin's theorisation of speech acts, long abjured
as fundamentally flawed since the publication of Jacques Derrida's
'Signature, event, context'.[39] To be sure, the recourse to Austin is somewhat grudging and decidedly instrumentalist (especially in the case of
Butler, who appears to have turned to Austin, largely by way of Derrida,
in an effort to clear up what she claims were misunderstandings and
misapplications of the theory of gender performativity she outlined in
her highly influential *Gender Trouble*). Nevertheless, both Sedgwick and
Butler single out the 'centrality of the marriage ceremony in . . . Austin's
examples of performativity' in order to suggest that 'heterosexualization
of the social bond is the paradigmatic form for those speech acts which
bring about what they name', and to ask 'what happens to the performative when its purpose is precisely to undo the presumptive force of the

---

38 'Support for the LGBT community', *Change.Gov: The Office of the President-Elect*,
    http://change.gov/agenda/civil_rights_agenda/ (accessed December 2008).
39 See Sedgwick, 'Queer performativity: Henry James's *The Art of the Novel*', *GLQ: A
    Journal of Lesbian & Gay Studies* 1:1 (1993), pp. 1-16; Butler, 'Critically queer', *GLQ: A
    Journal of Lesbian & Gay Studies* 1:1 (1993), pp. 17-32; and Derrida, 'Signature, event,
    context', in *Limited Inc*, ed. Gerald Graff, trans. Samuel Weber and Jeffrey Mehlman
    (Evanston: Northwestern University Press, 1988), pp. 1–24.

heterosexual ceremonial'?[40] Answering this question, for each theorist, means first 'undoing' the naturalness, stability, agency, and authoritative presence of Austin's speaking subject, the 'I' who names, and focusing instead on the discursive conditions, and conventions, that name that 'I', as, for example, heterosexual or homosexual, married or unmarried, ashamed or melancholy. Indeed, it is precisely by recuperating for analysis and discussion those specifically 'unhappy' conditions Austin enumerates as contributing to a given utterance's failure to do the thing it says it will do – a violation of accepted convention or procedure, the involvement of an inappropriate person or persons, the possession of an insincere thought or feeling[41] – that Sedgwick and Butler construct their affective and melancholic theories of sexual and gender identity as political and performative projects of disavowal, of ever fully or freely saying what one means or doing what one says. As Sedgwick remarks, so many of the references to marriage Austin invokes 'are offered as examples of the different ways things can go *wrong* with performative utterances' that his book perhaps warrants a different title altogether: '*I Do – Not!*'[42]

This points, in turn, as Sedgwick has elsewhere noted, to the witness role within spaces and contexts of performative utterance generally, and the spatial context of the wedding ceremony more specifically. In her more recent work on performativity, Sedgwick has outlined a theory of 'periperformative utterances'. This refers to utterances that are not in themselves explicitly performative in the referentially indicative and active sense described by Austin (i.e., they do what they say), but that 'cluster around', comment on, respond to, or even negate explicitly performative utterances (e.g., 'I do not'). In elaborating this distinction, Sedgwick returns to the marriage ceremony 'as a kind of fourth wall or invisible proscenium arch that moves through the world' demanding consensus from the community of compulsory witnesses it recruits to ratify 'the legitimacy of its privilege': 'Like the most conventional definition of a play, marriage is constituted as a spectacle that denies its audience the ability either to look away from it or equally to intervene in it'.[43] And yet, precisely by reminding us of the theatricality of the wedding ceremony, and by attempting to effect something of a rapprochement

40 Butler, 'Critically queer', p. 17.
41 See Austin, *How to Do Things with Words*, pp. 14–15.
42 Sedgwick, 'Queer performativity', p. 3.
43 Eve Kosofsky Sedgwick, *Touching Feeling: Affect, Pedagogy, Peformativity* (Durham: Duke University Press, 2003), p. 72; see also Andrew Parker and Eve Kosofsky Sedgwick, 'Introduction: performativity and peformance', in Andrew Parker and Eve Kosofsky Sedgwick (eds), *Performativity and Performance* (New York: Routledge, 1995), pp. 10–11ff.

between linguistic and dramaturgical theories of performance, Sedgwick demonstrates that it is possible to disrupt and decentre the authority and direction of the performative event itself, whether by changing the terms of its reference, the space of its enunciation, or the response of its addressees.

Of course, Austin famously dismissed theatrical utterance as 'parasitic' and 'etiolated', spoken not in 'ordinary circumstances' but as part of a 'non-serious', essentially fictive context, and so deliberately excluded from the purview of his analysis.[44] But even Butler, who would later distance herself from theatrical applications of performativity in, for example, her Austinian examination of the illocutionary force of hate speech,[45] first articulated her performative theory of gender (in *Theatre Journal*, no less) as a way of 'dramatizing' (her word) how gender functions. In Butler's now famous prescription, gender is '*a corporeal style*, an "act", as it were, which is both intentional and performative, where "performative" itself carries the double-meaning of "dramatic" and "non-referential"'.[46] Moreover, in that same article Butler draws equally from the phenomenological writings of Simone de Beauvoir and Maurice Merleau-Ponty *and* Victor Turner's important anthropological/ performance studies investigations of ritual social dramas (including weddings). In so doing, she points out that gender, like marriage, coheres as a normative concept and thus gains social legitimacy only to the extent that the 'mundane', everyday enactments that underscore this illusion of coherence and the 'mundane' social audience that places its faith in the power of that illusion are constituted in and ritually repeated over time.[47]

Thinking, in this way, about both the 'social temporality' (Butler) of the wedding ceremony, and the spatial relations of community witness it presupposes for its performative and political sanction (Sedgwick), forces us to acknowledge that the 'stylized repetition of acts' that help constitute marriage as perhaps *the* preeminent human social drama in Western culture also reveal the general arbitrariness, internal discontinuities, and potential misapplications of such acts. This in turn

---

44 Austin, *How to Do Things with Words*, p. 22. For two recent performance studies critiques of Austin's discussion of theatricality's antithetical relation to performativity, see Janelle Reinelt, 'The politics of discourse: performativity meets theatricality', *SubStance* 31 (2002), pp. 201–15; and Shannon Jackson, *Professing Performance: Theatre in the Academy from Philology to Performativity* (Cambridge: Cambridge University Press, 2004).

45 See Judith Butler, *Excitable Speech: A Politics of the Performative* (New York: Routledge, 1997).

46 Butler, 'Performance acts and gender constitution: an essay in phenomenology and feminist theory', *Theatre Journal* 40:4 (1988), pp. 521–2.

47 *Ibid.*, pp. 519–20.

suggests 'the possibility of a different sort of repeating, in the breaking or subversive repetition of that style'.[48] And here, let me suggest, that Turner's discussion of ritual as a liminal process, a threshold experience that has the potential to transform not just the participants involved, but also the larger social order in which it is embedded, is a useful way to begin thinking about the 'anti-structural' possibilities of queer weddings. That is, the same-sex wedding ritual need not simply reify the de facto equivalency of celebrant and legal subject, or of witness and compulsory arbiter of institutionalised norms, but might also earnestly imagine and playfully exploit different frameworks of everyday social relation and, by extension, political recognition. As Turner defines it, 'anti-structure' is that moment in a ritual's performance 'when the past is [temporarily] negated, suspended or abrogated, and the future has not yet begun, an instant of pure potentiality when everything, as it were, trembles in the balance'.[49] For Turner, such moments are played out not in the indicative mood, as Austin's theories of performativity would have us believe, but rather in the subjunctive mood, that which expresses a 'wish, desire, possibility or hypothesis'.[50] A fantasy of 'as if-ness' that corresponds roughly with Dolan's recent theorisation of the theatre as a utopian performative space,[51] a truly subjunctive performance of marriage demands a rewriting of the traditional wedding vows. In such a rewriting the repetition of 'I do take thee . . .' as an active expression of individual entitlement might be replaced by any number of activist invocations of collective possibility: 'If we were to do this . . .'; or 'If we were to do this differently . . .'; or 'If we decided *not* to do this . . . what might we become'? Let me then turn to some recent theatrical fantasies of 'as if-ness' to explore more closely the structure and anti-structure of same-sex marriage's ritual representation and repetition on stage.

48 *Ibid.*, p. 520.
49 Victor Turner, *From Ritual to Theatre: The Human Seriousness of Play* (New York: PAJ Publications, 1982), p. 44. See also his *The Ritual Process: Structure and Anti-Structure* (London: Routledge, 1969).
50 Turner, *From Ritual to Theatre*, p. 83. As I will demonstrate in the next chapter, Rosi Braidotti formulates a similar theory of 'as if' interconnectedness as the basis for a nomadic feminist consciousness; see her *Nomadic Subjects: Embodiment and Sexual Difference in Contemporary Feminist Theory* (New York: Columbia University Press, 1994).
51 Dolan writes (using the subjunctive): 'Utopian performatives describe small but profound moments in which performance calls the attention of the audience in a way that lifts everyone slightly above the present, into a hopeful feeling of what the world might be like if every moment of our lives were as emotionally voluminous, generous, aesthetically striking, and intersubjectively intense . . . Utopian performatives, in their doings, make palpable an affective vision of how the world might be better'; see Dolan, *Utopia in Performance*, pp. 5–6.

The moods of marriage

From classical Greek drama to Broadway mega-musicals like *Mama Mia* and contemporary audience participation shows like *Tony and Tina's Wedding*, marriage, and its consequences, have been central preoccupations of the western theatrical tradition. As often as not, those consequences are unhappy ones, especially for women. Murder, suicide, confinement, rape, physical and emotional battery: the list of what awaits many brides in the dramatic canon is enough to give any actress pause. Even Shakespeare's most famous comedies, which typically culminate in a marriage ceremony that not only properly unites hero and heroine, but also restores and reaffirms the larger social order, are filled with all manner of other 'broken nuptials', unconsummated relationships, and non-normative liaisons.[52] What, then, might a queering of this theatrical tradition have to say, in turn, about the tradition of marriage, both in terms of its institutionalisation by the state and its instantiation on the stage? I want to begin answering this question by looking at two adaptations, or queerings, of the Bard's work that throw into relief the anti-structural possibilities – and the structural constraints – posed by a ritual re-imagining of the act of marriage on stage.

Long before Edward Hall's Propeller Theatre made a vogue of the return to all-male casting in contemporary productions of Shakespeare, another British company devoted to bold re-interpretations of the classics, Cheek by Jowl (CBJ), wowed audiences with its same-sex take on *As You Like It*. Originally staged by co-artistic directors Declan Donnellan (director) and Nick Ormerod (designer) as part of CBJ's 1991-92 season, the production was revived for a world tour in 1994, with Adrian Lester reprising his star turn as Rosalind. That tour rolled into the Brooklyn Academy of Music's Majestic Theatre at the beginning of October for a week-long run that neatly coincided with Canadian Thanksgiving, thus affording my partner, Richard, and me, on one of our earliest theatrical long weekends in New York City as a couple, a first glimpse of a company whose work we would come to follow most devotedly (see the next chapter). At the time, as a new Ph.D. student only beginning to immerse myself in the emergent field of queer theory, what struck me was how simply – and how compellingly – CBJ's same-sex casting conceit laid bare (quite literally) the play's structural ambiguities and asymmetries around the theatricality of gender. This was exploited from the outset, with the

---

52 The phrase 'broken nuptials' comes from Leo Salinger; see his *Shakespeare and the Traditions of Comedy* (Cambridge: Cambridge University Press, 1974), pp. 302–5. Carol Thomas Neely adapts and extends the term in *Broken Nuptials in Shakespeare's Plays* (New Haven: Yale University Press, 1985).

entire cast assembling on stage as house lights dimmed, dressed in identical masculine uniforms of black pants and white shirts. As the actor who will eventually take on the role of Jaques (a swishy Michael Gardiner) here transposes and utters the famous lines from his 'Seven Ages of Man' speech in act two, scene seven – 'All the world's a stage,/And all the men and women merely players' – the actors playing Rosalind (Lester) and Celia (Simon Coates) cross stage left and stand apart from the rest of the company, their imposing male physiques impressed upon us visually in order to make all the more incongruous their subsequent transformation into demure ingénues of court, replete with full-length white gowns. And, indeed, when in Arden we are finally presented with the scenes of Rosalind (disguised as Ganymede) instructing Orlando (Scott Handy) in the art of wooing (see figure 9), it is hard not to interpret the spectacle of a man (a six-foot tall black one, at that) playing a woman playing a man playing a woman as an explicit comment on the fluidity of gender and sexuality, and on the homoerotics of early modern theatrical practice more generally.

And so the production has been analysed by a host of other scholars.[53] In retrospect, however, what strikes me as most bold (unwittingly so, perhaps) about this production is the implicit commentary on and critique of the institution of marriage it offers through the ritual 'recasting' of the play's final scene in a same-sex paradigm. In so doing, Donnellan and Ormerod, partners off stage as well as on, cannily insert their work into the discourse around gay marriage only then beginning to gather momentum in North America (as in the UK and Europe).[54] They also bring out (again, quite literally) the performative and political impediments to marriage's successful enactment already embedded within Shakespeare's play.

Of particular importance, in this regard, is the fact that none of the four marriages that are to be celebrated at the play's conclusion – between Rosalind and Orlando, Celia and Oliver, Silvius and Phebe, and Touchstone and Audrey – is actually given, in Lisa Hopkins's words,

---

53 See, in particular, Alisa Solomon, *Re-Dressing the Canon: Essays on Theater and Gender* (New York: Routledge, 1997); and James C. Bulman, 'Bringing Cheek By Jowl's *As You Like It* out of the closet: the politics of gay theater', *Shakespeare Bulletin* 22:3 (2004), pp. 31–46.

54 Of interest, in this regard, is that in their program notes, Donnellan and Ormerod quote from John Boswell's *Christianity, Social Tolerance, and Homosexuality: Gay People in Western Europe from the Beginning of the Christian Era to the Fourteenth Century* (Chicago: University of Chicago Press, 1980). There Boswell lays the groundwork for the thesis around the blessing of pre-modern same-sex unions he would advance more powerfully – and controversially – in his last book, *Same-Sex Unions in Pre-Modern Europe* (New York: Villard, 1994), published the year of CBJ's revival of *As You Like It*. I will return to Boswell below.

9 Scott Handy (left) as Orlando and Adrian Lester as Rosalind in the Cheek by Jowl production of *As You Like It* at the Brooklyn Academy of Music, October 1994

'performative validity'.[55] That is, no one actually pronounces (in Austin's sense of the illocutionary function of the linguistic performative) any of the couples husband and wife: not the god Hymen, whom Rosalind (now divested of her Ganymede costume) initially drags on stage with the express purpose of accomplishing said task; and not Duke Senior,

55 Lisa Hopkins, *The Shakespearean Marriage: Merry Wives and Heavy Husbands* (London: Macmillan, 1998), p. 20.

to whom Hymen just as quickly transfers the responsibility. As Hopkins notes, traditional comic closure is deconstructed in *As You Like It*, with the structural telos of the epithalamium seemingly set in motion by the Duke's closing rhyming couplet – 'Proceed, proceed. We'll so begin these rites,/As we do trust they'll end, in true delights' (V.iv.186-7) – immediately forestalled and undercut by Rosalind's epilogue. Her concluding address to the audience takes us out of the ritual temporality of Arden's free-play of anti-structural sexual possibility and returns us to the mundane social temporality of the play's real-world production.[56] Equally important is the fact that this temporal switch is accompanied by a corollary shift in grammatical mood, with the actor playing Rosalind invoking the subjunctive: 'If I were a woman I would kiss as many of you as had beards that pleased me' (V.iv.202-3). This switch gestures playfully to 'the homoerotic foundations of the play's marital structure',[57] but also highlights both the dramaturgical and the social constraints imposed by the normative regulation of the sexed body in contemporary society. Given that all four of the couples about to be married in the fictional world of CBJ's production were, in reality, of the same sex, I read Donnellan and Ormerod's staging of the impossible subjunctivity/subjectivity of this scene (retrospectively, to be sure) as an explicit statement about the limits, at least at that historical juncture, of a different sort of marital relation/repetition. And here I take Shakespeare himself, as much as the institution of marriage, to be a performative stand-in for the problem of ever fully or completely re-stylising or breaking with tradition.

The general seriousness with which I also recall these interrupted nuptial proceedings being played (Orlando thinks long and hard before finally acceding to Rosalind's proposal, and Lester's Rosalind delivers her final epilogue soberly, in the harsher, more striated lighting previously associated with the closed social world of the court) also bears examination. Indeed, the subdued comic tone can be interpreted as offering audience members wont to embrace the production as a participatory plea for sexual tolerance and social recognition of gay relationships a cautionary warning about the potential costs of institutionalised marriage for any of its celebrants. To this end, that old school queer Jaques's jibe to Touchstone (Peter Needham) that his 'loving voyage/Is but for two months victualled' (V.iv.180-1), and his postponing, in this production, of his withdrawal to the Duke's former cave hideaway in order to indulge his own favourite 'pastime' of picking up men, should

---

56 *Ibid.*, p. 21.
57 Mario DiGangi, 'Queering the Shakespearean family', *Shakespeare Quarterly* 47 (1996): p. 286.

not merely be dismissed as sour grapes or unseemly and outmoded behaviour. Rather, what Jaques has earlier identified (in act four, scene one) as for all intents and purposes his gender melancholia needs to be evaluated carefully in terms of what of queerness's political past (cf. Duke Senior's plangent homosocial reflections on his genuine affection for Orlando's recently deceased father, Sir Rowland), and what of its performative present (cf. the pansexual Eden Duke Senior creates out of his forest hideaway in Arden), must be sacrificed to the futurity of marriage as sanctioned by the state (where, for instance, in the court of Duke Frederick, hetero-patriarchal customs like primogeniture still hold sway). Again, in CBJ's production of the play, the slipperiness of this particular slope is signalled by a trick of casting, with the benevolent libertine Duke Senior and the power-mad opportunist Duke Frederick both performed by the same actor (David Hobbs).

If the civil wars (between the two Dukes, and between Orlando and Oliver) that underpin much of the action in *As You Like It* are ultimately contained by the play's overarching teleology of marital (en) closure, the opening prologue of *A Midsummer Night's Dream* reminds us that marriage can in fact be a literal spoil of war. Theseus, Duke of Athens, has won Hippolyta, Queen of the Amazons, in battle, and he can barely contain himself in counting down the 'four happy days' to their 'nuptial hour' (I.i.1-2). By contrast, Hippolyta sees the future tense of marriage 'bending' time to a social contract that seems to foreclose on woman's desire (Theseus likens the moon, which he casts as the main impediment to the dawning of his wedding day, to 'a stepdame or a dowager') and open out only onto the 'young man's revenue': 'Four days will quickly steep themselves in night,/Four nights will quickly dream away the time', is how Hippolyta describes her own suspended state (I.i.5-8).

However, in Charles Mee's updating of Shakespeare's *Dream* in his recent multicultural romp, *A Perfect Wedding*, it is the groom who gets cold feet. When Amadou disappears into the forest adjacent his fiancée Meridee's family compound, she fears he intends to leave her at the altar, and so promptly gives chase. She is joined by the various members of her large and complicated family: her divorced parents, Maria and Frank; the parents' new lovers, François and Edmund; siblings Jonathan and Tessa; and their respective partners, Ariel and James. Amadou's own parents, Djamila and Vikram, and his younger brother, Willy, soon turn up, as does a posse of gay wedding planners, here updating Shakespeare's mechanicals in more ways than one. The play received its premiere in 2004 in Los Angeles, in a Center Theatre Group production directed by Gordon Davidson. Its Canadian premiere took place two years later, at Vancouver's Studio 58, a student-training programme at Langara College that produces some of the most provocative theatre in the city (see chapter 4). The Studio 58 production was guest-directed and designed by Sherry Yoon and Jay Dodge, respectively; together, they form the artistic director and producer team behind Boca del Lupo, another highly respected local company known for its environmental, collaborative, and intensely physical approach to theatre-making, and about whom I will also have more to say in the coda of this book.

Charles Mee is perhaps best known as the resident playwright of Anne Bogart's SITI Company, for whom he has written several memorable 'artists' plays', including *bobrauschenbergamerica*, *Hotel Cassiopeia* (about Joseph Cornell), *soot and spit (the musical)* (about James Castle), and *Under Construction* (about Norman Rockwell and Jason Rhoades). Alongside this work, however, Mee has also been quietly rewriting the canon of ancient Greek drama as part of his 're-making project', pillaging the plots of Euripides and Aeschylus especially to make bold theatrical statements about love and war that might be relevant to twenty-first-century audiences. In the case of *Big Love*, for example, Mee scored the biggest success of his career by updating Aeschylus' *Suppliants* as a romance about mariticide set in a fantasy villa on Italy's Amalfi Coast, where forty-nine of the fifty Danaids eventually murder their would-be husbands rather than submit to arranged marriages of which they want no part. Indeed, in Mee's work death always closely shadows love, and funeral rites have an uncanny way of interrupting and upstaging the best-laid wedding plans.

So it is with *A Perfect Wedding*, whose dramatic climax centres, in act two, around an impromptu burial ceremony for Meridee's grandmother, Georgette, who has suffered an untimely heart attack on her way to officiate Meridee's wedding. This formal reversal involves a kinship ritual that momentarily suspends both audience and characters between life and death, with the rival sets of in-laws trading the literal mudslinging that closed act one for a more dignified coming together to aid a disconsolate Frank (Raphael Kepinski) in digging his mother's grave. In this respect, one of the most thrilling aspects of Yoon and Dodge's production of the play at Studio 58 was in fact how 'earthy' they made things, with Dodge bringing something of Boca del Lupo's site-specific outdoor aesthetic to his improvised black box recreation of a forest floor, and Yoon clearly instructing her young actors to get as down and dirty as possible. Meridee's (Trisha Cundy) white wedding dress becomes an important symbol here; crisp and clean when she slips into it just prior to going off in search of Amadou (Hamza Adam), by the end of the play it is tattered and streaked with black mud. This,

I would argue, is a subtle visual telescoping of the subjunctive mood embedded in the more archaic version of the performative wedding vow included in *The Book of Common Prayer*, 'Till death us do part', which just happens to be cited by Tessa (Emmelia Gordon) at the outset of the play as a promise impossible to keep.

The gay wedding planners, it turns out, also do funerals and know all the 'basic rituals', and so they lead the assembled party in a Tibetan mourning chant for Georgette. Ever practical, planners Isaac (Jon Lachlan Stewart) and Dieter (Jason Andrews) also decide they shouldn't let all of their preparations for Meridee and Amadou's wedding go to waste, that they should, in Isaac's words, 'have it for ourselves'. And so Isaac, who had earlier in the play claimed he was 'not the sort who wants to just be leaping into the mainstream/and losing my/specialness',[58] formally proposes to Dieter, and Dieter duly accepts. This culminates in a grand, Bollywood-style dance number which in turn inspires Meridee to declare her true feelings for Ariel (Miriam Westland), and Tessa for Amadou. And yet while all of this was performed with joyously infectious abandon by Yoon's young, rainbow-coloured cast, I couldn't help feeling that embedded within the mish-mash of ceremonial rites on offer in Mee's play is a caveat about the risks faced by minority groups, in particular, who seek to adapt their own 'special' ways of being and becoming to dominant cultural traditions. I base this assessment, in part, on Djamila's (Melissa Oei) earlier attempts, in act one, to describe her ritual deflowering and female circumcision. What for her is a legitimate sexual and religious rite of passage is for the other characters – and presumably for most in the audience – only intelligible within a paradigm of 'patriarchy and property/and handing girls over to new owners', to whom they are thereafter bound. In other words, there might be something fundamentally gay about planning a wedding, but the institution of marriage remains resolutely strait laced.

That the North American wedding industry is serviced largely by the labour of a queer creative class is the central ironic premise of Paul Rudnick's recent play, *Regrets Only*. A bagatelle of a comedy as thin as the Nan Kempner-like frame of its female lead, Christine Baranski, and shamelessly exploiting the prevailing cultural zeitgeist around same-sex marriage, the play premiered at the Manhattan Theatre Club in October 2006 under the direction of longtime Rudnick collaborator Christopher Ashley. Having just seen Raul Esparza's brilliant turn as the ambivalent,

---

58 All quotations from Mee's text, which preserve his syntax and line breaks, are
     taken from the version posted to his *(Re)Making Project* website; see Mee, *A Perfect
     Wedding*, *The (Re)Making Project*, www.charlesmee.org/html/perfectwedding.html
     (accessed September 2007).

commitment-wary Bobby in John Doyle's stripped-down Broadway revival of Stephen Sondheim's *Company*, I admit to being especially eager to receive what I hoped would be the sharper edges of Rudnick's apercus about the not-so genteel protocols of marriage among polite society (to quote Sondheim's Joanne, 'It's the little things you do together'). Michael Yeargan's set, with its hard right angles, gleaming surfaces, and abundance of cut crystal, seemed to bode well, in this regard. That the political critique I was seeking from *Regrets Only* was, in the end, more muted than militant is perhaps a function as much of the play's strict formal adherence to the surface dramatic conventions of the drawing-room comedy as it is Rudnick's failure, on the level of content, to explore in any real depth the social and sexual inequities embedded within the bourgeois conventions of marriage.

Nevertheless, as I surveyed the moneyed, mostly white, mostly straight, mostly post-boomer audience laughing appreciatively at Rudnick's rapid-fire wit, I wondered how many of them were actually in on the play's biggest joke. That is, how many of them understood that amid all the gentle barbs and light comic banter exchanged by the characters, Rudnick was actually reflecting back to them – as he did in an equally safe and non-threatening way in the screenplay for *In and Out* – the queer foundations of their companionate marriages? Enough to extend the run at City Center (and allow Richard and me a chance to catch a performance over the Christmas holidays), but not enough, apparently, to send the production to Broadway.

The play focuses on the relationship between Hank Hadley (George Grizzard), a successful fashion designer in the mould of Bill Blass, and his best friend and frequent muse, Tibby McCullough (Baranski), a Park Avenue society hostess. Tibby's busy lawyer husband, Jack (David Rasche), has for many years been more than happy to cede his marital duties as Tibby's social escort to Hank, and as act one opens Hank is slowly returning to his role as Tibby's chaste gay walker following the death of his longtime partner. However, before Tibby and Hank can get out the door, the McCulloughs' daughter, Spencer (Diane Davis), hijacks the proceedings, announcing her recent engagement. The ensuing family celebrations (in which Hank is warmly included) are in turn interrupted by a phone call. It's the President, and he wants Jack to come to Washington to help draft a potential constitutional amendment banning gay marriage. Jack's resolve to do so and, moreover, Spencer's eagerness to apply her own legal mind to the endeavour, chafes against Hank's hitherto quiescent political sensibilities. As a result, he sets in motion a 'what if' scenario designed to underscore the invisible (and illegitimate) sexual citizenship of an entire economic subgroup that

works to ensure the smooth operation of bourgeois culture's presump-
tively heteronormative social rituals. In other words, Hank uses his
own myriad connections in the fashion world to call for a queer general
strike. What would happen, Rudnick satirically (and subjunctively) asks,
if all the florists, hairdressers, caterers, designers, make-up artists, and
personal assistants in New York suddenly walked off the job?

The answer to this question, in act two, comes mostly in the form
of a series of sight gags: Tibby in a fright wig; Tibby's mother, Marietta
(played by the incomparable Sîan Phillips), somehow managing to look
chic in garbage bags; the McCulloghs' wisecracking maid, Myra (Mary
Testa, taking over from Jackie Hoffman), suddenly out of uniform, surprising everyone but Hank with the revelation that she will be joining
in the job action. If these images do not cumulatively add up to an
entirely satisfying examination of the differential rights that accrue to
minority groups through the social contract, the play does theatricalise
just how expansively the family compact can be opened up to different
forms of affective attachment and peformative belonging through its
ceremonial rites – not least the cocktail hour. In this, as several reviewers have noted, Rudnick has crafted a *Philadelphia Story* for the twenty-
first century, with Tibby and Hank's devotion to each other, like Cary
Grant's and Kate Hepburn's, comprising perhaps the queerest form of
marriage of all.

It was in Philadelphia, in the summer of 2006, that Terrence
McNally premiered *Some Men*, his non-chronological, episodic take on
North American gay history from the 1920s to the present. However,
by the time the play arrived at New York's Second Stage Theater, in
March 2007, it had undergone substantial revision. Originally conceived as a play-cum-revue about gay men and the musical divas they
supposedly worship (the Judys, the Barbras, the Lizas), the Philadelphia
version of the play featured a larger ensemble (including two female
actors, Suzanne Douglas and Barbara Walsh) and its serial structure was
anchored by as many live as canned musical moments. In tinkering with
the show for its New York opening, McNally reduced the cast size (elim-
inating completely the female roles) and turned the remaining show
tunes into a kind of incidental mood music for his *Cavalcade*-like exploration of eight decades of modern gay life. As a result, his diachronic
take on that life comes across as an uncharacteristically glib rhetorical
representation of successive moments of historical struggle that the
playwright had previously mined in much more satisfyingly synchronic,
and even dialectical, ways in earlier all-male cast plays like *Love! Valour!
Compassion!* and *Corpus Christi* (which I will explore at greater length
in chapter 4). That marriage is represented in *Some Men* as the de facto

– and dramaturgical – culmination of this struggle accounts in no small measure for my initial negative reaction to the play's overly hortatory tone. Re-watching the play eight months later in a local production mounted by the Vancouver queer company Raving Theatre did nothing to alter that reaction. What the experience did do was confirm an earlier suspicion that the overwhelmingly New York-centric focus of *Some Men* would not travel well.

That said, the play's particular (anti-)structure can be viewed, in some senses, as a staged battle between the indicative and subjunctive moods of performance. For while *Some Men* opens with the assembled company (and, tacitly, the audience – hence the rows of simple white chairs that recur throughout successive scenes of the play, frequently pointing outward) gathered to witness and celebrate a same-sex wedding in a swank ballroom at the Waldorf, the solemnisation of the vows is interrupted by the theatrical equivalent of Sedgwick's periperformative relays. A series of chronologically and spatially itinerant scenes ensues, imagining all that might have been, or all that might have been done differently, prior to the present-day frame of marital concupiscence. To his credit, McNally does offer up multiple 'as if' scenarios for the ways in which relationships of same-sex eroticism and kinship might be conceived as temporarily suspending the ritual repetition of straight time (most clearly and productively in the bathhouse and cyber-chat scenes); however, the fact remains that the play, aided in part by director Trip Cullman's swift pacing and liberal use of blackouts, moves, in Jill Dolan's words, 'inexorably toward marriage as its final, most meaning-ful, right, true act of faith'.[59]

In concluding his play with 'an emphatic "I do"',[60] McNally forces his audience to accede dramaturgically and ideologically to the inevi-table conflation of the theatrical rite this speech act performs and the political right it consequently stands in for. He also very nearly suc-ceeds in evacuating previous scenes of the force of their periperforma-tive protest, in which the failure to say, or the constraints placed upon saying, explicitly what one means, who one is, what or who one desires, paradoxically enacts a referential evasion of dominant regimes of social regulation and sexual prohibition. I am referring, here, to what for me remains the play's most powerful scene, when a gay veteran of the Iraq war (played by Frederick Weller) approaches the ex-army general father (Don Amendolia) of his closeted dead lover at the latter's military

59 Jill Dolan, 'Terrence McNally's *Some Men* at Second Stage', *The Feminist Spectator* (14 April 2007), http://feministspectator.blogspot.com/2007_04_01_archive.html (accessed September 2007).

60 *Ibid.*

funeral. Struggling to convey to the older man just what exactly his son meant to him within the rhetorical limits imposed by 'Don't ask, don't tell' becomes a productive circumlocutionary way for the younger soldier to preserve something of the alternative possibilities heralded by their relationship, of ensuring that that relationship, in Butler's evocative phrasing, avoids 'capture' within a circuit of heteronormative interpellation and legibility. As Butler puts it, in connection with her own analysis of the 'incommensurability between performativity and referentiality' in the US military's policy on homosexuality, 'one of the tasks of a critical production of alternative homosexualities will be to *disjoin* homosexuality from the figures by which it is conveyed in dominant discourse'.[61] Who would have thought that one of those figures might some day be marriage?

And who would have thought that legendary 'post-porn performance artist' Annie Sprinkle would one day end up exploring both the personal politics and the performative possibilities afforded by the ritual repetition of this institution? So far in my analysis of recent theatrical representations of same-sex marriage, I have been focusing exclusively on male playwrights/theatre artists working within a more or less conventionally naturalistic style. These works have also not afforded much opportunity to discuss the specific performative dynamics of the queer wedding ceremony itself, which is repeatedly postponed, interrupted, or only ever imagined as a hypothetical possibility. In turning to analyse Sprinkle and partner Beth Stephens' ongoing seven-year *Love Art Laboratory* project, not only do questions of gender difference, and of women's different social, political, and economic investments in the institution of marriage, per force come to the fore; the careful grounding of each of their successively staged weddings in explicitly feminist and Fluxus performance art traditions also asks us to consider how the very form of the evolving ceremonial contributes to a ritual re-imagining of the various forms of belonging said ceremonial both calls into being and into question. And, here, I would argue that one very successful part of that evolution has been the gradual merging – via, among other things, a strategic use of the Internet and a variety of satellite installations and shows – of Sprinkle and Stephens' at once private and public, local and global, audiences into an expressly theatrical counterpublic, a participatory wedding party (in all senses of that word) that just might succeed in altering 'the ways we understand marriage and the subjects who produce and are produced by it'.[62]

61 Butler, *Excitable Speech*, pp. 108 and 125; my emphasis.
62 Conway, 'A becoming queer aesthetic', p. 168.

Sprinkle, the porn-star-turned-performance-artist-turned-sexolo-gist best known for exposing her cervix on stage in her one-woman illustrated performance piece *Post-Porn Modernist* (1989-95), first met Stephens, a multimedia artist and Associate Professor in the Department of Art at the University of California, Santa Cruz, in New York in 1989. The two became reacquainted in 2001, shortly after Sprinkle relocated to the west coast to pursue a Ph.D. in sexology at San Francisco's Institute for Advanced Study of Human Sexuality. In 2003, following the United States' invasion of Iraq, the couple registered as legal domestic partners under California state law in order 'to propose love as an alternative vision to the war' (loveartlab.org). When San Francisco mayor Gavin Newsom started handing out marriage licences to gay and lesbian couples in early 2004, Sprinkle and Stephens made an appointment to tie the knot at City Hall, only to have the Superior Court of San Francisco put a stop to these ceremonies a day before their scheduled wedding. And so they decided to draw on their own artistic training, and on their many contacts in the overlapping theatre, activist, and sex communities of which they are both a part, to create a series of 'performance art wed-dings' to be staged in different locations across North America over the next seven years. Thus was born the *Love Art Laboratory*, a collaborative theatrical experiment based on the themes and colors of the chakras (the ancient Sanskrit system of body–mind energy wheels stretching from the base of the spine to the top of the head), and structurally (and politi-cally) modelled on Linda Montano's important performance piece, *14 Years of Living Art*.

Year one (2005) of Sprinkle and Stephens' project was focused, as a direct counterpoint to the war in Iraq, around the themes of 'secu-rity' and 'survival', and was inaugurated by the Red Wedding that took place at New York's Collective Unconscious Theater on 18 December 2004. The collaborative participation not only of Montano, but also of legendary Fluxus artist, Geoffrey Hendricks, in the ceremony is key to understanding how Sprinkle and Stephens are attempting to disrupt and displace the socially mundane act of marriage, turning its ritual repetition into an over-the-top, performative spectacle precisely in order to force us to examine how, as an institution, it comes to police the boundaries of acceptability in everyday life. Including, then, the preeminent performance artist of 'everyday life' as part of one's nuptial celebrations makes perfect sense. In the best known of her durational art/life performance pieces, Montano spent the years 1984-98 in upstate New York following a rigid daily routine: she wore only clothes that were colour-coded to match the chakra she was exploring that year; for three hours a day, she stayed in a similarly coloured space; for seven hours a day she listened to a sound pitch associated with that colour/ chakra; and, at least for the first seven years of the project, she spoke in an accent chosen to evoke that colour/chakra. Included as part of the project, each year Montano, an ex-nun, invited others to collaborate with her as part of an art/life residency she called 'Summer Saint Camp'. In the summer of 1987, Veronica Vera and Annie Sprinkle spent two weeks at the camp wearing only yellow and, not surprisingly, getting in touch with their 'sex chakras'. At the end of the two weeks, Montano baptised the two women 'artists', an 'intensely emotional' event for Sprinkle, then just making the transition from porn star to performance artist.[63] Above all, what Montano taught Sprinkle was that by living one's life entirely in 'art time', by attending to the ritual possibilities of each moment, no matter how banal or quotidian, one begins to 'wake up' to how the bourgeois public sphere, for example, insulates itself from critique in part through the privatisation and normatisation of habit.[64] Thus, some rituals relating to sex, gender, and kinship, such as opposite-sex marriage, are elevated to the status of an event – and one presumably worth repeating – while others are relegated the non-indicative, *sub rosa* category of caprice.

For Sprinkle and Stephens, then, each of their weddings inaugurates a new subjunctive temporality. The particular anti-structure of their annual live art/art-life nuptial celebrations – where the performative witnessing of Sprinkle and Stephens' exchange of vows is always second-ary to the witnessed performances of their friends and collaborators (see figure 10) – sets the stage (quite literally) for the multiple 'as if' scenarios of their life together that they will document throughout the coming year in still more performative modalities. These have so far included live body art and video installations (*Cuddle* and *Kissed*), full-scale touring theatrical productions (*Exposed*), happenings (*Zen for Head*), sex workshops, sermons, various lectures and talks, and year-end reports and photo collages posted to their website. One of the 'as if' scenarios encountered in the first year of the project was Sprinkle's diagnosis with stage one breast cancer; true to Montano's 'art time' credo, and in an effort to expose some of the more material effects of the gendering of everyday married life, even this was turned into a performance. Among other things, Sprinkle turned the papers used to blot the iodine injected into the lymph nodes of her breast into a set of her famous 'tit prints'.

63 See the scrapbook of the residency compiled by Vera and Sprinkle, 'Our week at Sister Rosita's summer saint camp', and published in *TDR: The Drama Review* 33:1 (1989), pp. 104–19.

64 See Linda M. Montano, *Letters from Linda Montano*, ed. Jennie Klein (New York: Routledge, 2005), p. 164.

10 Annie Sprinkle (left) and Elizabeth Stephens watching the performances at
the Red Wedding, New York, December 2004

Sprinkle and Stephens celebrated their first (red) wedding almost six
years to the day after Montano completed her *14 Years of Living Art*
durational performance; fittingly, an audience participation version of
Montano's poem/chant, *Amore*, has been used to start the proceedings
of each of their weddings celebrated thus far.

Officiating as Flux Priest at that first Red Wedding was Geoffrey
Hendricks. His presence on stage with Sprinkle and Stephens says much
about how their project, far more than any of the other performances
examined in this section, successfully decouples marriage as a legal
institution from the wedding as a ritual event that makes possible a
collective re-imagining of various forms of sexual and social belonging.
This subjunctive process of community-making has a long artistic and
queer genealogy, one in which, appropriately, straight divorce is ante-
rior to gay marriage. I am referring to the fact that in 1971 Hendricks
and his then-wife, Bici, celebrated the dissolution of their ten-year marriage in a collaborative performance event known as the *Fluxdivorce*;
they invited friends and family to their New York apartment, where
they had assembled various items they had accumulated during their
life together – wedding documents, clothes, furniture, photographs, and
other mementoes. Using everything from scissors to a power saw, they
then proceeded to cut all of these items in two. The guests then decamped

to the Hendricks' backyard for a symbolic tug-of-war, in which husband and wife were themselves separated, with the men pulling him and the women pulling her, a gendered allusion to the fact that each partner was about to enter into a new, same-sex relationship. Present at that event was the lesbian author and art critic, Jill Johnston.[65] When, twenty-two years later, she decided to take advantage of Denmark's recently passed civil union law for gays and lesbians and marry her Danish partner, Ingrid Nyeboe, Hendricks, who was to visit the country for a retrospective of his work, proposed that they turn the event into another *Fluxwedding* (the first such event, at which Hendricks also officiated, took place in 1977 between George Maciunus and Billie Hutching, both resplendent in matching white gowns and attended by a cross-dressed best man and maid of honour, respectively). The highlight of Johnston and Nyeboe's *Fluxwedding* was an improvised public procession, from Odense's city hall to the Kunsthallen museum showcasing Hendricks' retrospective. The procession featured, among other things, a Great Dane as majorette; a red wedding chair borne aloft by attendants whose bodies were painted Hendricks' signature sky blue; duelling boom boxes; a violist playing Danish folk tunes; and an enormous blue wedding dress designed by Danish Fluxus artist Eric Andersen and worn by thirty of Nyeboe's teenage cousins and assorted friends.[66]

In her account of the event, Johnston is critical of only one element of Hendricks' masterminding of the nuptial rites, namely that the requisite wedding video did not include shots of the traditional family portrait session. His response was that 'the real family wasn't part of his script, only the "art family" who helped create the event'.[67] I mention this because Hendricks' script seems to have found a decidedly more receptive audience in Sprinkle and Stephens, and their co-creators. Indeed, part of what is being 'undone' in their wedding project is the idea that marriage is the institutional (and biological) precondition of the normative, nuclear family structure as it has variously been celebrated, defended, lamented, and mourned by religious fundamentalists,

65 My description of Hendricks' *Fluxdivorce* and Johnston's own subsequent *Fluxwedding* is derived from two accounts provided by Johnston. See her 'In the meantime, art was happening', in Geoffrey Hendricks (ed.), *Critical Mass: Happenings, Fluxus, Performance, Intermedia and Rutgers University, 1958–1972* (Rutgers, NJ: Rutgers University Press, 2003), pp. 169–71; and 'Wedding in Denmark', in Nayland Blake *et al.* (eds), *In a Different Light: Visual Culture, Sexual Identity, Queer Practice* (San Francisco: City Lights Books, 1995), pp. 215–21.

66 For an excellent analysis of how these 'indeterminate and unharmonizable' aspects of the *Fluxwedding* produce an oppositional aesthetic that 'queers' the traditional marriage ceremony through inversion, chance, and the sublime, see Conway, 'A becoming queer aesthetic', pp. 179–88.

67 Johnston, 'Wedding in Denmark', p. 220.

political pundits, and talk show hosts across North America. As I have already suggested, the five weddings that have been performed so far have been as much – if not more – about celebrating and collectively experiencing the quirky talents of their extended art (and sex) families (the recombinant inter-relations of which are truly mind-boggling) as they have been about singling out for approval and sanction Sprinkle and Stephens as a couple. To this end, when in the Red Wedding we finally get around to the exchange of marriage vows, Barbara Carrellas, tantric sex educator, theatre artist, partner of Kate Bornstein, fellow Montano collaborator, and the director presiding over the whole event, interrupts the proceedings and, in her self-styled role as the 'anti-marriage fairy', hands out pieces of red paper to the assembled guests, instructing them to list ten reasons why marriage is wrong. And, in his role as Flux Priest, Hendricks crucially asks Sprinkle and Stephens to pronounce each other '*un*lawfully wedded wife and love/art collabora-tor', thereby subsuming the illocutionary force of their social and sexual relationship to the presumably more felicitous perlocutionary outcomes of their artistic collaboration.

I do not have the space to examine in depth all of Sprinkle and Stephens' subsequent nuptial ceremonies. (At the time of this writing, their fourth, Green Wedding, had been celebrated in Santa Cruz on 17 May 2008, just two days after the California Supreme Court handed down its decision on same-sex marriage equality in that state, and then again in Zagreb, Croatia, on 9 October 2008, less than a month before the passing of Proposition 8 effectively scuttled that decision. A fifth, Blue Wedding, took place in Oxford in June 2009, and then again at the Venice Biennale in August 2009.[68]) I do, however, want to remark on one feature of their Orange Wedding of 2006 that stood out for me. Structured around the themes of Sexuality and Creativity, the ceremony took place on 2 July 2006 at San Francisco's Center for Sex and Culture, with sex educator and Good Vibrations owner Carol Queen officiating. At one point during the course of various orgiastic rites that make up the event, a collaborator wearing a George W. Bush mask assists in a sym-bolic birthing of a flower. I single out this, among many other similarly surreal theatrical moments, as a reminder that Sprinkle and Stephens' project began, first and foremost, as a performative protest against the war in Iraq – and the coincidence of the colours of their first three wed-dings corresponding with the 'Severe', 'High', and 'Elevated' levels of the Homeland Security Advisory System is no doubt intentional. I'd also like to suggest that this particular act of reproduction not only visually locates

68   See the loveartlab.org website for full details.

participants within the 'make love, not war' epicentre of the US, but also neatly alludes to a queer performance tradition local to San Francisco. I am referring to the legendarily goofy drag send-ups performed by The Coquettes, who in 1971 made their own queer plea for peace by spoofing, on Super-8 film, Tricia Nixon's White House wedding, complete with drag incarnations of Jackie and Rose Kennedy, Mamie Eisenhower, and Lady Bird Johnson. Just as The Coquettes' gender parody sent up an institution that now made Tricia's husband, 24-year-old Harvard law student Edward Cox, doubly exempt from the Vietnam draft, so do Sprinkle and Stephens' anti-mimetic wedding ceremonies remind us that Bush's defense of traditional marriage was but one more weapon of mass distraction regarding the ongoing debacle in Iraq.

Finally, in concluding this section, I think it is important to point out that Sprinkle and Stephens' third Yellow Wedding (2007), organised around the themes of Courage and Power, marked a departure from the ritual patterns established in their previous two ceremonies in a number of significant ways. Chief among them is the fact that this wedding was the first to be celebrated outside the US, with Sprinkle and Stephens taking advantage of Canada's same-sex marriage statutes to get legally married for the first time in a ceremony performed as part of One Yellow Rabbit Theatre's annual High Performance Rodeo, an international festival of the performing arts held every January in Calgary, Alberta (see figure 11). To a certain extent this shifts the focus from subjunctive performative rites of the sort I have been examining above (i.e., what a wedding might suggest about and through the ties that bind) back to indicative political rights (i.e. how a marriage defines one, and what it gets one). Sprinkle acknowledges as much when she comments to Calgary's gay newspaper on the different benefits accrued through California's domestic partnership laws and Canada's same-sex marriage laws.[69] In this respect, Sprinkle and Stephens are also acutely aware (or were made aware) of the local political resonances of their choice of Calgary as the site of their third wedding. For while same-sex marriage is indeed the law of the land in Canada, and while oil-rich Calgary is an increasingly diverse and cosmopolitan city, the traditionally conservative province of Alberta (home to Prime Minister Harper) was for a long time the lone holdout in complying with the revised parameters of the Civil Marriage Act brought into effect in 2005. Then Premier Ralph Klein threatened to invoke the notwithstanding clause, a provision in Canada's Charter that allows federal and provincial legislatures to override certain

---

69   See Kaitlyn S.C. Hatch, 'One yellow wedding: Annie Sprinkle comes to town!' *GayCalgary Magazine* 39 (January 2007), p. 10.

11 Sprinkle and Stephens hold up their marriage certificate at the Yellow
Wedding, Calgary, January 2007

legal, expression, and equality rights for a temporary period of time. As
Sprinkle and Stephens retail all of this in their own inimitable way on
their website, 'We are told that while Calgary has gay marriage rights,
there are still a lot of people against gay marriage and who want to abolish

it. So we will make our wedding into a public relations fest and a unique performance art event to celebrate our queerness and generate more love for each other and with the Calgary community' (loveartlab.org).

To be sure, the question of rights remained largely moot at the time of the Yellow Wedding, not least because the 1996 Defense of Marriage Act explicitly exempts states from recognising same-sex unions entered into in other regions (New York has since enacted legislation allowing for such recognition).[70] Thus, while acknowledging that the battle over gay marriage is far from over on either side of the Canada–US border, it seems to me that to best understand – as Sprinkle and Stephens wish us to understand – how this battle is linked to other battles being fought over, or in the name of, difference in other parts of the world, we need to redirect our attention, in the above quote from the two brides, and in the wedding rites it announces, to how publicity is conjoined with festivity to suggest a possible reimagining of human social relations, including the relation of marriage. In this regard, it is important to note that another major difference between the Yellow Wedding in Calgary and the preceding ones was that Sprinkle and Stephens were not collaborating with their familiar American circles of friends, family, and fellow artists. Instead, they worked with the staff of High Performance Rodeo, especially curator and director Michael Green, production manager Ian Wilson, associate producer Johanna Schwartz, and stage manager Kenna Burima, to marshal a group of local talent (action poet Sheri-D Wilson, dancers Matthew Popoff and Emmanuel Piron, video artist Liss Platt, aerial performer Stephanie Norn, and the drag king troupe The Fake Mustaches, among others) to 'make a wedding' through the *doing* of their performances (loveartlab.org). This element of creative surprise, combined with the fact that the entire event was also open to the public for the first time – a public that is asked to accede formally and actively to its receptive role – suggests, finally, that the marital proscenium is breechable, that it is possible to join ritual performance with activist spectatorship to reconfigure both marriage's modes, and its moods.

On being blessed

Most proponents, and even a significant number of opponents, of gay marriage argue that it is a civil rather than a religious matter and, following from this, many countries, including the UK, have chosen to pursue

70 See the Library of Congress electronic record of the text of DOMA (Bill Number H.R. 3396), from the 104th Congress of the US: http://thomas.loc/gov/cgi-bin/bdquery/z?d104:h.r.03396 (accessed September 2007).

the somewhat easier path of legalising same-sex civil or domestic partnerships rather than full-fledged marriage. However, it is important to
remember that, historically, marriage law in North America, as inherited
from English common law practice, was rooted in Christian doctrine.
This meant, among other things, the loss of legal personhood for women
upon marriage (as they no longer had the right to own property); the
establishment of consummation as the limit test for a marriage's viabil-
ity/voidability (as the central purpose of the union between husband and
wife was the procreation of children); and, until the middle of the nineteenth century, the impossibility of divorce (as, until that time, marriage
law was governed by the ecclesiastical rather than the secular courts).[71]
Ignoring how this legacy necessarily frames current debates around the
question of legally and politically authorising civil marriages/unions
for queers is to be disingenuous. It is also to ignore the religious rituals
(some largely benign and meaningless, others deeply felt and symbolic)
that continue to inform a great many of the Christian-inspired weddings, whether gay or straight, performed around the world to this day.
Long before couples announced their engagements in the pages of their
local newspaper's social register, they published their banns in church,
announcing their intent to marry before the assembled congregation
on three successive Sundays, and inviting any objections to the proposed union. And, indeed, it was through the repetition of just such
an arcane religious performative that two Toronto couples, Elaine and
Ann Vatour, and the aforementioned Kevin Bourassa and Joe Varnell,
attempted, in 2000, to bypass the courts and circumvent provincial
and federal laws that at that time still prohibited same-sex marriage.[72]
While the Attorney General of Ontario, to whom the marriage banns of
the two couples were sent for official legal registration, refused the *post
hoc, ergo propter hoc* logic of the Metropolitan Community Church of
Toronto, it is interesting to note that with the legalisation of same-sex
marriage in Canada, many other religious congregations and denomi-
nations now find themselves in a similar moral and ethical quandary:
do they offer their blessing, after the fact, to same-sex unions already
sanctioned by law? This question has proved especially divisive for the
Anglican Church, and I want to conclude this chapter by exploring very

71 See, in the American context, Nancy F. Cott, *Public Vows: A History of Marriage and
the Nation* (Cambridge, MA: Harvard University Press, 2000); and, in the Canadian,
William Peter Ward, *Courtship, Love, and Marriage in Nineteenth-Century Canada*
(Montreal: McGill-Queen's University Press, 1990).
72 For further discussion of how this particular event speaks to 'the dialectical potential of the wedding as a form', see the concluding coda to Freeman's *The Wedding
Complex*, pp. 210–20.

briefly its performative and political articulations in various local, transnational, and global contexts.

While the pioneering queer historians John Boswell and Alan Bray have, in separate weighty tomes published just prior to and just after their respective deaths, argued that there has long existed both Greek and Latin liturgical rites that were performed publicly to celebrate erotic and/or kinship relationships between people of the same sex,[73] debates around religious blessings for gay and lesbian couples in long-term relationships have largely ebbed and flowed alongside the successive legal victories and setbacks around same-sex marriage in predominately secular societies around the globe. When, however, in May 2003, Bishop Michael Ingham, head of the Anglican diocese of New Westminster, British Columbia, threw his support behind such blessings, my hometown of Vancouver suddenly became the local epicentre of a larger battle looming within the worldwide Anglican Communion. Together with Katharine Jefferts Schori, Presiding Bishop of the Episcopal Church of the United States, who the same year confirmed the openly gay Gene Robinson as bishop of the diocese of New Hampshire, Ingham thrust simmering antagonisms within the Church over homosexuality firmly into the spotlight (see figure 12), pitting more liberal parishes in North America against conservative and even stridently anti-gay dioceses in Africa, Asia and Latin America. Not that such binary antagonisms should be seen as in any way absolute or stable. Indeed, as the war of words that erupted among Anglicans following Robinson's confirmation and Ingham's issuing of a rite of blessing for people in 'committed same-sex unions' threatened to spill over into a wholesale schism, one immediate and very local performative consequence of Ingham's act was the seceding of eight conservative Vancouver-area parishes from his diocese, with four of them subsequently joining the Anglican Church of Rwanda. Following this, Vancouver's largest (and richest) Anglican congregation, St John's Church in Shaughnessy, voted to join three Ontario Anglican congregations in forging a formal relationship with the Anglican Church of the Southern Cone of the Americas. This pattern has been repeated throughout the United States and Canada, prompting Archbishop Rowan Williams, at the July 2008 Lambeth Conference, to call for a moratorium not only on same-sex blessings and the consecration of gay bishops, but also on the intra-provincial poaching of Anglican members and congregations.[74]

One does not envy the enormous task faced by Williams in conven-

---

73 See John Boswell, *Same-Sex Unions in Pre-Modern Europe*; and Alan Bray, *The Friend* (Chicago: University of Chicago Press, 2003).
74 See Kim Westad, 'Anglican Diocese of B.C. reps favour same-sex blessing', *Vancouver Sun* (2 June 2007), p. A1; Douglas Todd, 'Same-sex opposed Anglicans to split',

12 Bishop Michael Ingham and Archbishop Katharine Jefferts Schori in Vancouver, May 2007

ing the 2008 iteration of Lambeth, the once-a-decade meeting of the 800-plus bishops that make up the worldwide Anglican Communion, who gather in Canterbury at the Archbishop's invitation to discuss both local and global concerns relating to worship, doctrine, and mission. Not only did Williams have to contend with a boycott by more than 200 of those bishops – most, again, staunch traditionalists from the global south, but several evangelicals from North America as well – who just weeks before had held their own anti-Lambeth Global Anglican Future Conference in Jerusalem, but he was also dealing with controversy relating to the Anglican Church's stance on gender and sexuality that hit much closer to home. I refer to the fact that only a week before the opening of Lambeth the General Synod of the Church of England, after much debate, voted to allow the ordination of women as bishops and to reject calls by more traditional members for an accompanying compromise that would see the creation of new male-only 'super-bishops'. Add to this the uproar over the 'gay' wedding service between two Anglican priests that took place earlier in June at one of London's most venerated and recognisable churches, St Bartholomew the Great (it has been featured in many films, including

Vancouver Sun (22 November 2007), p. A9; and Michael Valpy, 'Anglicans likely to sidestep decision on gays', *Globe and Mail* (31 July 2008), p. A7.

Four Weddings and a Funeral), and one can see that however carefully Williams's approached questions of spirituality and sexuality at Lambeth, he had to do so in a way that played both intra- and transnationally. In this regard, and with reference to earlier discussions of the subjunctive moods of marriage, it is worthwhile noting that opposition to the St Bartholomew wedding apparently had as much to do with the fact that the liturgy for the service hewed too closely to the one printed in the 1662 Book of Common Prayer as with Reverend Martin Dudley's open defiance of his superiors in agreeing to conduct the service in the first place.[75]

In the end, Williams, who is at once intellectually and socially progressive *and* fairly traditional in matters relating to church hierarchy and the instruments of communion, seemed to read his constituent audiences adeptly. That is, he and his advisers recognised that achieving any coherence or agreement pertaining to the Anglican Church's position on homosexuality first of all required separating the issue of pastoral care from that of ordination, and further understanding that the Church's approach to each will necessarily differ locally and globally depending on contrasting national and civil provisions concerning sexual and gender orientation. Politically, Williams seems also to have intuited that much of the heightened rhetoric emerging from African provinces, in particular, can be related to internal power struggles in several countries, and within the African Union more generally, that have led to a thorough muddying of matters of church and state. Thus, Robert Mugabe's denouncement of the Anglican Church as a homosexual fifth column in league with the recidivist colonialism of Britain is directly related to his own precarious leadership in Zimbabwe, with ousted former Bishop of Harare Nolbert Kunonga (a fervent Mugabe supporter) doing his best to paint his replacement, Sebastian Bakare, as a de facto spokesperson for the opposition Movement for Democratic Change.[76] And at Lambeth itself the Archbishop of Sudan, Daniel Deng, followed up his appeal for international aid for his war-torn country with a venomous attack on Robinson's ordination, suggesting that more liberal attitudes toward homosexuality within North American branches of the Anglican Church have actually exacerbated ethnic and religious differences in his country.[77]

75 Jonathan Wynne-Jones, 'Male priests marry in Anglican church's first gay "wedding"', *Sunday Telegraph* (15 June 2008), www.telegraph.co.uk/news/uknews/2130668/Male-priests-marry-in-Anglican-church's-first-gay-'wedding'.html (accessed November 2008).

76 Connie Levett, 'Anglicans feel the brunt of Mugabe's many hatreds', *Sydney Morning Herald* (23 June 2008), www.smh.com.au/news/world/anglicans-feel-the-brunt-of-mugabes-many-hatreds/2008/06/22/1214073053808.html (accessed December 2008).

77 Robert Pigott, 'Gay bishop "should quit"', *BBC News Online* (23 June 2008), http://news.bbc.co.uk/2/hi/uk_news/7520711.stm (accessed December 2008).

Then, too, it is fairly clear that many of the pronouncements against homosexuality emanating from bishops overseeing dioceses in the global south have been exacerbated, in the years since the invasions of Afghanistan and Iraq, by an uncritical anti-Americanism. Thus, despite the Archbishop of Canterbury's own vigorous opposition to the war in Iraq, it can be argued that a residual effect of Tony Blair's support of the Bush doctrine has been growing disenchantment within the Anglican Communion of the Church of England's leadership on doctrinal matters. For this reason, and with a nod to those local audiences he most needs to win over, Williams attempted to play down his own presiding role at Lambeth, cannily structuring the conference around a series of small working groups modelled on the Zulu tradition of *indabas*, or 'purposeful gatherings'. These groups produced no formal resolutions, but instead talked through their differences, agreeing in the end to continue working through those differences as part of an ongoing Covenant process, and to abide for the time being by the aforementioned moratoria brokered by Williams and his Windsor Continuation Group.[78]

The idea of an Anglican Covenant 'which would make explicit and forceful the loyalty and bonds of affection which govern the relationships between the churches of the Communion' was first broached in 2004, in the Windsor Group's final report on possible ways forward from the Communion's current impasse on matters of human sexuality, an impasse that reached crisis-level proportions as a result of Robinson's ordination and Ingham's authorising of a public rite of blessing for same-sex unions (both explicitly referenced by Archbishop Robin Eames in his foreword to the report).[79] The key issue in both the Windsor Report and the subsequent St Andrew's Draft Text of the Covenant[80] is how to allow for individual churches' autonomy in local ecclesiastical matters while also ensuring respect for and adherence to the mutual commitments of global communion, and – perhaps more to the point – who has final say

---

78 Valpy, 'Anglicans', p. A7. By late 2008, however, there were already signs that the moratoria would not hold, with bishops in Ottawa and Montreal indicating they would allow same-sex blessings in their dioceses, and with the Archbishops of Nigeria, Uganda, and South America all declaring that they would continue to welcome parishes in North America upset with the positions of their national church hierarchies. See Valpy, 'Same-sex blessings to further split Anglicans', *Globe and Mail* (30 October 2008), p. A13.

79 'Section C – Canon Law and Covenant', *The Windsor Report 2004*, www.anglican-communion.org/windsor2004/section_c/p9.cfm (accessed November 2008); see also Robin Eames, 'Foreword', *The Windsor Report 2004*, www.anglicancommunion.org/windsor2004/index.cfm (accessed November 2008).

80 *An Anglican Covenant – St Andrew's Draft Text*, (February 2008), www.anglicancommunion.org/commission/covenant/st_andrews/draft_text.cfm (accessed November 2008).

when disputes arise between the two? The negotiations governing the creation of the Anglican Covenant are not unlike those that took place in preparing the draft of Iraq's new constitution post-Saddam, approved in a nationwide referendum in October 2005. I am thinking, in this regard, of the latter document's need to strive for a general balance between universal equality provisions with the 'established rulings' of Islam (*shari'a*), and a more particular codification of minority (Sunni and Kurdish) versus majority (Shiite) religious and secular beliefs regarding personal status, including marriage.

Adopted in 1959, Iraq's personal status law (covering gender equality, marriage and divorce, and family inheritance) guaranteed Iraqi women some of the most progressive legal rights and freedoms in the region, and made significant advances in education and employment possible as a result. However, Shiite clerics viewed the law as yet another manifestation of Sunni and Baathist oppression and vowed to remove the provision from the new constitution, replacing it instead with the much more restrictive personal prohibitions dictated by *shari'a*.[81] In the end a compromise was reached, and Article 39 of the 2005 constitution states that Iraqis are '"free in their obligations respecting personal status, according to their religions, sects, beliefs, or choices", but leaves it up to subsequent legislation to define exactly what this means'.[82] As Isobel Coleman has recently noted, on the one hand the provision 'could lead to a confusing but relatively benign system (not unprecedented in the region), under which Iraqis with legal questions could choose among different codes and court systems – Sunni, secular, or Shiite – depending on which they thought would give them the most favorable treatment'.[83] And, in matters of marriage there is evidence that this is already happening, with many observers, for example, noting a marked rise in the incidence of *mutaa*, or 'enjoyment marriages', previously outlawed under Saddam, but now gaining renewed popularity in part as a material consequence of more than five years of armed conflict and sectarian violence. An ancient Shiite custom allowing a man to obtain a 'temporary' spouse in exchange for a monetary payment or help with household expenses or upkeep, these marriages (which can last for a few hours or several months) are said to have originated as a way of providing for war widows, while simultaneously allowing unmarried men out of work or married men with pregnant wives a sanctioned

81 Isobel Coleman, 'Women, Islam, and the new Iraq', *Foreign Affairs* (January/February 2006), www.foreignaffairs.org/20060101faessay85104/isobel-coleman/women-islam-and-the-new-iraq.html (accessed November 2008).
82 *Ibid.*
83 *Ibid.*

form of sexual release.[84] However, women's rights activists argue that *mutaa* marriages are really just a cover for prostitution, and in this case the vagueness of Article 39 – especially in terms of who one appeals to in terms of a perceived violation of personal freedom – might actually be severely limiting for women. So too for a church seeking clarification on the 'exercise' of autonomy and the 'management' of communion. Entering into a covenant, like a marriage, might be voluntary, but opting out can prove more difficult.

In fact, another local version of this very performative severing, or 'undoing', of church ties as a result of the blessing of same-sex relationships was rehearsed more than a decade before Lambeth 2008 when the congregation of St Alban's, in the northern Vancouver Island town of Port Alberni, voted in 1996 to 'disaffiliate' themselves from the Anglican Church. The event received relatively scant attention at the time, but subsequently came back to the fore of local public consciousness when in 2001 it served as the basis of a docudrama developed by playwright Mark Leiren-Young at the behest of Savage God Theatre Company, a resident performance ensemble at Vancouver's Christ Church Cathedral best known for its staged readings of Shakespeare. Employing the approach to the creation of theatrical character developed and refined by Anna Deavere Smith in her ongoing 'On the Road' series of multi-character documentary solo performances (of which *Fires in the Mirror* and *Twilight Los Angeles* remain the most famous examples), Leiren-Young conducted a series of interviews with members of the St Alban's congregation, former and current pastors, as well as a number of interested observers. He then assembled a short one-act play consisting of a series of monologues that reproduce verbatim the speech of a representative selection of interview subjects on both sides of the issue. In Savage God's production of the play a total of eleven roles, plus a Brechtian-style Reporter/Narrator who regularly reads from published newspaper accounts and diocese statements/proclamations to historicise events for the audience, were played by five actors. Under John Juliani's stripped-down direction, these actors formed a quasi-Greek chorus, harmonising a hymn of spiritual unity at the start and close of the play that made all the more compelling the literal breaking of ranks that occurred in between, with each actor stepping forward into a solo spot at certain designated points to express a given character's point of view on the issue of same-sex marriage. As in the work of Deavere Smith, beats, pauses, repetitions, malapropisms, and the halting search to express

---

84 Nancy Trejos, 'Temporary "enjoyment marriages" in vogue again with some Iraqis', *Washington Post* (20 January 2007), p. A1.

clearly what one means are used strategically throughout *Articles of Faith*,[85] with manner of speech and the loss or failure of words over time becoming the 'graphic evidence' for the audience not simply of a character's ideological position, but of how that position is constituted in and by history. In this, the production performatively reproduces, both dramaturgically and at the level of individual speech acts, the process of 'disaffiliation' undertaken by the St Alban's Church. That is, we in the audience are interpellated, regardless of our own subjectivities, by the particular interviewee structure of the characters' address, our contract as theatrical interlocutors at once inviting and immediately foreclosing on a response.

Recognising this, Leiren-Young and Savage God provided audiences with a subjunctive, anti-structural second act in the form of a post-performance talk-back session, in which playgoers and churchgoers alike were invited to engage in a dialogue on the blessing of same-sex unions, and to imagine scenarios that would both recognise the diversity of local faith communities and respect the canons of the worldwide Anglican Communion. The night I attended, this 'conversation' contained far more dramatic fireworks than the deliberately understated performance that preceded it. Men and women on both sides of the debate quoted scripture and then engaged in rigorous exegetical interpretation; cited historical precedents and then countered with liturgical impediments; offered impassioned personal testimonials and then made sweeping group generalisations. They harangued, admonished, accused, appealed, celebrated, and praised. As I listened to the rhetoric swirling around me, and absorbed its illocutionary force, I was variously chagrined, angered, disgusted, elated, overjoyed, and moved. What I wasn't was ever less than fully engaged, and to this day the entire event remains for me one of the clearest expressions of how the theatrical public sphere can ritually re-animate the bourgeois public sphere, in this case sparking an ongoing discussion about, among other things, the bounds of religious tolerance and the bonds of sexual citizenship.

What is more, in all the voluminous internal and external reporting on the crisis within the Anglican Church, I have so far failed to see reflected in any depth two important points – one we can for all intents and purposes label political, the other mostly performative – that came up in the post-performance discussion of *Articles of Faith*, and that encapsulate the main parameters of this chapter. The first, expressed by

---

85 See, in this regard, the 'Author's notes' to the published version of the play: Mark Leiren-Young, *Articles of Faith: The Battle of St Alban's* (Vancouver: Anvil Press, 2001), p. xii.

an avowed 'queer non-believer', was that a precondition of the proposed Anglican rite of blessing same-sex unions was that the gay and lesbian individuals in such unions were acknowledged to be part of committed, monogamous relationships, and that this prioritisation of monogamy over other sex and kinship models merely reinscribed the institutional prejudices already inherent within heterosexual marriage. The second objection, raised by an 'Anglican dissenter', had, or at least has in my recollected estimation, more to do with the form any such rite might take; that is, while this particular individual had 'no problem with gay people, per se', he wondered why 'their relationships' should be 'singled out' for blessing. While, at the time, the implication of his remarks seemed clear to everyone – that minority rights equalled 'special rights' – in hindsight it appears to me that, as per the argument I have been developing throughout this chapter, the performative act of blessing needs to be analysed alongside whatever abstract or material changes in status that blessing confers. And here, in closing, it is perhaps worthwhile to return to J. L. Austin and the 'unhappy' relationship between saying and doing in the marriage ceremony.

At the end of *How to Do Things with Words*, in summarising how his earlier distinction between constatives and performatives should be collapsed into a larger theory of language focused more on locution (meaning and reference) and illocution (convention and force), Austin outlines five general classes of speech acts into which he groups a number of 'explicit performative verbs': verdictives 'are typified by the giving of a verdict' (e.g. acquitting, convicting, ruling); exercitives 'are the exercising of powers, rights, or influences' (e.g. appointing, voting, ordering); commissives 'are typified by promising or otherwise undertaking' (e.g. proposing, pledging, espousing); behabitives 'have to do with attitudes and *social behaviour*' (e.g. apologising, congratulating, condoling); and expositives 'make plain how our utterances fit into the course of an argument or conversation' (e.g. replying, conceding, illustrating).[86] According to Austin's taxonomy, 'blessing' would be a behabitive, a speech act that expresses 'the notion of reaction to other people's behaviour and fortunes and of attitudes and expressions of attitudes to someone else's past conduct or imminent conduct'.[87] To bless, in other words, is to morally approbate according to what Austin calls 'like conduct'; to be blessed is to commit oneself to conduct likely to receive such approbation. Leaving aside the mechanisms of social regulation built into this kind of linguistic performative, behabitives are all

---

86 Austin, *How to Do Things with Words*, pp. 150–1.
87 *Ibid.*, p. 159.

the more troublesome for Austin because they have 'a special scope for insincerity',[88] like the serial confessor who needs to be repeatedly blessed for his or her sins. As applied to the act of marriage, gay or otherwise, one begins to see, then, that behabitive utterances like blessings lack the requisite illocutionary force; their saying does not seem to be equal to their doing. So too with the more usual commissives, like 'I promise', which structure the marriage ceremony; the gap between the declaration of intention and the actual undertaking can be very wide indeed. That leaves expositives, a broad category of performative utterances that Austin admits is difficult to define, and that overlaps with the other groups, but that nevertheless includes a whole list of important verbs central to the acts of communication and argumentation themselves.

What would an expository queer wedding ceremony look like? Here we might look again to the example of religious performatives, and in particular to the 'public act of repentance' called for by the Church of England in a blistering 2005 report condemning the war in Iraq.[89] While repentance, in the sense of expressing regret or contrition, looks suspiciously like a behabitive, it also carries with it notions of correction, revision, repudiation, a resolve not to continue doing something. And it was just such a performative (dis)avowal that the Archbishop of Canterbury himself presided over when he conferred, in April 2005 at St George's Chapel in Windsor, a rite of blessing on the union of one of the queerest couples in all of England, namely the Prince of Wales and the Duchess of Cornwall. Charles and Camilla, having both committed acts of adultery during their previous marriages, first 'earnestly repented' these 'grievous' wrongdoings before pledging their troth to one another. The event was televised and it was a curious sight, to say the least, watching the future King of England abase himself like this in front of his solemn-faced mother, Queen Elizabeth, and hundreds of guests, although certainly no less humiliating than having to reschedule the proceedings as a result of the death of Pope John Paul II – or having to relocate the site of the civil marriage ceremony that preceded the blessing from Windsor Castle to the nearby Guildhall as a result of licensing problems. To be sure, the low-key media exposition that accompanied Charles and Camilla's exit from the Guildhall contrasted sharply with the frenzy of fans and paparazzi that greeted Elton John and his long-time Canadian boyfriend David Furnish when they formally registered their union at the same venue on 22 December 2005 following adoption

---

88 *Ibid.*, p. 159.
89 See Ruth Gledhill, 'Bishops want to apologise for Iraq war', *Timesonline* (19 September 2005), www.timesonline.co.uk/tol/news/uk/article568282 (accessed September 2007).

of the UK's Civil Partnership Act by parliament earlier that month. Even in England there's royalty and then there's royalty.

Now far be it from me to suggest, at the end of this chapter, that the public assent to the *rights* that come with marriage be structured around a *rite* of repentance – presumably for other social/sexual bonds that do not conform to marriage's monogamous model. Indeed, as I hope I have made clear, this is precisely what I am arguing against in terms of the politics of marriage as an institution. And on this I am quite sure Sir Elton would support me. But what if, for one moment, we also give poor lovesick Charles his due? What if we read the strange spectacle that was his second wedding as in part an attempt to wrest an institution more or less created by one of his royal forebears for the express purpose of annulling one marriage and consecrating another into the twenty-first century? After all, this is a man who, upon ascending to the throne, would prefer to be known, among other titles, as Defender of Faith rather than Defender of *the* Faith. Indeed, following the Church of England's own mixing of the martial and the spiritual throughout its volatile history, what if built into the performative structure of the wedding ceremony itself, one had to make the case for its legitimacy and felicity as one might have to make the case for war? This, as we have seen with a Bush-governed America, no less than with Tudor England, would not necessarily be any safeguard against (il)locutionary insincerity. But it might compel additional forethought as to the potential perlocutionary consequences.

3

Travels with Tony Kushner and David Beckham

History is always written from a sedentary point of view and in the name of a unitary State apparatus, at least a possible one, even when the topic is nomads. What is lacking is a Nomadology, the opposite of a history. (Gilles Deleuze and Félix Guattari[1])

[P]ublic becomes private becomes public. People who work in the theater, which is never pure, should be comfortable with this dialectical impurity, this seesaw mixing-up of spheres, this paradox. And it is a paradox: the personal is the political, and yet it is important, somehow, to maintain a distinction between the two. Which is to say that the personal and the political are the same, and aren't. (Tony Kushner[2])

It may be hard to remember amid the World Cup clamour, but the beauty of football, like other games, lies in its sublime pointlessness. It is an end in itself with no higher purpose. The paradox is that precisely because it is utterly trivial, sport becomes saturated with meanings. (Mike Marqusee[3])

The published version of Tony Kushner's *Homebody/Kabul* contains seven epigraphs.[4] In this chapter, I have only three. They outline the

---

1 Gilles Deleuze and Félix Guattari, *A Thousand Plateaus: Capitalism and Schizophrenia*, trans. Brian Massumi (Minneapolis: University of Minnesota Press, 1987), p. 23. Subsequent references will be cited parenthetically in the text as *TP*.
2 Tony Kushner, 'Notes about political theater', *Kenyon Review* 19:3–4 (1997), p. 21.
3 Mike Marqusee, 'Football's phoney war', *Guardian* (6 June 2002), p. 17.
4 See Tony Kushner, *Homebody/Kabul* (New York: Theatre Communications Group,

general parameters of this chapter and serve as a textual frame for the travelogue that follows. The word is chosen strategically; in what follows I use the personal narrative of a trip I took in the spring of 2002 to Europe with my partner, Richard, as the starting point for a political and performative analysis of some of the events we experienced while there, as well as for a reflection on how, in the years since, those events continue to resonate both globally and locally. The trip was initially conceived as a chance to meet up with old friends in London and to revisit with one of those friends, Cathy, some familiar haunts in Lombardy and the Veneto: thus the dramatis personae and the setting for our trip.

There was, as well, a play within this play (as theatrical history might lead us to expect). As an academic (one, moreover, who had only recently secured a tenure-track job), I was at that very moment just beginning to think past my current research project (on literature and film), wanting to focus – then only vaguely, I admit – on contemporary drama and performance studies as a way of making political sense of how the world had changed since 9/11 and, more immediately and locally, how my own place in that world had changed as well. In planning the trip, I thus had a secondary interest in scouting out with Richard and Cathy some of the theatre then playing in Europe, particularly Kushner's controversial new work, which, following its premiere in New York the previous fall, was due to open in London while we were there. Since publishing an earlier version of this chapter (in a special issue of *Theatre Journal* on 'Theorizing Globalization through Theatre'), I have discovered that scholars who work in cross-disciplines such as cultural studies and performance studies are not always comfortable with these dialectical impurities, with the mixing of the personal and the professional, the social and the scholarly, the theatrical and the touristic. And yet isn't this precisely the paradox we routinely wield in both our intellectual and physical peregrinations? Adepts of travel *and* theory, migration *and* mimesis, we have been taught to saturate all cultural and experiential phenomena, all performative spaces, with multiple meanings. Thus it is – as I hope to demonstrate more clearly by the end of this chapter – that I nominate a travelling theory of performance, and performative writing, as a way of intervening in and accounting for the places (material and imaginative) of connection and transformation between local bodies and global politics. And thus it is that I found myself sitting in the audience at London's Young Vic Theatre on 14 May

2002), pp. 7–8. Subsequent references, unless otherwise noted, are to this edition and will be cited parenthetically in the text as *H/K*.

2002 listening to Kushner's Homebody quote Frank Sinatra singing a
song by Sammy Cahn and Jimmy Van Heusen:

> It's very nice to go trav'ling
> To Paris, London and Rome.
> It's oh so nice to go trav'ling,
> But it's so much nicer yes it's so much nicer
> To come home. (*H/K*, p. 29)

What follows, then, is my attempt to (re)construct the nomadology of that moment. Drawing on the work of Gilles Deleuze and Félix
Guattari – particularly their suggestion in *A Thousand Plateaus* (1987)
that the nomadic rhizome functions as a space of negotiation between the
globally relative and the locally absolute claims of history – I juxtapose
the Homebody's gloss on the 'war machine' that is Afghanistan with my
own critical and representational responses to some of the political and
media performances engulfing Europe around the time of my viewing
of Kushner's play. Taking centre stage, in this regard, are the theatrics
accompanying the 2002 version of the planet's biggest sporting spectacle
after the Olympics, the World Cup of Football. It might seem like a critical stretch to place the franchising of David Beckham, or his apparently
carefree globetrotting ways, on par with what I suggest is the resistant
nomadism of Kushner's Homebody. However, the local and national
diasporas and quixotic kinship relations produced both by Beckham's
and his fellow players' routine migrations between teams, their mix of
fraternal and martial behaviours on the pitch, and the at times equally
fickle migration of fan loyalty and/or complete collapse of spectator
civility, suggests that a global regulatory body like FIFA has at best only a
partial understanding of how the game of football intersects with travelling concepts of place and audience to foster communities of sentiment
that do not easily respect fixed boundaries, either on or off the field.

Indeed, to the extent that Beckham's successive migrations since
2002 – from Manchester to Madrid to Los Angeles to Milan – seem to
be coextensive with his successive humiliations on football's world stage
(in Japan in 2002, Portugal in 2004, and Germany in 2006), and his
consequent attempts to reclaim a place on that stage (by being named to
the English team that heads to South Africa in 2010), we might say that
the fluctuating fortunes of the Beckham brand enact one of the most
important yet inadequately theorised paradoxes of globalisation, namely
the 'retribalisation' of the local.[5] In *How Soccer Explains the World*,

---

5 Although, as Richard likes to remind me, this dynamic interrelationship between the
   global and the local is precisely what Marshall McLuhan was getting at in coining the

Franklin Foer, editor of *New Republic*, has attempted to deal with some of the more vexatious local consequences of the sport's globalising tendencies (which he reads primarily in terms of an escalation in 'lunatic' fan behavior, 'local blood feuds, and even local corruption').[6] He does so by making a special plea for renewed attention to the 'discreet charm of bourgeois nationalism', arguing, for example, that the pride of place, language, and culture that helps establish a metonymy between a club like FC Barcelona and an intra-national region like Catalonia is sufficiently cosmopolitan to allow even non-Catalans with 'liberal politics and yuppie tastes' to find 'a corner of the soccer firmament that feels like home'.[7] However, I want to suggest that it is precisely Beckham's *homelessness* as a player that allows his various local audiences – those in Vancouver included – to come together across national (and other) differences in an approximation of deterritorialised 'unknowing' that might yet provide a starting point for a mutual rethinking of the global contests for power that have so far bedevilled this new (yet wearisomely familiar) century. It is in this context that I conclude this chapter by offering a few final comments on my migratory experience of a subsequent, and greatly revised, New York production of Kushner's play in 2004, as well as my attendance at a local staged reading benefiting Amnesty International and Vancouver's Firehall Theatre in 2008. In this way, I use my 'itinerant' witnessing of the Homebody's and daughter Priscilla's repeated journeys to Afghanistan, not to mention Mahala's equally determined flights from it, as a 'place' from which to evaluate my own evolving armchair relationship with the country since Canada first deployed combat troops to Kabul in the spring of 2002. That relationship, I contend, has been influenced as much by successive changes in national government in Canada as by the precarious but surprisingly tenacious leadership of Hamid Karzai in Afghanistan; as much by mounting Canadian casualties as by stories of detainee transfers that very likely resulted in torture; as much by re-watching with a class I was teaching in 2004 Moshen Makhamalbaf's searing docudrama *Kandahar* (about an Afghan-born Canadian journalist who returns to the Taliban-controlled region to search for her sister) as by re-experiencing the local roots and global routes of Vancouver's own peculiarly addictive relationship with Afghanistan through that final staged reading of *Homebody/Kabul* in 2008.

term 'global village'. See McLuhan and Quentin Fiore, *War and Peace in the Global Village* (New York: McGraw-Hill, 1968).

6 Franklin Foer, *How Soccer Explains the World: An (Unlikely) Theory of Globalization* (New York: HarperCollins, 2004), pp. 5 and *passim*.

7 *Ibid.*, p. 194.

In structure, methodology, and tone, the entire chapter attempts to enact the theory of 'as if' interconnectedness and nomadic becoming outlined by Rosi Braidotti in *Nomadic Subjects*, deterritorialising the different levels and locations of my own experiences as they flow into and merge with other sites of embodiment, performance, and knowledge production.[8] Following Braidotti, in the ensuing sections I adopt a 'theoretical style based on nomadism', crossing and mixing different disciplinary epistemes and speaking voices as 'a way of inscribing my work in a collective political [moment]'.[9] Thus, while the autobiographical reflections in the first section provide a point of entry into my discussion of Beckham's performance of a reflexive nomadism in global sporting culture, they provide a point of exit (quite literally) from my hermeneutics of close reading, as applied to Kushner's play, in section two. This in turn allows me, in section three, to remap, via a return to Vancouver and questions of the local, still more of the critical connections I see between Beckham's, the Homebody's, and my own different brands of nomadic consciousness. As such, the metatheatrical, theme-and-variations movement of the chapter – what Deleuze and Guattari refer to as the nomadic 'intermezzo' (*TP*, p. 381) – also aims, in the words of Braidotti, to construct 'reading positions outside or beyond the traditional intellectual ones. In this process I hope to be constructing my potential readers as nomadic entities as well'.[10]

Act 1: Venice and Milan

If one consequence of globalisation is an increased flow of financial capital, then another is an increased flow of human capital. While large-scale migrations of peoples have always been a part of world history,[11] in today's globalised age both the patterns of and reasons for migration have changed. Middle- and upper-class religious, environmental, and war and terrorism refugees from Africa, Southeast Asia, Eastern Europe, the Middle East, and Latin America have joined the traditional migratory poor and ethnic and sexual minorities from these same regions in seeking supposed asylum in the so-called advanced capitalist and demo-

---

8 See Rosi Braidotti, *Nomadic Subjects: Embodiment and Sexual Difference in Contemporary Feminist Theory* (New York: Columbia University Press, 1994), especially pp. 5–8.

9 *Ibid.*, pp. 36 and 37.

10 *Ibid.*, p. 38.

11 See Wang Gungwu, 'Migration history: some patterns revisited', in Wang Gungwu (ed.), *Global History and Migrations* (Boulder: Westview, 1997), pp. 1–22; and Robin Cohen, 'Diasporas, the nation-state, and globalisation', in Wang (ed.), *Global History and Migrations*, pp. 117–44.

cratic nations of Western Europe, North America, Australia, Japan, and elsewhere. The addition of economic and 'disaster' refugees from within and between these latter regions has made for fierce competition between immigrants for both jobs and political and social favour among their host countries' citizens.[12] This was brought home to me (so to speak) most viscerally in Venice. Just off the Piazza San Marco or in front of the Accademia Bridge I nightly saw groups of North African, Russian *and* Southern Italian men competing to sell Louis Vuitton and Chanel knock-offs to tourists. Later I'd hear the hostess at the *osteria* we liked to frequent denounce all three groups with equally phobic fervour.

In Italy we spent a lot of time in restaurants in order to escape the rain. The worst in twenty years, we were routinely told by the locals, and we believed them. The night we flew into Milan the Po had overflowed, a foretaste of the flooding and displacement that was to affect so much of Eastern Europe that spring. At the time, however, I could only marvel to my Italian Canadian boyfriend at the extraordinary inefficiency with which his compatriots loaded a shuttle bus. Fortunately, we attached ourselves to a Japanese couple who looked like they knew what they were doing. We followed their gigantic Samsonite suitcases assiduously; this strategy eventually paid off in a shared cab ride from Milan's Stazione Centrale to the *locanda* where it turned out we were all staying. This happy coincidence was discovered in a typically intercultural moment, with Richard speaking Italian to the cab driver, the Japanese couple speaking even better Italian to the cab driver, who then astounded us all by speaking Japanese back to them. I kept silent. When, passing the Pirelli Building, the cab driver mimed a plane flying into the side of it, and pointed out the hole it had left behind, it was at last a language I could understand.

Another truism of current thinking regarding globalisation, that transnational social movements – including the physical movement of peoples – have created a hybridised culture that has sounded the death-knell of the individual nation-state as a political entity,[13] perhaps is in need of reconsideration (and by someone far more nuanced in their thinking than Franklin Foer). This need is especially urgent in the wake of 9/11. At every turn on that same trip to Europe we seemed to be witnessing not the waning of nationalism but its forceful, vengeful, and xenophobic rearticulation: in the National Front victories in local

---

12 See James H. Mittelman, *The Globalization Syndrome: Transformation and Resistance* (Princeton: Princeton University Press, 2000), p. 58.
13 See Cohen, 'Diasporas, the nation-state, and globalisation', p. 135.

elections in northern England; in Jean-Marie Le Pen's presidential run in France; in the rhetoric that swirled around the aftermath of Pim Fortuyn's assassination in Holland; in the debates in the press about which countries (including Canada) would agree to take in the thirteen remaining Palestinian hostage-takers from the siege of the Church of the Nativity in Bethlehem. For us, nowhere were Europe's divided loyalties more forcefully played out than in the plethora of media stories about the impending World Cup that steadily accrued throughout the course of the trip. No matter the publication or language, the story was always the same: over their baguette or brioche or bangers or bratwurst, men and women from all over Europe hotly contested the fact that their nation's World Cup aspirations often hinged on a star striker from elsewhere.

As Joseph Maguire and Robert Pearton have argued, 'Elite labour migration is now an established feature of the sporting "global village"'.[14] This phenomenon is perhaps nowhere more evident than in what we in North America call soccer, but which everyone else in the world calls football. Thus, in the lead-up to the 2002 World Cup, we heard much about the Nigerian phenom (Emmanuel Olisadebe) who was playing for Poland; Japan's fleet-footed Brazilian import (Alessandro dos Santos); the so-called divided loyalties of English coach Sven-Göran Eriksson (a Swedish national); Cameroon's coach Winfried Schafer (from Germany); and Japanese coach Philippe Troussier (a Frenchman). For some commentators writing in the European press in advance of the event's kickoff, this was a sign of football's 'benign' globalism, with the World Cup 'as important as the United Nations in promoting international understanding'.[15] Never mind that as one consequence of this 'international understanding' Japan was preparing to defend its shores and citizenry against an anticipated influx of barbaric hordes of English football hooligans.[16]

Other pundits looked forward theatrically to what they saw as the almost certain 'battles between professionalism and patriotism [that would] provide an intriguing sideshow' to the matches themselves.[17] As,

14 Joseph Maguire and Robert Pearton, 'Global sport and the migration patterns of France '98 World Cup finals players: some preliminary observations', in Jon Garland et al. (eds), The Future of Football: Challenges for the Twenty-First Century (London: Frank Cass, 2000), p. 175. See also Maguire, Global Sport: Identities, Societies, Civilizations (Oxford: Polity, 1999).

15 'Football is so much more than just a game', Independent (1 June 2002), p. 20.

16 See Michael Sheridan, 'Japan on red alert for the barbarians from England', The Times (3 February 2002).

17 Bill Edgar, 'Cameroon coach confronts conflict of loyalties', The Times (5 March 2002).

indeed, they proved to be. Thus, while Japan and South Korea's unique cohosting duties were being trumpeted as auguring a new era of 'Asian détente' for the region,[18] as both countries' teams progressed through their respective round-robin play, with Japan making it to the round of sixteen and Korea all the way to the semifinals, the gloves eventually came off. Old enmities were played up in the press, with South Korea being accused of match fixing and referee bias, and many wishing that Japan could have gone it alone in hosting the event.[19] But even this took a back seat to the frenzy of anticipation around the second-round meeting between bitter rivals Argentina and England in Sapporo. Not only did Beckham's winning penalty kick allow him the chance to relive and redeem his personal humiliation at being ejected from the match against Argentina four years earlier, it also allowed all of England a chance to re-fight – and win all over again – the Falklands War.[20]

Writing in the *Guardian* the day before the much-heralded England–Argentina rematch, Mike Marqusee argues that '[s]ports patriotism is often misleadingly described as "tribal". In the age of globalisation, it is less rooted and more malleable than that. Whether paroxysmic and febrile, or laid-back and ironic, it remains curiously hollow and . . . can easily be turned against imagined national enemies, within and without'.[21] However, there is one place in football (as in most organised sport, including the Olympics) where the virtues of a borderless world are regularly trumpeted: corporate sponsorship. Coca-Cola, for example, covered its assets nicely by backing both England and Argentina at the 2002 World Cup.[22] The market imperative was also very much on display in FIFA president Sepp Blatter's fight to secure re-election amid a bribery and corruption scandal that made the International Olympic Committee look like choirboys. In the same way that western democratic powers routinely threaten rogue states with economic sanctions unless they clean up their acts, major sponsors were threatening to pull out of the 2006 World Cup in Germany unless Blatter stopped treating FIFA as his own personal fiefdom.[23]

18 See John Gitting and Jonathan Watts, 'World Cup scores for Asian detente', *Guardian* (26 March 2002), p. 15; and Doug Struck, 'Japan, S. Korea: World Cup's strange bedfellows', *Washington Post* (28 April 2002), p. D01.

19 See Richard Pendlebury, 'Conspiracy theory in the land of the bribing sons', *Daily Mail* (25 June 2002), p. 64.

20 See Ian Cobain, 'We sang, screamed, sighed, then we celebrated as one', *The Times* (8 June 2002).

21 Marqusee, 'Football's phoney war', p. 17.

22 *Ibid.*

23 See Erskine McCullough, '"Blattergate" throws World Cup future in doubt', *Agence France Presse* (9 May 2002).

However, in European football the potential conflicts between tribal nationalisms and global economics, between players' various competing affiliations and fans' equally mercurial franchise loyalties, are further complicated by another more localised site of sporting imagination and cultural contestation. As the bidding war between Real Madrid and bitter rival Barcelona escalated during the summer of 2003 to sign Manchester United's most famous (and most costly) superstar, the global sporting community witnessed the city emerge (as it would four years later when he was signed by the LA Galaxy) as the most imme-diate and manifest locus for the production and circulation of what Michel Foucault would call 'bio-power in its many forms and modes of application'.[24] That is, the globe-trotting Beckham – on a product-placement tour of Asia at the time his trade was announced – suddenly found his subject-body, so used to transcending national borders, being disciplined, regulated, administered, and managed at a very metropoli-tan level, as he was ordered to report to Real Madrid's headquarters by the first week of July for a medical.[25] At the same time, alongside fellow travellers Zinedine Zidane, Ronaldo, Luis Figo, and Raul, Beckham's occupation, re-invention, and transformation of the urban centre of Madrid (if only for the duration of the Champions League's regulation season) must also simultaneously serve as an instructive lesson in global citizenship and/as spectatorship.

But I'm getting ahead of myself here. At the time of our trip, the English team was just preparing to decamp for Dubai for climate-specific training, and media reports (when they weren't focusing on his new haircut) were fretting over the status of Beckham's heavily taped foot. Meanwhile, the French press had conscripted the globalised face of football for much more urgent political ends. In the lead-up to Le Pen's presidential runoff with Chirac, members of France's defending World Cup Championship team, including Ghana-born captain Marcel Desailly and 1998 hero Zinedine Zidane, whose father is Algerian, urged voters to turn out en masse and vote against Le Pen. It was a powerful indictment of the National Front leader's racist policies and an embar-rassing reminder of remarks he had made four years earlier in criticis-ing France's football team, because many players were immigrants and apparently couldn't even sing the *Marseillaise* (thereby putting a public – and expressly political – spin on the general undercurrent of racism that

---

24 Michel Foucault, *The History of Sexuality, Volume One: An Introduction*, trans. Robert Hurley (New York: Vintage, 1990), p. 141.

25 Beckham offers an account of this in the introduction to his autobiography (written with Tom Watt), *Beckham: Both Feet on the Ground* (New York: HarperCollins, 2003), pp. 1–15.

pervades the football world, from players to fans to commentators).[26] Several days after Le Pen made these remarks in 1998, France beat Brazil 3–0 in the final; Zidane, who scored two of the winning goals, had his picture projected on the Arc de Triomphe under text that read variously 'Merci Zizou', 'La victoire est en nous', and 'Zidane President', which seemed to signal for the country a moment of multiracial harmony.[27] The extent to which Zidane, since that moment, has been conscripted as football's default face of global political resistance – much in the same way that former Real Madrid teammate Beckham has become a symbolic extension of the game's corporate capitalist reach – can be seen in an extraordinary image from the assemblage of news stories that make up the 'halftime sequence' of Douglas Gordon and Philippe Pareno's recent *Zidane, un portrait du 21e siècle*. A combination art film and sports documentary that premiered at Cannes in May 2006, and that uses some seventeen cameras to track Zidane (and only Zidane) in real time throughout the course of a 23 April 2005 match between Real Madrid and Villereal, Gordon and Pareno's celluloid portrait is simultaneously mesmerising and enervating, not least as a result of one haunting still image that briefly arrests the montage of same-day newsreel footage from around the world spliced in between the game's two halves. In it we see a young Iraqi boy, back turned toward the camera, wearing a black (that is, away) Zidane jersey, and making his way through what the subtitles tell us is the chaos and carnage that attended an escalation in anti-occupation violence following a car bombing in Najaf that killed nine people. A twenty-first-century portrait, indeed.

The fine line between heroic resistance and violent provocation that Gordon and Pareno set up with their juxtaposition of Zidane's intense and embodied involvement in the localised events on the field and his simultaneous prosthetic involvement in world events off the field makes all the more compelling the film's shocking denouement. In it we witness Zidane being unceremoniously ejected from the game after throwing a punch during a minor fracas between the two teams. An uncannily prescient rehearsal of the famous head butt launched at Italian player Marco Materazzi in the final minutes of regulation play during the 2006 World Cup championship match, Zidane's open displays of brutality in a sport saturated with the gamesmanship of faked fouls and feigned

26 See Jon Garland and Michael Rowe, *Racism and Anti-Racism in Football* (New York: Palgrave, 2001); and Richie Moran, 'Racism in football: a victim's perspective', in Garland *et al.* (eds), *The Future of Football*, pp. 190–200.
27 See Lisa Marlowe, 'Le Pen and French soccer hero clash in war of words', *Irish Times* (1 May 2002), p. 1; and Peter Wilson, 'World Cup champs urge voters to deliver Le Pen the red card', *Australian* (30 April 2002), p. 6.

injuries makes a martial reading of such contests almost unavoidable. Perhaps it was only fitting, then, that in between the glory of Zidane's and France's victories in the 1998 World Cup and the ignominy of their respective exits in 2006, they should lose their first-round match during the 2002 World Cup to the unevenly matched team from one of France's former African colonies, Senegal. A historic past was running up against a nomadic present.

Act 2: London and Kabul

In terms of my own nomadic present in London in May 2002, it was not an image of David Beckham kitted out for the globalised football pitch that I took with me into the Young Vic Theatre the night I saw Kushner's *Homebody/Kabul*, but rather one of him in a sarong. This was because earlier that afternoon Richard, Cathy, and I had attended the 'Men in Skirts' exhibition at the Victoria and Albert Museum, which featured the Jean Paul Gaultier-designed silk sarong that Beckham wore as a signifier of his confident metrosexuality during the 1998 World Cup. Beckham's nomadic fashion sense, in which his exportable celebrity image within the global marketplace (particularly in Asia) allows him to import and appropriate emblems of the orientalist and feminine other through mechanisms of aesthetic adornment and commodity fetishism, is a reminder of the Homebody's assimilation as an other in Kushner's play. More pertinently, her apparent decision to go native, disappearing underneath a burqa and settling placidly into her new role as dutiful Muslim wife, is first preceded by her exoticisation of the other – via her description and eventual display of the ten 'fezlike pillboxy attenuated yarmulkite' hats purchased from a 'Third World junk shop' in London to add 'something catalytic, some fizz' to a party for her husband (*H/K*, pp. 16, 17, and 15). Here, I draw on a brilliant article by Framji Minwalla, who argues that the Homebody's 'allegory of the hats' is paradigmatic of a tension that exists between two kinds of history being staged in Kushner's play: one in which the Homebody is positioned, as a result of the 'outdated guidebook about the city of Kabul' from which she quotes at length (*H/K*, p. 9), as an 'indiscreet observer' of the imperialist and 'picturesque' history of Afghanistan; and one in which she is 'interpellated', through her encounter with the Afghan merchant who sells her the hats, as 'a post-colonial subject' in her own right.[28] Although Minwalla's reading restricts itself to the Homebody's opening

---

28 See Framji Minwalla, 'Tony Kushner's *Homebody/Kabul*: staging history in a post-colonial world', *Theater* 33:1 (2003), pp. 31–3 and 40.

monologue, his nuanced observations on the many paradoxes operating therein – not least its apparent twinning of narratives of cultural tourism and political engagement – overlap with my own take on the play in many ways. Moreover, the issues raised by Minwalla in his article are a sobering reminder that – theories of nomadism notwithstanding – what most connects my autobiographical musings on David Beckham in the previous section with the scholarly dissection of Kushner's play that I am about to undertake here is that both were occasioned by my occupation, first and foremost, of the roles of cultural tourist and cultural consumer. Thus, this chapter, however localised I attempt to make it, cannot help but reproduce the rhetoric of a globalised (and globalist) souvenir narrative.

Extraordinarily perspicacious, fiercely intelligent, and thrillingly verbose, *Homebody/Kabul* explores, among other things, contradictions and confrontations between the local and the global, the past and the present, the personal and the political, history and nomadology. The play first began life as an hour-long monologue commissioned by the actress Kika Markham (see figure 13) and London's Chelsea Theatre Centre in 1997. In this early version, an unnamed, middle-aged, upper-middle-class British woman too much in love with both the world and with words, an armchair traveller whose 'borders have only ever been broached by books' (*H/K*, p. 12), reads from the aforementioned

13 Kika Markham as the Homebody in the Cheek by Jowl production of *Homebody/Kabul* at the Young Vic, London, May 2002

guidebook to Kabul. She slowly describes the process of empathic connection – what she calls 'touch' – she achieves with an Afghani hat salesman in London, an encounter with her postcolonial other that eventually propels her to leave the safety of her comfortable kitchen, 'her culpable shore' (*H/K*, p. 27), and join 'the drowning' (*H/K*, p. 28) of Afghanistan's 'awful Present' (*H/K*, p. 11). However, between the summer of 1999 and the summer of 2001, Kushner added several more characters and two more entire acts to the play. In them we discover how, in the wake of the Homebody's sudden and precipitous journey to Afghanistan, her bewildered husband, Milton Ceiling, and her angry daughter, Priscilla, have followed. As they struggle to discover whether or not the Homebody is in fact dead, as the Taliban government claims, Milton and Priscilla cross the paths of, occasionally tangle with, and are forever changed by, several individuals who together encapsulate the paradoxes of Kabul: what it once was, what it has become, and what it has always been (see figure 14). Khwaja Aziz Mondanabosh, a Tajik Afghan man who serves as Priscilla's guide and interpreter, agrees to help her find her missing mother in exchange for Priscilla's transporting back to London several poems he has written in Esperanto. Quango Twistleton is a British aid worker and government liaison officer who shows Milton how to heal his broken heart through heroin. Mahala is a Pashtun Afghan woman

14 Left to right: Jacqueline Defferary (Priscilla), Silas Carson (Zai Garshi), and Nadim Sawalha (Khwaja) in the Cheek by Jowl production of *Homebody/Kabul* at the Young Vic, London, May 2002

and former librarian unable to work under the Taliban who pleads with the Ceilings to help her immigrate to England. Finally, Mullah Aftar Ali Durranni is the very real face of Taliban authority, advising Milton and Priscilla to return to London as quickly as possible early in the play, only to return at the end just as they are about to leave, accusing Priscilla of smuggling coded documents destined for the Northern Alliance in the form of Khwaja's poems, and threatening to shoot Mahala in retaliation.

Written before 9/11, this version of the play has, since that time, had a fascinatingly nomadic production itinerary. It opened at the New York Theatre Workshop on 19 December 2001, just three months after the collapse of the World Trade Center, in a production directed by Declan Donnellan and designed by Nick Ormerod (see chapter 2), featuring Linda Emond in the pivotal role of the Homebody. Donnellan and Ormerod also oversaw the production I attended at London's Young Vic in May 2002, with Kika Markham once again in the title role. Throughout 2002, with the West suddenly clamoring for informa- tion about Afghanistan and its complicated political history, Kushner's play became one of the most produced in the United States, starting with Oskar Eustis's Trinity Rep production in March of that year. Over the course of this period, Kushner, despite having already published a version, continued to revise and rework the play. This resulted in an acclaimed co-production by Chicago's Steppenwolf Theatre Company and Los Angeles' Mark Taper Forum in the summer and fall of 2003, under the direction of Frank Galati. Capitalising, it would seem, on Kushner's success with the HBO television adaptation of *Angels in America*, and the off-Broadway premiere and subsequent Broadway transfer of his first musical, *Caroline, or Change*, this revised version of the play opened at the Brooklyn Academy of Music (BAM) in May 2004, with several members of the original New York production – including Linda Emond as the Homebody – reprising their roles. Thus, as with any discussion of the globe-trotting Beckham, who in early 2004 was himself jetting back and forth between Madrid and London in a desperate bid to save his marriage, a critical analysis of Kushner's play must remain in flux, adopting its own nomadic perspective. Nevertheless, while I will have occasion to comment on the BAM production and the revised text at the end of this chapter, as I hope to demonstrate in what follows, my reading of *Homebody/Kabul* crucially corresponds to the original loca- tion of my own itinerant viewing of it.

The play's 'timeliness' and 'prescience' (two words used repeatedly in reviews) stem not so much from Kushner's definitive explanation of 'The Source' of Afghan/Anglo-American relations – what Deleuze and Guattari deride in *A Thousand Plateaus* as 'arbolic' thinking – as from an examination, in the words of the Homebody, of 'all that which was dropped by the wayside on the way to The Source' (*H/K*, p. 9). For example, the lines that Mahala screams in act two, scene six – 'You love the Taliban so much, bring them to New York! Well, don't worry, they're coming to New York!' (*H/K*, p. 83) – and that virtually every review published since the play's opening has dutifully quoted, are part of a much larger peroration. She locates the United States' complex (and at one point CIA-funded) relationship with the Taliban not simply in the latter regime's willingness to serve as a bulwark against the Soviet Union in the dying days of the Cold War, but even more importantly, in the US's need for compliance from Afghanistan – and Pakistan – over a proposed oil pipeline from the Persian Gulf that cannot go through Iran. (Just as it cannot, for obvious reasons, go through Iraq, which is why the United States has to continue to tread carefully in its relations with Saudi Arabia, Jordan, Syria, and perhaps most importantly, Turkey.) As the Homebody suggests throughout the course of her monologue, sooner or later most everyone and most everything passes through the Hindu Kush. And, like the Homebody's gloss on the guidebook she reads, the history lesson offered by Kushner in this play proceeds '[e]lliptically. Discursively' (*H/K*, p. 12). Nomadically. In this, *Homebody/Kabul* continues the 'Great Work' begun by the playwright in *Angels in America*.[29]

The connections between the two plays are multiple and manifold, not least in their epic and dialectical approach to dramatising both the global and local histories of our awful present, of which AIDS and Afghanistan serve as Brechtian metonyms, iterable 'interruptions' that, rather than standing in supercessional place of, instead 'quote' intercessionally from historical incidents and lived lives, in order that they might be examined critically. Here, Kushner is, as several critics have noted, very much a student of Bertolt Brecht and of Brecht's great interpreter, Walter Benjamin.[30] In *Angels in America*, the storm 'blowing

29 Tony Kushner, *Angels in America, Part One: Millennium Approaches* (New York: Theatre Communications Group, 1993), p. 119.
30 Kushner himself acknowledges his debt to both men in the Afterword to *Perestroika*, 'With a little help from my friends', in *Angels in America, Part Two: Perestroika* (New York: Theatre Communications Group, 1994), pp. 149–58. On 'interruption', 'quotation', and 'historicisation' in epic theatre, see Bertolt Brecht, 'Short description of a new technique of acting which produces an alienation effect', in *Brecht on Theatre: The Development of an Aesthetic*, ed. and trans. John Willett (London: Methuen, 1964), pp. 136–47; and Walter Benjamin, 'What is epic theater?', in *Illuminations*, ed. Hannah Arendt, trans. Harry Zohn (New York: Schoken, 1968), pp. 147–54.

from Paradise'[31] finds its visual corollary in a Heaven designed to look like San Francisco after the 1906 earthquake and fire.[32] It's a space which Prior Walter, infected with the AIDS virus but very much wanting to live, is anxious to flee; it's also a space, at least in its contemporary earthly manifestation, towards which Harper Pitt – who shares with the Homebody a wildly empathic imagination, as well as a healthy appetite for barbituates and an acute case of agoraphobia tempered by a sudden urge for travel – consciously makes her way at the end of the play.[33] Harper could not have known then (February 1986, according to the play's chronology) what awaited her at the other end of her journey, the 1989 San Francisco earthquake in many ways as devastating to the city psychologically as its 1906 predecessor – just as the Homebody could not have known that her precipitous departure for Kabul would coincide with the American government's August 1998 resumption of bombings in the region in response to attacks on its embassies in Nairobi and Dar es Salaam. Instead, both of these unlikely nomads fly obliviously – but no less bravely – into the eye of the storm. "'The dust of Kabul's blowing soil smarts lightly in my eyes"', recites the Homebody at the end of her monologue, quoting from the seventeenth-century Persian poet Sa'ib-I-Tabrizi,

> But I love her; for knowledge and love both come from her dust.
> [...]
> I sing to the gardens of Kabul;
> Even Paradise is jealous of their greenery. (*H/K*, p. 30)

These are the last words spoken by the Homebody; she then walks off the stage and, in some senses, out of the play altogether. In Donnellan and Ormerod's staging of the play at the Young Vic, the shock of the Homebody's sudden exit after sixty minutes of enthralling verbal pyrotechnics was accompanied by a simple yet equally thrilling bit of design magic: the lush mauve fabric that had up until this point been covering the raised thrust stage was suddenly retracted inward through a hole in the stage, revealing the bare, unfinished plywood beneath. We had been transported, in a single swift stroke, to the dusty streets of Kabul.

As discussed in the last chapter, Donnellan and Ormerod are the husband-and-husband director/designer team who serve as co-artistic directors of Cheek by Jowl Theatre Company. The two men followed up the critical success of their 1991 all-male production of *As You Like It*

31 Benjamin, 'Theses on the philosophy of history', in Arendt (ed.), *Illuminations*, p. 258.
32 Kushner, *Angels in America, Part Two: Perestroika*, pp. 50–1 and 122.
33 *Ibid.*, p. 144.

by staging the British premiere of Kushner's *Angels in America* in 1992 and 1993 at the National Theatre. As Art Borreca asserts, that production seemed to reveal an intuitive understanding on the part of both director and designer of the Brechtian/Benjaminian dialectics at work in Kushner's play.[34] In the staging of *Homebody/Kabul*, playwright, director, and designer appeared to be on a similar dramaturgical wavelength. This time, however, everyone seems to have been reading Deleuze and Guattari's theories of nomadology.

Like Beckham's deterritorialised soccer pitch, both the form and content of Kushner's play are rhizomatic, an 'assemblage' of 'muliplicities', to use Deleuze and Guattari's terminology, in which there are no fixed 'points or positions', only multidimensional – and multidirectional – 'lines of flight', each laid out on a single 'exteriorized' plane: 'lived events, historical determinations, concepts, individuals, groups, social formations' (*TP*, pp. 8 and 9). The Homebody's opening monologue is paradigmatic; while, as Minwalla rightly argues, the Homebody's reading from her guidebook follows a fairly linear, positivist-historicist trajectory,[35] her tale about buying the party hats is for the most part composed of 'nomadic thoughts' that are 'anti-genealogical' (*TP*, p. 21) in the extreme. These thoughts erupt from and interrupt her narrative, a result of her desire to summon up for us in her 'salt-wounded mind's eye' (*H/K*, p. 17) 'every animate and inanimate thing, corporeal or incorporeal, actual or ideational, real or imagined, every, every discrete unit of . . . of *being*' (*H/K*, p. 10; ellipsis in original), a process which she herself admits exceeds her 'capacity for syncresis – is that a word? – straying rather into synchisis, which is a word' (*H/K*, p. 12): 'I . . . seem forever to be imploding and collapsing and am incapable it would seem of lending even this simple tale to the Universal Drift, of telling this simple tale without supersaturating my narrative with maddeningly infuriating or more probably irritating synchitic expegeses. Synchitic expegeses. Jesus' (*H/K*, p. 14). Nowhere are the multiple lines of flight in the Homebody's thinking more apparent – 'more detachable, connectable, reversible, modifiable' (*TP*, p. 21) – than in what she imagines to be the hat merchant's response to her query about the missing fingers on his right hand:

34 Art Borecca, '"Dramaturging" the dialectic: Brecht, Benjamin, and Declan Donnellan's production of *Angels in America*', in Deborah R. Geis and Steven F. Kruger (eds), *Approaching the Millennium: Essays on* Angels in America (Ann Arbor: University of Michigan Press, 1997), pp. 252–4. On *Homebody/Kabul* as a similar Benjaminian allegory of 'cultural and political apocalypse', see M. Scott Phillips, 'The failure of history: Kushner's *Homebody/Kabul* and the apocalyptic context', *Modern Drama* 47:1 (2004), pp. 1–20.

35 See Minwalla, 'Tony Kushner', pp. 30ff.

I was with the Mujahideen, and the Russians did this. I was with the Mujahideen, and an enemy faction of Mujahideen did this. I was with the Russians, I was known to have assisted the Russians, I did informer's work for Babrak Karmal, my name is in the files if they haven't been destroyed, the names I gave are in the files, there are no more files, I stole bread for my starving family, I stole bread *from* a starving family, I profaned, betrayed, according to some stricture I erred and they chopped off the fingers of my hand. (*H/K*, p. 23)

Earlier in her monologue, the Homebody describes how, when she had first caught sight of the merchant's ruined right hand as he accepted her credit card to process payment for the hats, she had recoiled from it, retreating from this immediate and proximate bodily imprinting of Afghanistan's history to the safely retrospective and relatively empirical compendium of so-called facts she has culled from her dry and dusty tomes: 'I know nothing of this hand, its history, of course, nothing. I did know, well I have learnt since through research that Kabul [. . .] was it was claimed by the Moghul Emperor Babur founded by none other than Cain himself. Biblical Cain' (*H/K*, p. 21). Indeed, this episode culminates in the Homebody's reading from her guidebook for the last time, relating the birth of 'modern Afghanistan' under the coalitionary leadership of Ahmed Shah Durrani, before adumbrating successive post-eighteenth-century invasions of the country by the British and the Russians, leading to the rise of both the Mujahideen and the Taliban (see figure 15). But the Afghan hat merchant's own tale, the Homebody soon realises, remains unassimilable within such a narrative. Indeed, it remains defiantly apposite to it (as its appearance on the facing page in the published playtext brilliantly illustrates), forcing the Homebody to revise her previous conceptions about the simultaneously 'sad' and 'marvelous' dislocations of global history (*H/K*, p. 18), and how those dislocations reterritorialise the local. If one cannot adequately explain, in a linear, cause-and-effect manner, the history of a single ruined hand, how can one hope to account for the history of an entire ruined city, country, continent, globe? The Afghan hat merchant, speaking through the Homebody, continues, issuing a direct challenge to his medium:

Look, look at my country, look at my Kabul, my city, what is left of my city? . . . only God can save us now, only order can save us now, only God's Law harsh and strictly administered can save us now, . . . save us from God, from war, from exile, from oil exploration, from no oil exploration, from the West, from children with rifles, carrying stones, only children with rifles, carrying stones, can save us now. You will never understand. It is hard, it was hard work to get into the U.K. I am happy here in the U.K. I am terrified I will be made to leave the U.K. I cannot wait to leave the U.K. I despise the U.K. I voted for

15 Linda Emond as the Homebody in the Steppenwolf/Mark Taper Forum production of *Homebody/Kabul* at the Brooklyn Academy of Music, May 2004

John Major. I voted for Tony Blair. I did not, I cannot vote, I do not believe in voting, the people who ruined my hand were right to do so, they were wrong to do so, my hand is most certainly ruined, *you will never understand*, why are you buying so many hats? (*H/K*, pp. 23–4; italics in original)

After this, there is no chance of the Homebody returning to her guidebook. Rather, after some literal wringing of her own hands and worrying about 'degrees of culpability' versus 'degrees of action', of the difference that 'agglutinates between Might and Do' (*H/K*, p. 24), she describes for us how she accepts the offer of the hat merchant's outstretched right hand, holding on tightly as he magically leads her through a parted curtain and on a guided tour of Kabul, eventually letting him touch her in the most intimate of places: 'We kiss, his breath is very bitter, he places his hand inside me, it seems to me his whole hand inside me, and it seems to me a whole hand' (*H/K*, p. 26). With what Minwalla describes as her literal internalisation of the other,[36] the Homebody completes her own process of 'supercessional displacement' (*H/K*, p. 27), of nomadic transformation. Significantly, as with Beckham's surprisingly affecting and deterritorialised conclusion to his autobiography – sitting in a hotel room in Thailand watching on television his new team playing several time zones away, he refers to himself as 'a boy from Chingford, England. United born and bred. And going to play for Real Madrid'[37] – this transformation is narrated in the third person: 'Where stands the Homebody, safe in her kitchen, on her culpable shore, suffering uselessly watching others perishing in the sea . . . Never *joining* the drowning. Her feet, neither rooted nor moving. The ocean is deep and cold and erasing. But how dreadful, really unpardonable, to remain dry' (*H/K*, pp. 27–8).

Deleuze and Guattari argue that '[a] rhizome has no beginning or end; it is always in the middle, between things . . . *Between* things does not designate a localizable relation going from one thing to the other and back again, but a perpendicular direction, a transversal movement that sweeps one *and* the other away, a stream without beginning or end that undermines its banks and picks up speed in the middle' (*TP*, p. 25). This description applies not only to the speech from the Afghan hat merchant that I have just quoted, but arguably to the Homebody's entire 'schizoanalysis'[38] of Afghanistan's – and her own – many paradoxes.

36 *Ibid.*, p. 40.
37 Beckham, *Both Feet*, p. 366.
38 'Schizoanalysis' is the term developed by Deleuze and Guattari in *Anti-Oedipus*, the companion volume to *A Thousand Plateaus*, to describe the process by which Freudian psychoanalysis, with its focus on the neurotic ego and the unconscious as the locus of repressed desire, is deterritorialised, liberating individual desires and mobilising their flow into a collective subjectivity (the 'desiring-machine') that makes a revolutionary politics possible; see Deleuze and Guattari, *Anti-Oedipus: Capitalism and Schizophrenia*, trans. Robert Hurley, Mark Seem, and Helen R. Lane (Minneapolis: University of Minnesota Press, 1983), pp. 296ff. In *A Thousand Plateaus*, 'schizoanalysis' is used as a synonym for nomadic thought.

And, just as arguably, it can be applied to the structure of Kushner's play, which steadily picks up speed in its middle scenes, documenting, with increasing urgency, what happens when the deterritorialising and nomadic tendencies of both the 'desiring machine' (what Deleuze and Guattari here and elsewhere refer to as the 'body without organs' [*TP*, p. 4]) and the 'war machine' (what, in a Foucauldian reading of Deleuze and Guattari, we might call power without government)[39] come up against the reterritorialising impulses of the state. Nowhere is this more apparent than in the operations of language and other systems of communication in the play. For Rosi Braidotti, the polyglot is the nomad par excellence, someone who 'knows that language is not only and not even the instrument of communication but a site of symbolic exchange that links us together in a tenuous and yet workable web of mediated misunderstandings, which we call civilization'.[40]

Thus, not only does the Homebody magically find herself able to communicate with the Afghan hat merchant in fluent Pushto, but Khwaja, who speaks Dari, Pashtun, and English, chooses to write his love poems in Esperanto because, as he tells Priscilla, 'It is a language that has no history, and hence no history of oppression' (*H/K*, p. 65). Having learned the language while in prison following the military coup against the democratically elected People's Democratic Party of Afghanistan (PDPA) in 1978 that preceded the Soviet invasion of Afghanistan, when a common 'international language, spoken in every country on earth' still looked like a marvelous possibility, Khwaja continues to write in Esperanto because he finds he has 'an ear for its particular staccato music [. . .]. I love its modern hyperrational ungainliness. To me it sounds not universally at home, rather homeless, stateless, a global refugee patois' (*H/K*, p. 67). But to Mullah Durranni and the Taliban government, Khwaja's attempts at Deleuzean 'decoding', his hymns to a world free from hierarchy and opposition, look suspiciously like secret plans to attack and attempt to dismantle the state. 'These papers are not of poems but Tajik informations for Rabbani and Massoud', he tells a frightened Priscilla, Milton, and Mahala at the climax of the play. 'Placements of weapons and this' (*H/K*, p. 130).

Just prior to this scene, while waiting for Priscilla to emerge from

---

39 In their 'Treatise on nomadology', Deleuze and Guattari take great pains to distinguish the war machine, which they admit in its 'pure form of exteriority' 'remains difficult to conceptualize', from the 'magic violence of the State', especially as that violence is institutionalised in the military (*TP*, p. 354). In its directionless 'flows and currents that only secondarily allow themselves to be appropriated by the State', in its existence 'only in its own metamorphoses', the war machine is resistance, the '*nomos*' that is outside the 'law' (*TP* p. 360).

40 Braidotti, *Nomadic Subjects*, p. 13.

a private interrogation by the Mullah, Milton, the computer network engineer, and Mahala, the librarian – who in a bravura scene at the end of act two decries the successive state apparatuses that have ruled Afghanistan (and the country's women in particular) in a mix of Dari, Russian, French, and English, and who now struggles to make herself understood (even attempting German) to the man who just might save her life – discover that they can communicate numerologically. Their respective 'strange languages' are reduced to a simple binary code that crosses boundaries and banishes 'confusion' (*H/K*, pp. 124–6). Excited by their discovery of a common link, Milton and Mahala proceed to apply their networking, or deterritorialisation, model to Afghanistan, the 'passing-through place' that serves as a 'perfect metaphor', according to Milton, for the 'intersection' of opposing forces: 'Afghanistan! Armies, and, and gas pipelines, licit and illicit markets, and even Islam, communism, tribes, the incommensurable interests of the West and the East, heroin, missiles, refugees, and each in a language, moving chaotically' (*H/K*, p. 127). The machine that Milton would make to banish such confusion is the war machine described by Deleuze and Guattari. Its 'numerical composition' – what they call the 'numbering number' – replaces the 'lineal' or territorial organisation of the state and redistributes power, not as hierarchical 'segments' or 'centers' but as relational 'series' – much like Beckham trading his number 7 Manchester United jersey for Real Madrid's number 23 (which he carried with him to the LA Galaxy). 'Arithmetic composition, on the one hand, selects, extracts from the lineages the elements that will enter into nomadism and the war machine and, on the other, directs them against the State apparatus, opposing a machine and an existence to the State apparatus' (*TP*, pp. 392 and 390–1).

In the production of *Homebody/Kabul* that I saw, what I have been describing as the nomadic form and content of Kushner's play found its visual corollary in the design and staging of Ormerod and Donnellan. Ormerod transformed the Young Vic's theatre-in-the-round studio space into a raised thrust stage extending, rhizomatically, into the audience as a walkway that connected with a doorway in the south wall of the theatre. This arrangement, together with the ingenious system of moveable brick walls at the back of the stage, allowed for multiple points of entry and exit, deftly exploited by Donnellan in the swift pacing of the transitions between scenes, when the actor-driven set changes foregrounded the stage as a space of intersection and contestation. In this regard, it is worth remembering that Donnellan and Ormerod founded Cheek by Jowl in 1981 as a touring company, staging classic plays in a stripped-down, anti-spectacular style that travels well and showcases actors hitting – and occasionally missing – their targets. In this, their first production since returning to England following a long hiatus working in Russia, director and designer are staging as much their own cultural and professional itinerancy as they are that of playwright Kushner's characters.[41]

Like Deleuze and Guattari, in their 'anticultural' book, and like Beckham in his autobiography, Kushner has given his play 'a circular form', although presumably not 'only for laughs' (*TP*, p. 22). Rather, the play ends with a quietly moving scene between Priscilla and Mahala. They are back in London, in the same room occupied by the Homebody in act one. It is the only scene to which Kushner, in the published text, gives a title: 'Periplum'. The word, we are told courtesy of Hugh Kenner in the fourth of Kushner's seven epigraphs to the play, 'is Pound's shorthand for a tour which takes you round then back again. And such a tour is by definition profitable, if not in coins then in knowledge' (Kenner, quoted in *H/K*, p. 8). I will return to the significance of this final scene shortly; for the moment, let me explain how Richard, Cathy, and I experienced our own curious form of periplum the night we saw *Homebody/Kabul*.

Place and displacement, location and dislocation: these are central concerns in Kushner's play. The audience is aware, given her plummy accent and accompanying narrative, that the Homebody is meant to reside in one of London's tonier enclaves. But we are never entirely sure of where, or even if, her encounter with the Afghan hat merchant takes place. For, as one of the playwright's notes makes explicit, 'When the Homebody, in Act One, Scene 1, refers to the street on which she found the hat shop, she doesn't mention its name; instead, where the name would fall in the sentence, she makes a wide, sweeping gesture in the air with her right hand, almost as if to say: "I know the name but I will not tell you." It is the same gesture each time' (*H/K*, p. 5). This mysterious London non-location finds its Kabuli corollary in the Homebody's obsession, noted above, with '[t]he Grave of Cain. Murder's Grave' (*H/K*, p. 21). Later we learn that the Homebody, at the time of her disappearance in Kabul, had apparently been searching for the grave site in Cheshme Khedre, which she had noted with a question mark in her guidebook. As Khwaja summarises to Priscilla, 'This says, not "Grave of Cain," but rather, "Grave of Cain?" She was pursuing a rumor. On no official map is there ever a question mark. This would be an entirely novel approach to cartography. The implications are profound. To read on a map, instead of "Afghanistan," "Afghanistan?" It would be more accurate, but –' (*H/K*, p. 63).

41 See Declan Donnellan, *The Actor and the Target* (London: Nick Hern, 2002).

Eventually Khwaja leads Priscilla to what is supposed to be the gravesite itself, which is in the middle of a minefield, presided over by a resigned Sufi marabout, and which, perhaps befitting the final resting place of a marked man, is unmarked. Priscilla is typically despondent, unable to express exactly what she hoped to find there: 'I thought I'd, I dunno, there'd be some sort of sign . . . for me here. That she'd marked the map for me' (*H/K*, p. 110). What Priscilla fails to understand is that her mother, in moving from her sedentary life in London to her nomadic one in Kabul, can only announce her presence in terms of an absence, can only locate herself in relation to a question that cannot be answered. As Deleuze and Guattari summarise,

> If the nomad can be called the Deterritorialized par excellence, it is precisely because there is no reterritorialization *afterward* as with the migrant, or upon *something else* as with the sedentary (the sedentary's relation with the earth is mediatized by something else, a property regime, a State apparatus). With the nomad, on the contrary, it is deterritorialization that constitutes the relation to the earth, to such a degree that the nomad reterritorializes on deterritorialization itself . . . The earth does not become deterritorialized in its global and relative movement, but at specific locations, at the spot where the forest recedes, or where the steppe and the desert advance. (*TP*, pp. 381–2)

Or where a city vanishes beneath the horizon line of the rubble it has become. Cheshme Khedre, an area on the outskirts of Kabul littered with undetonated land mines, is quite literally a no man's land. Even less so, as Priscilla is repeatedly reminded, a woman's.

In their treatise on nomadology and the war machine in *A Thousand Plateaus*, Deleuze and Guattari note, among other things, that nomadic space is 'a tactile space, or rather "haptic," a sonorous much more than a visual space' (*TP*, p. 382). To this end, at the close of this scene, as '*A muezzin's call for prayers*' sounds (*H/K*, p. 115), Priscilla gives Khwaja the Discman retrieved from the site where the Homebody is supposed to have disappeared, or where the remnants of her body were supposed to have been found. Either way, it is the sole remaining possession she has of her mother, one she now instructs Khwaja to pass on to Zai Garshi, an Afghan actor-turned-hat salesman who has previously testified before Priscilla that her mother is alive but does not want to be found, and who shares with the Homebody a love of Frank Sinatra. In exchange, Khwaja gives Priscilla '[o]ne last packet of poems' for delivery to London (*H/K*, p. 116), a city whose 'striated space[s]', in Deleuze and Guattari's terminology, represent a migratory beginning or end point rather than a nomadic 'intermezzo', a space of the '*relative global*', of assigned

direction (coming or going), rather than of the '*local absolute*', or polyvocal direction (always moving) (*TP*, pp. 380–2). Thus, for both Khwaja
as a former migrant, and Mahala as a future one, London's geography is
very tangible, the minutest of locations within it absolutely pinpointable,
despite its vast urban sprawl. To this end, when Khwaja asks Priscilla to
transport his poems back to his friend and fellow Esperantist, Mr Sahar,
in London, he alone among the characters in the play names a specific
address: '17 Pindock Mews, Maida Vale' (*H/K*, p. 65). It's a street that
very much exists, one of those typically English lanes that emerges out
of nowhere and that doesn't seem to go anywhere else. It's about a block
and a half from the Warwick Avenue tube stop, on the Bakerloo Line,
just off Castellain Road. It's also fewer than five hundred metres from
Cathy's flat. We had passed it, oblivious to its significance, on our way to
dinner and the theatre earlier that night. Returning home, we couldn't
help but pause in front of it, and count from the corner to what we
guessed would likely be the shuttered windows of number 17.

Act 3: Vancouver, New York, and Kandahar

The multiple journeys enacted in Kushner's play point to the fact that
theatre, like football, is a contact sport. The stage, like the stadium, is
a space of nomadism, of global wandering and local encounter, where
intersecting and polyvocal points of arrival and departure give rise to
what Jill Dolan calls further 'geographies of learning'. As Dolan puts it,
theatre can be 'a site of world traveling and world building', especially
when political theatre is also a theatre of empathy, in which 'the emotion
theater inspires [is used] to move people to political action, to desire
reconfigured social relations, to want to interact intimately with a local
and a global community'.[42] This harnessing of emotion to action – or
even activism, as Dolan notes in the subtitle to her book – is the key. In
this sense, it is important to distinguish empathy from what Kushner
identifies as the bugbear of catharsis, which, in a neat little capitalist
equation, involves an initial expenditure of emotion for a guaranteed
return of transcendence.[43] In contrast, empathy implies a reciprocal
exchange between producer and consumer (or actor and spectator), an
acknowledgement that both are in the event, that the liveness of theatre
creates a space in which we can collectively 'engage with the social in
physically, materially embodied circumstances'.[44] As Kushner puts it,

42 Jill Dolan, *Geographies of Learning: Theory and Practice, Activism and Performance*
    (Middletown: Wesleyan University Press, 2001), pp. 91 and 90.
43 Kushner, 'Notes about political theater', p. 22.
44 Dolan, *Geographies of Learning*, p. 90.

'Theater, like dialectical materialist analysis, examines the magic of perception and the political, ideological employment to which the magic is
put'.[45]

So too with global sporting culture, where any drama performed
by Beckham on the field cannot be separated from its economic contexts and cultural consequences off the field. In this respect, I truly feel
for Beckham, as I have followed, from my home in Vancouver over
the past several years, first his uneasy exile in Madrid and then, more
proximately, his much-heralded arrival in Los Angeles. In Madrid not
only did he have to deal with those nasty tabloid rumours about marital
infidelities, but, even more seriously, with open criticism from English
and Spanish fans alike about his uncharacteristically sluggish play. This
reached a nadir with the double ignominy of Real Madrid's quarterfinal
exit in the Champions League knockout round in March 2004, followed
by England's quarterfinal defeat by the Portuguese host team at the
UEFA Cup in late June. The latter match was decided on penalty kicks,
with Beckham, normally a precise dead-ball striker, crucially missing
on his attempt. Former English manager Sven-Göran Eriksson nevertheless remained loyal to Beckham, tapping him once again to serve as
team captain at the 2006 World Cup in Germany. However, Eriksson's
successor, Steve McClaren, unceremoniously passed Beckham over
completely when naming the player roster for his first national squad
in August 2006, a much-anticipated though no less humiliating move
whose longer-term negative effects Beckham himself had managed to
pre-empt by resigning as team captain in a teary press conference following England's quarter-final defeat by nemesis Portugal at the World Cup
the previous June. That game was once again decided on penalty kicks,
with Beckham unable even to attempt his following an injury substitu-
tion soon after halftime. To be sure, McClaren would eventually recall
Beckham to the English squad in 2007, with the midfielder distinguishing
himself by setting up four goals in as many games. And England's new
manager, Fabio Capello (who succeeded McClaren following the team's
failure to qualify for the 2008 Euro Finals), quickly granted Beckham his
much coveted one-hundredth international appearance 'cap' by naming
him to the English lineup in a friendly match against France in March
2008, adding that he saw no reason why the footballer couldn't continue
to play for his country through the 2010 World Cup.[46]

Capello has stated that any future decisions, in this regard, will be

45 Kushner, 'Notes about political theater', p. 27.
46 'David Beckham makes 100 caps for England', *The Daily Telegraph* (25 March 2008),
    www.telegraph.co.uk/sport/football/international/england/2295455/David-Beckham-
    makes-100-caps-for-England.html (accessed April 2008).

based solely on Beckham's fitness, something that was not very much in evidence during the footballer's abbreviated and injury-prone first season with the LA Galaxy. With his matinee idol looks, pop star wife, and international celebrity status, it was almost inevitable that Beckham would one day end up in Hollywood. And yet while Beverly Hills royalty (including Tom Cruise and Will Smith) rolled out the red carpet to welcome Becks in July 2007, and while wife Posh attempted to build on the hype by doing what every talentless beautiful person in LA does, that is, starring in her own reality television show, the Galaxy owners had something far more prosaic and instrumental in mind in hiring the Beckham brand: they wanted him to sell tickets and related merchandise, a lot of it, not to mention boost interest in a sport relegated to at best fifth-tier status – after baseball, basketball, American football, and hockey – in North America. Early indications are that he has delivered, at least initially, on the first promise, with the Galaxy racking up more than 2,000 season-ticket sales within hours of Beckham's signing, and selling in excess of 300,000 jerseys (priced at $79.99 a piece) before his first appearance in a game.[47] Major Soccer League ticket sales are up elsewhere as well, as fans across North America (and not necessarily of soccer) have dutifully clamoured for an up-close and personal glimpse on their local JumboTrons of a face they have hitherto likely only seen on TV, or in a magazine or on a billboard selling cologne or sunglasses or underwear.

Count me among the clamourers. For when it was announced that Beckham and the Galaxy would be visiting Vancouver to play an exhibition match with the local Whitecaps franchise at BC Place in early November 2007, I promptly purchased a ticket. And watched, along with friend, running partner, football enthusiast, and hard-core-anti-globalisation-Beckham-cynic, Jamie, as what should have been an outclassed Whitecaps team (they play in the lesser United Soccer League) drew Beckham and his fellow Galaxy players to a thoroughly uninspiring 0-0 tie (see figure 16). Not that this seemed to perturb most of the 40,000-plus fans, who roared with approval every time Beckham touched the ball during his 25 minutes of regulation play. While traces of Beckham's celebrated brilliance at bending the ball could be glimpsed in the few corners he was given and, most notably and entertainingly, in the kick he cheekily lobbed at the backside of a male streaker who momentarily halted play during the second half, what emerged most powerfully for me in watching this spectacle of travelling exhibitionism

47 Daniel Workman, 'World's richest soccer import: footballer David Beckham sells tickets & boosts merchandise sales', *suite101.com* (2 August 2007), http://internationaltrade.suite101.com/article.cfm/worlds_richest_soccer_import (accessed April 2008).

16 David Beckham at BC Place during an exhibition match between the LA
Galaxy and the Vancouver Whitecaps, November 2007

was a sense that the world's most famous itinerant footballer could,
finally, never go home again. Or at least not in the manner that he might
wish.

That is, not only are the playing styles of England's big three
Premier League teams – Chelsea, Arsenal (with whom Beckham trained
during the start of 2008), and Manchester United – somewhat at odds
with Beckham's unique strengths, but management's finances and
players' egos are such that none of them can really afford him. And
so, mindful of Capello's injunction to stay match fit, Beckham found
himself, during the Galaxy's off-season at the beginning of 2009, back
in Europe, this time on loan to AC Milan. At first he mostly watched

from the sidelines, but then he took the odd free kick ceded to him by Ronaldinho, and eventually found himself starting and scoring goals, prompting open speculation about a more permanent transfer to Milan. To be sure, Beckham's particular refugee status needs very much to be distinguished from the diasporas of terror and despair that have, respectively, propelled Mahala and the Homebody to swap places by the end of Kushner's play. Nevertheless, the emotions that his movements both on and off the field inspire in his deterritorialised viewing audience – myself included – can work proportionately to prompt a rethinking, at the local level, of one's transnational, globalised identifications and affiliations.

Thus it was, during the course of the Galaxy–Whitecaps match, as I found myself explaining to Jamie the circuitous global connections and strange local detours I was trying to track between Beckham and Kushner, and as I listened in turn to his own fascinating research on Esperanto that he was conducting as part of an upcoming collaborative art project, that I began to reflect, more generally, on my country's own evolving relationship, since 9/11, with another Afghan city that started with the letter 'K'. To be sure, the recent twinned histories of Canada and Kandahar were very much at the forefront of public discussion at that moment due to a number of factors: the publication the previous month of Janice Gross Stein and Eugene Lang's *The Unexpected War*, outlining in meticulous detail the series of steps (or missteps) that led to Canada's current military presence in the heartland of Taliban-controlled Afghanistan, the country's first deployment of combat troops since the Korean War, and its first time fighting an insurgency since the Boer War;[48] the registering, earlier that fall, of Canada's seventieth combat fatality, once again drawing attention to the fact that, due to its lone presence in the volatile southern region of Kandahar, Canadian casualties were disproportionately higher than those of other coalitionary forces in Afghanistan (the number of deaths has now surpassed 130); Conservative Prime Minister Harper's announcement in October that he was appointing an Independent Panel, led by former Liberal Foreign Affairs Minister John Manley, to explore 'Canada's Future Role in Afghanistan', with a view to making recommendations that would sustain Canadian troops in the region through to 2011; and the political imbroglio then just breaking as a result of the Harper government quietly ceasing the Canadian army's transfer of insurgent detainees to local Afghan custody after receiving credible evidence of torture.

Like most Canadians, I was only vaguely aware of how Canada had

---

48 Janice Gross Stein and Eugene Lang, *The Unexpected War: Canada in Kandahar* (Toronto: Viking, 2007).

gone from a small deployment of 800 troops stationed mostly around the already Northern Alliance-secured region of Kabul in early 2002 to assuming sole command of NATO forces in Kandahar, epicentre of the Taliban insurgency, in 2005. As Stein and Lang persuasively point out, Canada 'slid' into war in Afghanistan, the result, on the one hand, of Ottawa wanting to make nice with Washington following its post-9/11 refusals to join the invasion of Iraq or sign on to a strategic missile defence system, and, on the other hand, of successive changes in government (Jean Chretien to Paul Martin to Stephen Harper) struggling to put some cohesive and purposeful spin on Canada's hitherto amorphous (and largely toothless) foreign policy in a changed twenty-first-century world.[49] My connection to Afghanistan, and to Canada's role in Kandahar, in particular, conformed largely to what Stein and Lang refer to as the country's collective 'suspended disbelief',[50] my nightly consumption of news stories and images about the latest suicide bombing or diplomatic discussions between the Afghan and NATO leaderships too often leading to a reflexive invocation of the postmodern theory of a Paul Virilio, or to an ironic quip about Hamid Karzai's hat. And yet, following from the hard questions posed by Stein and Lang at the end of their book, just as the Homebody's search for party hats culminated in 'an extraordinary act of imagination' that moved her (quite literally) to find an embodied connection to Kabul, so do Canadian troops in Kandahar (no matter how they got there and no matter how long they stay) force me to confront 'the limits of [my own] liberal imagination', considering the extent to which I, in Vancouver, 'share a common fate, a destiny, with people who live halfway around the globe',[51] and whether that shared humanity extends beyond finding common cause in matching the brutality of an extremist regime with superior displays of armed force. For beyond hypothetical end dates to Canada's combat mission and the even more hypothetical possibility of a workable peace agreement with the Taliban, we must ask how far and how deeply our commitment to Afghanistan's reconstruction extends: to a revitalisation of its agricultural industry? to increased education and employment opportunities for women? to an elimination of much of the country's abject poverty? to ferreting out corruption in government and international aid agencies? to securing the country's border with Pakistan?

These and other questions were on my mind when, influenced by my viewing and reading of *Homebody/Kabul*, I taught an undergraduate

49 *Ibid.*, pp. 21 and *passim*.
50 *Ibid.*, p. 301.
51 *Ibid.*, p. 302.

course in the spring of 2004 called 'Histories of the Present', in which I paired a discussion of Kushner's play with a screening of Moshen Makhamalbaf's award-winning 2001 film *Kandahar*. In putting together the course, which included similar pairings of literary works and films that spatialised – through, among other things, palimpsestic metaphors of mental trauma, archaeology, travel, translation, mapping, and mirroring – the connections between different historical events and geopolitical regions (including the Holocaust, the AIDS pandemic, the bombing of Hiroshima, government-sanctioned genocides in Armenia and Sri Lanka), I was hoping for a similar interface between the spaces represented in the texts and the space of the classroom. That is, in thinking about the bodies in these texts, and their histories, I wanted my students to think about their own embodied histories; to think about what it means to be both a local resident and a local reader of a particular place, *and* to be a resident reader of this planet; to make imaginative connections between their occupation of a specific site of intellectual inquiry in British Columbia and other sites of knowledge production about which they may have been reading for the first time, or were maybe told never to visit, or might in fact find themselves travelling to one day.

Kandahar is a fictionalised account of Afghan–Canadian journalist Nelofer Pazira's real-life search for her childhood friend, Deanna, who has written her a letter describing the Taliban government's brutal suppression of the women of Afghanistan, and declaring that she intends to commit suicide rather than endure any more suffering. (In a 2003 follow-up documentary, called *Return to Kandahar* and co-directed by Pazira, we learn that her friend does indeed eventually kill herself.) In *Kandahar*, Pazira is cast as Nafas, and she is searching for her sister rather than her friend; additionally, we are told that the planned suicide is to take place during the final eclipse before the dawn of the twenty-first century, lending the film and Nafas's journey an apocalyptic urgency and prophetic symbolism similar to that bestowed, through the coincidence of historical timing, on Kushner's play and Priscilla's quest in search of her mother. The film's basis in reality is likewise reflected in the film's quasi-documentary feel; all the actors were non-professionals who largely improvised their roles under the direction of Makhmalbaf. These include an Afghani man (Ike Ogut) who agrees to smuggle Nafas across the border from Iran as his burqa-clad fourth wife; the boy Khak (Sadou Teymouri), whom Nafas meets soon after crossing the border, and who agrees to accompany her to Kandahar following his expulsion from a Taliban-run school; Tabib Sahid (Hassan Tantai), an African-American masquerading as an Afghani doctor whom Nafas consults for a stomach ailment, and who then agrees to drive her and Khak to a nearby Red Cross station; and, finally, Haya (Hayatala Hakimi), an armless man they meet at the camp who is looking for prosthetic limbs for his legless wife, and who eventually joins the unlikely caravan.

I chose to pair the film with *Homebody/Kabul* first and foremost because of the obvious parallels between the two texts' narrative focus on a journey to war-torn Afghanistan in search of a missing relative, and the issues around gender and religious and cultural conflicts that arise as a result. However, I also found the way in which the film was shot and edited, and the very recent history it captured on screen, to be an equally compelling example of Deleuze and Guattari's theory of nomadology. That is, the film's sequencing suggests no real beginning or end, in the standard narrative sense that most Western readers and spectators have come to expect. Rather, there is only the representation of the journey itself: a succession of scenes of Nafas wandering the desert spaces of Iran and Afghanistan like a nomad, moving through their virtually indistinguishable topographies with no sense of assigned direction (manifested beautifully in a scene near the end when the wedding party Nafas has joined splits in two, with Nafas not knowing which group to follow), and, significantly, never arriving at her chosen destination. Indeed, by the end of the film, we, as viewers, end up spatially back where we started, only at this point realising that the opening shot of Nafas lifting the veil of her burqa, reciting her name, and claiming affiliation with the bride's family actually comes at the end of her journey (at least the journey we see), when she and the rest of the wedding party are stopped and interrogated by members of the Taliban.

Moreover, the sequencing of scenes documenting Nafas's encounters with various locals, each intent on his or her own concerns (whether it be making money, treating the ill, getting prosthetic limbs, or journeying to a wedding), is illustrative of what I earlier referenced as Deleuze and Guattari's characterisation of the 'locally absolute' claims of nomadic spaces like Afghanistan. Here (where?) we see that there is no opportunity or even purpose to pause reflectively and put things into the 'globally relative' terms of official state history, where x cause produces y effect (as the Homebody attempts to do, initially, by reading from the guidebook, or as Nafas, in her own way, attempts to do by documenting her journey in a step-by-step, linear manner via her tape recorder). Rather, one can only deal with one's immediate and present situation and circumstances. This is revealed in a number of ways in the film, but perhaps nowhere more dramatically than in the surreal Red Cross scene, where Nafas's desire to find someone to transport her to Kandahar must take a backseat (quite literally) to the workers' attempts to deal with the more pressing local concern of trying to fit all of the men who have lost limbs to landmines with prostheses, which we have earlier witnessed being parachuted to the ground from helicopters in an almost Felliniesque homage. To put this another way, Nafas is fundamentally fixated on time as it delimits both the past and future horizons of expectation concerning her sister and herself (figured in the film by the recurring motif of the impending solar eclipse, with the metaphor of looming darkness receiving a crucial gendered interpretation via the aforementioned opening shot, which superimposes an image of said eclipse over a monocular point of view shot from the embroidered eye slit of Nafas's burqa); in contrast, all those around her, including Khak and Haya, are concerned with a more immediate spatial present (grounded for us in the film's gorgeous cinematography of the ubiquitous desert landscape).

In our discussions of *Kandahar*, and its connections to *Homebody/Kabul* and to our own lives, students and I inevitably focused a great deal on religion, and in particular on the global reach of religious extremism. Here, once again, Deleuze and Guattari proved useful. For in their treatise on nomadology in *A Thousand Plateaus*, they have much to say about the relationship between religion and nomadism, and the way in which absolutist monotheistic religion (be it Islam and its *jihads* or Christianity and its past and present crusades) has tended to 'convert' (somewhat counter-intuitively) the locally absolute and deterritorialised concerns of the political war machine into state-sponsored holy wars that compete to reterritorialise the globally relative centre of the world by, for example, trumpeting the primacy of 'prior' claims to the Holy Land (*TP*, pp. 383-4). We see this most dramatically in the film in the scene of the mullah supervising the class of boys learning the Koran, where, in between reciting passages of holy scripture, they are also charged with detailing the workings of a semi-automatic weapon and what it should be used for – namely killing Americans. Khak, the nascent nomad committed to the more immediate local concern of finding food for his mother, does not fit into this space, and so is cast out. However, religion's conversion of nomadism results not simply in the reconstitution of spatial, rhizomatic history into official state, arbolic history, but arguably in the end of history altogether. Next to the absolute authority of the word of God, why are any other voices necessary? Hence the confiscation of Nafas's tape recorder at the end of *Kandahar*. And hence one of Mullah Durranni's early comments to Milton and Priscilla in *Homebody/Kabul*; referencing the Homebody's recovered guidebook, he notes dismissively: 'But in Kabul there is no history. There is only God . . .' (*H/K*, p. 36).

In this, Mullah Durranni, like his counterpart in *Kandahar*, is, in his own way, an excellent pedagogue. And Kushner, in turning to the East in *Homebody/Kabul* for dramatic inspiration, is, like Brecht before him, also wanting to make his play a teaching text. How do we, I asked my class, make sense of and ideally put in dialogue competing fundamentalisms? How do we work through and beyond our own self-shattering grief to seek reconciliation with rather than retribution for an other? Theatre, I suggested, can help. For, the crux of the personal/political dialectic – or paradox – in modern performance is that empathic identification must lead inevitably to cathetic alienation, and finally to critical analysis and ethical responsibility. It's something Kushner recognises when he follows the Homebody's rapturous paean to the beauties of Kabul with Doctor Qari Shah's clinical – but no less vivid – description of a body's (presumably the Homebody's, now quite literally a 'body without organs') brutal dismemberment in act one, scene two. A burqa 'draped over the arm of a chair' on this stage suddenly crowded with men (including Milton, Quango, and the Mullah) bespeaks not only the Homebody's absent presence but also, more proximately, that of Priscilla, whose shadow we gradually see emerge in hunched profile against 'a bedsheet which has been hung across one corner of the room' (*H/K*, p. 31). Indeed, Priscilla's emergence from the long shadow of her mother's ghost – her '*corpus vile*', the 'body, alive or dead, of no regard to anyone' (*H/K*, p. 113) – and effecting her own slow, painful identification across difference, her own corporeal connection with Mahala, is the central conflict of *Homebody/Kabul*. This in part explains the nature of the changes Kushner has made in the revised text of the play, where the background to Priscilla's domestic estrangement from her parents, and from her self (the result of an attempted suicide that killed her unborn fetus), is fleshed out in longer scenes with Milton, and where the shrill tone and petulant anger that had previously dominated many of Priscilla's exchanges with Khwaja are replaced by a new openness and sense of wonder toward her own 'sad and marvelous' cultural dislocation in Kabul: '*Look* up there! Look at that sky! Black! Black! Those stars! Crikey. We could be on the moon! Oh sweet Christ it's . . . Unearthly! [. . .] Kabul has changed me. I've listened'.[52] This also explains the casting of Hollywood ingenue Maggie Gyllenhaal as Priscilla in the Steppenwolf Theatre/Mark Taper Forum production of the play that arrived at BAM in May 2004. At the very least, her star wattage would ensure that audiences kept watching, even if, despite Kushner's changes, nothing else in the four-hour evening still quite measured up to the verbal brilliance of the Homebody's opening monologue (see figure 17).

---

52 Tony Kushner, *Homebody/Kabul*, rev. ed. (New York: Theatre Communications Group, 2004), p. 112; first ellipsis in original.

17 Reed Birney as Milton and Maggie Gyllenhaal as Priscilla in the
Steppenwolf/Mark Taper Forum production of *Homebody/Kabul* at the
Brooklyn Academy of Music, May 2004

And yet, in revising his play so that it might – in the words of
Steppenwolf Artistic Director Martha Lavey – survive 'the sensational-
ism of its public birth', and 'receive a reading that concentrated on its
intrinsic force as a human drama (instead of as a record of extrinsic
world events)',[53] Kushner would not deny that its return to New York
shouldn't also provoke a renewed local debate about the United States'
unsettled and unsettling role as global law enforcer. This was especially
true in light of the US invasion of Iraq and the images of torture that
were at that very moment emerging from Abu Ghraib prison, and the
strange spectacle of the Republican National Convention that would
descend on the city later that summer, in addition to the far-from-
resolved situation in Afghanistan. In this regard, I would argue that
locally produced live theatre, as much as any electronically mediated
global sporting event on the scale of FIFA's World Cup, can function as
a 'disaporic public sphere' of the sort envisioned by Arjun Appadurai, a
space of connection and contestation where 'mobile texts and migrant
audiences' come together to produce 'communities of sentiment', transnational sodalities 'capable of moving from shared imagination to collective action'.[54] Thus I found myself sitting in the audience at BAM's

53 See Martha Lavey, 'A foreword', in Kushner, *Homebody/Kabul*, rev. edn, p. ix.
54 Arjun Appadurai, *Modernity at Large: Cultural Dimensions of Globalization*
    (Minneapolis: University of Minnesota Press, 1996), pp. 8–10.

Harvey Theater on 12 May 2004, little over a month after completing the 'Histories of the Present' course, and almost two years to the day since I had first followed the Homebody through a parted curtain to Kabul. Fresh from having seen her crosstown sister, Caroline, on Broadway the night before and – still on Vancouver time – acutely conscious of my own sense of displacement in a city I was visiting for the first time since the Twin Towers fell, I kept thinking about the politics and performance of mourning. Not that *Homebody/Kabul* hasn't always been a play about grief. But in the revised version, the recreative and regenerative possibilities of mourning, the productive transformation of loss into a new model for social action and intercultural connection, are emphasised through the addition of a key speech by Priscilla in her closing scene with Mahala:

> I miss her. I love her. She was my mother. But . . . Can I say this?
> In the space she's left . . . Some . . . joy? or something has been rising. Something unpronounceable inside is waking up. I . . . I've no words for this.
> [. . .]
> Y'see Mum? One sharp goad from a terrible grief and . . . the soul is waking up.[55]

As Judith Butler has likewise written, with special reference to 9/11, 'tarrying with grief', exposing oneself to the unbearable 'dispossession' of *self* that comes with it, might in fact provide an alternative 'resource for politics' and human understanding, one that, proceeding from a recognition of our common 'corporeal vulnerability', counters the historical countering of violence with still more violence: 'Is there something to be gained in the political domain by maintaining grief as part of the framework within which we think our international ties? If we stay with the sense of loss, are we left feeling only passive and powerless, as some might fear? Or are we, rather, returned to a sense of human vulnerability, to our collective responsibility for the physical lives of one another? Could the experience of a dislocation of First World safety not condition the insight into the radically inequitable ways that corporeal vulnerability is distributed globally?'[56] For Butler, the 'transformative effect of loss' has to do with its capacity to expose us to our own 'foreignness', our own 'unknowingness', and that this constitutes 'the

55 Kushner, *Homebody/Kabul*, rev. edn, p. 139; ellipses in original, except where indicated.
56 Judith Butler, *Precarious Life: The Powers of Mourning and Violence* (New York: Verso, 2004), p. 30.

source of [our] ethical connection with others': 'I am as much constituted by those I do grieve for as by those whose deaths I disavow, whose
nameless and faceless deaths form the melancholic background for my
social world, if not my First Worldism'.[57] I will be taking up the social,
political, and performative implications of Butler's ethical model of
mourning at greater length in the next chapter; for the time being, let
me suggest that the difficult questions Butler poses with respect to global
violence and localised/individualised grief are precisely those worked
through by Priscilla over the course of *Homebody/Kabul*, something that
is especially foregrounded in the revised version of the play. Without
her mother's body to recover and grieve over, Priscilla is forced to take
back home with her 'the spectacle of [Kabul's] suffering': 'she's scattered all over Kabul. The whole city. It's her'.[58] Moreover, in following
Khwaja's advice and not '[holding] her [mother] back from traveling',
Priscilla is gently encouraged to shrug off her own dry despondency and
join humanity's drowning. This is what, we discover (in one of the few
revisions to the Homebody's monologue), her mother had wished for
her all along: 'I so wanted her to be out in the world, my daughter. Of
use'.[59] In the end, Priscilla can no more make sense of what her mother
hoped to find in the ruins of Kabul than Mahala can understand what
clues she might have left behind in her neglected English garden and in
her 'strange' library. Rather, the Homebody's 'strangeness', her undeci-
pherability, become the means by which Priscilla and Mahala together
plant their dead and reflect on their own cultural estrangement, on the
knowing that comes through not knowing, and on the nomadism they
are allowed to experience through the Homebody's proxy.

Which is, finally, what motivates this (re)writing of that moment:
my own desire to stage an encounter with the moving target of our awful
present that resists the arriviste claims of interpretation but that nevertheless risks the corrupting touch of critical incorporation. In other words,
I am offering up for analysis the various migrations of Beckham and
Nafas and the Homebody in order, ultimately, to retrace my own steps
back home. Only fitting, then, that the opportunity to take in Beckham's
exhibition match at BC Place in November 2007 should be followed by
a similarly felicitous chance to attend an impromptu staged reading of
Homebody/Kabul at the Firehall Arts Centre – the only production of the
play in Vancouver so far – in March 2008. The third in a series of readings of four contemporary plays linked thematically through their focus

57 *Ibid.*, pp. 21 and 46.
58 Kushner, *Homebody/Kabul*, rev. edn, pp. 115 and 60.
59 *Ibid.*, pp. 116 and 28.

on oil, war, power, politics, and terrorism,[60] and organised to mark the fifth anniversary of the invasion of Iraq, Kushner's play brought together several of Vancouver's local theatre talent, including Susan Hogan as the Homebody, David Adams as Milton, Tamara Hamilton as Priscilla, Parm Soor as Khwaja, Lorena Gale as Mahala, Shaker Paleja as Quango Twistleton, and Jerry Wasserman as Zai Garshi and Mullah Durranni. The event also doubled as a benefit for the Firehall's community arts programmes and Amnesty International, who only the week before had, together with the British Columbia Civil Liberties Association, lost a bid to have the Federal Court of Canada issue an injunction halting the transfer of military detainees from Canadian Forces to Afghan jails, which had quietly resumed in February following a government investigation of torture allegations. That same week the opposition Liberals, as widely expected, joined the ruling Conservative party in voting to extend Canada's combat mission in Afghanistan through to 2011[61] – a date that, despite assurances by the Conservatives to the contrary, might yet be up for further negotiation, especially given the US's scheduled pullout from Iraq the same year and Barack Obama's pledge to increase NATO's presence in Afghanistan and Pakistan.

After introducing the cast, assembled before us at a long, makeshift trestle table – the separate placement of Hogan's Homebody at her own smaller table downstage left the only gesture toward the play's imaginative geography – Firehall Artistic Director Donna Spencer announced that the actors had only had one prior run-through of the play earlier that afternoon, and even then they didn't make it all the way to the end. And yet despite, or maybe because of these constraints, this local reading was perhaps the most affecting of the three performances of the play described in this chapter. Undoubtedly this had something to do with the intimacy of the setting: the Homebody's insistence on the interlocutory role we in the audience play as participants – regardless of our silence or censure – in the conversation she is having with us was made all the more palpable by Hogan's physical proximity and, I would say, attendant vulnerability (and here I make no distinction between actor and character). Indeed, Hogan gave what strikes me as a more shattered – and, for that, shattering – performance as the Homebody than those of Markham or Emond. In this, Hogan's desire for a witness to her/the

---

60   The other plays included David Hare's *Stuff Happens*; Stephen Sewell's *Myth, Propaganda and Disaster in Nazi Germany and Contemporary America*; and Robin Soans's *Talking with Terrorists*.

61   See Paul Koring, 'Tories stalling abuse probe, watchdog says', *Globe and Mail* (13 March 2008), pp. A1 and A11; and Mike Blanchfield, 'Commons votes to extend Afghan mission to 2011', *Vancouver Sun* (14 March 2008), pp. A1 and A4.

Homebody's witnessing, her almost compulsive need to look up from her text and seek out and hold our gaze, to solicit (again, at once in and out of character) our sympathy as she (only very) occasionally stumbled over some of the more vexingly complex of the Homebody's phrasings, and, most importantly, her decision to join us in the audience upon completing her monologue and exiting Kushner's play suggested, it seems to me, a keen understanding of the dis-placements any body must suffer to be 'at home' in the world.

Then, too, the positioning of the other actors in a single horizontal line at the same table meant that quite often they were literally speaking across difference, the physical hamstringing of their bodies making all the more expressive and felt their *verbal* efforts to connect with and understand one another. This was most vividly apparent in the bravura scene where we are first introduced to Mahala, as she pleads with Priscilla to take her to London. Gale, who is fluent in French, forwent any attempt at the passages in German and Dari, speaking instead the italicised English translation as glossed in Kushner's text. Nevertheless, Soor's Khwaja, seated between Gale and Hamilton, still acted as interpreter for Priscilla and the audience, with his accented English overlapping Gale's accented English becoming an apt metaphor for another type of confusion Milton's networking machine might not have anticipated: the difference in sameness. Finally, there was the venue, with the Firehall's location in the heart of Vancouver's impoverished and addicted Downtown Eastside complicating Spencer's statement regarding the motivation for the reading series as a whole: 'Theatre is a great medium for stimulating discussion and it is important that we don't become complacent about the world beyond our own beautiful city'.[62] What the Homebody teaches by painful example is that such complacency more often than not begins at home. I thought about this especially as I made my way to the bus stop following the reading, a span of two short blocks that nevertheless takes me through what I have already described (in chapter 1) as Vancouver's own no man's land, effluent to the rest of the city's post-Expo/pre-Olympic efflorescence, where used hypodermic needles substitute for unexploded landmines. Indeed, beyond the presence of Canadian soldiers in Kandahar and, more proximately, the recent appointment of University of British Columbia agricultural researcher and Afghan expat Tooryalai Wesa as the new governor of the region, there is another very material way in which Vancouver is bound up with the catastrophic recent history and equally uncertain future of Afghanistan: the

---

62 'Stuff's happening at the Firehall during the 25th anniversary season', www.firehallartscentre.ca/index.php (accessed March 2008).

international opium trade.[63] Attending to such a worldly isomorphism requires those of us in the West to realign ourselves corporeally with the place we call home. By this I mean, first and foremost, that we should concentrate less on curtailing global supply routes by, for example, fumigating the crops of Afghan farmers forced to turn to poppy production in the wake of the collapse of the country's agriculture industry and more on the roots – systemic poverty, homelessness, racism, misogyny – of local demand for the product refined from those crops. We need, in other words, to do some travelling in our own city.

'You need an idea of the world to go out into the world', announces Hannah Pitt at the end of the second part of Kushner's *Angels in America*. 'But it's the going into that makes the idea. You can't wait for a theory, but you have to have a theory'.[64] It's a paradox that Hannah herself has had to live in making her way uncertainly from the safety and sameness of Salt Lake City to the chaotic clash of difference in New York City. It's once again enacted for us by the Homebody in the extraordinary performance of her transformation into a nomad. And a version of it is repeated in the mantra of metaphysical questions that bookend Beckham's autobiography: 'Who are you? Where have you come from? How did you come to be here? Where are you going?'[65] In using theatre and performance to theorise the embodied relationship between local experience and global politics, we need to ask such questions not only of the mobile texts we study, but also of ourselves as migratory audience members and critics. Above all, we who fancy ourselves scholar gypsies, itinerant cultural workers, nomadic intellectual labourers, sojourner-artists; we who purport, in our work, to negotiate between the local and the global, between place and the performance of place, between the ethnographic gaze and the tourist gaze; we would do well, when descending from our towers, aeries, and studios to wander the lost and forgotten spaces of our own cities, or to board planes for London or New York or Kabul or———, to make sure that whatever theories we may have packed will travel well.[66]

---

63 On Wesa's appointment as governor of Kandahar, see Graeme Smith and Robert Matas, 'Afghan–Canadian the top choice for governor of Kandahar', *Globe and Mail* (18 December 2008), pp. A1 and A17. For an astute op-ed linking poppy farming in Afghanistan to the local drug trade in Canada's inner-cities, see David Eaves and Taylor Owen, 'Failed strategy connects Afghan fields, city streets', *Toronto Star* (7 December 2007), p. A8.

64 Kushner, *Angels in America, Part Two: Perestroika*, p. 147.

65 Beckham, *Both Feet*, pp. 15 and 364.

66 On the uses (and abuses) of travelling theories, see Edward Said, 'Travelling theory', *Raritan* 1:3 (1982), pp. 41–67; and 'Travelling theory reconsidered', in Robert Polhemus and Roger Henkle (eds), *Critical Reconsiderations: The Relationship of Fiction and Life* (Stanford: Stanford University Press, 1994), pp. 251–65.

4

Brothers' keepers, or, the performance of mourning: queer rituals of remembrance

One cannot hold a discourse *on* the 'work of mourning' without taking part in it, without announcing or partaking in death, and first of all in one's own death. (Jacques Derrida[1])

What grief displays . . . is the thrall in which our relations with others hold us, in ways that we cannot always recount or explain, in ways that often interrupt the self-conscious account of ourselves we might try to provide, in ways that challenge the very notion of ourselves as autonomous and in control. (Judith Butler[2])

But it may well be that theatre and performance respond to a psychic need to rehearse for loss, and especially for death. (Peggy Phelan[3])

Cities of the dead are primarily for the living. (Joseph Roach[4])

Judith Butler's *Precarious Life: The Powers of Mourning and Violence*, a text I have had occasion to refer to in other sections of this book

1 Jacques Derrida, 'By force of mourning', trans. Pascale-Anne Brault and Michael Naas, *Critical Inquiry* 22:2 (1996), p. 172.
2 Judith Butler, *Precarious Life: The Powers of Mourning and Violence* (New York: Verso, 2004), p. 23.
3 Peggy Phelan, *Mourning Sex: Performing Public Memories* (New York: Routledge, 1997), p. 3.
4 Joseph Roach, *Cities of the Dead: Circum-Atlantic Performance* (New York: Columbia University Press, 1996), p. xi.

(including the last chapter), was written as an impassioned and urgent response to the events of 9/11, and to the culture of unexamined violence those events seemed to precipitate on the part of several Western democracies – the United States chief among them – supposedly committed to the basic principles of liberal humanism. But *Precarious Life* actually picks up the threads of an argument first sketched by Butler three years earlier in *Antigone's Claim*. In both books, Butler asks how one moves beyond the preoccupation with individual human agency implicit in the question, 'What *makes for a grievable life?*', to a recognition that '[l]oss has made a tenuous "we" of us all'.[5] Acknowledging the terrible and terrifying effects of violence to which sexual and other minorities are routinely subjected, Butler nevertheless posits that

> each of us is constituted politically in part by virtue of the social vulnerability of our bodies – as a site of desire and physical vulnerability, as a site of publicity at once assertive and exposed. Loss and vulnerability seem to follow from our being socially constituted bodies, attached to others, at risk of losing those attachments, exposed to others, at risk of violence by virtue of that exposure.[6]

For Butler, then, the more important question becomes how we 'transform' or 'translate' (to use her words) this loss into a new social ethics and political responsibility, reconfiguring a model of the human that accounts for the 'you' in 'me', and that moves 'the narcissistic preoccupation of melancholia . . . into a consideration of the vulnerability of others', helping us to 'critically evaluate and oppose the conditions under which certain human lives are more vulnerable than others, and thus certain human lives are more grieveable than others'.[7]

In this chapter, I want to build on Butler's insights here and elsewhere (especially in *Antigone's Claim*), connecting them to my arguments around performance, place, and politics in the preceding chapters by theorising the political responsibility and social vulnerability that specifically attend queer rituals of remembrance, as well as some of the masculine – and masculinist – teleologies at the heart of these rituals. How do I grieve for the 'man' lost in 'human', when it is mostly straight white men who have insisted historically that the latter category is one whose loss as a mode of address must be rehearsed over and over again by all the rest of us? How could I ever call such a man my brother? I explore these and related questions by returning to the genealogical approach to memory and performance outlined by Joseph Roach in *Cities of the Dead*,

5 Butler, *Precarious Life*, p. 20; emphasis in original.
6 *Ibid.*
7 *Ibid.*, pp. 49 and 30.

stressing both the *performative* substitutions and the *local* embodiments of a queer theory of mourning. As such, I begin the chapter with a brief survey of some spaces of remembrance that in many respects constitute 'a landscape of memorialization'[8] particular to Vancouver, and that thus serve as the immediate backdrop to my thinking about the larger issues circulating in the ensuing pages. In suggesting a 'nervous mutating catastrophic reach' to these spaces, and the traumatic events they commemorate, a reach that extends beyond Vancouver and, more importantly, my own immediate experiencing of them, I am structuring this chapter, as I implicitly have each of the preceding ones, along the lines of the model for 'performative writing' adopted by Peggy Phelan in her brilliant book *Mourning Sex: Performing Public Memories*. There, Phelan notes that '[p]erformative writing is an attempt to find a form for "what philosophy wishes all the same to say"'. She continues:

> Rather than describing the performance event in 'direct signification', a task that I believe to be impossible and not terrifically interesting, I want this writing to enact the affective force of the performance event again, as it plays itself out in an ongoing temporality made vivid by the psychic process of distortion (repression, fantasy, and the general hubbub of the individual and collective unconscious), and made narrow by the muscular force of political repression in all its mutative violence. The events I disclose here sound differently in the writing of them than in the 'experiencing' of them, and it is the urgent call of that difference that I am hoping to amplify here.[9]

In the main sections of this chapter, then, I am likewise seeking to amplify a difference, focusing on four specifically theatrical performances of mourning in order to note how their respective Vancouver stagings speak both to my own evolving memorialisation of the city in which I live, and to a communal history of global queer witnessing whose narrative lacunae are precisely what constitute the act of memorialisation itself. As Butler puts it, 'I tell a story about the relations I choose, only to expose, somewhere along the way, the way I am gripped and undone by these very relations. My narrative falters, as it must'.[10] To this end, I look initially, and most extensively, at the performance work of Margie Gillis and Paula Vogel, women who have

8 I borrow this phrase from Sharon Rosenberg, who coined it in correspondence with me regarding an earlier draft of this chapter. I am extremely grateful to Sharon for the guidance and engaged colloquy she has provided on my work, and on the work of mourning more generally.

9 Phelan, *Mourning Sex*, pp. 11–12.

10 Butler, *Precarious Life*, p. 23.

both lost biological brothers to AIDS (Christopher Gillis and Carl Vogel, respectively), and who, moreover, have both sought to memorialise their brothers' lives in specific works of art: Gillis in the solo dance piece *Torn Roots, Broken Branches*; and Vogel in the Obie Award-winning play *The Baltimore Waltz*. The public performance of bereavement by these two women, its ritual repetition, is not, I argue, a narcissistic capitulation to grief – as Freud's notion of melancholia would have it – but rather an acknowledgment of community, a symbolic representation of collective struggle in response to an unprecedented social crisis, one that allows for the sharing of loss and the ritualisation of remembrance as a precursor to organisation and a demand for change.

Here, in theorising the performance of mourning *contra* Freud, I will be drawing primarily on the work of two of his more important contemporary interlocutors. In particular, I apply Butler's influential notion of 'gender melancholia', as she initially developed the concept in the 1990s over the course of *Gender Trouble, Bodies That Matter*, and *The Psychic Life of Power*; as she later refined its political and ethical applications in *Antigone's Claim, Precarious Life*, and *Undoing Gender*; and as she has consistently used it to (re)read Freudian (and Lacanian) psychoanalysis in order to demonstrate that homosexual cathexis must precede ego identification and the successful resolution of the Oedipal complex. This will aid in unpacking how performative memorialisation overlaps with queer kinship in the works by Gillis and Vogel. Relatedly, I will also be working from the model for social praxis on offer in Douglas Crimp's important essay 'Mourning and militancy', which takes as its central premise (one that I share) the absolutely necessary connection between mourning/remembrance and activism, especially in the context of the queer community's responses to the AIDS pandemic and decades of unabated anti-gay violence.

I conclude the chapter with a very brief analysis of two queer plays which each, in their own way, seek to memorialise – in order to attempt to make sense of – the 1998 murder of Matthew Shepard. Terrence McNally's *Corpus Christi*, an intensely homoerotic retelling of the Biblical passion story, was the subject of bomb threats and picketing when it opened at the Manhattan Theatre Club in the fall of 1998. Following Shepard's murder in October of that year, McNally included a preface in the published version of the play that makes a direct link between the crucifixion of the play's fictional gay protagonist, Joshua, and that of the real-life Shepard. Moisés Kaufman and Tectonic Theater's *The Laramie Project* is based on interviews with residents of Laramie, Wyoming, in the immediate aftermath of Shepard's killing; a dozen or so actors voice the words of more than fifty distraught, angry, uncomprehending, and media-weary citizens – as well as their own – in an effort to tell the story of this community to the world and, in the words of one resident/ character, 'say it right'.[11] The play was subsequently made into an HBO movie with a who's who of high-profile Hollywood stars.[12]

Both plays are large ensemble pieces that eschew explicit focus on the homosexual victim-as-martyr in favour of a dissection (McNally allegorically, Kaufman documentarily) of the community that produced his homophobic killers. These men, equally our brothers, how do we remember them? I attempt to answer this question by first focusing on a key theatrical convention employed by each play, and then by returning to my opening framing discussion of the specific orientations of queer remembrance in Vancouver via references to performances both near (local stagings of *Corpus Christi* and *The Laramie Project* in May and October 2002, respectively) and far (analogous dance-theatre pieces created by UK companies Stan Won't Dance and DV8 Physical Theatre in 2004 and 2008). There, I will offer some final Butlerian remarks on mourning and melancholia – and what often remains 'unspeakable' in each on the world stage (including the frequent incommensurability of sexual, racial, and religious difference) – within the context of the Vancouver queer community's determined efforts to remember Aaron Webster, killed by gay bashers in the same park from which an AIDS memorial has been barred as unsuitable.

The landscape of remembrance

This last point refers to a particular confluence of the local, the global, and the performative that has necessarily influenced my thinking about the issues addressed in this chapter. I am referring to the completion (in July 2004) and dedication (on 1 December 2004, in a ceremony that coincided with World AIDS Day) of a long-planned, and long-delayed, memorial to British Columbians who have died of AIDS. The site of the memorial is Sunset Beach West, along a grassy and lightly treed knoll at the foot of Broughton Street and Beach Avenue, in the heart of down-town's west end and a short walk east of English Bay and the Stanley Park seawall. Its design consists of a series of twenty steel panels, each close to a metre in width, cut into and winding through the adjacent landscape like a ribbon unfurling in the wind. The memorial's foundation, like

---

11 Moisés Kaufman, and members of Tectonic Theater Project, *The Laramie Project* (New York: Vintage, 2001), p. 100. Further references will be cited in-text as *LP*.

12 *The Laramie Project* (2002). Directed by Moisés Kaufman. Written by Kaufman and members of the Tectonic Theater Project. Produced by Declan Baldwin. New York: HBO Home Video, 96 min.

Maya Lin's famous Vietnam Veterans' Memorial in Washington, DC, follows the natural grade level of the site, resulting in a height ranging from 0.75 to 1.5 metres. Again much like Lin's design, the panels that comprise the Vancouver AIDS Memorial have been laser cut with the names of those who have died from the disease, signifying 'their absence from our lives'.[13] Small holes have been placed next to each name so that mourners and visitors to the memorial might leave flowers or other tokens of remembrance for lost loved ones. Finally, the following stanza from Spanish–American writer George Santayana's 1896 commemorative verse 'To W.P.' scrolls above the names, at the top of the memorial:

> With you a part of me hath passed away,
> For in the peopled forest of my mind
> A tree made leafless by the wintry wind
> Shall never don again its green array
> Chapel and fireside, country road and bay,
> Have something of their friendliness resigned;
> Another, if I would, I could not find,
> And I am grown much older in a day.
> But yet I treasure in my memory
> Your gift of charity, your mellow ease,
> And the dear honor of your amity;
> For those once mine, my life is rich with these.
> And I scarce know which part may greater be, –
> What I keep of you, or you rob of me.[14]

Despite the performance of civic harmony that attended the official ground-breaking ceremony for the memorial in May 2002, and that was likewise featured prominently at the official dedication ceremony in December 2004, public goodwill surrounding the project has not always been very much in evidence. Nor was Sunset Beach, chosen only after an especially arduous and acrimonious two-year public consultation process in June 1998, the site originally proposed for the memorial. Indeed, when the then fledgling AIDS Memorial Committee, working in an ad hoc manner under the auspices of AIDS Vancouver and the Pacific AIDS Resource Centre, first approached the Vancouver Parks Board in 1996 about installing a public monument to the memory of those who have died from AIDS, they proposed a site adjacent Ceperley

---

13 Remarks drawn from the website of the *Vancouver AIDS Memorial: A British Columbia Landmark of Hope and Courage*, www.aidsmemorial.ca (accessed September 2004).

14 George Santayana, 'To W.P.', *Sonnets and Other Verses* (New York: Stone and Kimball, 1896), p. 62.

Park, near the Second Beach entrance to Stanley Park. This proposal was endorsed by the Parks Board at an in-camera meeting in November 1996. However, when word of the planned memorial and its proposed location leaked to the press, there was an immediate public outcry. Ostensibly, debate centred around the *lack* of public consultation surrounding the process, but various media polls conducted during the period repeatedly suggested that what people most objected to was the choice of Stanley Park as the site for the AIDS Memorial – and precisely because the spot was deemed *too* public.[15]

Ceperley Park, a highly trafficked part of Stanley Park, popular with both locals and tourists alike, and home to a playground, pool, and picnic area frequented by young children and families, was deemed inappropriate for a memorial to AIDS victims. Wasn't it enough that the area was annually turned into the start and end point for the Vancouver AIDS Walk each September? A more discreet location should be found for a permanent memorial. Of course what remained unacknowledged throughout this public discourse on the discourse of publicness was that the woods just north of Ceperley Park are highly trafficked in another way – namely, as a late-night cruising ground for gay, bisexual and otherwise identified men seeking sex with other men. In the homophobic equation of 'gay sex = AIDS' that frequently subtended the fractious debates in late 1996 around erecting a memorial at Ceperley, what remained palpable – even when unspoken – was the feeling that the gay community wished to flaunt itself in broad daylight yet again. Less than four months after the Eleventh International AIDS Conference in Vancouver had ostensibly announced to the world the 'end of AIDS' (via the discovery of protease inhibitors and a combination of powerful antiretroviral drugs that came to be known as the 'AIDS cocktail'), here were local activists wishing to resurrect the dead, rubbing normal citizens' noses in a killing field of their own making, one that had best remain hidden away in the dark.[16] Never mind that the killings that go on in this field in Stanley Park under cover of darkness, killings that remain un- or under-memorialised within Vancouver public discourse, have nothing at all to do with the human immunodeficiency virus, and everything to do with 'normal' boys who carry baseball bats – a point to which I will return at the end of this chapter.

---

15 See Keith Fraser, 'AIDS wall's site at issue', *Vancouver Province* (1 December 1997), p. A2.
16 Focusing on dances by Neil Greenberg and Bill T. Jones, David Román has analysed the consequences for performance of the shift in AIDS discourse following the 1996 Vancouver Conference in 'Not about AIDS', a chapter in his book *Performance in America: Contemporary US Culture and the Performing Arts* (Durham, NC: Duke University Press, 2005), pp. 49–77.

Vancouver's recent history has been particularly vexed on the subject of public memorials. For example, the fallout attending the December 1997 unveiling of artist Beth Alber's *Marker of Change* memorial in Thornton Park, commemorating the lives of the fourteen women murdered by Marc Lepine at Montreal's École Polytechnique eight years earlier, rehearsed in many ways the same debates around intentionality and appropriateness that have characterised the AIDS Memorial. The conservative local press, led by *Vancouver Sun* columnist Trevor Lautens, and North Vancouver Reform Party MP Ted White, were particularly aggrieved by the fact that the Women's Monument Project (a feminist collective working out of Capilano College overseeing the design competition, fundraising, and eventual installation of Alber's sculpture), like the Vancouver AIDS Memorial Society, saw the *Marker of Change* not merely as commemorative but also as explicitly educative, a way of focusing immediate local attention on the ongoing global phenomenon of male violence against women.[17] Clearly the memorial was meant as a feminist indictment of men, the argument went, and, as such, could not be seen as representative of a spirit of shared remembrance in any way. In this regard, critics pointed to the phrase 'for all women who have been murdered by men' in the memorial's dedication plaque as unnecessarily provocative.

That same year, Vancouver resident Don Larson angered many in the First Nations community when he spearheaded a campaign to create a monument honouring the memories of the women (many of them Aboriginal sex trade workers) who began disappearing from the DTES at a statistical rate of approximately two per year in the early 1980s, a phenomenon that was met with what now seems willful inattention on the part of police and the local media. Indeed, despite substantial evidence and ongoing pressure from the local community and relatives, Vancouver police refused throughout the 1980s and most of the 1990s to acknowledge a connection between the missing women from the DTES, or to entertain the possibility that a serial murderer might be preying upon them. It was only in 2001 that the police, in conjunction with the RCMP, set up a special Missing Women Task Force, eventually compiling the names of more than sixty-five women who had disappeared. A year later, in February 2002, Robert 'Willie' Pickton, a fifty-three-year-old pig farmer from Port Coquitlam, was finally arrested in connection with the case after the most comprehensive forensic search in Canadian

17 See Trevor Lautens, 'Monument against too many', *Vancouver Sun* (24 June 1993), p. A13; and Ann Duncan, 'Politics threaten massacre tribute', *Montreal Gazette* (10 September 1994), p. I5.

policing history turned up DNA evidence linked to the remains of several of the missing women on his property. Initially charged with twenty-six counts of murder, the judge presiding over the case, BC Supreme Court Justice James Williams, eventually split the indictment into two parts, fearing that a single murder trial involving so many counts would overburden the jury. Pickton thus went on trial in January 2007 for the first-degree murder of just six women – Sereena Abotsway, Marnie Frey, Andrea Jonesbury, Georgina Papin, Mona Wilson, and Brenda Wolfe – less than one-tenth of the total number of missing. After a nearly year-long trial that saw 193 exhibits entered as evidence, and that heard the testimony of 128 witnesses, on 9 December 2007 the jury returned a guilty verdict on all six counts. However, in doing so the jury had reduced the charge to second-degree murder on all counts, leaving many to question how what had been described in the media as one of the worst serial killings in recorded history could not be planned and premeditated, and others to speculate that the lack of evidence presented by the defence on how exactly Pickton had lured and killed his victims meant that the jury had no choice but to return the verdict they did. With life in prison an almost certainty for the killer, many – including the Attorney General of BC – have since questioned the need for a second trial, something that has angered friends and family of the twenty other victims whose murders Pickton has been charged with. A final terrible irony hovering over the entire case is that Pickton had been in police custody back in 1997 on charges of stabbing a local prostitute; however, the charges were stayed, and Pickton was released, free to prey upon the women of the DTES for another four years.[18]

Unable to count on the resources, support, or even compassion of local municipal power structures, grassroots activists in the First Nations community thus began in 1991 to stage a public performance of remembrance and a call to action for these same women in the form of an annual 'smudge ceremony' and accompanying memorial march and demonstration that was held each Valentine's Day.[19] Nevertheless, in the face of what was by then an ongoing embodied and collective performance of remembering, organised by and for the Aboriginal women of Vancouver, in 1997 Larson – who is male and white – went ahead and unilaterally commissioned the design of a memorial boulder. The boulder was installed in CRAB (Create a Real Available Beach) Park at

18 For a comprehensive summary of the entire case, see Lori Culbert's six-part expose, 'Pickton', *Vancouver Sun* (1 December 2007), pp. E1-8; and Lori Culbert, Neal Hall, and Jeff Lee, 'Emotional end to Pickton trial', *Vancouver Sun* (10 December 2007), pp. A1 and A4.

19 Caffyn Kelley, 'Creating memory, contesting history', *Matriart* 5 (1995), pp. 6–11.

Portside – 3.3 hectares of reclaimed land along the waterfront at the foot of Main Street, and the closest approximation of a 'real beach' available to residents of the DTES.[20] The fact that the monument's dedicatory inscription appropriates a traditional First Nations' 'form of address ["All my relations"] . . . used to begin or end a prayer, speech, or story'[21] only added insult to injury for many in the community. In an attempt to make amends, Larson worked directly with members of the First Nations community three years later to rename another nearby park, on Alexander Street, and to dedicate a separate boulder and park bench in memory of Wendy Poole, a First Nations woman whose murdered body was discovered nearby in 1989.

In June 2002, three blocks away from the site of both of these memorial rocks, mute witnesses as much to a majority community's silence as to a minority community's suffering, celebrated Anishinabe–Canadian artist Rebecca Belmore (she was Canada's representative at the 2006 Venice Biennale) insisted not just on speaking, but on shouting, the names of the dead and missing women when she performed the site-specific endurance piece *Vigil* as part of the tenth anniversary of Vancouver's Talking Stick Festival, an annual festival of Aboriginal arts organised by the legendary Margo Kane, Artistic Director of Full Circle First Nations Performance. Planting herself on the corner of Gore and Cordova Streets, in the heart of the DTES, Belmore, clad in faded blue jeans and a wife-beater, began the performance with a ritual cleansing of the material space of remembrance, donning pink rubber gloves and getting down on her hands and knees with a bucket of soapy water to scrub away the trace signs of the collected detritus of three squares of sullied urban sidewalk – graffiti, garbage, saliva, urine, used chewing gum, used condoms, used needles, used women. Literally embodying the social and sexual stratification of this no-go zone of the city via the imprinting of the first names of these women in magic marker on her arms, Belmore then lit several votive candles, before yelling out the names on her arms one by one, drawing a rose, replete with thorns, through her lips and teeth after each ecstatic invocation. The performance concludes with Belmore changing into a bright red dress, which she proceeds to nail methodically to a nearby telephone pole; in the subsequent struggle to free herself, the fabric of the dress is torn from

20 In their article '"How might a women's monument be different?"' (*Essays on Canadian Writing* 80 [2003], pp. 17–35), Christine Bold, Ric Knowles, and Belinda Leach discuss in more detail the public debates that greeted both Alber's *Marker of Change* and Larson's efforts to remember the missing women from Vancouver's DTES, situating those debates within the context of a larger project about feminist memorialisation in Canada.
21 *Ibid.*, p. 24.

18 Still from the 2002 video installation of Rebecca Belmore's *Vigil*

her body bit by bit, her dispossession and dishabille in the moment of performance's own disappearance standing in for the tattered remains, and what remains in tatters, of the lives of so many women so many of us in the audience had long ago forgotten. To this end, when the video of the performance was subsequently included as part of Belmore's 2003 solo exhibition *The Named and the Unnamed*, at the Morris and Helen Belkin Art Gallery, its installation included a unique sculptural feature that doubled as something of a cognitive prompt to the viewer. I am referring to the fact that the screen on which the video was projected was dotted with several dozen light bulbs (see figure 18). As curator Scott Watson summarises the effect, 'The light bulbs might be metaphorical extensions of the candles [Belmore] lights in *Vigil*. They create an unusual optical effect, dividing a viewer's perception so that we can see simultaneously the depth of field in the space of the projections and also upon its surface ... The lights are figuratively in our way, disrupting our vision the way the memory of these women ought to trouble our conscience'.[22]

A year after Belmore's original performance of *Vigil*, the DTES

---

22 Scott Watson, 'Foreword', in *Rebecca Belmore: The Named and the Unnamed* (Vancouver: Morris and Helen Belkin Art Gallery/University of British Columbia, 2003), pp. 7–8.

once again became the site of conflicts around competing performances of memory. More specifically, in the summer of 2003 Vancouver armed forces veterans reacted with outrage when a loose coalition of youthful protestors wishing to focus attention on homelessness, poverty, and City Hall's repeated delays in converting the abandoned Woodward's Building to social housing, set up an impromptu squat at Victory Square, site of the cenotaph commemorating British Columbians who lost their lives in World Wars I and II. The veterans saw the squatters' actions as a desecration and a violation of public memorial space devoted to the preservation of the past; they also worried that the protest would delay plans by the city to renovate and spruce up the memorial site in time for November Remembrance Day activities. For their part, the squatters argued that their occupation of the square constituted a different kind of (re)memorialisation, a protest against the city's active forgetting of its spatial present.[23] Ironically, when forced by a police injunction to vacate Victory Square, the protesters split their forces, with half decamping to CRAB Park, and the other half to Thornton Park.

And, finally, this genealogy of the recent performance of public memory in Vancouver would not be complete without us also returning to Ceperley Park. This is where a memorial to the victims of the bombing of Air India Flight 182, which exploded over the Irish Sea while en route from Vancouver to Sahar, India in June 1985, was finally unveiled in July 2007. The choice of Ceperley for the memorial (like the AIDS memorial, a sloping wall 18 metres in length featuring the names of the victims), and the use of the federal monies pledged to pay for it to simultaneously upgrade the adjacent playground, momentarily revived debate around the rejection of the area as a site for an AIDS memorial ten years earlier, with some in Vancouver's queer community accusing the Vancouver Parks Board of a double standard.[24] And yet many within Vancouver's South Asian community would no doubt argue that they had the prior claim to the space, with its prime view of the mouth of English Bay. For looming behind the scandal that was that very summer emerging as a result of the public inquiry into Canada's worst terrorist attack (and, until 9/11, the deadliest instance of aviation terrorism) was the memory of an earlier incident in which the good citizens of Vancouver sent Indians – fellow colonial subjects of Britain – to unwitting slaughter. However, the vessel this time was a boat rather than an airplane.

23 See Petti Fong, 'Veterans demand tenters end Victory Square protest', *Vancouver Sun* (17 July 2003), p. B3.
24 See Lori Kittelberg, 'Air India tribute proposed for Ceperley Park', *XTRA! West* (6 July 2006), pp. 7 and 9.

On 23 May 1914 the Komagata Maru, a Japanese ship chartered
from Hong Kong, arrived in Vancouver's English Bay carrying 376
passengers from India (340 Sikhs, 12 Hindus, and 24 Muslims) who
were intent on challenging Canada's then racist and exclusionary
immigration policies. Local government officials refused the passengers permission to land, and for two months there was a tense stand-
off. In the end, only 24 passengers were allowed to disembark and
remain in Vancouver, and on 23 July the Komagata Maru departed for
Hong Kong, and from thence back to Calcutta. There they were met
by gun-toting British officials, who promptly impounded the boat, and
announced that the remaining passengers would be deported by train
to the Punjab. The passengers protested and another fraught waiting
game ensued, eventually resulting in the senseless deaths of twenty of
those who had originally made the arduous journey to Vancouver.[25]
An ugly episode from Vancouver's 'circum-Pacific' past that continues
to haunt its performative present, also crucially oriented toward the
Pacific Rim (as I demonstrated in chapter 1), the events surrounding
the Komagata Maru have inspired plays, films, novels, and a nascent
protest coalition that has taken its cue from the larger Asian redress
movement in Canada.[26] Indeed, as Vancouver geared up to 'commemorate' the one-hundredth anniversary of the 1907 anti-Asian riot, and
in the wake of the federal government's successive apologies and agreements to compensate the Japanese–Canadian and Chinese–Canadian
communities for the historical wrongs of internment and head taxes,
respectively, many in the South Asian community were reviving
memories of the Komagata Maru, and deliberately playing them off of
Air India, in order to demand an official apology of their own.[27] That
apology eventually came, but not as a formal declaration in Canada's
House of Commons, as most expected; rather, Prime Minister Stephen

25 For a full redaction of the details of the incident, see Hugh J.M. Johnston, *The Voyage
    of the Komagata Maru: The Sikh Challenge to Canada's Colour Bar* (Delhi: Oxford
    University Press, 1979).
26 See the radio play by Sugith Varughese, *Entry Denied*, in Damiano Pietropaolo (ed.),
    Where is Here?: The Drama of Immigration, Volume I (Winnipeg: Scirocco, 2005); the
    stage play by Sharon Pollock, *The Komagata Maru Incident* (Toronto: Playwrights
    Co-op, 1978); the documentary film by Ali Kazimi, *Continuous Journey* (Peripheral
    Visions Film and Video, 2004); a feature film currently in development by Deepa
    Mehta, *Exclusion*; and the novel by Anita Rau Badami, *Can You Hear the Nightbird
    Call?* (Toronto: Knopf, 2006), which makes an explicit link between the Komagata
    Maru incident and the Air India bombing. See also the Komagata Maru Heritage
    Foundation, which has long lobbied the Canadian government for compensation:
    www.komagatamaru.ca (accessed February 2008).
27 See Kim Bolan, 'Komagata Maru kin want amends', *Vancouver Sun* (23 May 2006),
    p. B1.

Harper tacked it on to the end of a speech he delivered in August 2008 to Indo-Canadians gathered in another park – this one in the Vancouver suburb of Surrey – on the occasion of British Columbia's 150th birthday. The move was immediately decried as a slap in the face.[28]

'The protocols of mourning'

At the heart of these debates are some fundamentally difficult and necessarily polarising questions about public memory, memorialisation, and mourning: Who gets to publicly remember, for whom, where, in what ways, and how? What constitutes an appropriate (there's that word again) display – psychically, materially – of mourning? When does respectful remembrance cross the line into social activism? And how are all of these rituals further complicated by what Marianne Hirsch and others have called the phenomenon of 'postmemory',[29] in which the 'performance' of remembrance via Internet sites, television shows, and other media technologies designed to remember for us, produces a constant – though necessarily simulacral and ersatz – condition of reminiscence and retrospection that signals not so much a felt connection with the past (including the very recent past) as a profound *dis*connection from it? For Andreas Huyssen, this globalised penchant for instant memorialisation – in everything from hurried architectural competitions to rebuild Ground Zero in New York City to more populist expressions of remembrance, such as roadside displays of flowers marking the site of a car crash – has, paradoxically, produced what he calls a 'culture of amnesia', whose primary symptom is the 'atrophy' of historical consciousness, aided and abetted by a high-tech 'media world spinning a cocoon of timeless claustrophobia and nightmarish phantasms and simulation', in which there is 'nothing to remember, nothing to forget'.[30] However, as my partner, Richard, likes to remind me – pointing to his own recent work on literary representations of Canadian cultural memory – Huyssen's argument is profoundly 'normative': 'there are good memories and there are bad memories for [Huyssen], and bad memories usually tend to be associated with populist expression – what one might call "history from

28 Nicole Tomlinson, 'Indo-Canadians "deceived" by Komagata Maru apology', *Vancouver Sun* (5 August 2008), p. A1.
29 See especially Marianne Hirsch's *Family Frames: Photography, Narrative and Postmemory* (Cambridge, MA: Harvard University Press, 1997).
30 Andreas Huyssen, *Twilight Memories: Marking Time in a Culture of Amnesia* (New York: Routledge, 1995), pp. 7 and 9.

below" as opposed to the official or institutional histories most often valorised by the state'.[31]

Although Huyssen has since revised his take somewhat in his book *Present Pasts*, even there his critical perspective 'is guided by the conviction that too much of the contemporary memory discourse focuses on the personal',[32] especially with respect to episodes of trauma. Such sentiments issue from the statist view that nations, for example, primarily build public monuments to – and organise museums around – great events and great men. These spatial aids to memory (what Pierre Nora has theorised, in the French context, as *les lieux de mémoire*[33]), so the theory goes, in turn help citizens remember iconographically, ensuring that, in the present, we will not forget the past, lest we repeat its mistakes. But this somewhat naively holistic and ameliorative view of historical memory as a collective cultural repository from which humanity progresses forward is, it seems to me, undercut by precisely the more populist, impromptu, localised, and, yes, performative forms of memorialisation that Huyssen eschews from his analysis. Indeed, as Roach has pointed out so powerfully in the introduction to *Cities of the Dead*, Nora formulated his notion of *lieux de mémoire*, or 'places of memory', precisely in order to distinguish these 'artificial sites of the modern production of national and ethnic memory' from *milieux de mémoire*, 'environments of memory' that were made up of 'the largely oral and corporeal retentions of traditional cultures', a '"true memory"' or '"living memory"' comprised of 'patterned movements made and remembered by bodies, residual movements retained implicitly in images or words (or in the silences between them), and imaginary movements dreamed in minds', and that remain 'variously resistant' to official discourses of forgetting 'through the transmission of gestures, habits, and skills'.[34]

Take, for example, a queer ritual of remembrance such as the Names Project Memorial Quilt, and its relation to how bodies (as opposed to monuments) re-member space, be it the space of a national government capital or the space of history. What the formerly semi-regular unfurling of the quilt on the grounds of the National Mall in Washington,

31 Richard Cavell, 'Histories of forgetting: Canadian representations of war and the politics of cultural memory', in Serge Jaumain and Éric Remacle (eds), *Mémoire de guerre et construction de la paix: Mentalités et choix politiques: Belgique – Europe – Canada* (Brussels: Peter Lang, 2006), p. 68.

32 Andreas Huyssen, *Present Pasts: Urban Palimpsests and the Politics of Memory* (Stanford: Stanford University Press, 2003), p. 8.

33 See Pierre Nora (ed.), *Les Lieux de mémoire* (Paris: Gallimard, 1997).

34 Roach, *Cities of the Dead*, p. 26. See also Nora, 'Between memory and history: *Les Lieux de mémoire*', *Representations* 26 (1989), pp. 7–25.

DC[35] demonstrated most vividly was that recovering a narrative of collective memory need not be at the expense of all of the individual bodies and personal stories subsumed within that narrative; nor must memorialisation's pedagogical function be separated from its political one.[36] Each vibrantly sewn and personalised panel seeks to preserve individual eccentricities and encapsulate the life story of its memorial subject, lest his or her death fade into a roll call of anonymous statistics about AIDS' human toll. At the same time, the display of this individual *privation* is undertaken as part of a highly theatrical, ritualised, and intensely *public* act: each panel is laid out for viewing in an elaborately choreographed manner as the names of persons who have died from the disease are read out by alternating participants at a microphone. Carried out in the shadow of a nation's ultimate folly (the hyper-phallic Washington Monument), just a short distance away from the rows of indistinguishable white crosses at Arlington National Cemetery and from the equally white seat of world democracy from which issued the edict 'Don't ask, don't tell', such a memorial project is a defiantly personalist resistance of the attempts by governments to muzzle and displace grief through monumentalist abstraction. The Quilt insists not only on telling, but also on showing; it is a performance of mourning that doubles as a political occupation. As Elinor Fuchs notes in a 1993 article originally published in *American Theatre* (and reprinted in her book *The Death of Character*), the whole idea of the Quilt,

> combining monumentality with patchwork, expresses at once the scale of the leaping world AIDS crisis and its assault on humanist faith in order and social continuity. Pastiche and defiant disunity are by now familiar hallmarks of the postmodernist artwork, but here they are returned to a humanism which insists that this exuberant life not be forgotten. In the way it remembers, the Quilt is more relaxed, more inclusive, more sensual, more human, more *theatrical* than anything previously imagined in the protocols of mourning.[37]

---

35 The Quilt, which now comprises some 45,000 panels, weighs more than 54 tonnes, and covers approximately 1,270,350 square feet (or roughly the equivalent of forty-seven football fields if laid end to end), was last displayed in its entirety in October 1996. While portions of the Quilt continue to tour the US and the world, for obvious logistical reasons there are no immediate plans to assemble and display the whole thing again; see the AIDS Memorial Quilt website at www.aidsquilt.org (accessed September 2004).

36 On this point, see especially the essays collected in Roger Simon, Sharon Rosenberg, and Claudia Eppert (eds), *Between Hope and Despair: Pedagogy and the Remembrance of Historical Trauma* (Lanham: Rowman and Littlefield, 2000).

37 Elinor Fuchs, *The Death of Character: Perspectives on Theater after Modernism* (Bloomington: Indiana University Press, 1996), p. 196.

I want to link up what Fuchs singles out here as the Quilt's inherent 'theatricality', its necessary 'imaginativeness', with Huyssen's speculative hand-wringing about the 'cultural amnesia' that he sees as a worrisome by-product of such memorial projects. At a physiological level, of course, the cognitive condition of forgetting must in some senses always precede, even prompt, the cognitive condition of remembering. That is, an irony that seems to be lost on Huyssen is that we can only remember something that we have first forgotten. And how do you remember that which official or institutional histories of the sort privileged by Huyssen have refused to record, and thereby literally make impossible to forget? I overstate my case, to be sure, but I do so in order to make an important point about the necessarily performative nature of queer rituals of remembrance and mourning. Phelan puts it this way: 'As an art form whose primary function is to meditate on the threshold that heralds between-ness, theatre encourages a specific and intense cathetic response in those who define themselves as liminal tricksters, socially disenfranchised, sexually aberrant, addicted, and otherwise queerly alienated from the law of the father. Queers are queer because we recognise that we have survived our own deaths'.[38]

When hate crimes against queers go unreported, when the names of gay men and lesbians killed in Nazi death camps are nowhere to be found at the Holocaust Memorial at Yad Vashem,[39] when the archiving of gay life – let alone gay death – has been and continues to be so scant and piecemeal, how does one remember? One remembers by sewing a piece of fabric onto another, by staging kiss-ins and die-ins at public institutions in major urban metropolises, by placing flowers and placards and talismans in a fence in Wyoming (for a Matthew Shepard) or along a forest path in Vancouver (for an Aaron Webster), by writing plays and choreographing dances for lost brothers. In the absence of built monuments, queer acts of remembrance, witnessing, and mourning necessarily become ritualised through performance, just as they per force get linked to local manifestations of grassroots activism. Indeed, a key element of the organisational success of groups such as ACT UP, AIDS Action Now, Queer Nation, and Outrage! since the 1980s has been their recognition of the co-extensiveness of activism and

38 Phelan, *Mourning Sex*, p. 16.
39 This is not meant to deny the efforts of other memorialisations of the Holocaust, both from within and without the queer community, to record this history of persecution. See, in particular, the permanent special exhibit at the United States Holocaust Memorial Museum in Washington, DC, on the 'Nazi persecution of homosexuals, 1933–1945', www.ushmm.org/museum/exhibit/online/hsx/ (accessed September 2006); and Rob Epstein and Jeffrey Friedman's documentary film *Paragraph 175* (New Yorker Films, 1999).

memorialisation, and their ability to adapt the performance of each to a specific situational context. A march and rally in New York, a charity concert in London, a candlelight vigil in Toronto or Vancouver: at some level, with each event, street theatre segues into social protest, just as the mourning of an individual loss helps to clarify the 'fundamental dependency and ethical responsibility' of our participation in a 'political community of a complex order'.[40]

Thus, in much the same way that Fuchs has examined how the Quilt necessarily sunders 'mourning's ancient links to church, family, class and state' and 're-imagines a connection between politics and the sacred',[41] I want now, in the remainder of this chapter, to turn to an analysis of the post-AIDS rituals of grieving, remembrance, art, and social activism in two other performative contexts: dance and theatre. In so doing, I want to link up Butler's theorising of the relationship between mourning and (queer) kinship with a notion of vigilant remembrance that is both situationally contingent and relationally binding – if not always politically transformative. Christopher Gillis, Carl Vogel, Matthew Shepard, Russell Henderson, Aaron McKinney, Aaron Webster: How am I connected to these men? Why is it incumbent upon me to remember them? How, to use Butler's language, does the rehearsal of their deaths, or the deaths they caused, both constitute me and the other in me? And how does it undo me?[42]

Queer kinship: Gillis and Vogel

Following the 1993 death of her brother, Christopher, who was himself a member of the Paul Taylor Dance Company in New York, Margie Gillis added two new pieces to her staple of solo dances: *Landscape*, a stark meditation on impending death choreographed for her by Christopher from his hospital bed, and *Torn Roots, Broken Branches*, a frenzied outpouring of grief that she herself created. In the first, Gillis enters the stage down right. She wears a simple white shift reminiscent of a hospital gown and is dragging a bare tree branch on the floor behind her. A solitary strip of torn cloth has been tied to one of the branch's outermost limbs, and before the piece is over Gillis will add another. As the haunting sounds of an Edvard Grieg composition rise and fall, Gillis begins her long painful walk across the stage, progressing slowly, in halting and unsure steps. Her movements, normally Duncanesque in their

40 Butler, *Precarious Life*, p. 22.
41 Fuchs, *The Death of Character*, p. 197.
42 See Butler, *Precarious Life*, pp. 22–3.

expansiveness, are here tiny and contained and precise. Indeed, Gillis's solidity as a dancer, the generous shape of her arms and legs, makes the frailty of her gestures in this piece even more powerful and poignant; when, in the middle of the stage, she stumbles and falls, for example, we know that something more inevitable and inexorable than mere gravity is weighing her down. Near the end of *Landscape*, Gillis glances back over her shoulder, measuring the distance she has travelled, trying to bridge the gap between where she has come from and where she is going. The psychological and spiritual isolation that Christopher Gillis has attempted to convey with this piece is encapsulated in this one brief moment and the effect is devastating – knowing this, devastated herself, his sister, Margie, picks up the branch and continues on her journey, exiting the stage upper left.

The image of the broken branch is what links Christopher's vision of his own death with Margie's performance of her mourning. Brother and sister's respective choreographic styles, however, could not be more different. In *Torn Roots, Broken Branches*, the dull grey backdrop of *Landscape* is replaced by one that is blood red. The piece begins with Gillis in the middle of the stage, hands covering her face, dressed head to toe in black: black hat, long-sleeved black bodice buttoned to the throat, full-length black skirt – a formal funereal shroud that will serve alternately as a prop and a shield, parts of which Gillis will gradually shed, throughout the next four minutes. To the keening wail of Sinéad O'Connor's 'I am Stretched on Your Grave', a contemporary arrange-ment of a traditional Irish dirge, Gillis performs her own dance of mourning, beginning slowly and precisely with small circular steps and slowly unfurling arm and finger extensions. As the song picks up speed, particularly in the closing fiddle section, so too does Gillis, whirling about in faster and wider circles, shaking her skirts and hair in fierce fury, her pain and anger and guilt registering ever more profoundly, ever more clearly, on her face and body – in the wild, despairing look of her eyes, the tight clench of her jaw, the lowered outstretched palms that rhythmically grasp at and release only empty air. To label the combined effect as cathartic does not nearly go far enough in describing what both Gillis and the audience have been through by the end of the piece. Indeed, as with Gillis's iconic predecessor in the dramatisation of sisterly grief, Antigone, cathartic release is arguably replaced by something more akin to what Butler would call 'melancholic *incorporation*',[43] with Gillis

43 Judith Butler, 'Melancholy gender/refused identification', in *The Psychic Life of Power: Theories in Subjection* (Stanford: Stanford University Press, 1997), pp. 134 and *passim*. For a specific application of Butler's theory of melancholic incorporation to AIDS choreography, see David Gere, *How to Make Dances in an Epidemic: Tracking*

preserving, through her choreography, the loss of her brother – who was, crucially, her first dance partner – as constitutive of her very being as a grieving subject (a point to which I will shortly return). And this, to allude to my opening epigraph from Derrida, constitutes the 'force' of each sister's mourning, as well as the force of her protest.

That double force, I would argue, is transferred, as well, to the audience. Often accused of sacrificing technique for emotional intensity in her performances, in this case it is precisely Gillis making transparent her corporeal vulnerability on stage that allows for a concomitant empathic identification on the part of her spectators. I speak from experience, having attended successive solo recitals by Gillis over the years, dating back to a 1994 benefit in support of the Canadian AIDS charity Dancers for Life at the Vancouver Playhouse, where I first saw both *Landscape* and *Torn Roots, Broken Branches* performed in repertory. Sedimented in my own body's memory from that time is an image – of the woman seated next to me weeping quietly – and a reflexive motor response – of me reaching silently for her hand and her letting me take it and both of us squeezing together, neither one of us wanting to let go. This at once private and public moment of shared intimacy – as apt a starting place as any for a reconstituted notion of sexual citizenship in the age of AIDS – was triangulated through our mutual witnessing of – and partaking in – Gillis's own equally intimate expression of the emotional and physical labour involved in the work of mourning.

We witness something similar in Paula Vogel's *The Baltimore Waltz*, which, as Vogel states in her 'Playwright's note', was written as a direct result of her brother Carl's death from AIDS in 1988. The published play-text reprints a hilarious and touching letter from brother to sister regarding the former's wishes for his memorial service, and Vogel's dedication reads '*To the memory of Carl – because I cannot sew*'.[44] The play premiered at New York's Circle Repertory Company in January 1992 under the inspired direction of Anne Bogart, and featured memorable performances by Cherry Jones and Richard Thompson as siblings Anna and Carl (the two actors would team up again three years later in the Tony Award-winning revival of *The Heiress*), and Joe Mantello (soon to star as Louis in the Broadway premiere of Tony Kushner's *Angels in America*) in a succession of supporting roles. Like the best eulogies, Vogel's tribute to her brother is confined to one economical ninety-minute act, and combines moments of unbearable pathos with side-splitting laughs. It opens

Choreography in the Age of AIDS (Madison: University of Wisconsin Press, 2004), especially chapter 2, pp. 91–137.
44 Paula Vogel, *The Baltimore Waltz and other plays* (New York: Theatre Communications Group, 1996), p. 3. Further references will be cited in-text as *BW*.

in a Baltimore, Maryland, hospital. While sitting in a starkly lit waiting room, Anna imagines a final journey to Europe with her brother, Carl, who is slowly dying in another room from AIDS-related pneumonia. It is this dream voyage that comprises most of the play, and in it Anna, and not Carl, is sick, having contracted Acquired Toilet Disease, or ATD, a fatal illness spread through contaminated potty seats that seems to afflict mostly single female elementary school teachers. Having learned from Anna's doctor about the experimental research of one Dr Todesrocheln, a Viennese urologist, and having packed, upon the instructions of his old university pal, Harry Lime, his childhood stuffed rabbit, Carl whisks his sister off to Europe for what she thinks will be a final fling, but what he hopes will result in a cure.

In a swift progression of thirty short scenes Anna and Carl hop from Paris to Amsterdam to Berlin to Vienna, all the while trailed by a shadowy figure referred to in the text only as the 'Third Man', a composite character who has the disconcerting habit of metamorphosising, depending upon the specific locale, into either a potential lover for Anna or a possible enemy for Carl. In these scenes Vogel skewers every conceivable stereotype and convention, from the linguistic trials of American tourists to the new age wisdom of Elizabeth Kubler-Ross:

> CARL: Calm down, sweetie. You're angry. It's only natural to be angry. Elizabeth Kubler-Ross says that –
> ANNA: What does she know about what it feels like to die?! Elizabeth Kubler-Ross can sit on my face. (*BW*, p. 27)

Here, Anna's potty mouth, speaking from and to the pathogenesis *and* the pathologisation of her disease, expresses what Kubler-Ross has no room for in her strictly delimited five stages of grief, namely the *eros* of loss. Indeed, one of the things that was so refreshing about Vogel's play when it first appeared was how exuberantly 'unchaste' it was in its AIDS dramaturgy, with Anna responding to her diagnosis, for example, by taking up sexually with virtually every man she encounters in Europe. This superabundance of libidinal energy was something that director Sandhano Schultze and star Patti Allan brought to the proceedings in spectacularly theatrical fashion during Pink Ink Theatre's local Vancouver production of the play in the spring of 1993. In so doing, they reminded me, precisely at the moment when I was beginning to get worn down as a result of my volunteer work with the Pacific AIDS Resource Centre, that 'mourning presupposes desire and cannot proceed without it'.[45] By contrast, reviews

---

45 Gere, *How to Make Dances in an Epidemic*, p. 99.

of the 2004 New York revival of *The Baltimore Waltz* as part of Signature Theatre's Paula Vogel season tended to see the play's manic zaniness as evidence of the datedness of its satire, reading the play as an artefact from the early days of AIDS rather than as a ritual performance of mourning, which, as we have seen, never goes out of fashion.[46] And would that we could, in 2004, actually consign some of the play's set pieces, such as the homophobia that attends out gay teachers in public schools and the clandestine efforts still required in many parts of the world to secure potentially life-saving AIDS drugs, to the global dustheap of history.

The production notes for *The Baltimore Waltz* call for a lavish, wildly varied, and deliberately clichéd musical score. And, as with Gillis's performance, dance becomes the carapace both of a brother's death and a sister's mourning. In the final three scenes, for example, Vogel carefully choreographs the climax and rapid denouement of the play around the hackneyed violin strains of three successive Strauss waltzes. In the first of these scenes, a conscious homage to the climactic confrontation between Orson Welles and Joseph Cotten in the 1949 film version of *The Third Man*, Carl and his friend-turned-nemesis, Harry Lime, 'waltz-struggle' for Carl's stuffed rabbit on the Prater ferris wheel in Vienna. Harry eventually gives Carl a final, and presumably fatal, push and 'waltzes off with the rabbit' (*BW*, p. 51). In the next scene, the urine-swilling Dr Todesrocheln asks a frightened Anna 'WO IST DEIN BRUDER?' before transforming before her eyes into the Baltimore doctor from the play's opening scene. Anna, suddenly realising that she is now 'awake', rushes to Carl's bedside, only to find him 'stiff beneath a white sheet' (*BW*, p. 55). To the tempo of 'The Emperor Waltz' Anna tries to revive her dead brother, but to no avail. In the play's closing sequence, however, we are briefly transported back to the realm of fantasy. As the stage directions read, '*Softly, a Strauss waltz begins. Carl, perfectly well, waits for Anna. He is dressed in Austrian military regalia. They waltz off as the lights dim*' (*BW*, p. 57). This final tableau, reminiscent as it is of the scene near the end of the first part of Kushner's *Angels in America*, where Prior is permitted one last dance with Louis,[47] is of course doubly encoded with meaning. The waltz, traditionally a dance of courtship, is here inverted as the *danse macabre*, in which Anna is literally partnered with death

---

46 See, for example, Helen Shaw, 'The Baltimore schmaltz', *The New York Sun* (6 December 2004), www.nysun.com/article/5841 (accessed May 2007).

47 See Tony Kushner, *Angels in America, Part One: Millennium Approaches* (New York: Theatre Communications Group, 1993), p. 114. Again, a further connection between the two plays is that actor/director Joe Mantello originated, within the space of a year, the roles of Louis and The Third Man in the initial New York productions of *Angels in America* and *The Baltimore Waltz*. Mantello also directed the New York premiere of Terrence McNally's *Corpus Christi*, discussed below.

in the form of her brother, their rehearsal of a familiar, repetitive, and circular two-step a moving attempt on Anna's – and Vogel's – part to forestall the return to 'reality' that Freud, for one, sees as the normative end point of the work of mourning.

Freud certainly hovers uncannily behind much of the psycho-sexual satire and parodying of biomedical etiology in Vogel's play. Not only does the Viennese setting of much of the interior fantasy sequence of the play necessarily evoke the analyst's ghost, but Dr Todesrocheln's ('death rattle') repeated confrontations of Anna from within the melancholic space of that fantasy regarding the whereabouts of her brother can be seen as a self-conscious theatricalisation of the talking cure, an attempt (potentially harmful, as Freud himself notes) to wrest Anna's ego from its excessively morbid identification with her lost love object, in this case Carl. In his famous essay on 'Mourning and melancholia', Freud distinguishes between two types of mourning. What he labels so-called 'normal' mourning manifests itself initially in individuals as opposition to the abandoning of libidinal attachment to the deceased or lost object, but whose work is eventually completed through first the hyper-cathecting and then the detachment of 'memories and expectations . . . bound to the [lost] object', resulting in a return to 'reality'.[48] By contrast, the so-called 'pathological' condition of mourning, what Freud refers to as 'melancholia', arises essentially from a narcissistic prolonging of libidinal attachment, or ego-identification, with the lost object.[49] As Freud pithily summarises, 'In mourning it is the world which has become poor and empty; in melancholia it is the ego itself'.[50]

Following the Freudian model, then, Gillis's addition of *Landscape* and *Torn Roots, Broken Branches* to her repertoire, her apparently *compulsive repetition* (to allude to another of Freud's famous theories) of them on stages across the world, suggests that she is performing 'melancholia' rather than 'mourning'. Even the lyrics of O'Connor's song – 'So I'm stretched on your grave and will lie there forever/If your hands were in mine, I'd be sure we'd not sever' – are suggestive of deeper-than-'normal' attachment. So too with Vogel. In her 'Playwright's note', she states that she began writing *The Baltimore Waltz* as a way of exorcising her own personal demons *vis-à-vis* guilt about not accompanying her brother on his last tour of Europe. But while Freud insists that

---

48 Sigmund Freud, 'Mourning and melancholia', in *The Standard Edition of the Complete Psychological Works of Sigmund Freud*, vol. 14, trans. and ed. James Strachey (London: Hogarth, 1957), pp. 244–5.
49 *Ibid.*, pp. 250ff.
50 *Ibid.*, p. 246.

melancholia 'is marked by a determinant which is absent in normal mourning',[51] he also never defines what 'normal' signifies in this context (nor even what a return to 'reality' might look like). And while Freud would later, in *The Ego and the Id*, revise slightly his strict division between proper mourning and improper melancholy, noting that the identification with the lost love object in the latter might in fact be a pre-condition to the successful resolution of the former, he does still seem to insist that a giving up of that object must finally occur.[52] However, as Butler has persuasively shown, it is precisely this coextensiveness of the ego with its disavowed object choices that makes melancholia the constitutive condition of normative social relations in Western culture, a process which sees heterosexual genders, for example, institutionalise and memorialise themselves precisely through a *refusal* of the identifica-tions involved in mourning, including the renunciation of the loss of *homosexual* genders as 'a possibility of love'.[53]

Butler's theorisation of heterosexual gender identification as a kind of melancholia, in which unresolved same-sex desire is internalised as a prohibition that precedes the incest taboo, has been articulated in differ-ent ways across the body of her work, including most representatively *Gender Trouble, Bodies That Matter, The Psychic Life of Power*, and *Undoing Gender*.[54] However, it is in *Antigone's Claim*, via her reading of Sophocles' play (structurally the concluding part of his *Oedipus* trilogy, but, crucially in terms of chronology of composition, the first part to be written), and its treatment in Western philosophical discourse, that Butler demonstrates most forcefully how gender melancholia has helped

---

51 *Ibid.*, p. 250.
52 Freud, 'The ego and the id', in *The Standard Edition of the Complete Psychological Works of Sigmund Freud*, vol. 19, trans and ed. James Strachey (London: Hogarth, 1961), pp. 12–66.
53 Butler, *Bodies That Matter: On the Discursive Limits of 'Sex'* (New York: Routledge, 1993), p. 235. See also Butler, 'Melancholy gender/refused identification', pp. 132–50; and *Precarious Life*, pp. 20–1.
54 See Butler, *Gender Trouble: Feminism and the Subversion of Identity* (New York: Routledge, 1990), pp. 63ff.; *Bodies That Matter*, pp. 235–6ff.; and *Undoing Gender* (New York: Routledge, 2004), pp. 152–60. See, as well, the following comments by Gayle Rubin in 'The traffic in women: "the political economy" of sex', in Rayna R. Reiter (ed.), *Toward an Anthropology of Women* (New York: Monthly Review Press, 1975): 'the incest taboo presupposes a prior, less articulate taboo on homosexuality. A prohibition against *some* heterosexual unions assumes a taboo against *non*hetero-sexual unions. Gender is not only an identification with one sex; it also entails that sexual desire be directed toward the other sex. The sexual division of labour is implicated in both aspects of gender – male and female it creates them, and it creates them heterosexual' (p. 180). And this from Monique Wittig's *The Straight Mind and Other Essays* (Boston: Beacon Press, 1992): 'the straight mind continues to affirm that incest, and not homosexuality, represents its major interdiction. Thus, when thought by the straight mind, homosexuality is nothing but heterosexuality' (p. 28).

structure and hierarchise kinship patterns in our society, patterns whose markers of exclusion only fully emerge in death and the performance of mourning. And, in whose normative constitution we also, per force, witness a perverse negation, or non-consummation of the family romance: as Butler puts it, 'Antigone, who concludes the oedipal drama, fails to produce heterosexual closure for that drama'.[55] At the same time, the prohibition against incest enacted in Sophocles' play, according to Butler, is really something of a red herring. What is more important is how that prohibition has symbolically come to be memorialised as standing in for other socially taboo, morally denigrated, and juridically invalid relationships, modes of gender expression, sexuality, and ways of being and loving in this world, ways that continue to be placed outside the bounds of the normalised nuclear family and the human, and thus subject to social scrutiny, regulation and policing by the state:

> When the incest taboo works *in this sense* to foreclose a love that is not incestuous, what is produced is a shadowy realm of love, a love that persists in spite of its foreclosure in an ontologically suspended mode . . . Do we say that families that do not approximate the norm but mirror the norm in some apparently derivative way are poor copies, or do we accept that the ideality of the norm is undone precisely through the complexity of its instantiation? For those relations that are denied legitimacy, or that demand new terms of legitimation, are neither dead nor alive, figuring the nonhuman at the border of the human. And it is not simply that these are relations that cannot be honored, cannot be openly acknowledged, and cannot therefore be publicly grieved, but that these relations involve persons who are also restricted in the very act of grieving, who are denied the power to confer legitimacy on loss.[56]

To put this in more familiar contemporary terms, what if today Antigone were attempting to mourn the death of her common-law husband, a former step-daughter from a second marriage that had ended but with whom she was still close, a gay male friend she cared for throughout a prolonged illness, her lesbian lover? In this respect, the force of Antigone's protest, like Gillis's and Vogel's, comes through the staging of their *private* sisterly grief in very *public* acts of ritualised remembrance, acting out, and up, performing the personal as political as a direct intervention against a state-sponsored discourse about who can and cannot be mourned, about what, to use Butler's phrasing, remains unspeakable, and unspeakably violent, about any encounter

---

55 Judith Butler, *Antigone's Claim: Kinship Between Life and Death* (New York: Columbia University Press, 2000), p. 76.
56 *Ibid.*, pp. 78–9; emphasis in original.

with difference.[57] As Phelan remarks, Antigone and – lest we forget – Ismene, both equally caught, in their different ways of mourning, between life and death, point 'to a different form of theatre sisters might one day invent. Such a theatre would be more precise than Sophocles's or Lacan's about the distinction between desire and love'.[58]

Moreover, as Douglas Crimp has pointed out, 'for Freud, [mourning] is a solitary undertaking';[59] at no time does he conceive of it as a shared activity. And it is on this account that I consider the works by Gillis and Vogel to challenge fundamentally the standard Freudian model of mourning. This is also where the concept of performance becomes crucial. For performance, it seems to me, whether we are using the term in a 'theatrical' or 'theoretical' (i.e., Austinian–Derridean–Butlerian–Sedgwickian speech act) sense, always requires an audience. Gillis's and Vogel's *public* performance of their bereavement, like Fuchs's description of the public displaying of the Quilt, their invitation to audiences to join the dance, as it were, is not a wilful surrendering to the singular oppression of grief; rather, it is an acknowledgment, to return to Butler, that in the spectacle of the self's 'undoing' that necessarily attends the process of mourning, also lies the possibility of remaking or refashioning new models of social collectivity, new networks of community action, and new patterns of intersubjective response.[60]

And yet, as Crimp has also pointed out, while collective public mourning rituals have their own affective and even political force, 'they nevertheless often seem, from an activist perspective, indulgent, sentimental, defeatist – a perspective only reinforced . . . by media

57 See Butler, *Precarious Life*, pp. 48–9.
58 Phelan, *Mourning Sex*, p. 16. In their remarks on Sophocles's play, both Phelan and Butler are drawing on and revising Lacan's famous reading of *Antigone* in his *Seminar VII*. For Lacan, Antigone bridges not only the divide between life and death, but also between the imaginary and the symbolic, her defiance of Creon and the law of the father in death a necessary consequence of her tainted birth. See Lacan, *The Seminar of Jacques Lacan, Book VII: The Ethics of Psychoanalysis, 1959–60*, ed. Jacques-Alain Miller, trans. Dennis Porter (New York: Norton, 1992).
59 Douglas Crimp, 'Mourning and militancy', in Russell Ferguson *et al.* (eds), *Out There: Marginalization and Contemporary Cultures* (Cambridge, MA: MIT Press, 1990), p. 236.
60 In this regard, it is important to remember that the dance and theatre communities have been at the forefront of mobilising in the fight against AIDS: think of the DIFFA Dance and Design Project or Equity Cares/Broadway Fights AIDS in New York; think of Dancers for Life or Theatre Cares Week here in Canada. See, as well, in this regard Marita Sturken's *Tangled Memories: The Vietnam War, the AIDS Epidemic, and the Politics of Remembering* (Berkeley: University of California Press, 1997), p. 201, which likewise discusses Freud's dismissal of 'the role of collective mourning' within the context of the 'conversations with the dead' enacted through the AIDS Quilt.

constructions of [both mourners and mourned] as hapless victims'.[61]
Crimp casts aside Freud's interdiction that 'any interference with
[mourning is] useless or even harmful',[62] and argues instead for an
active – and *activist* – channelling of grief and loss into the forceful
mobilising of the tenuous collective social body that AIDS has per force
made not just of the queer community, but of us all:

> We can then partially revise our sense . . . of the incompatibility between
> mourning and activism and say that, for many gay men dealing with AIDS
> deaths, militancy might arise from conscious conflicts *within* mourning
> itself, the consequence, on the one hand, of 'inadvisable and even harmful
> interference' with grief and, on the other, of the impossibility of deciding
> whether the mourner will share the fate of the mourned.[63]

As I have already intimated, my only revision to Crimp's comments here would be that I think it's important, in true Greek fashion,
to extend the 'shared fate' of mourning (and the militancy it might
inspire) in this context beyond 'gay men dealing with AIDS deaths'.
What the work of Gillis and Vogel teaches is that every remembering
self is inextricably connected to the production and circulation of larger
patterns of cultural memory; no act of remembrance can occur without
a simultaneous act of empathic identification and performative sub-
stitution, or 'surrogation', in Roach's genealogical formulation of the
'displaced transmission' of the work of memory. That is, in *Torn Roots,
Broken Branches* and *The Baltimore Waltz*, a sister uses the 'vortices of
behaviour' specific to dance and the theatre (the language of the body
and the language of words) to reconfigure time and space, 'kinaestheti-
cally imagining' herself into the restored experience of her brother's
death, which must also in some senses be her own – and, just as importantly, our own.[64] Moreover, in the repetition of these very personal,
localised performances of mourning we are witness, once again, to
memory's worldly, improvisational phenomenology; that is, as every act
of remembrance is necessarily preceded – and to some extent enabled
– by an imperfect act of forgetting, the insistent return of what will not
be repressed requires us, each time, to re-inventory and reinvent what
has been displaced, deferred, and lost. Which, in the context of a global
AIDS pandemic that, though far from over, many in Western queer

61 Crimp, 'Mourning and militancy', p. 234.
62 Freud, 'Mourning and melancholia', p. 244.
63 Crimp, 'Mourning and militancy', p. 237.
64 In *Cities of the Dead*, Roach lists 'kinesthetic imagination', 'vortices of behavior', and
    'displaced transmission' as the 'three principles' governing the practices of memory at
    work in his genealogy of circum-Atlantic performance; see pp. 26–9.

19 Margie Gillis in *A Complex Simplicity of Love*

communities pretend to have forgotten, must include the performative power of protest.

To this end, when Gillis returned to the Vancouver Playhouse in 2005 as part of the local Dancing on the Edge Festival, she had a new piece in her repertoire about her brother. Set to a gorgeous aria from the Handel opera *Rinaldo*, *A Complex Simplicity of Love* (figure 19) enacts the paradox of its title by setting Gillis's limbs in counterpoint to each other, with the restlessly shifting forward and backward movements of her legs and feet providing a muscular contrast to the sweeping lateral arcs created by her waving arms as they ride and shape the sound of the human voice. In the piece, she seems to be asking, in a manner akin to

Butler, how one's individual, reflexive, and restored response to grief might open out onto a more expansive dialogue on love – a point Gillis emphasised in an audience talkback following the performance by placing her memories of her brother within the context of the AIDS pandemic's continued spread in Africa, and by reminding us of the present-day currency of the historical backdrop to Handel's opera, about the battle between Christians and Saracens during the First Crusade.

Likewise, Vogel followed up the success of her Pulitzer Prize-winning *How I Learned to Drive* (1997) with *The Long Christmas Ride Home* (2003), at once a continuation of the earlier play's dysfunctional family themes and vehicular metaphors and an extension of its presentational/narrational style via an homage to the short plays of Thornton Wilder and an adaptation of the formal techniques of classical Japanese drama, especially Bunraku puppetry and Noh choreography. However, in her afterword to the published version of the play, Vogel states that she actually conceived *Christmas Ride* as 'a twin tribute and response' to *The Baltimore Waltz*, with the playwright this time giving Carl 'the last word', appending at the end of the former text a series of letters as florid and heartbreaking as the one containing his funeral instructions that prefaces the latter, and dramatising within the play itself, via the character of Stephen, the literal inspiration she draws from his memory.[65] In honouring that memory, Vogel has created an intensely affecting and highly theatrical work of hybrid performance, one that incorporates her brother's admiration for the emotional restraint and 'self-possession' of '[t]raditional Japanese aesthetics', but that in deliberately 'misunderstanding' their corporeal application – eventually the actor-puppeteers playing the children abandon their puppet-surrogates and at one point even manipulate the limbs of the actor-narrators playing their parents – paradoxically stages the work of mourning as an ongoing *dis*-possession, or undoing, of self.[66]

SILENCE = DEATH. The ACT UP activist slogan, like the performances of Gillis's dance movements and Vogel's play, gives voice to our rage and anger and profound sense of loss; but, its rhetorical power, again like the work of Gillis and Vogel, is ultimately choric rather than ventriloquised, encouraging us, inducing us, moving us, to lend our voices to the clarion call for action. We are all our brothers' keepers; and we could all do with sisters as keenly vigilant in reminding us of this point as Gillis and Vogel.

65 Paula Vogel, *The Long Christmas Ride Home: A Puppet Play with Actors* (New York: Theatre Communications Group, 2004), p. 80.
66 *Ibid.*, pp. 81 and 5.

Melancholic spectatorship: McNally and Kaufman

Terrence McNally's *Corpus Christi* recasts the Biblical passion play as
a coming-of-age story, set in the small Texas town of the playwright's
birth, with the role of Jesus as an initially socially leprous and later pro-
gressively more charismatic gay youth named Joshua, who spreads the
gospel of love with his 'chosen family' of twelve gay brothers, including
his sometime lover Judas. Previewing at the Manhattan Theatre Club
in late September 1998, the play, by virtue of its subject matter and not
least because of the bomb threats, hate mail and picketing that greeted
its premiere, became a proleptic and de facto memorialisation of and
performative mourning for Matthew Shepard when the latter's beaten
body was found tied to a fence outside Laramie, Wyoming, six days
before the play's official opening on 13 October. Lest we not see the
connection, the playwright himself makes it explicit for us in the preface
to the published version of the play: 'Beaten senseless and tied to a split-
rail fence in near-zero weather, arms akimbo in a grotesque crucifixion,
[Matthew Shepard] died as agonizing a death as another young man
who had been tortured and nailed to a wooden cross at a desolate spot
outside Jerusalem known as Golgotha some 1,998 years earlier. They
died, as they lived, as brothers'.[67]
The play's central theatrical conceit is that it makes explicit the
performative scaffolding of such narrative and historical equations
by having the actors in the company 'assume' their characters' roles
on stage in front of the audience. With house lights still up, and while
members of the audience are still finding their way to their seats, thirteen male actors, clad identically in white shirts and khaki pants (blue
jeans in the production I saw), slowly make their way to the stage as
if for a casual rehearsal rather than an actual performance, pausing to
chat with one another, greet members of the audience, check the props
table, and limber up with various physical and vocal exercises. At a pre-
arranged signal, one of the actors steps forward and speaks directly to
the audience, announcing that the story he and his cast mates are about
to tell is an 'old and familiar one', one we've 'all heard over and over,
again and again', but that 'bears repeating': 'The playwright asks your
indulgence, as do we, the actors. There are no tricks up our sleeves. No
malice in our hearts. We're glad you're here' (*CC*, p. 1). We then watch
as this same actor, who will shortly assume the role of John the Baptist,
calls forth each of his fellow actors in turn, blessing them first by their

---

67 Terrence McNally, *Corpus Christi: A Play* (New York: Grove, 1998), p. vi. Further
    reference will be cited in-text as *CC*.

real names before re-baptising them by the name of one of Joshua/Jesus' twelve disciples.

On a raked proscenium stage, such as the one at the Manhattan Theatre Club, the effect of this opening would, I imagine, be disconcerting enough. In the intimate confines of Festival House, on Vancouver's Granville Island, where I saw Hoarse Raven Theatre's production of the play in May 2002, the whole thing felt painfully voyeuristic: a spare studio space devoid of a raised stage, fixed seating, or anything even remotely resembling wings, means that actors and audience are quite literally on top of one another and – as McNally has staged things – wont to bump into each other in queuing to get into the room. Indeed, it left me, at certain moments, longing for the return of theatre's invisible fourth wall. This is, of course, precisely the point. In watching this play, as intensely moving and romantic and erotic as so many parts of it are, we are meant to feel uncomfortable, to question whether or not the performance has started, whether it has ended, who precisely is part of the action, whether the actors are playing a version of themselves or their characters or both, and how precisely we in the audience are meant to respond to such alienated and alienating transformations.

Something similar takes place in Moisés Kaufman and Tectonic Theater Project's (TTP) play, *The Laramie Project*. Famous for its documentary-style approach to historical moments in queer history, the company had previously scored an unexpected international hit with *Gross Indecency: The Three Trials of Oscar Wilde*. For *The Laramie Project*, which opened at the Denver Centre Theatre Company in February 2000, members of TTP travelled to the Wyoming town, then recently and unwantedly memorialised via the international media as the redneck locus of Matthew Shepard's brutal murder, in order to conduct interviews with its traumatised residents. A narrator who speaks directly to the audience (as, indeed, do all the 'characters' in the play) opens by summarising the process of its creation:

> On November 14, 1999, the members of Tectonic Theater Project traveled to Laramie, Wyoming, and conducted interviews with the people of the town. During the next year, we would return to Laramie several times and conduct over two hundred interviews. The play you are about to see is edited from those interviews, as well as from journal entries by members of the company and other found texts. Company member Greg Pierotti: (*LP*, p. 5)

The last line of this passage highlights an important feature of *The Laramie Project*'s docudrama – or, more properly, dramatised documentary – narrative aesthetic. That is, the TTP actors, in addition to

20 Cast members from the Studio 58 production of *The Laramie Project*, Langara College, Vancouver, September 2002

impersonating on stage the various real-life residents of Laramie whom they interviewed, turning each into a 'character' (in both the conventional dramatic sense of playing a part and the broader sense of conveying an individual's distinctive traits or eccentricities through manner of speech, mannerisms, style of dress, etc.), must also deal with the fact that the play likewise turns each of them into a character. This becomes all the more apparent if one attends a production of the play that is being performed by any company or cast other than the original TTP ones. Such was the case when I caught a performance of Studio 58's production of the play in October 2002. A respected actor training programme affiliated with Vancouver's Langara College that I had occasion to reference in chapter 3, Studio 58 presented audiences who attended its brilliant staging of *The Laramie Project* with the spectacle of student-actors playing professional actors playing real people, some of whom, as has been the case with many productions of the play across North America since its premiere, could potentially have been in the audience watching their surrogate-selves on stage on any given night (see figure 20).

The use of the narrator throughout the play to introduce both the speech of the actor-characters and the resident-characters is also integral in orienting – or disorienting – the audience's relationships with the action being portrayed on stage. It is akin to Brechtian quotation, in which lines are spoken not as if they were being spontaneously improvised but rather almost in the manner of reading a report. This distancing effect means that we, in the audience, are compelled not to judge the person doing the speaking but rather the words he/she speaks, and the larger social attitudes these words betray. In terms of the work of memorialisation and the performance of mourning operating in *The Laramie Project*, such a structural device again functions in two ways – on the one hand, disabusing potentially smug audience members of many of the prejudices they may have held towards the residents prior to the performance, and, on the other, dramatising the important educational process that the actors themselves must go through in confronting their own preconceptions about the individuals they were going to interview or portray.

In short, McNally and Kaufman, following from Brecht's famous theorisation of the Alienation-effect's application to the technique of acting, are asking each actor who speaks their words to 'invest what he [*sic*] has to show with a definite gest of showing', whereby gest refers to 'the mimetic and gestural expression of the social relationships between people of a given period'.[68] In so doing, these two queer playwrights are, like Brecht, urging both actors and audiences to adopt 'socially critical' attitudes: 'In his exposition of the incidents and in his characterisation of the person [the actor] tries to bring out those features which come within society's sphere. In this way his performance becomes a discussion (about social conditions) with the audience he is addressing. He prompts the spectator to justify or abolish these conditions according to what class [or gender or sexuality or race or nationality] he belongs to'.[69] 'Look what they did to Him. Look what they did to Him', the actor playing James the Less addresses the audience at the end of *Corpus Christi*, coming 'out of character' and gesturing to the naked body of Joshua crucified on a cross (*CC*, p. 80). The actor's Brechtian transposition of his speech into the third person and the past tense here[70] lets neither the actor playing Joshua nor us in the audience off the hook, as it were. Looking in this context becomes precarious – reinforced by the fact that, in the production I saw, all of the other actors exited the studio shortly after this point as the house lights once again came up, leaving the audience to gaze upon the twisted body of the actor playing Joshua for what seemed to be an excruciatingly long time, wondering this time if the 'performance' was over and, if so, whether or not we should clap or continue to sit in stunned silence. Similarly, in the epilogue to *The Laramie Project*, the actor playing TTP company member Greg Pierotti

---

68 Bertolt Brecht, 'Short description of a new technique of acting which produces an alienation effect', in *Brecht on Theatre: The Development of an Aesthetic*, ed. and trans. John Willet (London: Methuen, 1964), pp. 136 and 139.
69 *Ibid.*, p. 139.
70 *Ibid.*, p. 138.

playing gay Laramie resident Jonas Slonaker frames the question 'What's come out of this?' (and presumably this applies in equal measure to the play we are currently watching/reading and to the murder of Shepard memorialised by it) in terms of a juxtaposition between first and third person, past and present:

> Change is not an easy thing, and I don't think people were up to it here. They got what they wanted. Those two boys got what they deserve, and we look good now. Justice has been served. The OK Corral . . . The town's cleaned up, and we don't need to talk about it anymore.
>
> You know, it's been a year since Matthew Shepard died, and they haven't passed shit in Wyoming . . . at a state level, any town, nobody anywhere, has passed any kind of laws, antidiscrimination laws or hate crime legislation, nobody has passed anything anywhere. (*LP*, p. 99; second ellipsis in original)

Both speeches force us to interrogate in the present how we have memorialised similar scenes of trauma – in this case, most pertinently, but by no means only, anti-gay and lesbian violence – and our respective identifications or disidentifications with both the 'Him' and the 'they' – not to mention the 'we' and the 'you' – of such scenes.

Here I want to link up my all-too cursory redaction of the structural conventions of these two plays to the theoretical ruminations on mourning undertaken in connection with Gillis and Vogel. I suggest that part of the social discussion we in the audience are being asked to engage in by the performers has to do with critically unpacking the complex codes of masculinity operating within the heartland of rural America, and, more specifically, analysing with whom, in the ritualised violence that all too frequently accompanies the articulation of those codes, we empathise when we mourn. Here, too, I want to bring in the work of JoAnn Wypijewski, who in a 1999 *Harper's* article entitled 'A boy's life' has written what I believe to be the most critically astute analysis of Matthew Shepard's murder, wading through 'the quasi-religious characterisations of Matthew's passion, death and resurrection as patron saint of hate-crime legislation' to zero in on the 'everyday life of hate and hurt and heterosexual culture' that constituted the 'psychic terrain' of Aaron McKinney and Russell Henderson, Shepard's murderers.[71] Following from Wypijewski, then, it seems to me that the crucial question posed by *Corpus Christi* and *The Laramie Project* (albeit retrospectively in the case of McNally's play), is why is it that, in the ritual re-membering of this hate-crime (in the media and elsewhere), Shepard, as passive sufferer,

71 JoAnn Wypijewski, 'A boy's life', *Harper's Magazine* (September 1999), p. 62.

automatically becomes representative of *all* homosexual people, whereas McKinney and Henderson, as violent aggressors, are always discussed in terms of their *individual* predispositions towards delinquency? Why, in other words, aren't McKinney and Henderson seen, why aren't they remembered, as representative of the attitudes of a larger patriarchal-heterosexist culture, a 'socially instituted melancholia' that, to adapt Butler, prescribes 'how the condemnations under which one lives [e.g., to be gay is to be less than human] turn into repudiations that one performs [e.g., it is alright to kill what is not human]'?[72] A similar sentiment is expressed toward the end of *The Laramie Project* by Father Roger Schmit, the Catholic priest whose own attitudes queer TTP writers and cast members Leigh Fondakowski and Greg Pierotti were wont to prejudge upon their initial meeting; Schmit notes:

> I think right now our most important teachers must be Russell Henderson and Aaron McKinney. They have to be our teachers. How did you learn? What did we as a society do to teach you that? See, I don't know if many people will let them be their teachers. I think it would be wonderful if the judge said: 'In addition to your sentence, you must tell your story, you must tell your story'. (*LP*, p. 89)

Or, as the 'Actor Playing Judas' says about his own character at the close of *Corpus Christi*, 'Sometimes I mourn for Judas, too' (*CC*, p. 80).

Other brothers

One of the most daring and provocative attempts to tell a story, through performance, akin to that of Henderson and McKinney is the dance-theatre piece *Sinner*, created, choreographed, and performed by Liam Steel and Rob Tannion, in collaboration with playwright Ben Payne, and designers Ruth Finn and Ian Scott. The debut production of Stan Won't Dance, the London-based company formed by Steel, Tannion, and managing partner Ellie Beedham with a mandate to create original and topical works of art fully integrating movement, text, and design, *Sinner* premiered at the South Bank Centre in May 2004, before subsequently touring the UK and North America through 2006. The piece hypothesises, and dramatically exploits, the motivations behind David Copeland's 1999 planting of a nail-bomb in a crowded gay pub in Soho, the Admiral Duncan, that tore through the premises, leaving three dead

---

72 Butler, *Antigone's Claim*, p. 80. That our society largely rejects this kind of memorialisation is indicated by the negative reaction, noted above, to the inscription 'for all women who have been murdered by men' on Beth Alber's *Marker of Change* monument.

and more than eighty injured. That carnage, as with similar scenes of devastation and loss accompanying other acts of terrorism, is what remains impressed in our memories of the event, and this is brilliantly evoked by Finn in her set design for the piece, with tables and chairs overturned by the force of the bomb suspended in mid-air amid clouds of acrid smoke. What remains more murky are the details leading up to the bomb's detonation, and it is one possible version of that story that *Sinner* seeks to tell.

Subtitled 'a self-destructive solo for two men', the piece opens innocently, even parodically: 'A man walks into a bar . . .' Robert (Steel), short, wiry, and extremely nervous, is dressed – 'wrongly', he thinks – in jeans and a sweatshirt embossed with a faded Union Jack; he clutches a gym bag. He is soon joined by the taller, more muscular Martin (Tannion and later Ben Wright, taking over the role for the North American tour). Martin sports identical clothes and carries the same gym bag, but he oozes a languid, sexy confidence, and Robert is both attracted and intimidated. And so begins what appears to be a familiar ritual dance of flirtation and seduction, with the predatory Martin using his intense physicality to first charm and then menace the less experienced Robert, who responds with a combination of coy demurrals and hysterical spasms and recoilings. As *Sinner* gains momentum, bodily gesture and text – perfectly fused and precisely timed throughout the duration of the 70-minute piece – together move from playful insinuation to violent provocation, with the slow laying of a hand on a knee, or the casual rubbing of shoulders, giving way to increasingly furious sequences of contact improv-inspired grappling, tumbling, pinning; in this, the piece owes a marked debt to the work of Lloyd Newson (particularly his *Dead Dreams of Monochrome Men*), with whom Steel and Tannion apprenticed as members of DV8 Physical Theatre. Mirroring the increasing intensity of the movement, Robert and Martin's separately voiced private thoughts and insecurities eventually erupt into a shared torrent of racist and homophobic obscenities. Along the way, roles are exchanged, lines of dialogue and movement phrases repeated by different men, until the full meaning of the piece's subtitle becomes painfully clear: Robert and Martin are actually two sides of the same person. And if the latter's crucifixion at the hands of the former in the final minutes of the piece feels symbolically heavy-handed (by this point both men have shed their sweatshirts, revealing matching Jesus muscle shirts underneath) and thematically reductive (the closeted and self-loathing gay man who murders what he most desires), it makes for no less of an effective – and disturbing – *coup de théâtre*. Disturbing because, as shocking as *Sinner's* ending is (thanks in large measure to the lighting effects created by Scott and the horrifyingly imaginative uses to which Finn's set is put), it also manages to feel absolutely inevitable. Feel is the operative word here. 'To feel something for other people, even if it's hate, feels like something'. So says Martin at the outset of his seduction of Robert. And, when in a later scene that prefigures in reverse the piece's climax, Martin has Robert pinned to a table, both men agree that hate's execution, presumably even when self-directed, at least 'gives you something to believe in'.

Whereas its prosecution more often than not leaves one doubtful, if not completely incredulous. To this end, the Vancouver premieres of *Corpus Christi* and *The Laramie Project* in 2002 were all the more compelling because for many of us in the audience the brutal murder of Aaron Webster was still so fresh in our minds. At 2:30 a.m. on Saturday, 17 November 2001, the naked body of forty-one-year-old Webster was found by his friend Tim Chisholm battered and bleeding in a parking lot near Second Beach in Stanley Park. The victim of a vicious gay bashing, he died a few minutes later in Chisholm's arms as ambulance paramedics tried to save him. The next day, at an impromptu rally at the corner of Denman and Davie Streets, members of the gay community listened as police and politicians labelled the death a hate crime and vowed to act swiftly to apprehend the perpetrators.[73] In February 2003, a nineteen-year-old male suspect was finally arrested in connection with the crime. Seventeen at the time of the attack, he could not be identified, and pleaded guilty to manslaughter in juvenile court in July. On 18 December 2003 he was sentenced to two years in custody and one year house arrest, the maximum penalty Judge Valmond Romilly could issue; Romilly explicitly labelled Webster's murder a hate-crime and berated Crown prosecutors for not trying the case within this context. Another juvenile who also pleaded guilty to manslaughter was likewise sentenced to a maximum of three years in custody on 21 April 2004.[74] Ryan Cran and Danny Rao, two adults also charged in connection with the case were tried together in December 2004, with BC Supreme Court Justice Mary Humphries sentencing Cran to six years in jail for manslaughter and acquitting Rao due to lack of credible evidence. The verdicts, together with Humphries repudiation of Romilly's previous characterisation of Webster's murder as a hate crime, outraged the queer community and prompted renewed protests.[75]

73 See Yvonne Zacharias, 'Gays demand action in wake of brutal killing', *Victoria Times-Colonist* (19 November 2001), p. A12.
74 See 'Second youth connected to Webster beating sentenced to three years', *Vancouver Sun* (22 April 2004), p. B2.
75 See Gerry Bellett, 'Attacker gets six years for role in fatal beating', *Vancouver Sun* (9 February 2005), pp. B1 and B6.

As part of the community programming around Studio 58's pro-duction of *The Laramie Project*, Langara College organised a one-day public forum on gay bashing and hate crimes legislation, an issue that has been much in the air in local queer circles since Webster's murder, and especially since Judge Romilly's surprisingly forceful comments. To paraphrase Wypijewski once again, to the extent that 'hate-crime laws symbolize a society's values',[76] they can be viewed as a form of cultural memory work, a process of belatedly representing in juridical discourse a hitherto actively forgotten fissure in the social fabric of a community (note, in this regard, how relatively recently anti-gay violence was included under the purview of hate-crime legislation in Canada, and how most American states have no legal mechanism to recognise such violence as even constituting a hate-crime). This notion of belatedness points, in turn, to the fact that what hate-crime legislation actually memorialises is the crime itself, not the culture of hate and violence that produced the crime in the first place. To this end, Wypijewski notes, with characteristic bluntness, that such legislation 'means nothing for life and, because its only practical function is to stiffen penalties, eve-rything for death'; it also means, in the specific context of gay-related hate-crimes, where 'it's always the sexuality of the victim that's front and center, not the sexuality of the criminal or the undifferentiated violence he took to extremity', that 'straight people are off the hook'.[77] Similarly, as Judith Butler argues in *Excitable Speech*, proponents of hate speech regulation, in focusing on the injury such speech causes to the abjectly governed and agentless individual addressee (be it a woman, a queer, or a racial minority), tend to ignore the ways in which their arguments relocate notions of 'sovereignty' and 'universality' within a speaker, who not only says what he means, but whose utterances are immediately memorialised by others as simultaneously demarcating and overstep-ping the borders of what is acceptable. Even more pertinently, for Butler, proponents of hate speech laws fail to recognise how the iterability of such speech is to a large measure coextensive with and institutionalised within much official 'state speech'.[78]

Perhaps no other individual has come to represent so manifestly the paradoxes inherent within Butler's equation than Fred Phelps, founder and presiding pastor of Westboro Baptist Church in Topeka, Kansas. For it was his encouragement of his parishioners and supporters to picket, among other events, the military funerals of American soldiers

76 Wypijewski, 'A boy's life', p. 74.
77 *Ibid.*, pp. 74 and 75.
78 Judith Butler, *Excitable Speech: A Politics of the Performative* (New York: Routledge, 1997), p. 102.

killed in Iraq and Afghanistan as evidence of the righteous outcome of an iniquitous nation turning its back on God and embracing a militant homosexual agenda that actually led the US government to pass the 'Respect for America's Fallen Heroes Act',[79] which prohibits protests within 100 metres of the entrance of any cemetery overseen by the National Cemetery Administration. Phelps, of course, is most famous for the picket he organised outside Matthew Shepard's funeral, at which followers held aloft signs announcing 'God Hates Fags' and chanted that Shepard's murder was just punishment for a deviant lifestyle. The incident, as well as the ingenious 'angel action' devised by Shepard's friend Romaine Patterson to block out Phelps and crew when they again showed up outside Henderson and McKinney's murder trial, is depicted in *The Laramie Project*; as a result, Phelps has threatened all subsequent productions of the play with similar pickets. Sure enough, when Vancouver company Fighting Chance Productions announced that it would be mounting the play at the Havana Theatre in the fall of 2008, incorporating a new epilogue written by Kaufman and TTP members based on a return trip to Laramie to mark the tenth anniversary of Shepard's death, opening night at this tiny venue on the city's east side was immediately added to the rotating schedule of pickets listed on Phelps's website, godhatesfags.com. The local community responded quickly, announcing a counter-demonstration, and calling on border officials to use Canada's own hate speech laws to deny Phelps and his followers entry into the country (which has been a special target of Phelps's vituperation since the legalisation of same-sex marriage in Canada in 2005). In the end, the folks from Westboro were a no-show, although that didn't stop Richard and I from lingering in the rain amid the raucous melee outside the Havana, joining in the chorus of increasingly lewd chants, and surmising how some of the local significations on offer in the messages contained on several protesters' signs might resonate with cross-border and other global audiences (see figure 21).

Symptomatic, in this regard, is the way in which Shepard's death, a brutal hate crime that focused the eyes of the world on a culture of anti-gay violence in many ways specific to the heartland of late twentieth-century white, rural America, has simultaneously – and not unproblematically – been exported transnationally as standing in for an entire global history of attacks against sexual minorities. This has happened in no small way through the tireless efforts of the foundation created in Shepard's

---

79 See the Library of Congress electronic record of the text of the act (Bill Number H.R. 5037), from the 109th Congress of the US: http://thomas.loc.gov/cgi-bin/query/ z?c109:h.r.5037.eh: (accessed December 2008).

21 Protesting Westboro Baptist Church's planned picket of Fighting Chance's production of *The Laramie Project*, Havana Theatre, Vancouver, November 2008

memory by his mother, Judy, but also arguably because Shepard's whiteness (and middle-classness) has made his memory more assimilable – that is to say, in Butler's terminology, more grievable – within a theory of queer mourning that cannot easily account for those victims of homophobic violence whose presumed sexual identities must compete with the more visual markers of racial, ethnic, or religious difference – their own and that of their attackers. David Copeland's bombing of the Admiral Duncan, while the deadliest and most violent, was preceded by similar attacks in the predominantly black and South Asian communities of Brixton and Brick Lane, but the scope of the perpetrator's hatred does not necessarily translate into a shared capaciousness in the ways we remember and mourn his victims. Nor, as world events in this case continue to attest by speaking back quite pointedly to the ethical musings of various local academic audiences, in the presumed solidarity that exists between minority communities at risk of injury and violence.

This accounts, in the Vancouver context of built memorials with which I began this chapter, for some of the ill feeling within the queer community over the eventual siting of the Air India Memorial in Stanley Park: a number of recent gay bashings in the city have been linked to members of the local South Asian community. And this provides as well, in the repertoire of recent UK performance, the basis for another memorable show from Lloyd Newson himself. Like *The Laramie Project*, DV8's *To Be Straight With You* (2008) uses a large, and in this case multi-ethnic cast, to reproduce verbatim the text of interviews conducted with Londoners of various backgrounds on their attitudes to homosexuality, religion, and race, and demonstrates in the process the frequent incommensurability of each within the theory and practice of (in)tolerance. Spoken word is paired with ensemble dance and solo movement sequences that turn everyday actions – riding a chair like a horse, spinning across the stage like a top, skipping rope as if one's life depended on it – into virtuosic displays of learned bigotry and survival. What's more, through a series of stunning visual set pieces, including a transparent globe manipulated from within by a dextrous performer and illuminated from without by digital projections, Newson and his designers manage the difficult trick of situating the roots and repercussions of homophobia both locally and globally, without letting anyone completely off the hook. Jamaican Rasta culture comes in for some serious indictment, for example, but so implicitly do the London club kids who groove unthinkingly to hate-spewing rap tracks. In both cases, the sexed, sexual, and sexualised stranger becomes the unassimilable, abject limit that both constructs what is known and familiar about the citizen's identity *and* what threatens the very stability of that identity (cf., in this regard, the images from Abu Ghraib). By juxtaposing and complicating just what and who is domestic and foreign, familiar and strange, *To Be Straight With You* illustrates, among other things, how liberal democracies, no less than fundamentalist theocracies, formally deny certain bodies full membership in the national polity through a paradoxical process of anxious identification and reluctant estrangement, the labelling of someone as not like *me* being premised on an unspoken acknowledgement of similitude, of the uncanny possibility of being just like *you*. As the performance works discussed in this chapter make clear, moving beyond this kind of melancholic spectatorship to a shared process of mourning demands the full incorporation of the other, no matter how proximate or removed the claims to brotherly love.

Towards the end of *Antigone's Claim*, a text I have been using as one of my main critical touchstones throughout this chapter, and which comes as close as any recent treatise I can think of in articulating a socially relevant theory of global queer remembrance and mourning, Butler notes that what remains 'unspoken' in Antigone's grief for her brother Polyneices is her shared grief for her 'other brother[s]', Eteocles and, not least, Oedipus, both arguably responsible not only for the 'crime' of Polyneices' death, but also for the 'crime' of Antigone's defiant public mourning of that death. As Butler puts it, 'The "brother" is no singular place for her, though it may be that all her brothers (Oedipus, Polyneices, Eteocles) are condensed at the exposed body of Polyneices, an exposure she seeks to cover, a nakedness she would rather not see or have seen'.[80] Likewise, it seems to me that in our vigils for the Aaron Websters and the Matthew Shepards of this world, for the Christopher Gillises and the Carl Vogels, for all our 'named and unnamed' queer brothers and sisters lost prematurely to violent death or disease, or simply the violence of heteronormative historiography, we must be as, if not more, vigilant in our remembrance of the un- or underexposed melancholic keepers of that history, our 'other' brothers. For, if part of what is enacted in queer rituals of remembrance and queer performances of mourning not just in Vancouver and other parts of North America, but around the world, is a speaking of the unspeakable, then it is incumbent upon those of us who undertake such rituals to utter the silence, to outer the active forgetting, to counter the willful amnesia at the heart of heterosexual melancholia. That is, to adapt Wypijewski one last time, we must acknowledge that Aaron Webster and Matthew Shepard; Brandon Teena and Lisa Lambert and Philip Devine; Sakia Gunn and Lawrence King; Zoliswa Nkonyana and Sizakele Sigasa and Salome Masooa; Brian Williamson and Lenford 'Steve' Harvey; Mokhtar N. and Ali A.;[81] not

---

80 Butler, *Antigone's Claim*, p. 79.
81 Brandon Teena (aka Teena Brandon), a twenty-one-year-old preoperative trans-gendered man from Lincoln, Nebraska, was, along with housemates Lambert and Devine, murdered on New Year's Eve 1993, by former friends Thomas Nissen and John Lotter when it was discovered 'he' – at least in the eyes of his homo- and transphobic killers – was in fact a 'she'. Kimberly Pierce's award-winning narrative film *Boys Don't Cry*, starring Hilary Swank, chronicles the story, as does Gréta Olafsdóttir and Susan Muska's documentary *The Brandon Teena Story*. Sakia Gunn, a fifteen-year-old New Jersey lesbian returning from a night of partying in New York City with her girlfriend, was stabbed to death at a bus stop adjacent Newark's busiest intersection by twenty-nine-year-old Richard McCullogh in May 2003 after she rebuffed his sexual advances. Lawrence King, also fifteen, was shot in the head by a fellow junior high student in Oxnard, California, in February 2008 after announcing to assembled classmates that he was gay. In February 2006, Zoliswa Nkonyana, a nineteen-year-old lesbian from Khayelitsha, South Africa, was stoned to death by an angry mob outside her own home after identifying as homosexual. The following year the bodies of Sizakele Sigasa, thirty-four, and Salome Masooa, twenty-four, were found in a field in Meadowlands, Soweto. Sigasa had been shot six times, while Masooa had been shot once. Both women were openly lesbian and active in the local HIV/AIDS and LGBT movements. Brian Williamson and Lenford 'Steve' Harvey, gay activists in Jamaica, were murdered in 2004 and 2006, respectively. Mokhtar N. (twenty-four years old) and Ali A. (twenty-five years old) were executed by the government of Iran in November 2005 after they were found guilty, under the country's *shari'a*-based penal code, of the crime of '*lavat*', defined as penetrative and non-penetrative sexual acts between men. And this in spite of the fact that, according to Iranian president Mahmoud Ahmadinejad, homosexuality does not exist in Iran. For more on each of their stories, see the website of Human Rights Watch: http://hrw.org (accessed July 2007).

to mention the murdered women from the École Polytechnique in Montréal and from the Downtown Eastside in Vancouver, died not because they were queer or feminist or prostitutes, but because their killers were all men for whom straight maleness was presumably the only life worth living – and grieving. And it is this disavowal of brotherly love (of the self, of the same, of the other) at the heart of masculine identity formation that, above all, our world must mourn.

Coda: 1 December 2007 – changing direction/*Lost Action*

Was I sleeping, while the others suffered? Am I sleeping now? Tomorrow, when I wake, or think I do, what shall I say of today? . . . We have time to grow old. The air is full of our cries . . . But habit is a great deadener . . . At me too someone is looking, of me too someone is saying, He is sleeping, he knows nothing, let him sleep on . . . I can't go on! (Vladimir, in *Waiting for Godot*[1])

A pivot is a change of direction requiring precise execution: it allows for another point of view. It is a turning point, something of crucial importance. It is a repeatable, refinable action that extends our perspective of the possible. This accuracy and focus, in combination with the instinctual, chaotic and risky nature of improvisation, define both the process and the result. (Crystal Pite[2])

Everything that acts is a cruelty. It is upon this idea of extreme action, pushed beyond all limits, that theater must be rebuilt. (Antonin Artaud[3])

It is Saturday, 1 December 2007, World AIDS Day, and I am at the Vancouver East Cultural Centre – known affectionately as 'the Cultch' by

---

1 Samuel Beckett, *Waiting for Godot* (New York: Grove, 1982), pp. 104–5.
2 Quoted in Nancy Shaw, *Lost and Found: Kidd Pivot, Dance Documenta*, no. 2 (Vancouver: Eponymous Productions and Arts Society, 2006), p. 14. Subsequent references will be cited parenthetically in the text as *LF*.
3 Antonin Artaud, 'The theater and cruelty', in *The Theater and its Double*, trans. Mary Caroline Richards (New York: Grove, 1958), p. 85.

local live art aficionados – and the aging but much beloved site of many a memorable performance I have attended (see chapter 2). A crowd is gathering for the final night of the return engagement of *Lost Action*, a dance piece created by local choreographic wunderkind Crystal Pite and her company Kidd Pivot. Winner of the 2006 Alcan Performing Arts Award, a $50,000 prize that is awarded annually on a rotating basis to local theatre, music, and dance companies in order to facilitate the creation of a new work, *Lost Action* premiered to great acclaim in March of that year at the same venue. Then I attended alone, and was so transported by what I saw that I longed to share the experience with others. This time I am with Richard and three other friends, and I have talked up the piece so much that I worry it will fall short of expectations. Nevertheless, we are excited. Pite has been touring the work across the country with the same group of seven original dancers (herself included) for more than a year, refining sections, adding gestures and phrases, whole movements, jettisoning others, and the buzz among the cognoscenti is that she has arrived back home with an even tighter and more complex work. Plus, it's the end of term (four of us are academics). Our bellies are full after a pleasing meal. And it's snowing. Hard. Normally such anomalous meteorology would be worrisome to Vancouver audiences, especially given recent weather patterns around this time of year (see below). But tonight it feels strangely appropriate, and as we unbundle from our respective layers and stamp our feet and slowly unthaw in the crowded lobby, I remember a key prop that is used to great symbolic effect by Pite at recurring moments throughout the dance.

Pite's choreography has always been distinguished by its intensely self-reflexive approach to both narrative and bodily gesture (witness the titles of her other works: *Field: Fiction*; *Uncollected Work*; *Double Story*). But in *Lost Action* she takes this to a whole new level, using dance as 'an extreme expression' of the impermanence of performance, its necessary disappearance, its loss. In language that echoes Peggy Phelan's famous pronouncements about the present-tense, non-reproductive ontology of performance, whose 'after-effect of disappearance is', according to Phelan, 'the experience of subjectivity itself',[4] Pite notes, with reference to the work, that

> Dancers sculpt space in real-time, working inside a form that is constantly in a state of vanishing. We have no artifacts. I find it strangely beautiful to be creating something that is made of us – made of our breath and blood and bones and minds. Something that is made of the space we occupy and made of the space between us. We embody both the dance and its disappearance. (*LF*, p. 2)

4 Peggy Phelan, *Unmarked: The Politics of Performance* (New York: Routledge, 1993), p. 148.

In this, as well, Pite sees 'a perfect metaphor for life', with the body
and its improvised, repeated, and unconsciously remembered movements becoming the locus – 'through effort, articulation, torsion and
exhaustion' – of our reworking and rehearsal of a larger history of social
relations and movements (*LF* pp. 2 and 9). Including relations and
movements that sometimes lead to *unnecessary* losses, *wasted* actions.
In asking of her audience to grieve the ends of performance – both its
literal ending when the dancers stop dancing and the house lights come
up, and what the dancers accomplished in seeming to push their bodies
beyond the limits of extreme physical action – Pite, like the artists and
theorists discussed in the last chapter, is simultaneously fashioning 'a
story about the griever and the events that lead to her grief[. . .] The
viewer will seek out the narrative – find one, make one with what's
offered' (*LF*, p. 6).

For many in the audience that narrative was overlain by the fact
that these remarks by Pite were made in a brilliant essay on *Lost Action*
included with our programmes, an essay written by local poet, teacher,
and cultural critic Nancy Shaw, who had succumbed to cancer in the
time between the dance's premiere and this restaging. Indeed, this made
all the more powerful for me a section of the piece that I had somehow
forgotten from my first viewing, in which the four male dancers (Eric
Beauchesne, Malcolm Low, Yannick Matthon, and Victor Quijada)
work in concert, and with impossibly fluid grace, to lift, pass, carry,
caress, cradle, console, and, it seems, revive the smallest of the female
dancers (Anne Plamondon), whose limp body, in its total surrender to
the men's collective touch, choreographs for us the mutuality, the co-
implicatedness, of loss, that what we are witness to here in its multiple
relays is both the missing and the missed. For still others in the audience,
myself included, the men's attempts at rescue, here and elsewhere in
the piece – especially when, during a repeated sequence of movements,
three of the men pull the inert body of the fourth up off the floor, only
to have his borne and shared weight set off a chain of collapses and
slackenings in their own (see figure 22) – pivots on an understanding of
the missing preposition in Pite's title: lost *in* action (*LF*, p. 7). And here
the bulky parkas worn by the seven dancers at the outset of the piece,
and that they subsequently shrug off and don at various ensuing points,
telegraph multiple meanings: an army greatcoat; gang colours; a hospital gown. One of these parkas is also symbolically carried across the
stage at key junctures in the piece by the third female dancer (Francine
Liboiron), who bears the garment – now a winding-sheet or a widow's
weeds or the gifted flag from a soldier's coffin – in her outstretched arms
as she walks slowly and mournfully through the twin columns of her

22 Left to right: Victor Quijada, Malcolm Low, Eric Beauchesne, and Yannick
Matthon in Kidd Pivot's *Lost Action*

fellow dancers, exiting stage right. This repeated action, so simple, so
untechnical, was what I remembered most from my first viewing of the
dance, and alone among my companions I both looked forward to and
dreaded its final appearance, which I knew would signal that the piece
was well and truly over.

Except that it didn't. Wily and restlessly creative artist that she is,
Pite changed things up on me, dispensing with the final funeral march
(perhaps fearing it too heavy-handed) and the talismanic coat in favour
of a quieter ending focused on the spent body of the dancer for whom
both are presumably intended. That is, at the end of the final sequence
of structured improvisations shared by the quartet of men, and that Pite
has said explores, among other things, the 'kinetics of rescue' (*LF*, p. 7),[5]
the dancer whose prone body, once lifted up, sets off the chain reaction
of strivings and collapsings among his cohort, refuses to be resuscitated,
refuses to go on. And just as the body can't go on, so the dance is played
out, and thus the piece does not end, it just stops.[6]

As I sat there, not moving, through the three curtain calls, the
inevitable but certainly well-deserved standing ovation, the murmurs
of 'Shall we go?' circulating like evening vespers among my friends
(the Cultch was formerly a church), I mourned the action lost to this

5 Pite explores this subject further in her 'Ten Duets on a Theme of Rescue' (2008),
   created for Cedar Lake Contemporary Ballet, where she is an associate artist.
6 For a brilliant theatrical exploration of the difference between things that end and
   things that 'just stop', see Daniel MacIvor's play *In on It* (Winnipeg: Scirocco, 2001).

ending that wasn't an ending, and certainly not the one I was expecting, and struggled to improvise an interpretation worthy of this new narrative I had been given. Perhaps what I have since come up with was unduly influenced by the weather that night, the wonderfully associative musings contained in Shaw's text, my natural tendency to think in terms of gross calamity and dire emergency, the story about the latest iconic incarnations of Didi and Gogo I was to read in the *New York Times* the next day (again, see below). Nevertheless, in the days and weeks and months and now years that have passed since that second performance of *Lost Action*, I have come to read in the dancers' physical expenditures, their accumulated energy losses, their gasps for breath, their spent sweat, not just a metaphor for life and its inevitable expiration, but one that extends to the acts of extremity by which we are daily pushing our fatigued planet beyond the limits of possible rescue and resuscitation.

If, as Artaud famously wrote, theatre depends for its relevance and renewal on successive shocks to its system, recovering its lost necessity by staying ahead of world events and 'dominating the instability of the times' through a sensorial 'appeal to cruelty and terror . . . whose range probes our entire vitality, confronts us with all our possibilities', then it seems to me that we are at a pivotal point in history, one that requires extreme action to change direction, wake us up and, in both Vladimir and Artaud's terminology, recharge our nerves and heart.[7] I am referring to the fact that global climate change and ongoing environmental depredation present us precisely with the mass spectacle that, in Artaud's estimation, should logically send local audiences pouring out into the streets (or else ducking for cover – 'Artaud as Chicken Little', in the words of Una Chaudhuri[8]). At the very least, it presents the theatre, with a unique opportunity – as well as a unique set of challenges – to respond to 'the cataclysms which are at our door'[9] by revealing, cruelly, violently, everything we have to lose in this final and most spectacular of disappearing acts. I offer the following concluding remarks – by no means a formal ending – as a record of my thinking on these matters during the final stages of the writing and revising of this book.

Like the weather

The world got a lot hotter between December 2007 and December 2008: in war zones in Iraq, Afghanistan, and the Middle East; in the

7 Artaud, 'The theater and cruelty', pp. 84 and 86.
8 Una Chaudhuri, Comment, 'A forum on theatre and tragedy in the wake of September 11th, 2001', *Theatre Journal* 54:1 (2002), p. 98.
9 Artaud, 'The theater and cruelty', p. 87.

nuclear posturing of North Korea and Iran; in sectarian violence in India and Pakistan; in the truncheons raining down on rival political and ethnic protesters in Burma and Kenya and Tibet; in the swelling refugee and casualty lists resulting from the various proxy wars and civil violence engulfing the Congo and Darfur and Somalia and South Africa and Zimbabwe; in the Cold War-era rhetoric exchanged between the USA and Russia over the latter's invasion of Georgia; in the pools of sweat collecting under the collars of stockbrokers and bankers and politicians as the global economy spontaneously combusted. However, local weather conditions the past few Decembers notwithstanding, it was the literal heat associated with global warming that grabbed most of my attention during that year. It seemed that I couldn't open the newspaper or turn on the television news without daily being confronted by yet another dire scientific pronouncement about the increasingly sorry state of the environment, about what human inhabitants are continuing to do to accelerate its decline, and what we need to do, when, and by how much, to reverse course. Even Annie Sprinkle and Elizabeth Stephens, as we saw, gave their fourth Green Wedding an overtly environmental focus, 'vow[ing] to love, honor and cherish the earth till death do us part'.[10] Of course, maintaining such a commitment also means waking up to the reality that the sudden collapse of the world's financial markets, for example, is related not just to unregulated and dirty profiteers operating with impunity on Wall Street but also to the unsustainable consumption of dangerous and expensive dirty fuels in cars and homes on Main Streets the world over. Indeed, to the extent that the economy and the environment are inextricably linked, 2008 just might mark the year that 'energy security' eclipses 'national security' as the buzzword among mandarins in government.

Where once, in the capitalist West at the very least, we measured our premiums on futurity in terms of insurance rates, inheritance taxes, pension indexes, and cholesterol and body fat ratios, we have suddenly been told that there is really only one statistical – and suitably spectral – equation that matters. Calculating our individual carbon footprints has become part of the guesswork – or should I say ghostwork? – by which we account for the cumulative decimation of the once reliable prompts to the memory theatre that sustains our planet: melting ice caps; depleted water tables; eroded coastlines; clearcut forests. And if, after this, the numbers still seem somehow

---

10 See 'Artist's statement', *Love Art Laboratory Year 4: Love Compassion*, www.loveartlab. org/artist-statement.php?year_id=4 (accessed April 2008).

too abstract, there are the attendant images, some biblically apocalyptic in their raw visual impact (fires in Australia, southern California, and Greece; floods in northern England, the American Midwest, and southern China), others as enervating precisely because they require satellite imaging and digital magnification to see and register their effects (a shrinking Arctic ice cap, an expanding Saharan desert). Indeed, in making of the Earth a virtual dumbshow, a popular search engine like Google or a more sophisticated remote-sensing satellite used by industry and government agencies to track land use and disaster management, should ideally serve to prick the conscience of even the most jaded and skeptical of planetary playgoers: having, like Claudius, been given a colour commentary of the rot we have wrought on the world stage (in this case, blue for rising ocean levels and green for a receding tree line), we may yet imagine, as local audiences, scenarios in which a change of direction is possible and the inevitable denouement of recrimination and retribution forestalled (by, for example, zooming in on a government-run wind farm in China, or a collective urban garden in Vancouver). It's no longer enough merely to weep for Hecuba.

Harnessing the performative power of images was, of course, in large measure what elevated the shell game of numbers and statistics on offer in *An Inconvenient Truth* to the realm of political theatre (or absurdist comedy, depending on one's personal position). With the help of some deft editing, director Davis Guggenheim succeeded in turning a glorified power point lecture – with Al Gore doing his best Helen Caldicott and Michael Moore impressions – into a populist manifesto that rode (in a hybrid Prius, no less) a wave of general discontent with the administration and policies of George W. Bush (and regret, presumably, at not having elected Gore president) all the way to an Oscar for Best Documentary (note again the Caldicott and Moore connections). Eventually adding a Nobel Peace Prize to his collection of hardware, Gore suddenly emerged as the environmental movement's newest – and in some ways, unlikeliest – impresario. To this end, Gore used the success of *An Inconvenient Truth* as a launching pad for the much lampooned Live Earth series of concerts, where the performative rhetoric of environmental sustainability seemed at odds with the bloated excess of the event as theatrical spectacle. Several commentators and pundits, for example, took delight in calculating the total carbon emissions of stars arriving to perform on private jets, while audience members proved much more adept at conspicuous consumption than at recycling – at least to judge by mounds of non-biodegradable garbage, including several thousand plastic cups and drinks containers, left behind at

concert venues on seven continents.[11] Nevertheless, much to the churl-
ish chagrin of Bob Geldof, Bono, and other celebrity spokespersons for
African AIDS, debt, and refugee relief, the environment has suddenly
become the *cause du jour* (cf. Leo DiCaprio's own documentary take
on the subject, *The Eleventh Hour*). It is perhaps only appropriate, then,
that in advancing the Doomsday Clock to five minutes to midnight on
17 January 2007 – an advance of two minutes from its last adjustment
in 2002, and the closest the clock has been to midnight since 1984 – the
Board of Directors of the University of Chicago's *Bulletin of the Atomic
Scientists* cited not only the nuclear posturing of North Korea and Iran
alongside the US's own renewed emphasis on the military utility of
nuclear weapons, but also added climate change as a comparable threat
to the future of humankind for the first time in the Clock's thirty-year
history.[12]

I'm fond of saying to my students, and practically anyone else who
will listen, that while global climate change seems to be drying out most
of the rest of the planet, we here in North America's Pacific Northwest
seem only to be getting soggier. Vancouverites (and our Gore-Tex-clad
cousins in Seattle) are used to the rain: it's the price we willingly pay for
living in a temperate rain forest ringed by snow-capped mountain ranges
on one side and sandy ocean beaches on the other, making the best of
seasonal lifestyle choices accessible when we need them, but without the
extremes of temperature and freak weather patterns normally associated
with summer and winter in other parts of the continent. But even we
can be forgiven for wearying of what seem to be the increasingly lengthy
deluges of the past few years. In January 2006, for example, the city
and adjacent communities endured twenty-nine straight days of rain,
leading to a boil water advisory owing to excess turbidity in reservoirs
feeding municipal water supplies, prompting flood watches along the
Fraser River to the south, and triggering landslides on the north shore
that threatened to sweep away multi-million dollar homes. As I detailed
at greater length in chapter 1, local playwright James Long subsequently
used this confluence of rain and real estate to create a dystopic vision of
Vancouver's unsettled future in *The View from Above*.

Heavy rainfall also pummelled the Vancouver region in November
and December of 2006, only this time it was accompanied by severe
wind storms that felled power lines, tore off roofs, sent waves crashing
several hundred metres inland, and uprooted old growth trees by the

---

11 See David Smith, 'Rockin' all over the world (but just watch your carbon footprint)',
    The Observer (8 July 2007).
12 See 'Doomsday clock: timeline', *Bulletin of the Atomic Scientists*, www.thebulletin.org/
    content/doomsday-clock/timeline (accessed January 2008).

23 Lord Stanley welcoming all to the park that bears his name

thousands across the Lower Mainland and on Vancouver Island. One of the city's hardest hit areas was Stanley Park, the 400-hectare haven of green in the city's West End about which I had much to say in the last chapter of this book, and which the eponymous Lord Stanley, then Governor General of Canada, dedicated for the 'use and enjoyment of all colours, creeds, and customs, for all time' in 1888 – only after the local indigenous populations had first been displaced (see figure 23). Ringed by an 8.8 kilometre 'seawall' that affords pedestrians, joggers, cyclists, and rollerbladers spectacular views of English Bay, the Strait of Georgia, Burrard Inlet, Lion's Gate Bridge, and the north shore mountains, the park also boasts world-class gardens, hidden beaches, and several amenities – including pools and picnic areas, restaurants, hiking trails, tennis and lawn bowling courts, a mini golf course and yacht club, an aquarium and children's zoo, etc. – designed to appeal to both locals and tourists, who visit the park in numbers that swell to almost eight million each year. The park is also home to approximately 500,000 trees,[13] several of them toweringly majestic old-growth conifers with trunks the circumference of a small studio stage, trees that were cut down and lashed and broken in two like so many twigs as a result of the wind. I had seen the extent of the devastation via the aerial images broadcast on the nightly news, and eventually first-hand when the trails I like to run along were finally re-opened (some eight months later) and I saw up close the fallen totems. But somehow the sheer scale of the damage only fully registered when Boca del Lupo, a local theatre company whose work I briefly discussed in chapter 2, announced that its annual all-ages free show in the park was being moved for the first time in its ten-year history owing to ongoing clean-up operations from the storm and the continued danger posed by falling branches, exposed tree roots, and obstructed pathways.

Boca del Lupo, founded by Sherry J. Yoon and James Dodge, both alumni of the theatre programme at the university where I teach, is known for challenging physical productions, and for a broadly 'environmental' approach to theatrical space (more on this shortly). This is especially true of their summer Stanley Park shows, which each year see the troupe adapting a well-known work of literature into a roving spectacle that employs classic *commedia* techniques, including music, dance, acrobatics, and audience participation, and that makes splendid use of the park's natural setting to create stunning physical effects (the most famous of which usually involve cast members swinging from pulleys suspended from tree branches). For their tenth-anniversary 2007 show, Boca decamped to the Burrard Street Bridge underpass, on the south side of False Creek. The move was not a success, and this had, I think, only partially to do with a rare miscalculation in the choice of source material, in this case Victor Hugo's *Hunchback of Notre Dame*. Something about the new location and the company's necessary adjustments to the built environment resulted in what for me was a lacklustre and disappointing production. A number of factors contributed to this. First, the scale of the work had to compete unduly with the monumentality of the bridge's

---

13   See 'Welcome to Stanley Park', *Vancouver Park Board: Parks and Gardens*, www.city. vancouver.bc.ca/parks/parks/stanley (accessed February 2008).

infrastructure. Relatedly, audience members had to strain against the rumble of traffic overhead to hear the performers. Finally, the specifics of site here resulted in a paradoxical compression of signature Boca effects and meant that the 'roving' aspects of the production were in fact reduced to performers and audience members retracing their steps along a single horizontal plane. It was, in the end, like Shakespeare in the park without the park. Remove the main attraction, and things are bound to suffer by comparison.

A good portion of this book was written and revised in the aftermath of the storms that wreaked such havoc on Stanley Park, and as I worked on the preceding essays, and on the connections between world stages and local audiences I saw underscoring much of that material, I kept reflecting, somewhat guiltily I admit, on what great theatre extreme weather makes. Electrical storms that light up city skylines, tornados that rip through trailer parks, blizzards that shut down airports, flood waters that burst through levees and send people scrambling to rooftops: there is never a bad seat in the house. And yet while the image of Prospero conjuring the perfect storm is an iconic one in Western drama, the tempests of late have seemed increasingly unscripted, their effects altogether too cruel. What, one wonders, would Artaud have made of Hurricane Katrina? Or of the sensory re-experiencing of the event by local audiences witness to Paul Chan's November 2007 site-specific productions of *Waiting for Godot* in the devastated Lower Ninth Ward and Gentilly neighbourhoods of New Orleans? A celebrated video artist known for digital animated projections that blend political allegory and social activism, Chan worked with Creative Time, a New York-based nonprofit that provides resources and financial support to innovative public art projects, and the Classical Theater of Harlem to stage the play. Much in the manner of Susan Sontag's famous amateur production of *Godot* in war-torn Sarajevo in 1993, or in countless productions that have taken place in prisons since the play's premiere in 1953, Chan's mounting of the play in post-Katrina New Orleans must, inevitably, be read as a metaphor for a community in despair at having been abandoned by the powers that be and yet committed to creating something out of nothing. As Vladimir says at one point late in act two, lines that – spoken by actor Wendell Pierce, a New Orleans native – can't but be read as a forceful rebuke to FEMA and other aid agencies too mired in their own bureaucratic dysfunction and 'Nothing to be done' logic to help the people who need it most,

> Let us not waste our time in idle discourse! . . . Let us do something while we have the chance! It is not every day that we are needed. Not indeed

that we personally are needed. Others would meet the case equally well, if not better. To all mankind they were addressed, those cries for help still ringing in our ears! But at this place, at this moment of time, all mankind is us, whether we like it or not. Let us make the most of it before it is too late! Let us represent worthily for once the foul brood to which a cruel fate consigned us![14]

Heeding Didi's call, Chan collaborated with several local artists and community activists, devoted himself to several months of teaching in public schools and universities before and after the *Godot* run, and had Creative Time set up a special 'shadow fund', with the play's production costs matched dollar for dollar by anonymous donors, money that would stay in New Orleans and be distributed to local grassroots agencies involved in various recovery projects. He also worked with filmmaker Cauleen Smith on a documentary about the project, and with New Orleans writers on a commemorative book.[15] But arguably Chan's greatest gift to the city was his work as location scout/scene designer, that is, his decision to exploit two of the areas most devastated by the hurricane – a desolate intersection in the Lower Ninth, a gutted and condemned house in Gentilly – to create a 'ready-made theater' where the literal *performance* of the *place* of time's suspension dramatises what Tim Griffin has called the 'portable acuity' of the play's *political* allegory: that is, the audiences waiting to see the play were also local constituencies still waiting for restitution.[16] In this, as several commentators have noted, the cryptic signage that Chan created to advertise the production (in which Beckett's equally cryptic opening stage directions – 'A country road. A tree. Evening.' – were painted onto bits of industrial cardboard scattered across the city; see figure 24) 'obtains the public, poetic, political dimension of graffiti'.[17] The signs joined the messages – tallying the dead, the missing, the hazards that remain – spray-painted on so many condemned houses in offering material witness to that which, like the weather (indeed, like performance), can be fleeting, but no less furious.

The tragedy that was – still is – Katrina and its aftermath had a lot to do with the arrested oedipal relations between various municipal, state, and federal levels of US government; with a White House too focused on Iraq to notice the lack of emergency preparedness at home; and with enduring Jim Crow-era racial divisions that have been re-mapped

14 Beckett, *Waiting for Godot*, p. 90.
15 See Holland Carter, 'A broken city. A tree. Evening', *The New York Times* (2 December 2007), p. 34.
16 Tim Griffin, 'Editor's letter', *Artforum* 66:4 (December 2007), p. 51.
17 *Ibid.* See also Carter, p. 34.

24 Paul Chan advertises his post-Katrina production of *Waiting for Godot* in the Lower Ninth Ward of New Orleans, November 2007

along class lines. But, arguably, it had as much, if not more, to do with warmer ocean surface temperatures in the Atlantic and changes in the flows of the Gulf Stream that have contributed to an increase in the frequency and ferocity of hurricanes in the region.[18] Indeed, the world's continued fascination with New Orleans' devastation, and my own personal interest in Chan's theatre-making, illustrates that the performative dynamics, and political dialectics, of the global and the local are enacted no more materially than in the causes and effects of climate change – and, as importantly, in what small, specific steps can be taken by individual communities to begin fixing our broken planet. Every time the house lights go down and the stage lights come up at the Cultch, in Vancouver's east end, carbon molecules are released into the atmosphere in another part of the world, a particular problem in the theatre, as low-energy LED technology is not yet available in high enough wattage to illuminate with sufficient strength, or subtlety, the stage. These released carbon molecules might then, in turn, result in some future change in the local climate or environment in yet another part of the world. How do we apportion responsibility for this action? For similar actions performed in the past? And for future actions whose

18 See, for example, Richard A. Kerr, 'Atmospheric science: is Katrina a harbinger of still more catastrophic hurricanes?', *Science* (16 September 2005), p. 1807; and P. J. Webster *et al.*, 'Changes in tropical cyclone number, duration, and intensity in a warming environment', *Science* (16 September 2005), p. 1844.

effects might not be felt for generations to come? Who, as Pozzo might put it, owns the sky qua sky?

These were precisely the issues that were on the table in December 1997 when the Kyoto Protocol was ratified, committing the 175 member-nations of the United Nations Framework Convention on Climate Change (UNFCCC) who signed on to its binding targets – including Canada – to a reduction of Greenhouse Gas emissions by at least 5 per cent against 1990 levels by 2012. Using the principle of 'common but differentiated responsibilities', the Protocol places a heavier burden of responsibility for emissions reduction on developed than on developing nations, arguing that the former can more easily pay, and that they have historically contributed more to the problem while developing nations have disproportionately felt the consequences in the form of storms, floods, droughts, and the disease that inevitably follows.[19] Yet, ten years later, at the fourth Conference of the Parties to the UNFCCC in Bali, Canada, having undergone a change of government since Kyoto (the performative consequences of which I also analyse in chapters 2 and 3), was leading a coalition of nations – including Japan and the United States – that sought to rewrite the terms of Kyoto, indicating that Canada had no intention of meeting its reduced emissions targets by the specified five-year time frame of 2008–12; Canada's then Environment Minister, Jim Baird, further claimed that the economic burden of tackling climate change must be shouldered equally by all, including nations like China and India, whose booming economies have been matched by concomitant spikes in pollution.[20] To borrow a performance metaphor from the front of the house, admission to this bit of political theatre has suddenly gone from pay-what-you-can to a preferred customer, front-of-the-line premium designed to ensure all investors at the very least break even, if not in fact turn a tidy profit. Here we see the price of thinking 'planetarily' – to re-invoke a concept I first floated, courtesy of Gayatri Spivak, back in the introduction to this book[21] – following the 'peculiar algebra' of what Joseph Roach has recently called 'world-bank drama'. In such a zero-sum model, performances of local, preferably indigenous, cultural specificity become abstracted and revalued by transnational bodies like UNESCO or multinational corporations like Microsoft as a global asset,

19   See the terms of the Kyoto Protocol posted at http://unfcc.int/kyoto_protocol/
     items/2830.php (accessed January 2008).
20   This position was reiterated by both Baird and Prime Minister Stephen Harper at
     the G8 Summit in Japan in July 2008; see Campbell Clark, 'Climate-change goals fall
     short at G8', *Globe and Mail* (7 July 2008), pp. A1 and A4.
21   See Gayatri Spivak, *Death of a Discipline* (New York: Columbia University Press,
     2003), pp. 72–102.

a part of 'World Heritage' worth preserving and investing in. This in turn perpetuates the very real structural asymmetries that continue to exist between those who produce the 'authenticating narratives' of, for example, living in harmony with the natural environment, and those who rebrand those narratives as resources for tourism and trade.[22] One thinks, in this regard, of the images of traditional Balinese dancers – so instrumental to Artaud's theories of 'pure' or 'total' theatre – performing outside the various UNFCCC meetings in Indonesia, their ceremonial and religious specificity quite literally flattened by our TV screens into Club Med-style advertisements for Bali's renewal as a global tourist destination following the 2002 bombings in Kuta. One thinks, as well, of the images of New Orleans' Mardi Gras Indians – whose particular 'circum-Atlantic' performance genealogies are discussed by Roach so masterfully in *Cities of the Dead*[23] – exported around the world in the wake of Hurricane Katrina as evidence that the city, though devastated, was still open for business.

We here on the west coast of North America have our own long history of appropriating the voices and performances of the autochthonous other as part of our collective local heritage, especially when it comes to trumpeting how ecologically savvy we are. Organisations like Greenpeace (officially founded in Vancouver in 1972), the Sierra Club of British Columbia, the Rainforest Action Network, and the David Suzuki Foundation all routinely cite First Nations cultural traditions or deploy First Nations artifacts and symbols in lobbying government and industry in matters pertaining to the environment.[24] At the same time, the modern treaty process recently revived by British Columbia Premier Gordon Campbell (see chapter 1) has raised fears among members of several of these groups that settling historical land claims with First Nations peoples could lead to an increase in non-sustainable development projects undertaken by local bands eager to exploit prime real estate or valuable natural resources.[25] Campbell has also recently

22 See Joseph Roach, 'World bank drama', in Wai Chee Dimock and Lawrence Buell (eds), *Shades of the Planet: American Literature as World Literature* (Princeton: Princeton University Press, 2007), pp. 174–5. Roach adapts his term 'world-bank drama' from Amitava Kumar's edited collection *World Bank Literature* (Minneapolis: University of Minnesota Press, 2002).
23 See Roach, *Cities of the Dead: Circum-Atlantic Performance* (New York: Columbia University Press, 1996), especially chapter 5, pp. 179–237.
24 To this end, Greenpeace's famous boat, *The Rainbow Warrior*, derived its name from the book *Warriors of the Rainbow: Strange and Prophetic Dreams of the Indian People*, given to Bob Hunter in 1969. See Rex Weyler, *Greenpeace: How a Group of Ecologists, Journalists, and Visionaries Changed the World* (Vancouver: Raincoast Books, 2004).
25 See Bill Curry, 'Premier accused of rushing land claim', *Globe and Mail* (15 June 2007), p. S1; and Carlito Pablo, 'Development as colonialism', *The Georgia Straight*

enacted tough new legislation – including a carbon tax – aimed at reducing greenhouse gas emissions by 68 per cent by 2020. However, this seems to have had as much to do with the star-struck premier scoring photo ops with California Governor Arnold Schwarzenegger, on whose environmental policies BC's have been modelled,[26] as with redressing the dismal sustainability record of successive governments that, among other things, presided over the collapse of the province's resource industries due to years of clearcut logging and over-fishing. Likewise, Prime Minister Stephen Harper's own recent conversion to more green-friendly environmental planning policies was largely prompted by Barack Obama's election as US President.[27]

Even Vancouver City Council's recent adoption of an 'EcoDensity' blueprint for the metropolis can be read as a strategic move on the part of former Mayor Sam Sullivan to shore up our global credibility regarding questions of urban sustainability in advance of the 2010 Winter Olympics, and, in retrospect, to amass a degree of personal glory while hosting the World Urban Forum in June 2006, when the term was first coined.[28] Yet, as I sought to make clear in chapter 1, at the same time as Vancouver's municipal government has sped up the process of encouraging developers to build taller and greener in speculative real-estate markets like False Creek South, which via the canny positioning of the Olympics' Athletes' Village is poised to make the jump from light industry to residential usage, it appears to be approaching much more cautiously and slowly those areas of the city like the Downtown Eastside – our own Lower Ninth Ward – most in need of sustainable revitalisation. To say nothing of a more comprehensive and integrated recognition of the role that arts and culture might play in such revitalisation through, among other things,

Footnote no. 25 (*cont.*)
(3–10 July 2008), p. 15. More recently, First Nations-owned Ma-Mook Natural Resources and Coulson Forest Products have clashed with environmental groups over the companies' plans to log old-growth trees in several pristine watersheds on Vancouver Island's Clayoquot Sound, site of violent protests in 1993, when environmental and First Nations groups – then allies – blocked forestry giants MacMillan Bloedel and Interfor from clear-cutting the area; see Randy Shore, 'The new battle for Clayoquot Sound', *Vancouver Sun* (25 July 2008), p. B3.

26 See Miro Cernetig, 'California model for Campbell's Green Plan', *Vancouver Sun* (10 February 2007), pp. A1 and A14; and Jonathan Fowlie, 'Going green enshrined into law', *Vancouver Sun* (21 November 2007), pp. B1 and B6.

27 See Mike Blanchfield, 'Harper hints at Canada–US climate plan', *Vancouver Sun* (7 November 2008), p. B5.

28 In this regard, Sullivan caused a particular stir when it was revealed, in June 2007, that he had personally applied to the Canada Intellectual Property Office to trademark the term EcoDensity under his own name, rather than the city of Vancouver, as is normally the case; see Frances Bula 'Mayor seeks to trademark "EcoDensity" for himself', *Vancouver Sun* (23 June 2007), p. A1.

the development of training, employment, and volunteer opportunities, improvements to local facilities and amenities, and the creation of social cohesion among residents by providing positive images of their lives.[29]

Thinking about the performative contradictions inherent in recent local political pronouncements on the environment – the gap between saying and doing – leads me back to issues of performance and place, indeed the performance of place, and the role that theatre, and live art generally, have to play in bolstering community awareness and activism around questions of sustainability and renewable resources. For, indeed, who better than artists and performers and cultural producers of all stripes know about such questions – whether securing sustainable funding sources for cash-strapped companies or renewing one's body against the ravages of time and physical toil? Relatedly, the arts' ability to respond in a topical and timely manner to issues of pressing community importance, the diversity of its offerings and representations, the opportunities it provides for community participation (including vocational training for youth), and its necessary engagement with place (from production sites to targeted audiences), has led Jon Hawkes to rank 'cultural vitality' 'the fourth pillar' of sustainability, 'as essential to a healthy . . . society as social equity, environmental responsibility and economical viability'.[30] Finally, as theorists from Artaud to Grotowski to Schechner have taught us, theatre's 'poverty' is also its greatest resource: dispensing with unnecessary embellishments like sets and props and even text, and exploring instead the mutually sustaining, and transforming, core

29 At the community roundtable discussion I attended at the Chinese Cultural Centre to discuss Vancouver's EcoDensity Draft Charter on 16 February 2008, I raised the issue of what I perceived to be a lack of due attention to the place of culture in the city's stated commitments to sustainability, affordability, and livability. While a commitment to 'cultural sustainability' and to achieving 'sustainable strategies' for 'arts, culture and creativity' did eventually make it into the final draft of the Charter adopted by City Council on 10 June 2008, these terms do not figure in any of the sixteen initial policy actions adopted by the city at the same time. Granted, a separate 'Creative City Initiative' has been undertaken to develop a comprehensive ten-year Arts and Culture strategic plan for Vancouver; however, in terms of the promotion of a sustainable 'sense of place' emanating from Vancouver's municipal government, one wishes, at times, for a deeper ecological vision, in which commitments to an 'Eco City' and a 'Creative City' might be pursued simultaneously and interdependently. Copies of the Vancouver *EcoDensity Charter* and *Initial Actions* can be found at www. vancouver-ecodensity.ca/webupload/File/Charter%20Appendix%20A%20-%20June%2011%281%29.pdf and www.vancouver-ecodensity.ca/webupload/File/ Actions%20Appendix%20B-June%2011%284%29.pdf, respectively (accessed July 2008). The 'Culture Plan' of the Creative City Initiative can be accessed at http:// vancouver.ca/creativecity/ (accessed July 2008).

30 Jon Hawkes, *The Fourth Pillar of Sustainability: Culture's Essential Role in Public Planning.* (Victoria, Melbourne: Common Ground Publishing, 2001), p. vii. My thanks to Alana Gerecke for drawing my attention to this work.

relationship between actor and audience can lead to a reconfiguration of how we occupy and exploit various spaces of and in performance, a reconfiguration that ideally translates into a rethinking of our relationships with other, non-human, environments as well.

And yet, as Theresa J. May has recently argued, the tendency among some performance studies scholars to 'deploy ecology as a kind of aesthetic systems theory in order to describe the multifarious, dynamic, and interdependent relationships between, for example, production and reception, actors and space, or theatre and its social context' is a problematic by-product of 'theatre's habituated metaphorization of nature' on stage (cue, once again, Prospero's storm).[31] In such a system, reading worlds on stage, and the local relationships between people and place reproduced by/within those worlds, becomes a rhetorical exercise divorced from the very pressing 'material-ecological issues confounding society' (such as climate change) that always underscore the performance exchange; this, in turn, perpetuates a false nature/culture binary that not only flies in the face of taking the living, breathing organism of the human body as the ground of theatrical expression, but that, in May's opinion, has been definitively exploded in the wake of an event like Hurricane Katrina, which dramatised fiercely and inexorably 'a twenty-first century in which we humans will come to terms with our relationship to the natural world, come hell or high water'.[32] In developing her argument, May draws heavily on a ground-breaking essay by Una Chaudhuri published in *Theater* in 1994; there, addressing the dearth of plays and performance pieces confronting the environmental crisis and the lack of meaningful discussion of theatre ecology (broadly defined) among critics, Chaudhuri maintains that modern Western drama's humanist impulses, in 'complicity with industrialization's animus against nature', have produced 'a wholly social account of human life', resulting in a theatre that is 'programmatically anti-ecological'.[33] Calling for an equally 'programmatic resistance to the use of nature as metaphor', Chaudhuri advocates instead 'a turn towards the literal' in order to 'conceptualize our moral responsibility' for the environment, and in order to begin to address 'the deeply vexed problem of classification that lies at the heart of ecological philosophy: are we

31 Theresa J. May, 'Beyond Bambi: toward a dangerous ecocriticism in Theatre Studies', *Theatre Topics* 17:2 (2007), p. 100.
32 *Ibid.*, pp. 100 and 95; for a further discussion of how Hurricane Katrina forcefully dramatises the relationship between environmental justice and performance, see May's '"Consequences Unforeseen . . ." in *Raisin in the Sun* and *Caroline, or Change*', *Journal of Dramatic Theory and Criticism* 20:2 (2006), pp. 131–44.
33 Una Chaudhuri, '"There must be a lot of fish in that lake": toward an ecological theater', *Theater* 25:1 (1994), pp. 23 and 24.

human beings – and our activities, such as theater – an integral part of nature, or are we somehow radically separate from it'?[34]

Retaining what May calls 'the ontological [i.e. materialist] integrity of ecology' as applied to theatre and performance,[35] what we might call the life of liveness, means paying attention not just to the content of the work, but also to the ways in which that work is produced and consumed. Thus, while I can congratulate myself on the fact that every time I visited the Cultch over the past several years, a portion of my ticket price went towards a legacy fund aimed at renovating the cramped and energy-sucking edifice into a state-of-the art, LEED (Leadership in Energy and Environmental Design)-certified performance space (the first in Canada), and while I can also feel good about the fact that I likely got there via public transit (Richard and I don't own a car), and that I will recycle my programme when I get home, I have also, in the past, thought nothing of hopping on a plane to catch a 'must-see' production half way around the world. This is particularly true of my fifteen-year fetishisation of Tony Kushner's work, the global chasings after of which are only partly described in chapter 3 (suffice it to say that instead of joining David Román and friends at the Mark Taper Forum production of *Angels in America*, just down the coast, I chose instead to fly to New York to see it – twice). Then, too, there is the vexing little matter of how most performance-studies scholars, myself included, tend to disseminate our critical accounts of such productions: in print. To be sure, the ever-expanding blogosphere, combined with a steadily dwindling market for academic books (especially in the humanities) is slowly changing this picture, and one of the things this project has inspired me to do is to join the electronic conversation on performance (at performanceplacepolitics.blogspot.com, to be precise). Not that university administrators and government funding bodies necessarily count such things as research.

Of course, Phelan has famously argued that performance resists commodification. While she allows that the act of spectatorship does involve 'an element of consumption', its returns, she insists, are largely valueless and empty: performance 'saves nothing; it only spends'.[36] But for every *Lost Action* that escapes reproduction, there is also a big budget Broadway musical or Vegas spectacular that won't disappear, and that arguably helps fuel a largely waste-driven industry of theatre tourism by spawning not only authorised touring productions, but

34 *Ibid.*, pp. 29 and 27.
35 May, 'Beyond Bambi', p. 100.
36 Phelan, *Unmarked*, p. 148.

also spin-off products like CDs, coffee mugs, and T-shirts.[37] This is not an argument against live performance; nor is it, as Phelan herself has recently clarified, a naive claim that somehow 'performance is "beyond" the market'.[38] It is, however, an argument about rethinking how, what, why, where, for and with whom we experience performance. And for acknowledging that 'the *pivotal* oscillation between the ethical and the aesthetic' that Phelan sees occurring in the live art event can produce 'other kinds of capital'.[39] One of those other kinds of capital, I would argue, is environmental capital, a renewed attention to and investment in, if not the literal site-specificity of a given performance, the situated response of community-based theatre, for example, to the pressing environmental issues facing a given region. In this kind of 'grassroots' equation, as Downing Cless has astutely pointed out, ecology ('the study of home') is counterbalanced by economy ('the maintenance of home'), rather than subsumed by/within it.[40]

And here, let me stress, I am paradoxically arguing *against* parochialism in performance, in the sense of limiting or confining the possibilities or scope or forms of performance according to geographical locale. This would be the kind of thinking that insists that real, cutting-edge, avant-garde work only happens in New York or London and that, equally, leads to an internalised cultural cringe in places on the margins of those hubs, where fostering a quality local scene is de facto taken to mean creating a Shakespeare festival – and, in Vancouver's case, sticking it in a circus tent on a beach – or importing big box touring musicals from Broadway. The theatrical equivalent of industrialisation, such a production model is as bad for the local black box theatre ecology as it is for the global environment. Instead, I want to go see local acts committed to addressing local concerns in a globally relevant and reflexive manner, performances where any sense of safety I might take in feeling part of a recognisable audience witnessing familiar material presented in a tested idiom is exploded, expanded, and made strange by the boldness and uncertainty and sense of risk underscoring the ideas behind the work. Performances that, as Marshall McLuhan would insist, make of the proximate environment I *think* know, and thus take for granted, an 'anti-environment'.

37 Susan Bennett has recently analysed this aspect of the globalisation of commercial theatre, with a particular focus on New York and Las Vegas. See 'Theatre/tourism', *Theatre Journal* 57:3 (2005), pp. 407–28.
38 Peggy Phelan, 'Marina Abramović: witnessing shadows', *Theatre Journal* 56:4 (2004), p. 576.
39 *Ibid.*, pp. 575 and 576; my emphasis.
40 Downing Cless, 'Eco-theatre, USA: the grassroots is greener', *TDR: The Drama Review* 40:2 (1996), p. 80.

At the same time as the modern environmental movement as we presently know it was getting going in the 1960s, Canadian media theorist Marshall McLuhan, who coined the term 'global village', was reconfiguring his influential notion of the medium as message into a larger theory of media environments (be they natural, mechanical, or informational).[41] For McLuhan, environment, broadly defined, referred to the invisible, unremarked, and unconsciously perceived ground of human production and social relations, the context, matrix, or 'energy system' that structures and processes our actions and inter-relations, but of whose contours and patterns we remain largely unaware and indifferent, except as those contours and patterns get abstracted into artifacts or art objects, becoming the content of a new anti- or counter- environment (as when flowers or cut grasses are brought into the home for decorative display, or, in a favourite example of McLuhan's, earth is viewed from space via satellite images).[42] McLuhan thus saw the artist, and especially the performance artist, as having a special role to play in 'probing' our habituated and 'clichéd' relationship with 'the environment in which we live and of the environments we create for ourselves technically', producing anti-environments that 'archetypalize' and throw into relief repeated patterns/actions/behaviours of, for example, use and abuse, conservation and exploitation, interest and neglect.[43] In this regard, McLuhan reserved a special fondness for the Happenings of the 1960s, because in such performances the 'art materials' normally used by a single artist 'as a probe to direct and order perception' are here 'assumed by the audience directly', who manipulate 'the commonplace materials' of their immediate environment 'to draw vivid attention' to that environment's worth as 'the most invincible of teaching machines, and the most neglected'.[44] Let me thus conclude this chapter, and this book, by briefly describing a version of this kind of Happening I recently attended at a café in my neighbourhood, one that used the tools of performance and pedagogy to ask patrons to tackle, in very literal, non-metaphorical, and self-critical ways, some difficult questions about climate change,

41 On the profound effect that McLuhan's media theories had on the nascent environmental movement, and on Greenpeace in particular, see Weyler, *Greenpeace*; and Stephen Dale, *McLuhan's Children: The Greenpeace Message and the Media* (Toronto: Between the Lines, 1996).

42 Marshall McLuhan, 'The emperor's old clothes', in Gyorgy Kepes (ed.), *The Man-Made Object* (New York: Braziller), p. 90. See also, McLuhan, 'The relation of environment to anti-environment', *The University of Windsor Review* 2:1 (1966), pp. 1–10.

43 McLuhan, 'Address at Vision 65', in Eric McLuhan and Frank Zingrone (eds), *The Essential McLuhan* (Toronto: Anansi, 1995), p. 225. See also, McLuhan (with Wilfred Watson), *From Cliché to Archetype* (New York: Viking, 1970), pp. 198 and *passim*.

44 McLuhan, *From Cliché to Archetype*, pp. 198 and 199.

and to begin to think, in McLuhan's counter-environmental fashion, 'of the entire planet as a work of art'.[45]

Hypocrite acteur

Headlines Theatre is a Vancouver-based performance company founded in 1981 by a group of politically active local artists, and committed to producing community-specific, issue-oriented theatre. In 1984, David Diamond assumed the role of Artistic Director. Heavily influenced by Augusto Boal's Theatre of the Oppressed,[46] as well as the ecologically based network theories of physicist Fritjof Capra, Diamond has, since the mid-1980s, evolved his own unique approach to using theatre for community empowerment and social change, an organic, 'systems-based' theory of performance and/as dialogue that Diamond calls 'Theatre for Living'. For Diamond, communities, like the planetary ecosystem as a whole, are living organisms capable of responding and adapting to various social disturbances in complex, dynamic, and ulti-mately self-sustaining ways. As such, Diamond, in his appointed role as Joker – as derived from Boal, a combination *metteur en scène* and *agent provacteur* – uses the language of the theatre in much the same way as I outlined Darren O'Donnell's approach to performance as 'social acu-puncture' in the introduction to this book, that is, to probe at and render unstable various entrenched forms of social organisation in order to open up a space where new models and networks might be amplified and potentially incorporated into the system.[47] For example, building on Boal's notion of the 'spect-actor' – the audience member who, attending a community-based performance exploring a given social or political topic, becomes part of the dramatic action, offering different options, solutions, and suggestions for change[48] – Diamond and his company have repeatedly deployed their own version of participatory Forum Theatre to tackle a series of pressing local issues, including poverty, homelessness, domestic violence, Native rights, racism, drug addic-tion, safer sex, bullying in schools, and sustainability and the environ-ment. Indeed, in March 2002, for their twentieth-anniversary mainstage

45 *Ibid.*, p. 199.
46 According to Cless, much grassroots eco-theatre in North America borrows heavily from Boal; see Cless, 'Eco-theatre, USA', pp. 79–80.
47 See Diamond, *Theatre for Living: The Art and Science of Community-Based Dialogue* (Victoria, BC: Trafford Publishing, 2007); Boal, *Theatre of the Oppressed*, trans. Charles A. and Maria-Odilia Leal-McBride (London: Pluto, 1979); and Capra, *The Hidden Connections* (New York: Doubleday, 2002).
48 See Boal's discussion of this concept in his *Games for Actors and Non-Actors*, trans. Adrian Jackson (New York: Routledge, 1992), p. xxx.

production, Diamond and Headlines collaborated with MainDance Artistic Director Kathryn Ricketts to create *THIR$TY*, an interactive dance-theatre piece and consciousness-raising workshop about water privatisation that opened at the Roundhouse Community Centre on what the UN had decreed as World Water Day (March 21).

For their 2008 Forum Theatre project, Headlines had hoped to stage a production called *2° of Adaptation: Making Choices While the Climate Changes*. However, the piece had to be cancelled because the company could not raise the required amount of funding. On their website Headlines summarises the initial preparations for and subsequent cancellation of the project as follows:

> Our approach to possibly the most important issue facing humanity today, was regarded as innovative and extremely timely. 106 people had applied to us for places in the community workshop and cast; word about the project was spreading far and wide. And yet, we had a very difficult time raising funds for the production, which was to investigate the blockages we face in making core behavioural change in our lives in relation to climate issues. We believe that what we encountered is a sense from some funders that the environment is something 'out there' that we can go and fix, and that the solutions are 'top down'. What this misses is that *we are the environment*. The adaptations and mitigations that are necessary in the face of climate change lie inside.[49]

Adapting in their own way to the collapse of their mainstage show, Diamond and company members organised instead a series of grass-roots community workshops on global warming called *2° of fear and desire*. The first of these took place over three successive nights in early November 2007 at Rhizome, a café that is about fifteen minutes from my house and that, in addition to serving up tasty comfort food in a relaxed, suitably bohemian setting, also routinely partners with social justice organisations, community groups, and local artists to host events, forums, performances, and screenings on a range of issues. The positive response prompted Diamond to schedule ten additional workshops at various locations around the city between February and March 2008.

I attended the first of this second series of workshops, held once again at Rhizome. It was another snowy evening and the turnout was less than anticipated. Diamond kept looking forlornly at the rows of empty chairs. Nevertheless, at the appointed hour he took up the microphone, introduced himself, and told the assembled audience that we were going

49 See 'History of the project', *2° of fear and desire*, www.headlinestheatre. com/2Degrees08/history.htm (accessed March 2008).

to use an exercise adapted from Boal, called Cops in the Head, in order
to work through some of the dilemmas we face on a daily basis regarding
climate change. Diamond began by calling for three volunteers; I studi-
ously looked at the floor. The volunteers, meanwhile, were invited to tell
a story about a moment of decision in their lives in which their good
green intentions become paralysed or thrown off course by competing
voices counselling an easier or safer path. The audience then voted on
the story they wished to see dramatised. We chose single mom Molly's
story, which she titled 'The Hypocrite in Me'; it detailed her struggles
most weekdays to get her kids off to school and herself in to work, and
in particular how her plans to have the family ride their bikes to their
respective destinations are more often than not derailed by the voices
in her head that tell her they're going to be late, and wouldn't it just be
easier to take the car? After walking Molly through the conversation
she's having inside her head, Diamond called on three more volunteers
to give literal shape to a physical form that Molly had chosen to represent three of the more admonitory/regulatory voices she finds herself
arguing with every morning: a finger-wagging mother; a boss who
simply shrugs; a fellow single mother who offers a prayer on bended
knee (a pose, I remember thinking at the time, that Crystal Pite might
have choreographed). These three characters were subsequently invited
to construct their own monologues about why Molly should ditch the
bikes in favour of the car: it's safer for the kids; it's your career that's on
the line; who has the time or energy?

Then came the hard part. Molly was required to spar in turn with
each of the three characters about the best course of action, with audience members invited to intervene at pivotal moments to change the
direction of the conversation, replacing an ever-wearying Molly with
our own spoken and gestural representations of possible solutions for
diminishing the insistence of the antagonistic voices counselling the
status quo. We did this twice over for each conversation, after which
there was a general audience talk-back about what we had witnessed/
participated in, and how this related to larger issues impeding concrete
action on global climate change. The process was painful and slow-
going. Audience members, myself included, were loath to intervene,
and the solutions proposed seemed tentative and timid. I could tell
Diamond, normally amiable and encouraging, was getting increasingly
frustrated in his role as Joker; twice he stopped the action to remind us
of the participatory goals of forum theatre, and of our physical roles as
'spect-actors'. In the talk-back sessions, there were frequent silences.
When Diamond looked at me, in the front row with my notebook, I
looked away.

I certainly had things to say: about different generational responses to climate change; about the gender of labour; about the local specificities of place we were performatively reinscribing in our prioritising of Molly's story over the others (one of which was about the non-sustainability of a sustainable kibbutz in Israel). Afterwards the cops inside my own head tried to convince me that my silence owed to the fact that I was there primarily as a researcher rather than a participant, that I needed to take notes, record the process of the event as it unfolded. But really I was encountering, even abetting, some of the practical impediments to the theories of performance publics and audience formations, live art and livability, place-based spectatorship and global political consciousness, advanced in the preceding chapters. In this respect, the title of Diamond's workshop is an especially apt reminder that the performance event always stages the opportunity for response as one fraught with risk, as a moment that pivots between fear and desire. The Joker who has to work the room so hard is here encountering an audience afraid to move, to be moved, lest the joke be on them.

Lost action/last actions. At the end of the introduction I suggested that, as a teacher, I am fairly familiar – even comfortable – with failure. And so, as this coda likewise draws to a close, let me attempt to connect Pite's 'kinetics of rescue' with what we might call its analytics. I do so not on Diamond's behalf, but on my own. Specifically, in launching this book into the world, I also want to commit to resolving a bit more concretely, in my own performance practice, the gap between saying and doing that I ideally see it challenging. What better way to do this than to make use of a theatrical forum – the university classroom – in which I regularly serve as joker and joke? After all, I have a captive audience; various institutional resources and potential collaborators to draw upon; an upcoming international performance event that will allow us to scrutinise more closely questions of local spectatorship and global citizenship; and various electronic tools (including the aforementioned blog) through which to disseminate the archive of our thinking and activities about the relationship between performance, place, and politics. I can't predict what, exactly, will be staged out of all of this. But I invite the world to watch. And respond.

SELECT BIBLIOGRAPHY

Books, articles, and reports

Agamben, Giorgio, *Homo Sacer: Sovereign Power and Bare Life*, trans. Daniel Heller-Roazen, Stanford: Stanford University Press, 1998.

Amnesty International, 'People's Republic of China: the Olympics countdown – broken promises', www.amnesty.org/en/library/asset/ASA17/089/2008/en/8249b304-5724-11dd-90eb-ff4596860802/asa170892008eng.pdf (accessed July 2008).

Appadurai, Arjun, *Modernity at Large: Cultural Dimensions of Globalization*, Minneapolis: University of Minnesota Press, 1996.

Artaud, Antonin, *The Theater and Its Double*, trans. Mary Caroline Richards, New York: Grove, 1958.

Auslander, Philip, *Liveness: Performance in a Mediatized Culture*, New York: Routledge, 1999.

Austin, J. L., *How to Do Things with Words*, New York: Oxford University Press, 1962.

Badami, Anita Rau, *Can You Hear the Nightbird Call?*, Toronto: Knopf, 2006.

Badiou, Alain, *Being and Event*, trans. Oliver Feltham, London: Continuum, 2006.

——, 'Rhapsody for the theatre', trans. Bruno Bosteels, *Theatre Survey* 49:2 (2008), pp. 187-238.

Beckett, Samuel, *Waiting for Godot*, New York: Grove, 1982.

Beckham, David and Tom Watt, *Beckham: Both Feet on the Ground*, New York: HarperCollins, 2003.

Benjamin, Walter, 'Theses on the philosophy of history', in *Illuminations*, ed. Hannah Arendt, trans. Harry Zohn, New York: Schoken, 1968, pp. 253-64.

——, 'What is epic theater?', in *Illuminations*, pp. 147–54.

Bennett, Susan, *Theatre Audiences*, London: Routledge, 1990; 2nd edn 1998.

——, 'Theatre/tourism', *Theatre Journal* 57:3 (2005), pp. 407-28.

Black, David R. and Shona Bezanson, 'The Olympic Games, human rights and democratisation: lessons from Seoul and implications for Beijing', *Third World Quarterly* 25:7 (2004), pp. 1245–61.

Blau, Herbert, *The Audience*, Baltimore: Johns Hopkins University Press, 1990.

Boal, Augusto, *Games for Actors and Non-Actors*, trans. Adrian Jackson, New York: Routledge, 1992.

——, *Theatre of the Oppressed*, trans. Charles A. and Maria-Odilia Leal-McBride, London: Pluto, 1979.

BOCOG, *Supplement on Olympic Commitments*, Beijing: BOCOG, 2008.

Bold, Christine, Ric Knowles, and Belinda Leach, '"How might a women's monument be different?"', *Essays on Canadian Writing* 80 (2003), pp. 17–35.

Borecca, Art, '"Dramaturging" the dialectic: Brecht, Benjamin, and Declan Donnellan's production of *Angels in America*', in Deborah R. Geis and Steven F. Kruger (eds), *Approaching the Millennium: Essays on Angels in America*, Ann Arbor: University of Michigan Press, 1997, pp. 245–60.

Boswell, John, *Christianity, Social Tolerance, and Homosexuality: Gay People in Western Europe from the Beginning of the Christian Era to the Fourteenth Century*, Chicago: University of Chicago Press, 1980.

——, *Same-Sex Unions in Pre-Modern Europe*, New York: Villard, 1994.

Bourassa, Kevin and Joe Varnell, *Just Married: Gay Marriage and the Expansion of Human Rights*, Toronto: Doubleday, 2002.

Braidotti, Rosi, *Nomadic Subjects: Embodiment and Sexual Difference in Contemporary Feminist Theory*, New York: Columbia University Press, 1994.

Bray, Alan, *The Friend*, Chicago: University of Chicago Press, 2003.

Brecht, Bertolt, 'Short description of a new technique of acting which produces an alienation effect', in *Brecht on Theatre: The Development of an Aesthetic*, ed. and trans. John Willett, London: Methuen, 1964, pp. 136–47.

Brewster, Claire, and Keith Brewster, 'Mexico City 1968: sombreros and skyscrapers', in Tomlinson and Young (eds), *National Identity and Global Sports Events*, pp. 99–116.

Brownell, Susan, *Beijing's Games: What the Olympics Mean to China*, Lanham: Rowan and Littlefield, 2008.

Bulman, James C, 'Bringing Cheek By Jowl's *As You Like It* out of the closet: the politics of gay theater', *Shakespeare Bulletin* 22:3 (2004), pp. 31–46.

Butler, Judith, *Antigone's Claim: Kinship Between Life and Death*, New York: Columbia University Press, 2000.

——, *Bodies That Matter: On the Discursive Limits of 'Sex'*, New York: Routledge, 1993.

——, 'Critically queer', *GLQ: A Journal of Lesbian & Gay Studies* 1:1 (1993), pp. 17–32.

——, *Excitable Speech: A Politics of the Performative*, New York: Routledge, 1997.

——, *Gender Trouble: Feminism and the Subversion of Identity*, New York: Routledge, 1990.

——, *Giving an Account of Oneself*, New York: Fordham University Press, 2005.

——, 'Melancholy gender/refused identification', *The Psychic Life of Power: Theories in Subjection*, Stanford: Stanford University Press, 1997, pp. 132–50.

——, 'Performance acts and gender constitution: an essay in phenomenology and feminist theory', *Theatre Journal* 40:4 (1988), pp. 519–31.

——, *Precarious Life: The Powers of Mourning and Violence*, New York: Verso, 2004.

——, *Undoing Gender*, New York: Routledge, 2004.

Capra, Fritjof, *The Hidden Connections*, New York: Doubleday, 2002.

Cashman, Richard, *The Bitter Sweet Awakening: The Legacy of the Sydney 2000 Olympic Games*, Sydney: Walla Walla Press, 2006.

Cavell, Richard, 'Histories of forgetting: Canadian representations of war and the politics of cultural memory', in Serge Jaumain and Éric Remacle (eds), *Mémoire de guerre et construction de la paix: Mentalités et choix politiques: Belgique – Europe – Canada*, Brussels: Peter Lang, 2006, pp. 67–80.

Centre on Housing Rights and Evictions, *Fair Play for Housing Rights: Mega-Events, Olympic Games and Housing Rights*, Geneva: COHRE, 2007.

Chaudhuri, Una, Comment, in 'A forum on theatre and tragedy in the wake of September 11th, 2001', *Theatre Journal* 54:1 (2002), pp. 97–9.

——, *Staging Place: The Geography of Modern Drama*, Ann Arbor: University of Michigan Press, 1997.

——, '"There must be a lot of fish in that lake": toward an ecological theater', *Theater* 25:1 (1994), pp. 23–31.

Cless, Downing, 'Eco-theatre, USA: the grassroots is greener', *TDR: The Drama Review* 40:2 (1996), pp. 79–102.

Cohen, Robin, 'Diasporas, the nation-state, and globalisation', in Wang (ed.), *Global History and Migrations*, pp. 117–44.

Coleman, Isobel, 'Women, Islam, and the new Iraq', *Foreign Affairs* (January/February 2006), www.foreignaffairs.org/20060101faessay85104/isobel-coleman/women-islam-and-the-new-iraq.html (accessed November 2008).

Conway, Mary T., 'A becoming queer aesthetic', *Discourse* 26:3 (2004), pp. 166–89.

Cott, Nancy F., *Public Vows: A History of Marriage and the Nation*, Cambridge, MA: Harvard University Press, 2000.

Crimp, Douglas, 'Mourning and militancy', in Russell Ferguson, Matha Gever, Trinh T. Minh-ha, and Cornel West (eds), *Out There: Marginalization and Contemporary Cultures*, Cambridge, MA: MIT Press, 1990, pp. 233–46.

Dale, Stephen, *McLuhan's Children: The Greenpeace Message and the Media*, Toronto: Between the Lines, 1996.

de Certeau, Michel, *The Practice of Everyday Life*, trans. Steven Rendall, Berkeley: University of California Press, 1984.

de Kloet, Jeroen, Gladys Pak Lei Chong, and Wei Liu, 'The Beijing Olympics and the art of nation-state maintenance', *China Aktuell* 2 (2008), pp. 5–35.

Debord, Guy, *The Society of the Spectacle*, Detroit: Black and Red, 1983.

Deleuze, Gilles, and Félix Guattari, *Anti-Oedipus: Capitalism and Schizophrenia*, trans. Robert Hurley, Mark Seem, and Helen R. Lane, Minneapolis: University of Minnesota Press, 1983.

——, *A Thousand Plateaus: Capitalism and Schizophrenia*, trans. Brian Massumi, Minneapolis: University of Minnesota Press, 1987.

Derrida, Jacques, 'By force of mourning', trans. Pascale-Anne Brault and Michael Naas, *Critical Inquiry* 22:2 (1996), pp. 171–92.

——, 'Signature, event, context', in *Limited Inc.*, ed. Gerald Graff, trans. Samuel Weber and Jeffrey Mehlman, Evanston: Northwestern University Press, 1988, pp. 1–24.

Diamond, David, *Theatre for Living: The Art and Science of Community-Based Dialogue*, Victoria, BC: Trafford Publishing, 2007.

DiGangi, Mario, 'Queering the Shakespearean family', *Shakespeare Quarterly* 47:3 (1996), pp. 269–90.

Dirlik, Arif, 'Place-based imagination: globalism and the politics of place', in Roxann Prazniak and Arif Dirlik (eds), *Places and Politics in an Age of Globalization*, New York: Rowman & Littlefield, 2001, pp. 15–51.

Dolan, Jill, *Geographies of Learning: Theory and Practice, Activism and Performance*, Middletown: Wesleyan University Press, 2001.

——, *Utopia in Performance: Finding Hope at the Theater*, Ann Arbor: University of Michigan Press, 2005.

Donnellan, Declan, *The Actor and the Target*, London: Nick Hern, 2002.

Eby, David, and Christopher Misura, *Cracks in the Foundation: Solving the Housing Crisis in Canada's Poorest Neighbourhood*, Vancouver: Pivot, 2006.

Edelman, Lee, *No Future: Queer Theory and the Death Drive*, Durham: Duke University Press, 2004.

Fan, Di'an, and Zhang Ga (eds), *Synthetic Times: Media Art China 2008*, Beijing and Cambridge, MA: National Art Museum of China and MIT Press, 2008.

Foer, Franklin, *How Soccer Explains the World: An (Unlikely) Theory of Globalization*, New York: HarperCollins, 2004.

Foucault, Michel, *Ethics: Subjectivity and Truth*, ed. Paul Rabinow, trans. Robert Hurley and others, New York: New Press, 1997.

——, *The History of Sexuality, Volume 1: An Introduction*, trans. Robert Hurley, New York: Vintage, 1990.

——, *The History of Sexuality, Volume 2: The Use of Pleasure*, trans. Robert Hurley, New York: Vintage, 1990.

——, *The History of Sexuality, Volume 3: The Care of the Self*, trans. Robert Hurley, New York: Vintage, 1990.

——, 'Of other spaces', in Nicholas Mirzoeff (ed.), *The Visual Culture Reader*. New York: Routledge, 1998; 2nd edn 2002, pp. 229–36.

Freeman, Elizabeth, *The Wedding Complex: Forms of Belonging in Modern American Culture*, Durham: Duke University Press, 2002.

Freud, Sigmund, 'The ego and the id', in *The Standard Edition of the Complete Psychological Works of Sigmund Freud*, vol. 19, ed. and trans. James Strachey, London: Hogarth, 1961, pp. 12–66.

——. 'Mourning and melancholia', in *The Standard Edition of the Complete Psychological Works of Sigmund Freud*, vol. 14, 1957, pp. 243–58.

Fuchs, Elinor, *The Death of Character: Perspectives on Theater after Modernism*, Bloomington: Indiana University Press, 1996.

Garland, Jon, and Michael Rowe, *Racism and Anti-Racism in Football*, New York: Palgrave, 2001.

Gere, David, *How to Make Dances in an Epidemic: Tracking Choreography in the Age of AIDS*, Madison: University of Wisconsin Press, 2004.

Greenpeace China (Amy Zhang, lead author), *China after the Olympics: Lessons from Beijing: A Greenpeace Assessment of the Performance of the Beijing 2008 Olympic Games*, Beijing: Greenpeace China, 2008.

John R. Gold, and Margaret M. Gold, *Cities of Culture: Staging International Festivals and the Urban Agenda, 1851–2000*, Aldershot: Ashgate, 2005.

Griffin, Tim, 'Editor's letter', *Artforum* 66:4 (December 2007), p. 51.

Guttmann, Allen, 'Berlin 1936: the most controversial Olympics', in Tomlinson and Young (eds), *National Identity and Global Sports Events*, pp. 65–82.

Habermas, Jürgen, *The Structural Transformation of the Public Sphere: An Inquiry into a Category of Bourgeois Society*, trans. Thomas Burger, Cambridge, MA: MIT Press, 1989.

Halberstam, Judith, *In a Queer Time and Place: Transgender Bodies, Subcultural Lives*, New York: New York University Press, 2005.

Harvey, David, *Spaces of Capital: Towards a Critical Geography*, Edinburgh: Edinburgh University Press, 2001.

Hawkes, Jon, *The Fourth Pillar of Sustainability: Culture's Essential Role in Public Planning*, Victoria, Melbourne: Common Ground Publishing, 2001.

Hill, Christopher R., *Olympic Politics*, Manchester: Manchester University Press, 1992.

Hirsch, Marianne, *Family Frames: Photography, Narrative, and Postmemory*, Cambridge, MA: Harvard University Press, 1997.

Hopkins, Lisa, *The Shakespearean Marriage: Merry Wives and Heavy Husbands*, London: Macmillan, 1998.

Human Rights Watch, *'One Year of My Blood': Exploitation of Migrant Construction Workers in Beijing*, vol. 20, no. 3, New York: Human Rights Watch, 2008.

Huyssen, Andreas, *Present Pasts: Urban Palimpsests and the Politics of Memory*, Stanford: Stanford University Press, 2003.

——, *Twilight Memories: Marking Time in a Culture of Amnesia*, New York: Routledge, 1995.

Ingraham, Chrys, *White Weddings: Romancing Heterosexuality in Popular Culture*, New York: Routledge, 1999.

International Olympic Committee, *Olympic Charter*, Lausanne: IOC, 2007.

The International Performance and Culture Research Group of the University of California, 'Letter to the editor', *Theatre Survey* 47:2 (2006), pp. 169–73.

Jackson, Shannon, *Professing Performance: Theatre in the Academy from Philology to Performativity*, Cambridge: Cambridge University Press, 2004.

Johnston, Hugh J. M., *The Voyage of the Komagata Maru: The Sikh Challenge to Canada's Colour Bar*, Delhi: Oxford University Press, 1979.

Johnston, Jill, 'In the meantime, art was happening', in Geoffrey Hendricks (ed.), *Critical Mass: Happenings, Fluxus, Performance, Intermedia and Rutgers University, 1958–1972*, Rutgers: Rutgers University Press, 2003, pp. 169–72.

——, 'Wedding in Denmark', in Nayland Blake, Lawrence Rinder, and Amy Scholder (eds), *In a Different Light: Visual Culture, Sexual Identity, Queer Practice*, San Francisco: City Lights Books, 1995, pp. 215–21.

Kaufman, Moisés, and members of Tectonic Theater Project, *The Laramie Project*, New York: Vintage, 2001.

Kelley, Caffyn, 'Creating memory, contesting history', *Matriart* 5 (1995), pp. 6–11.

Kinsman, Gary, *The Regulation of Desire: Homo and Hetero Sexualities*, Montreal: Black Rose Books, 1987; 2nd edn 1996.

Kramer, Larry, *The Normal Heart*, New York: Plume, 1985.

Kumar, Amitava, (ed.), *World Bank Literature*, Minneapolis: University of Minnesota Press, 2002.

Kushner, Tony, *Angels in America, Part One: Millennium Approaches*, New York: Theatre Communications Group, 1993.

——, *Angels in America, Part Two: Perestroika*, New York: Theatre Communications Group, 1994.

——, *Homebody/Kabul*, New York: Theatre Communications Group, 2002.

——, *Homebody/Kabul*, revised edn, New York: Theatre Communications Group, 2004.

——, 'Notes about political theater', *Kenyon Review* 19:3-4 (1997), pp. 19–34.

Lacan, Jacques, *The Seminar of Jacques Lacan, Book VII: The Ethics of Psychoanalysis, 1959–60*, ed. Jacques-Alain Miller, trans. Dennis Porter, New York: Norton, 1992.

Large, David Clay, *Nazi Games: The Olympics of 1936*, New York: Norton, 2007.

Laroque, Sylvain, *Gay Marriage: The Story of a Canadian Social Revolution*, Toronto: Lorimer and Co., 2006.

Law Commission of Canada, *Beyond Conjugality: Recognizing and Supporting Close Personal Adult Relationships*, 2001, http://tabletology.com/docs/beyond_conjugality.pdf (accessed September 2007).

Leiren-Young, Mark, *Articles of Faith: The Battle of St. Alban's*, Vancouver: Anvil Press, 2001.

Lenskyj, Helen Jefferson, *Olympic Industry Resistance: Challenging Olympic Power and Propaganda*, Albany: SUNY Press, 2008.

Lévinas, Emmanuel, *Ethics and Infinity: Conversations with Philippe Nemo*, trans. Richard A. Cohen, Pittsburgh: Duquesne University Press, 1985.

MacAloon, John J., 'Olympic Games and the theory of spectacle in modern societies', in John J. MacAloon (ed.), *Rite, Drama, Festival, Spectacle: Rehearsals Toward a Theory of Cultural Performance*, Philadelphia: Institute for the Study of Human Issues, 1984, pp. 241–80.

MacIvor, Daniel, *In on It*, Winnipeg: Scirocco, 2001.

McLuhan, Marshall, 'Address at Vision 65', in Eric McLuhan and Frank Zingrone (eds), *The Essential McLuhan*, Toronto: Anansi, 1995, pp. 219–32.

——, 'The emperor's old clothes', in Gyorgy Kepes (ed.), *The Man-Made Object*, New York: Braziller, 1966, pp. 90–5.

——, 'The relation of environment to anti-environment', *The University of Windsor Review* 2:1 (1966), pp. 1–10.

McLuhan, Marshall, and Quentin Fiore, *War and Peace in the Global Village*, New York: McGraw-Hill, 1968.

McLuhan, Marshall, with Wifred Watson, *From Cliché to Archetype*, New York: Viking, 1970.

McNally, Terrence, *Corpus Christi: A Play*, New York: Grove, 1998.

Maass, Steven, 'Going green', *Olympic Review* 64 (2007), pp. 31–7.

Maguire, Joseph, *Global Sport: Identities, Societies, Civilizations*, Oxford: Polity, 1999.

Maguire, Joseph, and Robert Pearton, 'Global sport and the migration patterns of France '98 World Cup finals players: some preliminary observations', in Jon Garland, Dominic Malcolm, and Michael Rowe (eds), *The Future of Football: Challenges for the Twenty-First Century*, London: Frank Cass, 2000, pp. 175–89.

Mann, Bonnie, 'Gay marriage and the war on terror', *Hypatia* 22:1 (2007), pp. 247–51.

Martin, Biddy, 'Extraordinary homosexuals and the fear of being ordinary', *differences: a journal of feminist cultural studies* 6:2–3 (1994), pp. 100–25.

Massey, Doreen, *Space, Place, and Gender*, Minneapolis: University of Minnesota Press, 1994.

May, Theresa J., 'Beyond Bambi: toward a dangerous ecocriticism in theatre studies', *Theatre Topics* 17:2 (2007), pp. 95–110.

——, '"Consequences unforeseen . . ." in *Raisin in the Sun* and *Caroline, or Change*', *Journal of Dramatic Theory and Criticism* 20:2 (2006), pp. 131–44.

Minwalla, Framji, 'Tony Kushner's *Homebody/Kabul*: staging history in a post-colonial world', *Theater* 33:1 (2003), pp. 29–43.

Mittelman, James H., *The Globalization Syndrome: Transformation and Resistance*, Princeton: Princeton University Press, 2000.

Montano, Linda M., *Letters from Linda Montano*, ed. Jennie Klein, New York: Routledge, 2005.

Moran, Richie, 'Racism in football: a victim's perspective', in Jon Garland, Dominic Malcolm, and Michael Rowe (eds), *The Future of Football: Challenges for the Twenty-First Century*, London: Frank Cass, 2000, pp. 190–200.

Muñoz, José Estaban, *Disidentifications: Queers of Color and the Performance of Politics*, Minneapolis: University of Minnesota Press, 1999.

Neely, Carol Thomas, *Broken Nuptials in Shakespeare's Plays*, New Haven: Yale University Press, 1985.

Nora, Pierre, 'Between memory and history: *Les Lieux de mémoire*', *Representations* 26 (1989), pp. 7–25.

—— (ed.), *Les Lieux de mémoire*, Paris: Gallimard, 1997.

O'Connell, Lisa, 'Marriage acts: stages in the transformation of modern nuptial culture', *differences: a journal of feminist cultural studies* 11:1 (1999), pp. 68–111.

O'Donnell, Darren, *Social Acupuncture: A Guide to Suicide, Performance, and Utopia*, Toronto: Coach House Books, 2006.

Olds, Kris. 'Canada: hallmark events, evictions, and housing rights', in Antonio Azuela, Emilio Duhan, and Enrique Ortiz (eds), *Evictions and the Right to Housing: Experience from Canada, Chile, the Dominican Republic, South Africa, and South Korea*, Ottawa: International Development Centre, 1998, pp. 1–45.

——, *Globalization and Urban Change: Capital, Culture, and Pacific Rim Mega-Projects*, Oxford: Oxford University Press, 2001.

Parker, Andrew, and Eve Kosofsky Sedgwick, 'Introduction: performativity and performance', in Parker and Sedgwick (eds), *Performativity and Performance*, New York: Routledge, 1995, pp. 1–18.

Pavis, Patrice (ed.), *The Intercultural Performance Reader*, New York: Routledge, 1996.

Pearson, Wendy, 'Interrogating the epistemology of the bedroom: same-sex marriage and sexual citizenship in Canada', *Discourse* 26:3 (2004), pp. 136–65.

Pedersen Wendy, and Jean Swanson, *Nothing About Us Without Us: Interim Report on Community Visioning*, Vancouver: Carnegie Community Action Project, 2008.

Phelan, Peggy, 'Marina Abramović: witnessing shadows', *Theatre Journal* 56:4 (2004), pp. 569–77.

——, *Mourning Sex: Performing Public Memories*, New York: Routledge, 1997.

——, 'Performance, live culture and things of the heart: Peggy Phelan in conversation with Marquard Smith', *Journal of Visual Culture* 2:3 (2003), pp. 291–302.

——, *Unmarked: The Politics of Performance*, New York: Routledge, 1993.

Phillips, M. Scott, 'The failure of history: Kushner's *Homebody/Kabul* and the apocalyptic context', *Modern Drama* 47:1 (2004), pp. 1–20.

Pollock, Sharon, *The Komagata Maru Incident*, Toronto: Playwrights Co-op, 1978.

Rayside, David, *On the Fringe: Gays and Lesbians in Politics*, Ithaca: Cornell University Press, 1998.

Reinelt, Janelle, 'The politics of discourse: performativity meets theatricality', *SubStance* 31 (2002), pp. 201–15.

Roach, Joseph, *Cities of the Dead: Circum-Atlantic Performance*, New York: Columbia University Press, 1996.

——, 'World bank drama', in Wai Chee Dimock and Lawrence Buell (eds), *Shades of the Planet: American Literature as World Literature*, Princeton: Princeton University Press, 2007, pp. 171–83.

Robertson, Leslie A., and Dara Culhane (eds), *In Plain Sight: Reflections on Life in Downtown Eastside Vancouver*, Vancouver: Talonbooks, 2005.

Roche, Maurice, *Mega-Events and Modernity: Olympics and Expos in the Growth of Global Culture*, London: Routledge, 2000.

Román, David, *Performance in America: Contemporary U.S. Culture and the Performing Arts*, Durham: Duke University Press, 2005.

Rubin, Gayle, 'The traffic in women: "the political economy" of sex', in Rayna R. Reiter (ed.), *Toward an Anthropology of Women*, New York: Monthly Review Press, 1975, pp. 157–210.

Said, Edward, 'Travelling theory', *Raritan* 1:3 (1982), pp. 41–67.

——, 'Travelling theory reconsidered', in Robert Polhemus and Roger Henkle (eds), *Critical Reconsiderations: The Relationship of Fiction and Life*, Stanford: Stanford University Press, 1994, pp. 251–65.

Salinger, Leo, *Shakespeare and the Traditions of Comedy*, Cambridge: Cambridge University Press, 1974.

Santayana, George, *Sonnets and Other Verses*, New York: Stone and Kimball, 1896.

Schechner, Richard, *Between Theater and Anthropology*, Philadelphia: University of Pennsylvania Press, 1985.

——, *Performance Studies: An Introduction*, New York: Routledge, 2002.

Sedgwick, Eve, *Touching Feeling: Affect, Pedagogy, Peformativity*, Durham, NC: Duke University Press, 2003.

——, 'Queer performativity: Henry James's *The Art of the Novel*', *GLQ: A Journal of Lesbian & Gay Studies* 1:1 (1993), pp. 1–16.

Shaw, Nancy, *Lost and Found: Kidd Pivot, Dance Documenta*, no. 2, Vancouver: Eponymous Productions and Arts Society, 2006.

Sherman, Suzanne (ed.), *Lesbian and Gay Marriage: Private Commitments, Public Ceremonies*, Philadelphia: Temple University Press, 1992.

Simon, Roger, Sharon Rosenberg, and Claudia Eppert (eds), *Between Hope and Despair: Pedagogy and the Remembrance of Historical Trauma*, Lanham: Rowman and Littlefield, 2000.

Solomon, Alisa, *Re-Dressing the Canon: Essays on Theater and Gender*, New York: Routledge, 1997.

Spivak, Gayatri Chakravorty, *Death of a Discipline*, New York: Columbia University Press, 2003.

Stein, Janice Gross, and Eugene Lang, *The Unexpected War: Canada in Kandahar*, Toronto: Viking, 2007.

Sturken, Marita, *Tangled Memories: The Vietnam War, the AIDS Epidemic, and the Politics of Remembering*, Berkeley: University of California Press, 1997.

Sullivan, Andrew, *Love Undetectable: Notes on Friendship, Sex and Survival*, New York: Knopf, 1999.

—— (ed.), *Same-Sex Marriage: Pro and Con*, New York: Vintage, 1997; revised edn 2004.

——, *Virtually Normal: An Argument about Homosexuality*, New York: Knopf, 1995.

Taylor, Diana, *The Archive and the Repertoire: Performing Cultural Memory in the Americas*, Durham, NC: Duke University Press, 2003.

Taylor, Paul (ed.), *The Heart of the Community: The Best of the Carnegie Newsletter*, Vancouver: New Star, 2003.

Tomlinson, Alan, 'Olympic spectacle: opening ceremonies and some paradoxes of globalization', *Media, Culture & Society* 18 (1996), pp. 583–602.

Tomlinson, Alan, and Christopher Young (eds), *National Identity and Global Sports Events: Culture, Politics, and Spectacle in the Olympics and the Football World Cup*, Albany: State University of New York Press, 2006.

Turner, Victor, *The Anthropology of Performance*, New York: PAJ Publications, 1986.

——, *Dramas, Fields, and Metaphors: Symbolic Action in Human Society*, Ithaca: Cornell University Press, 1974.

——, *From Ritual to Theatre: The Human Seriousness of Play*, New York: PAJ Publications, 1982.

——, *The Ritual Process: Structure and Anti-Structure*, London: Routledge, 1969.

United Nations Environment Programme, *Beijing 2008 Olympic Games: An Environmental Review*, Nairobi: UNEP, 2007.

Varughese, Sugith, *Entry Denied*, in Damiano Pietropaolo (ed.), *Where Is Here?: The Drama of Immigration, Volume I*, Winnipeg: Scirocco, 2005.

Vera, Veronica, and Annie Sprinkle, 'Our week at Sister Rosita's summer saint camp', *TDR: The Drama Review* 33:1 (1989), pp. 104–19.

Vogel, Paula, *The Baltimore Waltz and Other Plays*, New York: Theatre Communications Group, 1996.

——, *The Long Christmas Ride Home: A Puppet Play with Actors*, New York: Theatre Communications Group, 2004.

Wallace, Keith, *Action-Camera: Beijing Performance Photography*, Vancouver: Morris and Helen Belkin Art Gallery, 2009.

Wang, Gungwu (ed.), *Global History and Migrations*, Boulder: Westview, 1997.

——, 'Migration history: some patterns revisited', in Wang (ed.), *Global History and Migrations*, pp. 1–22.

Ward, William Peter, *Courtship, Love, and Marriage in Nineteenth-Century Canada*, Montreal: McGill-Queen's University Press, 1990.

Warner, Michael, *Publics and Counterpublics*, New York: Zone Books, 2002.

——, *The Trouble with Normal: Sex Politics, and the Ethics of Queer Life*, New York: Free Press, 1999.

Wasserstrom, Jeffrey N., *Global Shanghai, 1850–2010: A History in Fragments*, New York: Routledge, 2008.

Watson, Scott, 'Exponential future', in Julie Bevan, Juan A. Gaitán, and Scott Watson (eds), *Exponential Future*, Vancouver: Morris and Helen Belkin Art Gallery, 2008, pp. 6–15.

——, 'Foreword', in *Rebecca Belmore: The Named and the Unnamed*, Vancouver: Morris and Helen Belkin Art Gallery/University of British Columbia, 2003, pp.7–8.

Weyler, Rex, *Greenpeace: How a Group of Ecologists, Journalists, and Visionaries Changed the World*, Vancouver: Raincoast Books, 2004.

The Windsor Report 2004, www.anglicancommunion.org/windsor2004/section_c/p9.cfm (accessed November 2008).

Wittig, Monique, *The Straight Mind and Other Essays*, Boston: Beacon Press, 1992.

Wolford, Lisa, and Richard Schechner (eds), *The Grotowski Sourcebook*, New York: Routledge, 1997.

Select newspaper, magazine, and Internet articles

Ai Weiwei, 'Ai Weiwei: fragments, voids, sections and rings', interview with Adrian Blackwell, *Archinect* (5 December 2006), http://archinect.com/features/article.php?id=47035_0_23_0_C (accessed December 2008).

Auld, Alison, 'Constables to wed, as Canada blogs', *Globe and Mail* (30 June 2006).

Bailey, Ian, 'Ahead of Games, Vancouver reaches out to Eastside homeless', *Globe and Mail* (15 September 2008).

Baines, David, 'The devil was in the details', *Vancouver Sun* (17 January 2009).

Barboza, David, 'Gritty renegade now directs China's close-up', *New York Times* (7 August 2008), www.nytimes.com/2008/08/08/sports/olympics/08guru.html?pagewanted=1&_r=1# (accessed August 2008).

Bellett, Gerry, 'Attacker gets six years for role in fatal beating', *Vancouver Sun* (9 February 2005).

Bermingham, John, 'Vancouver's future rising in the east', *Vancouver Province* (5 February 2006).

Blanchfield, Mike, 'Commons votes to extend Afghan mission to 2011', *Vancouver Sun* (14 March 2008).

——, 'Harper hints at Canada-US climate plan', *Vancouver Sun* (7 November 2008).

Blitz, Roger and Richard McGregor, 'Olympics chief warns west', *Financial Times* (26–7 April 2008).

Bolan, Kim, 'Komagata Maru kin want amends', *Vancouver Sun* (23 May 2006).

Bradsher, Keith and David Barboza, 'Pollution from Chinese coal casts a global shadow', *The New York Times* (11 June 2006), www.nytimes.com/2006/06/11/business/worldbusiness/11chinacoal.htm (accessed July 2008).

Bula, Frances, 'City opts for less social housing in False Creek', *Vancouver Sun* (21 January 2006).

——, 'Mayor seeks to trademark "EcoDensity" for himself', *Vancouver Sun* (23 June 2007).

Carter, Holland, 'A broken city. A tree. Evening.', *The New York Times* (2 December 2007).

Cernetig, Miro, 'California model for Campbell's Green Plan', *Vancouver Sun* (10 February 2007).

——, 'Vancouver has a pivotal role in the Tibet debate', *Vancouver Sun* (19 April 2008).

Cernetig, Miro and Kevin Griffin, 'Premier cringes at Games ceremony that presented icy image of Canada', *Victoria Times-Colonist* (1 April 2006).

'Chinese Canadians in Vancouver rally to support Beijing Olympics', *China Economic Net* (27 April 2008), http://en.ce.cn/National/Politics/200804/27/t20080427_15292385.shtml (accessed May 2008).

Clark, Campbell, 'Climate-change goals fall short at G8', *Globe and Mail* (7 July 2008).

Cobain, Ian, 'We sang, screamed, sighed, then we celebrated as one' *Times* (8 June 2002).

Conover, Ted, 'Capitalist roaders', *The New York Times Magazine* (2 July 2006), www.nytimes.com/2006/07/02/magazine/02china.html (accessed July 2008).

Culbert, Lori, 'Pickton', *Vancouver Sun* (1 December 2007).

Culbert, Lori, Neal Hall, and Jeff Lee, 'Emotional end to Pickton trial', *Vancouver Sun* (10 December 2007).

Curry, Bill, 'Premier accused of rushing land claim', *Globe and Mail* (15 June 2007).

'David Beckham makes 100 caps for England', *Daily Telegraph* (25 March 2008), www.telegraph.co.uk/sport/football/international/england/2295455/David-Beckham-makes-100-caps-for-England.html (accessed April 2008).

Duncan, Ann, 'Politics threaten massacre tribute', *Montreal Gazette* (10 September 1994).

Eaves, David and Taylor Owen, 'Failed strategy connects Afghan fields, city streets', *Toronto Star* (7 December 2007).

Edgar, Bill, 'Cameroon coach confronts conflict of loyalties', *Times* (5 March 2002).

Fallows, James, 'China's silver lining', *The Atlantic* (June 2008), pp. 36–50.

Fan, Maureen, 'Shanghai's middle class launches quiet, meticulous revolt', *The Seattle Times* (26 January 2008).

Fong, Petti, 'Veterans demand tenters end Victory Square protest', *Vancouver Sun* (17 July 2003).

'Football is so much more than just a game', *Independent* (1 June 2002).

Fournier, Suzanne, 'Native warriors admit to flag theft', *Vancouver Province* (9 March 2007).

Fowlie, Jonathan, 'Going green enshrined into law', *Vancouver Sun* (21 November 2007).

Fraser, Keith, 'AIDS wall's site at issue', *Vancouver Province* (1 December 1997).

Galloway, Gloria, 'Same-sex marriage file closed for good, PM says', *Globe and Mail* (8 December 2006).

Geller, Michael, 'Sydney's sustainability suburb', *Vancouver Sun* (10 March 2007).

George-Cosh, David, 'The man who built Vancouver has grand plan for Abu Dhabi', *National Post* (12 April 2008).

Gibson, Owen, 'Government forced to bail out major Olympic projects', *The Guardian* (21 January 2009), www.guardian.co.uk/uk/2009/jan/21/olympics-2012-funding-bailout (accessed January 2009).

Gitting, John, and Jonathan Watts, 'World Cup scores for Asian détente', *Guardian* (26 March 2002).

Gledhill, Ruth, 'Bishops want to apologise for Iraq war', *Timesonline* (19 September 2005), www.timesonline.co.uk/tol/news/uk/article568282 (accessed September 2007).

Gold, Kerry, 'Feist shines on the Olympic stage', *Globe and Mail* (14 February 2008).

Goldberger, Paul, 'Out of the blocks', *The New Yorker* (2 June 2008), pp. 68–71.

Gordon, Sean, 'Revive Kelowna accord, leaders urge', *Toronto Star* (17 July 2008).

Hartocollis, Anemona, 'Gay brother, straight brother: it could be a play', *New York Times* (25 June 2006).

Hatch, Kaitlyn S. C., 'One Yellow Wedding: Annie Sprinkle comes to town!', *GayCalgary Magazine* (January 2007).

Hertzberg, Hendrik, 'Distraction', *The New Yorker* (19 June 2006).

Hill, Mary Frances, 'Homeless swept from tent city to hotels', *Vancouver Sun* (16 August 2008).

Hulse, Carl, 'Gay-marriage ban faces loss in early vote', *New York Times* (14 July 2004).

Jacobs, Andrew, 'China to limit web access during Olympic Games', *New York Times* (31 July 2008).

Keating, Jack, 'Musqueam members ratify treaty', *Vancouver Province* (12 March 2008).

Kerr, Richard A., 'Atmospheric science: is Katrina a harbinger of still more catastrophic hurricanes?', *Science* 16 (September 2005).

Kittelberg, Lori, 'Air India tribute proposed for Ceperley Park', *XTRA! West* (6 July 2006).

Koring, Paul, 'Tories stalling abuse probe, watchdog says', *Globe and Mail* (13 March 2008).

Laurence, Robin, 'Landscapes beyond nature', *The Georgia Straight* (22–9 January 2009).

Lautens, Trevor, 'Monument against too many', *Vancouver Sun* (24 June 1993).

Lee, Jeff, 'Licence plates prove hot', *Vancouver Sun* (13 June 2007).

——, 'Who is lobbying who [sic] is the name of the game', *Vancouver Sun* (30 May 2008).

Lev, Elianna, 'Poverty Olympics carries the torch for social issues', *Globe and Mail* (4 February 2008).

Levett, Connie, 'Anglicans feel the brunt of Mugabe's many hatreds', *Sydney Morning Herald* (23 June 2008), www.smh.com.au/news/world/anglicans-feel-the-brunt-of-mugabes-many-hatreds/2008/06/22/1214073053808.html (accessed December 2008).

Lindsay, Bethany, 'Olympic exec not guilty in threat case', *North Shore News* (17 August 2008).

McCullough, Erskine, '"Blattergate" throws World Cup future in doubt', *Agence France Presse* (9 May 2002).

Macfarlane, Robert, 'Blitzed Beijing: why the Olympic city is set on abolishing its past', *Granta* 101 (spring 2008), pp. 79–94.

Mackie, John, 'Yip family legacy lives on in renovation by condo king', *Vancouver Sun* (1 August 2008).

Marlowe, Lisa, 'Le Pen and French soccer hero clash in war of words', *Irish Times* (1 May 2002).

Marqusee, Mike, 'Football's phoney war', *Guardian* (6 June 2002).

Mason, Gary, 'Another sickening sight for the man planning Vancouver's version', *Globe and Mail* (8 April 2008).

——, 'Hate is a learned behaviour', *Globe and Mail* (24 September 2005).

——, 'IOC sinks to new low by severing ties with charity', *Globe and Mail* (22 January 2009).

Matas, Robert, 'Ottawa aims to put its stamp on 2010 Games', *Globe and Mail* (22 August 2008).

Mickleburgh, Rod, 'Female ski jumpers to sue VANOC for inclusion', *Globe and Mail* (21 May 2008).

——, 'VANOC wins praise for social conscience', *Globe and Mail* (28 February 2008).

Pablo, Carlito, 'Development as colonialism', *The Georgia Straight* (3–10 July 2008).

Pendlebury, Richard, 'Conspiracy theory in the land of the bribing sons', *Daily Mail* (25 June 2002).

Penner, Derrick. 'Creating a first nations buzz', *Vancouver Sun* (28 July 2008).

Picard, André, 'Supporting Insite unethical, Clement tells doctors', *Globe and Mail* (19 August 2008).

Pigott, Robert, 'Gay bishop "should quit"', *BBC News Online* (23 June 2008), http://news. bbc.co.uk/2/hi/uk_news/7520711.stm (accessed December 2008).

Reevely, David, 'Surrey school board rejects same-sex books', *Vancouver Sun* (13 June 2003).

Riding, Alan, 'Olympics to Sydney; Beijing's bid fails for 2000 Games', *Montreal Gazette* (24 September 1993).

Savidge, Mariella, 'No, you don't: controversy continues to build over the right of gay couples to wed', *The Morning Call* (9 March 2004).

'Second youth connected to Webster beating sentenced to three years', *Vancouver Sun* (22 April 2004).

Shaw, Helen, 'The Baltimore schmaltz', *The New York Sun* (6 December 2004), www. nysun.com/article/5841 (accessed May 2007).

Sheridan, Michael, 'Japan on red alert for the barbarians from England', *Times* (February 2002).

Shimatsu, Yoichi, 'Tibetan cowboys' last stand: globalism sets grasslands on fire', *New America Media* (20 March 2008), http://news.newamericamedia.org/news/view_article. html?article_id=ee49c44cd49f7bca788fe2f284552696 (accessed July 2008).

Shore, Randy, 'The new battle for Clayoquot Sound', *Vancouver Sun* (25 July 2008).

Smith, David, 'Rockin' all over the world (but just watch your carbon footprint)', *The Observer* (8 July 2007), http://observer.guardian.co.uk/uk_news/story/0,,2121489,00. html (accessed January 2008).

Smith, Graeme, and Robert Matas, 'Afghan–Canadian the top choice for governor of Kandahar', *Globe and Mail* (18 December 2008).

Smith, Nicola and Flora Bagenal, 'Hitler architect's son redraws Beijing', *The Sunday Times* (12 August 2007), www.timesonline.co.uk/tol/news/world/asia/article2241705 (accessed July 2008).

Spencer, Jane and Juliet Ye, 'China eats crow over fake photo of rare antelope', *Wall Street Journal* (22 February 2008).

Struck, Doug, 'Japan, S. Korea: World Cup's strange bedfellows', *Washington Post* (28 April 2002).

Sullivan, Andrew, 'The conservative case for gay marriage', *Time* (22 June 2003), www.time.com/time/magazine/article/0,9171,1101030630-460232,00.html (accessed September 2007).

Todd, Douglas, 'Same-sex opposed Anglicans to split', *Vancouver Sun* (22 November 2007).

Tomlinson, Nicole, 'Indo-Canadians "deceived" by Komagata Maru apology', *Vancouver Sun* (5 August 2008).

Trejos, Nancy, 'Temporary "enjoyment marriages" in vogue again with some Iraqis', *Washington Post* (20 January 2007).

Valpy, Michael, 'Anglicans likely to sidestep decision on gays', *Globe and Mail* (31 July 2008).

——, 'Same-sex blessings to further split Anglicans', *Globe and Mail* (30 October 2008)

Ward, Doug, 'A national call for healing: Harper takes step to atone for a "sad chapter in our history"', *Vancouver Sun* (12 June 2008).

Watts, Jonathan, 'Olympic artist attacks China's pomp and propaganda', *The Guardian* (9 August 2007), www.guardian.co.uk/world/2007/aug/09/china.artnews (accessed July 2008).

Webster, P. J., G. J. Holland, J. A, Curry, and H.-R. Changet 'Changes in tropical cyclone number, duration, and intensity in a warming environment', *Science* (16 September 2005).

Westad, Kim, 'Anglican Diocese of B.C. reps favour same-sex blessing', *Vancouver Sun* (2 June 2007).

Wilson, Peter, 'World Cup champs urge voters to deliver Le Pen the red card', *Australian* (30 April 2002).

Winter, Henry, 'David Beckham given real hope of 100th cap', *The Daily Telegraph* (6 March 2008), www.telegraph.co.uk/sport/main.jhtml?xml=/sport/2008/03/06/sfnbec106.xml (accessed April 2008).

Wong, Edward, 'Parents of schoolchildren killed in China earthquake confirm lawsuit', *The New York Times* (23 December 2008), www.nytimes.com/2008/12/23/world/asia/23quake.html (accessed December 2008).

——, 'Families file suit in Chinese tainted milk scandal', *The New York Times* (21 January 2009), www.nytimes.com/2009/01/21/world/asia/21milk.html (accessed January 2009).

Wong, Jackie, 'City green-lights condo against community objections', *Carnegie Community Action Project Web Log*, (8 July 2008), http://ccapvancouver/wordpress/2008/07/08 (accessed July 2008).

Workman, Daniel, 'World's richest soccer import: footballer David Beckham sells tickets & boosts merchandise sales', *suite101.com* (2 August 2007), http://internationltrade.suite101.com/article.cfm/worlds_richest_soccer_import (accessed April 2008).

Wynne-Jones, Jonathan, 'Male priests marry in Anglican church's first gay "wedding"', *Sunday Telegraph* (15 June 2008), www.telegraph.co.uk/news/uknews/2130668/Male-priests-marry-in-Anglican-church's-first-gay-'wedding'.html (accessed November 2008).

Wypijewski, JoAnn, 'A boy's life', *Harper's Magazine* (September 1999).

Zacharias, Yvonne, 'Gays demand action in wake of brutal killing', *Victoria Times-Colonist* (19 November 2001).

Select website references

The AIDS Memorial Quilt, www.aidsquilt.org.

Amnesty International, www.amnesty.org.

Beijing 2008, http://en.beijing2008.cn/bocog/concepts/index.shtml.

Change.gov, http://change.gov.

Charles Mee: The (Re)making project, www.charlesmee.org.

City of Vancouver, www.city.vancouver.bc.ca.

The Feminist Spectator, http://feministspectator.blogspot.com.

Four Host First Nations Society, www.fourhostfirstnations.com.

Human Rights Watch, www.hrw.org.

Impact of the Olympics on Community Coalition, www.iocc.ca.

Komagata Maru Heritage Foundation, www.komagatamaru.ca.

London 2012, www.london2012.com.

Love Art Laboratory Project, www.loverartlab.org.

National Film Board of Canada, www.nfb.ca.

Pivot Legal Society, www.pivotlegal.org.

PuSh Festival, www.pushfestival.ca.

Squamish Lil'wat Cultural Centre, www.slcc.ca.
United States Holocaust Memorial Museum, www.ushmm.org.
Vancouver 2010, www.vancouver2010.com.
Vancouver AIDS Memorial, www.aidsmemorial.ca.

Select film references

Boys Don't Cry, dir. Kimberly Pierce, Hart-Sharp Entertainment, 1999.
The Brandon Teena Story, dirs Gréta Olafsdóttir and Susan Muska, Bless Bless Productions, 1998.
Continuous Journey, dir. Ali Kazimi, Peripheral Visions Film and Video, 2004.
FIX: The Story of an Addicted City, dir. Nettie Wild, Canada Wild Productions, 2002.
Kandahar, dir. Mohsen Makmalbaf, Bac Films, 2001.
The Laramie Project, dir. Moisés Kaufman, HBO Home Video, 2002.
Manufactured Landscapes, dir. Jennifer Baichwal, Mongrel Media, 2006.
Paragraph 175, dirs Rob Epstein and Jeffrey Friedman, New Yorker Films, 1999.
Zidane, un portrait du 21e siècle, dirs Douglas Gordon and Philippe Parreno, Anna Lena Films, 2006.

INDEX

0 1341 1378819 1

'F